D1538166

i

The Art & Science of Project Management

The Art and Science of Project Management

Attitude

Books, and

Conversations

Second Edition

by
Roger D. H. Warburton
Vijay Kanabar

RW-Press

Published in the United States of America by *RW-Press*, Newport, RI.

Second Edition:

Current Version: 2.4, July 19, 2016.

First Printing, August 15th, 2013.

First Edition:

April 2012.

ISBN: 978-0-9831788-4-2

www.projectmanagementartandscience.com

RW-Press

150 Eustis Avenue,

Newport, RI 02840. U.S.A.

www.RW-Press.com

Cover Design by Nye Warburton.

Cover Image: The White Rabbit, Sir John Tenniel (1890).

Tenniel created black and white illustrations for *Alice's Adventures in Wonderland* by Lewis Carroll (1865). He later created color versions for *Nursery Alice* in 1890.

This particular image is courtesy of Carol Eads at justartrageous@EBay.com.

The white rabbit appears at the very beginning of the book muttering, *"Oh dear! Oh dear! I shall be too late."* Alice follows him down the rabbit hole into Wonderland.

To Eileen and Dina
—for their patience.

CONTENTS

LIST OF FIGURES

LIST OF TABLES

PREFACE

I like prefaces. I read them. Sometimes I do not read any further.

Malcolm Lowry

Is project management an art or a science? *Both!*

In reality, there is an element of science within art. You can't expect to be good at communication without understanding technical issues. There is also an artistic aspect to the technical analysis.[1] In spite of the longstanding false dichotomy between art and science, within project management and the world at large, we hope you will value both the beauty of analysis and the precision of management.

There is a tendency for project management (PM) to be presented as *Plan, Do*, as if one can perfectly plan a project, and then with your shiny plan in hand, just go out and do it. Unfortunately, the real world doesn't work that way.

We believe that to be successful in PM requires an extra ingredient: *Challenge Everything!* Look at a paragraph, a chart, or a number and ask yourself if it makes sense. Examine it and formulate an opinion. Does your experience tell you something? It is a theme we will return to.

A magician makes the trick look easy, but it takes thousands of hours of practice to make it look effortless. Success in project management is not magic either. It takes hard work, training, practice and continuous education.

My customer is	unreasonable, too demanding, crazy always changing his mind
My boss is	relentless, unreasonable, meddling
My staff is	untrained, inexperienced
The project is	impossible.

We believe that as a project manager, there are no excuses. It is your problem, just get on with it.

[1] We find the earned value formulas particularly elegant.

Why Project Management?

At this point, many books about PM claim that using the book will allow you to: *Deliver your projects on time! Deliver on budget!* Unfortunately, most projects fail to meet their objectives in either cost, schedule, or more importantly, customer satisfaction. It seems self-serving, perhaps even arrogant, therefore, to guarantee that reading a book can cure this problem.

We prefer to say that there are excellent reasons for studying PM, and rather than make some outrageous claim about delivering on time, we prefer to tell you the truth, as in "Earned value tells you the amount of your cost overrun."

In our opinion, the excellent reasons for studying project management include:

- You are not alone, others have left breadcrumbs for you to follow.

- There are powerful tools and proven techniques that are pretty easy to use.[2]

- There are jobs for project managers.[3]

- The stress of project management can be reduced by working smart.[4]

The number of projects in the world is increasing. This is due to selection factors, changing industries, and a superb job of marketing by the Project Management Institute. Many companies are only recently realizing that they are project-oriented. Also, small, non-profit organizations, such as theaters, charities, and arts groups host fund raising events—all projects. We claim that the skills and techniques of project management are applicable to these small organizations. Project management need not be large and bureaucratic.

Project Management is revolutionizing business

The study of traditional management is at a cross roads.[5] Paul McDonald suggests that *Management 1.0* was founded on the manufacturing paradigm, which has reached the limits of its relevance, and that it is time to consider a new *Management 2.0* based on the global, information age paradigm in which modern businesses compete. [1] McDonald argues that six powerful forces will redefine the future of management, forces that will require a new kind of management thinking: The virtualization of work, open source practices, the decline of organizational hierarchy, the rise of Generation-Y values, the tumult of global markets, and the imperative of business sustainability.

[2] In fact, there's no excuse not to use them.

[3] OK, we admit this is pandering to the reader!

[4] The critical path might only involve 25% of the activities, so worry about those, and then enjoy the weekend.

[5] General Management, as distinct from Project Management.

Companies such as Apple and Google, who now overshadow one-time giants such as General Motors, typify the transition from an industry-driven economy to a knowledge-based economy. While some people view McDonald's theory as extreme and futuristic, we believe that the concepts underlying his six forces are woven throughout *current* project management thinking.[6]

We conclude that *project* management is at the forefront of modern management.

Project Management is revolutionizing education

Many of the most innovative and interesting ideas are emerging from the business sector, rather than from academia. Traditionally, the teaching of project management has been buried in a course on Operations. Therefore, the explosive growth in PM in the past two decades has left an academic vacuum, which has been filled by non-traditional academic units. The teaching of project management is dominated by online courses and professional, non-credit training.

Many people who seek project management education are working graduate professionals, and the best way to meet their needs is by offering online education. Project management is consequently at the forefront of an emerging trend: online education in non-traditional academic units.[7]

Acknowledgments

First, we thank all the students who have put up with our methods. "It's hard," they cry, but we don't apologize for relentlessly challenging our students. By challenging students, we are empowering them to succeed later—in real world projects where the stakes are higher.

We are fortunate to have worked for two brilliant and dedicated department chairs, Dr. Kip Becker and Dr. John Sullivan, both of whom constantly challenged us to innovate and grow. Our lives are made so much easier by the endless hard work of the superb Administrative Sciences department staff: Susan Sunde, Lucille Dicker, and Fiona Niven. Thanks! Our department's student services staff handle dozens of daily details in the non-academic lives of our students. Thank you Frank Cassidy and Bill McGue.

Our warm thanks go to both our previous Dean, Jay Halfond, and our current Dean, Tanya Zlateva, for their whole-hearted support of the PM program. We have benefited enormously from the efforts of the first-class Boston University Distance Education department. To everyone there, a huge, grateful *Thank You!* Jan Morris

[6]For more on this topic, see [2].

[7]We should explain, in the interest of honesty, that the authors both teach online courses in Boston University's Metropolitan College, a college whose mission has been redefined the past two decades to provide *Graduate Professional Education.*

tracked down the details of the quotations, and double checked their authorship. Her dedication, not to say zeal, for the task relieved us immensely.

Eileen Warburton copy-edited the entire book. Without her superb talents, there would be random commas and peculiar wording throughout. Any mistakes remain our responsibility.

Preface to the Second Edition

The primary motivation for the second edition was the publication of the 5th edition of the Project Management Body of Knowledge (usually referred to as the PMBOK) [3], which is now covered in Part IV, and to which we added examples and templates. We also added new chapters: The Graduation Picnic Party project and a tutorial in *Microsoft Project, 2013*. These were the topics most often requested by our students.

We also took the opportunity to revise the order of the chapters, which, we feel, is now more logical. We begin in Part I with the projects and their environment, including the relation of projects to their companies. We moved the Technical Skills (Scope, Work Breakdown Structure, Network, Earned Value, etc.) to Part II because it is logical to study these chapters directly after completing Part I. In the second edition we added, in Chapter 13, a section on *schedule estimation*, which, we believe, is a critical skill. Versions 2.3 and 2.4 are minor updates to correct typos.[8]

Part III is dedicated to examples and cases: The Kitchen project and a new chapter, The Graduation Picnic Party. Both cases illustrate the entire project management process and its deliverables. This Kitchen case follows the project life-cycle, while the Graduation Picnic follows the PMBOK process groups.

Part IV covers the PMBOK Process Groups in detail: Initiating, Planning, Executing, Monitoring and Controlling, and Closing. We also cover all 47 Processes, as well their inputs and outputs.

Part V is new to the second edition: A tutorial in *Microsoft Project® 2013*: The graduation picnic project described in Part III is implemented in *MS Project*.

Our students are our best critics and we listen carefully to all of their suggestions. Many students pointed out errors, ambiguities and typos in the first edition, and we sincerely thank them for taking the time to bring them to our attention.

Any remaining mistakes are still our responsibility.

[8]Many heartfelt thanks go to Meera and Anish.

INTRODUCTION

**The important thing is not to stop questioning.
Curiosity has its own reason for existence.**

Albert Einstein

Project management and Boston made us who we are. Despite our diverse backgrounds, Boston is where our project management grew to maturity. We love the Big Dig, baked beans, and the Red Sox. We really are Bostonians.

The subtitle of the book is an ABC:[9]

- *Attitude* . . . because we believe project management is about clear and strong communication, with an attitude. Challenge everything!

- *Books* . . . because books and research are the foundation of what we are.

- *Conversations* . . . because the book challenges the reader, and invites comment. Our reader is not a passive subject.

This book introduces the student to the world of project management. We assume nothing; we start from zero.

Most of our students know little formal project management. Our goal is to produce a useful reference, so we devote a good deal of effort to defining concepts and establishing first principles. We firmly believe that precision is important and have added lots of index entries, notes and references.

Many of our students are, in fact, project managers, but have never studied formal project management. We call such a person an *Accidental Project Manager.* Typically, you get called into your boss's office and are told, "Congratulations, you are now the project manager for the company's new project."

[9] Besides, ABC is a good metaphor for an introductory textbook, what's new, and Boston is "The New World."

xxxvii

Visions of pay raises and glory stream through your mind. Then you wake up early the next morning realize you know nothing about project management!

For the accidental project manager, our job is to define the concepts clearly and precisely. We hope that combining your valuable practical experience with the established, powerful theoretical concepts, all expressed in the correct vocabulary, will take your project skills to new heights.

The content on which this book was based has been tested in introductory and advanced courses. Whether our students are undergraduate or graduate, they are typically non-traditional, are usually older with families and careers, are committed to their education, and are motivated. Therefore, we have the luxury of assuming an intelligent and dedicated reader.

As a result, you will not find in this book sections entitled *What you will learn in this chapter*. Rarely will you find *Overviews*.[10] We believe all that just clutters up a book and adds useless pages.[11]

Our mission is to provide a readable, easy to understand book that carefully defines the tools and techniques of project management, is up to date in accepted wisdom (i.e., research), and can serve long-term as a reference for the working professional. To accomplish our mission we established the goals of covering all project management concepts, supporting the concepts with examples, explaining the technical tools and techniques and providing practical worked examples, pointing the reader towards relevant research if they want more depth, covering the PMBOK in detail, and eliminating junk.

Structure of the Book

The book is divided into five parts:

- *Part I: Projects and Their Environment:* We define a project, and explore the domain to which project management applies. We also cover the role of projects in accomplishing the mission of the company.

- *Part II: Technical Skills:* We cover the skills that a project manager must master to be effective. In Part II, we generally follow the project life cycle, and so it makes sense to follow them in the order presented here. When teaching a class, we follow these chapters in order, covering more or less one chapter per week in a one-semester course.

    This is complemented with selected examples from Part III. The chapters in Part II also generally follow the order in the PMBOK.

[10]When our students ask if we will provide a study guide for the exam, we reply "No. If it was important, it's in the book. If we thought it was unimportant, we left it out."

[11]We wrote the book, and then deleted almost 20%. We do try to practice what we preach. According to Stephen King: Rewrite formula: 2nd Draft = 1st Draft - 10%.

- *Part III: Examples and Cases* We cover two cases in detail, and they are presented in different styles:

  - *The "New Kitchen" Project*: This illustrates the entire project management process and its deliverables using a real-world example. This case follows the project life-cycle: requirements gathering, bid process, planning, design, implementation, cost and schedule tracking, and acceptance.

  - *The "Graduation Picnic" Project*: This also illustrates the entire project management process, but this case is presented differently: It follows the PMBOK® 5th Edition process groups: initiating, planning, executing, monitoring and controlling, and closing.

  These are the two major ways of approaching the presentation of project examples. Studies of the detailed technical aspects of project management tend to follow the life-cycle approach. Students more interested in certifications, such as the Project Management Professional (PMP®) and the Certified Associate in Project Management (CAPM®), tend to work sequentially through the process groups.

- *Part IV: Process Groups, Processes, and Knowledge Areas:* This part closely follows the 5th edition of the PMBOK®. The *process groups* are the activities that the project manager follows during the planning and execution of the project: Initiating, Planning, Executing, Monitoring and Controlling, and Closing.

  We discuss the *processes*[12] that make up each *process group*, as well as the inputs and outputs for each. We then explain the *Knowledge Areas* by providing examples of the deliverables. In-depth explanations of how to construct those deliverables are covered in Part II.

- *Part V: Microsoft Project 2013® Tutorial:* The graduation picnic project in Part III is implemented in *Project*. Assuming no previous knowledge, the tutorial gradually explains how to create the schedule and analyze the cost. Annotated screens and reports are used to explain the commands, data entry and outputs.

Advice to the Beginner

Projects surround us, but only recently have people begun to define carefully the characteristics of a project. Many people throw around the term "project" without understanding that it is a very precisely defined concept. Also, projects are often

[12]All 47 of them!

xxxix

confused with programs, which are totally different. As a result, there is a lot of confusion surrounding the word *project*.

Many students come to class having heard the word *project* bandied about in meetings, and often incorrectly.[13] This illustrates one of the problems of project management. Many of the terms are thrown around by people who do not understand their meaning.[14]

Advice to Teachers

The chapters stand alone, so they can be covered in any order.[15] We have successfully used the following approaches:

- *Undergraduate Courses:* We tell the students to ignore Part IV, the PMBOK chapters. We cover the introductory chapters on projects and then work sequentially through Part II, which generally follows the project life-cycle.

- *General Graduate Courses:* Graduate students who are not project management majors are usually taking the course as part of a core curriculum. We explain that Part IV—the PMBOK chapters—has useful examples, but we tell them to ignore the details, such as the inputs and outputs.

- *Graduate Project Managers:* These students need everything. Our goal, however, was to make the book easier to read than the PMBOK.

- *The Microsoft Project Tutorial:* This is a stand-alone chapter, and can be covered in a few hours, at the appropriate time, in any course.

Conventions

[13]We love it when that happens! Actual learning is going on.

[14]In that situation, we always give the same advice: Keep your mouth shut, no one likes a smarty pants.

[15]Actually, we didn't plan this, it just worked out that way.

[16]This is a page note. It falls towards the bottom of the page.

One of the challenges students face is to learn to master the large, intimidating terminology. Therefore, throughout the book, formal project management terms are italicized. This includes project management processes, e.g., *Define Scope*; key documents, e.g. *Risk Register*; and important terms, e.g., *critical path*. This should help the student become familiar with the terminology.

There are two types of notes, page notes and chapter notes. Page notes are numbered sequentially throughout each chapter.[16] Page notes appear on the same page as the number, and so are easy to find. They contain immediate information, mostly personal observations and comments.

Chapter notes are informal references; they provide explanatory and bibliographic information, and are collected at the end of the book in the *Notes* Chapter. Chapter notes explain where the reader can find more information on a topic, what the research says, and where to find more information. Chapter notes are also numbered sequentially throughout a chapter.[1]

While the appearance of two sets of numbers may at first appear confusing, they have completely different jobs to do.[17]

More practically, if you don't see a note at the bottom of the page corresponding to that number, it is a chapter note and you can find it at the back of the book. If you find two notes with the same number on a page, one is a page note, and its content is below. The other is a chapter note at the end of the book.

Formal references to other works are given by citations, and collected in the *Bibliography* section at the end of the book. Citations are provided as numbers in brackets. For example, our previous book on project management said that "this is a great time to study project management." [4]

Definitions appear as follows:

> *This is not a definition, but it sure looks like one.*

When we express an opinion, we want it to be clear that it is *our opinion*. We do not do this lightly. We have strong views that are backed by years of experience with both projects and teaching. Hopefully, we have backed our opinions with research supported by references.[18]

There is only one index, because we think that looking up authors separately is confusing. For example, should you look up *Maslow's Hierarchy* under *Maslow* in an author index, or in the subject index? In this book, everything and everyone is in a single index. Neither is there a separate glossary, as that duplicates information. Terms are defined in their context, and indexed.

The Cases

Throughout the book, we use cases to illustrate project management concepts. We also provide sample documents, which students can use as a model for their own projects. The following practical case studies are used throughout:

- *The PMA Case*

  The Project Management Association (PMA) is a small, Boston-based (hypothetical) organization dedicated to educating its members about project

[17] This is another page note. The superscript '1' at the end of the previous paragraph is a chapter note, and you can find it in the *Notes* section at the end of the book. The fact that there is no '1' at the bottom of this page, also indicates that it is a chapter note.

[18] But if you want to challenge our opinions, feel free to do so. Challenge everything.

management, to providing networking opportunities, and to making available useful summaries of the latest research. PMA would like to improve the services it offers to its members, and, so, is considering implementing a new web site with the following features: Administration of memberships; social networking and marketing emails to members; web pages of useful research materials; and a conference management system with online registration, as well as submission, review and acceptance of papers.

- *The New Kitchen*

    We follow the design and implementation of a new kitchen project through its life-cycle, discuss the issues involved, and give examples of the deliverables, tools and techniques.[19]

- *The Graduation Picnic*

    Students who have studied project management have decided to hold a picnic at the end of the academic year and selected a classic American theme of hamburgers, hot dogs and beer. The party is an informal, evening picnic with food and entertainment. The focus of this case is on document templates and generally follows the PMBOK process groups.

Challenge Everything!

We tell our students to challenge everything. When reading a paragraph, ask yourself: Does this make sense to me? Do I have experience that either reinforces or contradicts the premise of what I am reading?

To challenge everything is not to be a cynic. A cynical person is someone who denies the sincerity of people's motives, and is often sarcastic or sneering.[20]

But challenges must be backed up from an intellectual perspective. This means that you are expected to back up your challenge with facts, data and, preferably, references.[21] When it comes to citing references, the gold standard is to quote from an academic journal. We are not being pedantic here, but setting the standard. [22] Random quotations found in a quick Google search carry no weight.

In our previous book, Vijay wrote "A talented PM can work magic with a doomed project."[23] As his friend and colleague, I defend his use of the poetic word *magic* as an aspirational goal. You can challenge it, but you'd better come armed.

[19] Vijay was overheard to say that if he had to listen to Roger's obsessing over his new kitchen, at least he was going to make him put it to practical use as a case in the book.

[20] This is not a useful attitude.

[21] Otherwise, you are plagiarizing.

[22] Academic journals define the accepted state of the art, and contain the accumulated wisdom.

[23] This sure caused a lot of discussion among students.

xlii

Part I

Projects and Their Environment

1

PROJECTS

**Don't undertake a project unless it is manifestly important
and nearly impossible.**

Edwin Land

Projects are everywhere.

Examples of projects include building a house or skyscraper, organizing and holding a birthday or anniversary party, developing a new drug, designing a new airplane or ship, filming a movie or producing a play, or developing a new web site.

The chief distinguishing characteristic of projects is that they are new endeavors, they have never been attempted before. This is in contrast to routine activities, which are performed repetitively. Examples of routine activities include cutting your grass, cooking daily meals, manufacturing drugs, maintaining an airplane or ship, showing a movie or performing a play, and maintaining a web site.

The concept of a project is very old. The Pyramids of Ancient Egypt and the Roman Colosseum were magnificent, sophisticated and complicated projects. However, it is only recently that the precise definition of a project has emerged.

Projects are not necessarily large endeavors. Small, non-profit organizations also engage in projects, for example, when they conduct fund-raisers, or introduce new performances, such as plays and dances. They resort to routine activities when they take tickets and their performances go into a regular run.

The techniques of modern project management are applicable to both large and small projects. There is a tendency for students to look at the jargon, the vast quantity of information, and the diverse collection of tools and assume that project management only applies to large projects. Not so! The tools and techniques of project management can be easily adapted to small projects.

For example, a key lesson is that the scope document, which precisely describes the project, is a project's most important document. Therefore, taking time to carefully define the scope is worthwhile. Even for a small project, it is still worth the effort to produce a clear and concise scope document. The scope need not be a long, bureaucratic tome.

Also, modern network diagram tools operate on small computers and are relatively easy to learn. The application of such tools to manage cost and schedules is very cost effective, even for small projects.[1]

As you go about your daily life, you often hear people talking about their "projects," but not all of these activities will satisfy the precise definition, and as a result, there is considerable confusion as to what constitutes a project. This confusion is exacerbated by the fact that all organizations have their own terminology and procedures. Once the word "project" is embedded in a company, it is likely to stick, even if the outside world does not regard what they are doing as projects.

For example, almost all of the activities in a manufacturing plant are routine, non-projects: parts are ordered, delivered into inventory, and then assembled into products. These operations are much the same from week to week. However, people who work in manufacturing often describe their activities as projects. They may refer to the week's manufacturing target as their project for the week.

It is easy to develop standardized procedures for routine activities. Since projects typically have not been done before, it is much harder to develop a standardized approach, and this presents one of the challenges of project management.

1.1 The Project Management Institute

I think it's wrong that only one company makes the game Monopoly.

Stephen Wright

[1]We occasionally hear a comment like, "My project is too small to need a network diagram." To which we reply, "It's so small you don't need to know if it is behind schedule."

The Project Management Institute (PMI) is the professional organization devoted to the furthering of project management. PMI is growing rapidly, which is one indicator of the growing importance of project management.[2]

PMI has done an excellent job of defining the characteristics of projects through global standards. These standards are widely accepted and, as claimed by PMI, "when consistently applied, they help you, your global peers and your organization achieve professional excellence."

The most important standard published by PMI is known as the *PMBOK®*.[3] The official title of the *PMBOK* is *A Guide to the Project Management Body of Knowledge* [3]. PMI defines the *PMBOK* as the standard formal document that describes established norms, methods, processes, and practices.

> *The PMBOK® Guide is the standard for managing projects most[4] of the time across many types of industries. This standard describes the project management processes, tools, and techniques used to manage a project towards a successful outcome.*

The *PMBOK* mostly addresses project management, but it also contains information about the project environment, such as program and portfolio management. It also contains information from other disciplines, such as communications theory, risk management, and quality control.

While the *PMBOK* is the definitive standard, we do not feel obligated to slavishly follow every word. Project management is a complex endeavor and applicable to a wide range of industries. We are quite comfortable challenging the *PMBOK* when we have experience, data or research to suggest a better approach. In fact, we encourage our students to examine critically all their readings, not just the *PMBOK*.[5]

1.2 What is a Project?

We begin with the formal PMBOK definition of a project:

> *A project is a temporary endeavor undertaken to create a unique product, service, or result.*

A project is considered to be a unique endeavor, in that it has never been done before. Projects must be carefully distinguished from routine activities, which are repetitive in nature.

[2] The PMI website *pmi.org* has a massive collection useful information on all aspects of project management.

[3] *PMBOK* is usually pronounced as pim-bock.

[4] Most?! Some standard!

[5] Challenge Everything!

This is a somewhat cryptic definition that obscures a lot of important information.[6] For example, the word "temporary" is expanded to mean that a project has definite beginning and end dates.[7] The word "temporary" is also a little unusual because it implies a short duration activity while projects often continue for long periods. A skyscraper may take many years to build. Even so, the project to create the skyscraper is referred to as a *temporary endeavor*.

The word "unique" is also a loaded term. Here, the word means that the project has not been done before. There are of course, repetitive aspects of a project, even if the overall result is unique. In our skyscraper example, the building may be highly original in design, and therefore unique. Within the construction, however, many activities are quite routine, e.g., installing the light fixtures in each floor.

The uniqueness of projects requires further clarification. Suppose one is building several houses in a development, and all of the houses have the same design. One might argue that the first house is a project, since it is unique. Building the remaining houses might be considered routine, and not really projects. It is likely, though, that one would continue to treat the other houses as projects, and manage their construction in a disciplined way.

A definition should stand alone, and precisely define a concept. We believe the above definition does not work very well in this regard, e.g., it needed several paragraphs just to clarify the idea of "temporary." Therefore, we provide another definition that we believe is more helpful:

> *A project is unique, non-routine effort, limited by time and budget, defined by a performance specification, and designed to meet stakeholder needs.*

Rather than defining a project as temporary, we used the phrase "unique, non-routine." This clarifies the idea that a project is different from anything that went before. Also by avoiding the word "temporary," we eliminate the confusion about projects that take many years, or even decades to complete. The definition also clarifies the important distinction between routine activities and projects.

The limitations on cost and schedule are also important additions. Often, some of the first questions asked about a project are: How much will it cost? When will it be completed? Since every project is limited by cost and schedule, it is appropriate to include these ideas in the definition.

Including the performance specification explains how the project is defined. The performance specification is part of the scope, which is the most important document in the project, and highlighting it in the definition elevates its importance.

[6]And, therefore, we have no problem challenging it.

[7]An activity without an end date is technically, not a project. This is a favorite trick question on exams.

Finally, the project must meet stakeholder needs. We note the use of the word, "stakeholder," who is anyone with a stake in the project. Sometimes, the word, "customer," is used in the definition, but the customer is only one of many stakeholders.

It is not unusual to have stakeholders who would be happy to see the project fail, and managing such naysayers is a challenging activity. For example, in the construction of a new sidewalk, the owners of the stores lining the route may be negatively affected during construction, and might prefer that the project not be done at all.

Projects are characterized as follows:

- *Projects have an established objective.*

  In the early stages of a project's conceptual development, the project is defined by its charter, which is a short overview of the goals and objectives, and perhaps a desired schedule and rough budget. The first activity of the project is typically the development of the scope, which precisely defines the project.

- *Projects have a well-defined life span.*

  Projects have a beginning date and an end date. If activities continue indefinitely into the future, then technically it is not a project. In general, it is a good idea to break up long projects into several shorter projects, each with a well-defined objective, budget, and completion date.

- *Projects require staff participation from across the organization.*

  Projects are inherently multi-disciplinary. For example, when building a house, the project manager must interact with the architect and the contractor, as well as assorted subcontractors such as roofers, plumbers, electricians, and carpenters. There are also technical requirements such as the permitting process, gas company installation and approval procedures, and voluminous fire codes, electrical codes, and environmental regulations.

  Project managers must also interact with professionals such as accountants, lawyers, engineers, and human resources personnel. Project managers will quickly find themselves immersed in many disciplines.[8]

- *Projects have defined schedules and budgets.*

  No project has the luxury of an infinite cost or schedule. Customers always have an assigned budget and a preferred delivery schedule.

- *Projects have limited resources.*

[8]There is a fascinating debate about whether a project manager can be successful if he or she does not possess technical expertise in the project's discipline. Does a project manager need to be a subject matter expert, or are project management skills universally applicable?

7

Resources include staff and equipment, which must be managed. Other factors may limit the performance of the project, such as competition with other projects for staff and the availability of funds.

- *Projects have multiple, often competing, stakeholders.*

The project manager and the team are obvious stakeholders, but there are many more, including the sponsor (who pays the bill), customers, users, and trainers. Upper management also has a stake in the project's success, but if things are not going well, it may be in their best interest to cancel the project!

1.2.1 Project Time Scales

Projects have widely different time scales. Table 1.1 shows typical time scales for projects in different industries.

Table 1.1: Project time scales by industry.

Industry	Typical Project Time Scale
Military Jet	15-20 years
Mega Project Construction	10-15 years
Skyscraper Construction	3-5 years
House Construction	3-6 months
Software System	1-2 years
Web Site Construction	3-6 months
Insurance Product	1 month

1.3 Project Management

> **You want to study project management?**
> **Read more, sleep less!**
>
> *John Cable*

Project management is the term applied to the process of managing projects.

Because projects are unique, it is difficult to develop a completely standardized approach. There is seldom a "right" way to proceed, one is always dealing with uncertainty. On the other hand, standardized methods have evolved which reduce the risks associated with dealing with the unknown.

The Project Management Institute (PMI) defines project management as:

> *Project Management is the application of knowledge, skills, tools, and techniques to project activities to meet the project requirements.*

As with professions such as law, medicine, and accounting, the body of knowledge rests with the practitioners and academics who apply and advance it. The PMBOK includes proven traditional practices that are widely applied, as well as innovative practices that are emerging. As a result, the PMBOK is constantly evolving.[9]

> *The PMBOK Guide® provides guidelines for managing individual projects. It defines project management and related concepts and describes the project management life cycle and the related processes.*

How should the PMBOK be used? The project team should consult the PMBOK to identify the processes that are relevant to their own individual project objectives. Company and environmental factors may constrain project options and, therefore, affect the selection of relevant processes.

For example, it may be decided that from the planning process group, a process called *Identify Risks* is necessary and should be integrated into the specific project life cycle. When considering such a process for inclusion, it is useful to identify the relevant inputs and outputs, any forms or company templates that already exist, and any related documents.

The entire life cycle should be tailored to meet the project's and sponsor's requirements in the most efficient manner. The workload of including a process must be balanced against the elimination of the associated deliverables. Every project needs a well-constructed *scope*, and so eliminating the *Define Scope* process is a bad idea. On the other hand, if there are no subcontractors, then one can safely eliminate *Procurement Management Planning*.[10]

As an illustration of tailoring the PMBOK, for small projects we frequently combine the four PMBOK risk processes: *Identify Risks*; *Perform Qualitative Risk Analysis*; *Perform Quantitative Risk Analysis*; and *Plan Risk Responses*. We define a customized process that we call *Create Risk Management Plan*.[11]

Since every project is unique, no two life cycles will be the same. Also, the rigor with which each process is executed varies from one project to another. If the

[9] That the standard is evolving is often neglected. However, as a student of project management, your job is to question the standard, and to improve it, wherever possible.

[10] We do not recommend eliminating this entirely from the Management Plan. It is better to briefly state, "No subcontractors are planned." That way, if you later decide you need subs, you have a place to put the information in the plan.

[11] Note that we actually use the PMBOK as a checklist to ensure that we include all the necessary pieces. It would do no good if we forgot to plan the risk responses!

9

project is mission critical, or if the project team is not experienced, one should use more rigor in implementing and executing each process. An example of 'more rigor' is to enforce the processes and conscientiously review all deliverables and documentation.

Table 1.2 lists project management skills and classifies them. Fortunately, coming to the aid of the modern project manager is a discipline and methodology that provides support and professionalism in both arenas.

Table 1.2: The technical and sociocultural skills of project management.

Technical Skills	Sociocultural Skills
Scope Production	Stakeholder Management
Work Breakdown Structure	General Management
Cost & Schedule Management	Staff Management
Resource Contention	Leadership
Critical Path Management	Negotiation Skills
Earned Value Management	Politics

A project manager needs two types of skills:

1. *Sociocultural Skills:* A project manager interacts with diverse stakeholders, many of whom have different goals. The project manager reports to upper management and customers. Also, the project manager must acquire the team, and develop their skills. Communication skills are therefore a critical aspect of project management.[12]

   These are often referred to as "soft" skills, and include general management skills, interpersonal communications, and staff development.[13]

2. *Technical Skills:* A project manager must be able to perform a variety of technical analyses, such as determining the value of the project to stakeholders, performing a cost estimate, constructing a work breakdown structure, building a network diagram, determining if the project is on schedule, and whether it is over or under budget. These are essential skills, as every customer wants to know the cost and the schedule.[14]

[12]Vijay is often heard to say, "Communication is 90% of project management."

[13]We prefer to think of these as the *art* of project management.

[14]We prefer to think of these as the *science* of project management.

10

1.4 The Project Manager

> **Managing is essentially a loser's job, and managers are about the most expendable pieces of furniture on the earth.**
>
> *Ted Williams, The Splendid Splinter.*

Let's begin with the definition:

> *The project manager is the person assigned to achieve the project's objectives.*

In this book, we are always going to assume that you, dear reader, are the project manager. Whenever we ask a question, or expect you to analyze a problem, we always assume that you should answer it from the project manager's point of view.

The project manager must possess three characteristics: Knowledge about project management; the ability to perform as a project manager; and personal effectiveness, which encompasses both skills and personality traits.

The project manager often has responsibility without authority. Rarely does the project manager have the luxury of being able to order people around. The interdisciplinary nature of projects, and the diverse skills required, means that few, if any, of the staff work directly for the project manager. Therefore, one of the key skills required of a project manager is being able to *induce* the right people to do the right thing at the right time. This includes their staff, stakeholders, customers, and even upper management. This leads to one of our most cherished beliefs:

> Project managers *induce* people to perform.

The role of the PM is to:

1. Plan and organize the project from start to finish.

2. Manage relations with stakeholders and, in particular, customers.

3. Manage relations with the parent company.

4. Develop and manage the project team.

5. Monitor and control project progress, particularly the costs and schedule.

6. Deal with uncertainty and changes.

7. Deliver the product or service and get the customer's acceptance.

Project managers must exercise control and provide leadership to their team. At the same time, they cannot do everything and so must learn to delegate, follow up, and provide training and encouragement as needed.

Since projects have not been done before, project managers must deal with uncertainty. Almost everything in project management is a compromise, there are rarely correct answers. Projects are inherently messy, and change is a fact of life. Project managers must deal with complexity and ambiguity, and be able to prioritize.

Project managers live in a permanent competition for resources. They compete for staff and with other projects for resources. They referee stakeholders, all of whom have different goals, objectives and priorities.[15]

1.4.1 Interactions

The project manager interacts with many different constituencies:

- *Stakeholders.* This is the most important group. Failure to carefully manage stakeholders will jeopardize the project. Stakeholders are usually a diverse group with competing priorities.

- *Upper Management.* The project manager must understand the role of the project in the company's strategy, and be able to defend its budget.[16]

- *Sponsor.* The person who pays for the project will want regular cost and schedule updates.

- *Customers.* The people who set the expectations for the final product or service.

- *Project Team.* It is the project manager's job to *induce* the team to perform to the best of their ability.

- *Functional Areas.* These are typically the company departments that provide the staff to the project, and may include:

    - System designers and architects.
    - Subject matter experts.
    - Business analysts, lawyers, and accountants.

[15]Challenging enough for you?

[16]We regard this a nothing less defending one's job security!

12

     – Contractors and subcontractors.

     – Testers and quality control staff.

1.5 Benefits of Project Management

There are two main benefits to a disciplined approach to project management:[17]

- *You are not alone.* There is a mountain of information available: Literature, templates, and advice. You can access it, and learn from others. Someone has probably done something similar.

- *Powerful Tools.* The critical path tells you which activity is the most important one to work on now. Earned value tells you how much your project is over budget and behind schedule. You may not like the answers, but at least you'll know the truth.

1.5.1 Project Success

A significant challenge of project management is that every project must aim to be successful. In a routine manufacturing environment, the failure of a few products (out of a million) might not be regarded as catastrophic. However, the failure of a project critical to the mission of a company might lead to a crash of the entire company. Finally, projects are almost always produced to a tight deadline with constrained funds. This all adds pressure to the project manager to succeed.

When discussing "success," however, it is important to distinguish between: [5]

1. *Project management success.* . This is typically measured in terms of the quality of the process, e.g., whether the project was delivered on schedule and within budget.

2. *Project success.* This is usually defined in terms of product quality, and measured by whether the project met its overall objectives, e.g., its critical success factors.[18]

One should also distinguish between size and importance because the importance of a project is not necessarily related to its size. Small, mission-critical projects are much more important than their larger non-critical cousins. Neither is technical complexity related to size. Small, mission-critical, technically challenging projects will require the best from a project manager.

[17]As explained in the introduction, we are resisting the urge to say that you will deliver your project on schedule and on budget.

[18]Despite being over budget and late, did the project deliver value to the stakeholders?

13

The subject of project failure garners a lot of attention. First, we point out that *failure* is a complex concept: Is a project a failure if it successfully meets stakeholder needs but comes in late and over budget? Is a project successful that is on time and on budget, but leaves some stakeholders unhappy?

One of the most quoted sources of project failure is the *CHAOS Report* by the Standish Group who studied 365 companies with a total of 8,380 Information System applications. [6] The report divided projects into three distinct outcomes, as shown in Table 1.3.

Table 1.3: The CHAOS data on project failure.

Project Outcome	1994	2009	Definition
Successful	16%	32%	Completed on time and budget, with all features as specified.
Challenged	53%	44%	Completed, but were over cost, over time, and/or lacking features
Impaired/Failed	31%	24%	Abandoned or canceled **Total losses!**

The first percentage is for the original data from 1994, and the second is for 2009. While these are Information Technology (IT) projects, similar data exists for other types of projects in other countries and industries. The point is that while things have improved somewhat in 15 years, the CHAOS data suggest that most projects fail!

There are major criticisms, however, of the Standish interpretation of "failure." [7] For example, a project 25% over budget that meets stakeholder needs and is on time is a failure according to the Standish criteria.

Another interesting factor is the forecast bias. The data is biased in that it ignores projects that under-run in cost and time. Since most people underestimate their forecast,[19] without taking these biases into account the Standish data are highly suspect.

These are excellent examples of a technique that we wish to inculcate into our reader: Challenge Everything! [20]

[19]Whether by design or ignorance is another fascinating question

[20]Just because you read it in a fancy report, you don't have to take it for granted. Ask questions. Examine assumptions. Find your own data.

2

THE PROJECT ENVIRONMENT

**There are two ways of being creative. One can sing and dance.
Or one can create an environment in which singers and dancers flourish.**

Warren G. Bennis

A project manager must be aware of the external environment surrounding the project, as well as creating a positive internal environment for the team.

2.1   The Internal Environment

The internal project environment influences team members' attitudes and their desire to perform. For a project to succeed, team members must be committed to the project's goals and care about producing a quality product or service.[1] A positive internal environment includes:

1. A corporate culture that acknowledges and appreciates the efforts of team members.

2. Good working relationships among team members.

3. Clear and open communications.

[1] Again, we see the idea that you cannot 'order' someone to succeed, you can only create an environment that helps them to succeed.

15

4. An environment of trust.

5. A willingness to take risks.

6. Recognition of efforts and achievements.

Apart from the first item, which depends on the corporate climate, these qualities are the responsibility of the project manager. They are important because they relate directly to the characteristics of a project. Since projects are unique, the project manager must ensure that everyone understands both the objectives and their own roles. A willingness on the part of the team to take risks is required because they are venturing into uncharted territory.

2.2   The External Environment

The external environmental influences include:

1. The parent company, including upper management.

2. Organizational assets, including policies and procedures, lessons from previous projects, etc.

3. The company culture, existing staff, and company investment in tools and technologies.

4. The political environment, including government policies, tax incentives, etc.

5. The business climate, including company strength, business strategies, and access to funds.

6. The geographical setting, including environmental issues.

7. Social commitments, including benefits and working conditions.

2.3   The Project's Rationale

An important and critical aspect of the external environment is the business need of the project—its rationale for existence. This need is documented in the business case, and must be aligned with company objectives. (This is covered in the section on portfolio management 2.4.2.)

If the need for the project disappears, the project will also disappear. A threat to all projects is the evolution of the business that eliminates the need for the project. Project managers must be on the lookout for this.[2]

2.4 Programs

Programs are collections of projects that have a natural association, and are managed together for mutual benefit. The definition of a program is:

> *A program is a group of related projects managed in a coordinated way to obtain benefits and control not available from managing them individually.*

Suppose a company's marketing department creates a program to launch a new product. That program might include the following projects:

- Launch the product at a national trade show.

- Plan and implement a marketing campaign.

- Create the supply chain for the product.

- Create new marketing channels for the product.

Sometimes a program has routine activities as part of its mission. In the above example, routine activities might include updating the marketing materials and publication of a weekly sales brochure to selected clients.

An organization that uses the term "program" in the way we have defined it is NASA. For example, NASA's Mars exploration program consisted of many projects, including Spirit and Opportunity Launches, 2001 Mars Odyssey, Mars Express, and the Mars Reconnaissance Orbiter.

2.4.1 The Program Management Office

Program management is often accomplished in a Program Management Office (PMO).[3] A Project Management Office is responsible for the coordinated management of projects. The job of the PMO is to:

- Develop and manage the company standards, policies and procedures that apply to projects.

[2] No project, no job!

[3] Note: The PMBOK defines the PMO organization as the *Project* Management Office. A program is a collection of projects, and managing them collectively is the job of the PMO. Therefore, we believe it is more correct to call it the *Program* Management Office. Besides, almost all companies call it that.

17

- Invest in project management technology, best practices, tools and techniques, and implement them across projects.

- Manage the information technology system

- Supervise functions that are managed centrally, such as the portfolio selection system, and risk pools.

- Collect and manage lessons learned.

2.4.2 Portfolios

A portfolio is an entity that is managed from a business perspective. A comparison of portfolios, programs and projects is shown in Table 2.1, which is based on a similar table in the PMBOK.

> *A portfolio is a collection of programs, projects, products, and routine activities managed together for mutual benefit.*

That is, a portfolio consists of all the activities necessary to make a product (or line) successful. Portfolios, therefore, include projects, programs, as well as routine activities.

Table 2.1: A comparison of portfolios, programs, and projects.

	Projects	**Programs**	**Portfolios**
Scope	Clearly defined objective	Wider scope with corporate objectives	Business objectives aligned with corporate strategy
Planning	Progressive elaboration of project objectives	Program plan	Business Plan
Management	The project	The program	The portfolio
Success	Meets stakeholder objectives, within cost & schedule	Meets business objectives	Meets corporate objectives

Developing a new product is a project, but the activities to make the product successful include many routine activities such as marketing, product maintenance, inventory control, and customer service. A new product cannot be successful without all of these non-project activities, so it makes sense for a company to manage it all as a coherent whole.

2.5 Mission, Goals, Objectives, and Strategy

A project manager must be able to define and articulate clearly the link between their project and the company's mission, goals, and objectives. Projects compete for both client and company funds and resources, and projects without a clear link to the mission are at risk of cancellation.[4] Every project manager should have an "elevator speech" about why the company cannot possibly survive without their particular project.[5]

Therefore, it is important to understand the precise difference between mission, goals, objectives, and strategy, as well as their relation to portfolios, programs, and projects.

2.5.1 Mission

The mission is the company's reason for existing. The mission statement is often aspirational, providing the vision and values for the company. It defines who you are, what you do, and why. Every project must have a clear link to the mission and strategy. Otherwise, why do it?

For example, Google's mission is to "organize the world's information and make it universally accessible and useful." Notice that this does not say anything about search engines. If I had asked you what Google is known for, you'd probably say something about web searching.

Google's is an excellent example of mission statement. It is concise and clear, and sets out their goals for everyone to see. An excellent example of how that mission statement helped to guide Google is to think about what happened when digital mapping became available. If the Google mission had been to create a great search engine, then digital mapping might have been viewed as outside the realm of their mission. But since their mission is to 'organize information,' and maps are an organizational tool, digital mapping was clearly within their domain.

Many companies had the capabilities to include mapping in their portfolios, but failed to see the link to the organization of information. Google understood that mapping was clearly linked to their mission and became one of the leading mapping companies.

[4] Again, it is simply job security to be able to defend your project.

[5] The notion of an elevator speech is that if you find yourself in the elevator with the President of the corporation, you have about 60 seconds to justify your existence. Practice it.

2.5.2 Goals

The goals are what you wish to accomplish. For example, a company goal might be to: *Diversify our products to get into new markets.*

19

2.5.3 Objectives

Objectives are detailed, specific statements about what the company wishes to achieve. When listing objectives, the acronym SMARTO is often used—see Table 2.2[6]

An example of a specific objective related to the above goal of diversifying into new markets is *Increase market share by 15% in 3 years.* This objective satisfies all of the SMARTO criteria.

Table 2.2: SMARTO objectives.

S	Specific	in the target objective
M	Measurable	indicators of progress
A	Assignable	to a specific person
R	Realistic	in what can be done
T	Timed	with schedules and deliverables
O	Open	for everyone to see

2.5.4 Strategy

The strategy defines precisely how the company will accomplish the objectives. For example, the strategy to accomplish the above objective of increasing market share by 15% in 3 years might be:

- Invest $50,000 in new product development.

- Set up a new portfolio evaluation method.

- Develop 3 new innovative products and dramatically enhance the existing lines.

- Diversify the portfolio into 2 totally new product areas.

[6]Actually, most textbooks use the acronym SMART (without the 'O' at the end). We believe that a vital part of successful project selection and evaluation is openness. Everyone in the company should see what is being funded and what rejected.

2.6 Portfolio Management

Which projects should a company select? If the literature is to be believed, most companies are very poor at this. Also, there is a huge difference in effectiveness between the best and worst companies in selecting projects. In this section, we briefly describe the key aspects of the scoring matrix, which is the most appropriate tool to use for portfolio management.

A portfolio consists of many different projects, all with different goals, stakeholders, and priorities. Projects must align with corporate objectives, and choosing between projects is a vital skill.

Projects may spring up in unexpected areas. For example, when tax and environmental regulations change, systems and processes must be upgraded. These so-called "compliance projects" are not glamorous, they cost money, and do not improve the bottom line. However, the project selection mechanism must also permit the selection of these types of projects.

But what makes for a successful project? Research has established that there are a few *critical success factors* (CSF).[1]

A good portfolio is characterized by:

- *The right number of projects.* Many companies take on too many projects. The result is that their projects do not have enough resources, either money or staff, and it should therefore come as no surprise that their portfolio performs poorly. Therefore, one of the essential aspects of good portfolio management is *killing projects.*

- *Good balance.* Portfolios need to have a mix of highly innovative projects, moderate extensions to existing lines, and compliance projects. One of the excellent attributes of the scoring matrix is that it achieves a balanced portfolio.

- *Clearly tied to the business mission and strategy.* Company spending and investment are linked to corporate goals, so the portfolio of projects had better be also.

There are many ways of prioritizing and selecting projects. Financial methods are popular and until recently dominated the selection process. However, selecting a project based on its return on investment is generally considered to be the *worst* way to select projects. Early in the life of a project quantities such as cash flow, profitability, and return on investment are very difficult to estimate.

21

2.6.1 Critical Success Factors

I don't know the key to success, but the key to failure is trying to please everybody.

Bill Cosby

Many studies have been conducted on what makes a successful product.[2] Successful products have a few *Critical Success Factors* in common. The most important CSFs are:

1. *A unique, differentiated product that provides significant benefits and superior value to the customer.* This is the most important CSF and is much more important than any other factor in the eventual success of a product.

2. *A strong market-driven, customer-focused orientation aimed at an "attractive market."* An attractive market is one in which there is lots of money[7] and, preferably, no competitors. Also an attractive market is defined from the customer's perspective and so it is vital to build in the voice of the customer. That is, solicit opinions from potential customers: Customers, not the project manager, determine the project's value. Also, one should carefully assess the competition and their potential responses.

3. *Solid up-front project definition.* The project's most important document is the scope, so investment of time up front is critical. Don't rush in. Clearly define the project.

4. *Don't stray from core competencies.* What are you good at? You can branch out into new areas, but if you do, be sure you know that it is risky.

5. *Execute a disciplined process.* Practice good project management and garner upper management support. Implement a portfolio management system with tough Go/Kill decisions. Continually check costs, margins, and revenues.

2.7 The Scoring Matrix

If it doesn't matter who wins or loses, then why do they keep score?

Vince Lombardi

[7]If there is not lots of money, why bother?

A sample scoring matrix is shown in Table 2.3. The top row lists the evaluation criteria, which are the factors against which projects will be scored. The CSFs established above are the foundation of the evaluation criteria in the scoring matrix. For example, knowing that a unique, differentiated project is the #1 CSF, we need a way to evaluate projects against this criterion. Other company goals may be added as criteria.

Table 2.3: A sample scoring model.

Criteria	Unique	Innovative	ROI	
Weight	5	4	2	Score
Project #1	9	8	4	85
Project #2	6	2	3	44
Project #3	9	9	9	99
Project #4	6	4	5	56

The projects to be evaluated are listed down the left hand side. Each projects is given a score out of 10 for each of the criteria. For example, Project #1 is assigned a score of 9/10 for the *Unique* criterion, and a 4 in Return on Investment (ROI).

The total project score is obtained by multiplying the weights by the scores. For example, the Project #1 score is:

$$9 \times 5 + 8 \times 4 + 4 \times 2 = 45 + 32 + 8 = 85. \tag{2.1}$$

Once all projects have been scored, they can be ranked and dollars assigned.

Scoring models are efficient: They fit management's style in that they are simple to understand, do not take a lot of time, and do not require a tedious bureaucracy. While that is useful, it is more important that scoring models:

- yield portfolios with high value projects,

- support go/kill decisions,

- assign investment that reflects strategic priorities, and

- result in well-balanced portfolios.

23

2.7.1 PMA Project Selection

As an example, suppose the Project Management Association (PMA) is considering implementing several new projects. Proposed new projects usually emerge from strategy sessions, internal solicitations throughout the company, and the marketing department. Each project has a project manager[8] and a *Charter*, which briefly describes the project, its budget, and the primary objectives. PMA's list of proposed projects is as follows:

1. A new web site to communicate with members.

2. A fundraiser solicitation by email to members.

3. A course in project management for members.

4. A membership drive to increase the membership.

The CSFs

The mission and goals of PMA are as follows: PMA is dedicated to project management research and to the education of its members. We might establish, therefore, the following criteria to evaluate the proposed projects:

- **Research.** Projects will be scored high if they increase the research knowledge of members and, since this is the primary mission, this will carry a weight of 5.

- **Education.** Projects will be scored high if they increase the education of members. This is important, but not quite as important as the research goal, and so it is assigned a weight of 4.

- **Growth.** Projects will be scored high if they grow the membership of the organization. This is not so important as research and education, and so it is assigned a weight of 2.

Each CSF should be carefully defined, and the definition is elaborated during discussions. For example, the **Research** CSF might be scored as in Table 2.4:

The Scoring Matrix

Once the CSF scoring criteria are defined, each project is given a score for each CSF–see Table 2.5. The projects are then ordered by their score (high scores at the top) to rank the projects. This is shown in Table 2.6.

[8]At this stage, the project manager is the person who will champion the project.

24

Table 2.4: Scoring values defined for the Research CSF.

Score	Definitions for Scoring the Criteria
9-10	Valuable research information for most members.
7-8	Valuable research information for many members, or useful research capabilities for majority of members.
4-7	Research information useable by a few members.
0-3	No useful research information.

Table 2.5: The scoring matrix for the PMA project.

Criteria	Research	Education	Growth	
Weight	5	4	2	Score
#1. Web Site	9	8	4	85
#2. Fundraiser	2	2	9	36
#3. PM Course	0	10	7	54
#4. Membership	0	0	8	16

The Budgets

When the projects were initially proposed, a rough budget was included. So far, we have not considered the budgets, we have evaluated them solely on their match to the CSFs. The next step involves the costs of the projects, which are entered in the *Budget* column in Table 2.6.

The final piece of data we need is the total funds allocated to be spent on projects by the organization. Suppose for PMA, this amount is $10,000. In the *Allocated* column in Table 2.6, we calculate the running total of the funded amount. The top project gets funded, so at this point we have spent $5,000. Then the next highest score is funded, and the total allocated at this point is $10,000.

25

Table 2.6: PMA Winners and Losers.

Criteria	Research	Education	Growth	Score	Budget	Allocated
Weights	5	4	2			
Funded Projects						
#1. Web Site	9	8	4	85	5,000	5,000
#3. PM Course	0	10	7	54	5,000	10,000
Losers						
#2. Fundraiser	2	2	9	44	1,000	11,000
#4. Membership	0	0	8	16	1,000	12,000

Winners and Losers

Projects are funded until we reach the allocated amount, which here is $10,000. The Fundraiser and Membership projects do not get funded.

The Strategy

The final step in the process is to decide if the funded projects make sense from a strategic perspective *as a group*. To do that, we look at the overall match to the company mission, and also such things as synergy between projects. At this stage, the committee evaluating the projects often makes changes, such as:

- *Cut the budgets.* Budgets are not sacred. Project managers may have padded their bids, assuming they would get cut. Very expensive projects need to be looked at carefully, even if they score high. Sometimes, we can do several small projects instead of a single expensive one. If the scores are close, then the decision becomes one of strategy, not scoring.

- *Combine similar projects.* The fund-raiser and the membership drive look very similar. We could ask the project managers to rebid with synergy.

- *Beware of "false precision."* That is, projects with similar scores should be considered to be equally valuable, after all there is a lot of guesswork in the scoring process. Also, a high score in one highly weighted category can dramatically affect the ranking of a project.

- *Conduct a sensitivity analysis.* After the projects are ranked, you should examine the scores to see if small changes affect the order. If so, think about the score to make sure that it is reasonable.

2.7.2 Calibration

Projects are funded based on their ranking in the scoring matrix, and the major factor that affects the ranking is the weight. While the weights are somewhat subjective, they are defined in a way that is meaningful to the company.

However, the weights are somewhat arbitrary: They are assigned based on what the company *thinks* is important. For a company starting out on the project selection process, this is about the best that can be done. Over time, however, the weights can be calibrated, making the selection process more reliable.[9]

Calibration is accomplished by having the organization go through the scoring process using historical projects. Typically, several small teams are assigned to score a dozen or so projects, including several successes, several failures, and other projects of interest that will help calibrate the matrix. The teams first suggest values for the weights, and then come together to negotiate their differences.

Next, the teams use the agreed upon weights to score selected historical projects. This must be done by returning to what the opinion of the projects was when they were first proposed.[10] The teams then rank the projects so that the highest score projects are at the top.

If the weights are correct, the company's most successful projects will be at the top of the list. Or, as is often the case, the projects that people thought were going to be successful, but that failed for surprising reasons.

In practice, the process usually works surprisingly well in that successful projects do tend to float to the top, and the failures to the bottom. The weights, the project scores, and the relative rankings should all be analyzed and discussed, and if appropriate, some of the weights might be adjusted.

2.7.3 Setting Up a Selection Process

A company can set up a project selection process as follows:

- *Calibration of the weights:* This is performed first. A dozen projects that the company performed in the past are chosen for the calibration step. These historical projects should be selected so as to provide a representative sample of company projects, including spectacular successes and failures, as well

[9] Remember, we are predicting the future, so nothing is guaranteed.

[10] Otherwise, hindsight on successes and failures will corrupt the process.

27

as a wide range of ordinary projects. The scoring matrix process is followed through using the historical projects.

The objective is to determine a set of weights that allow the best projects to float to the top, while the poor projects congregate at the bottom. Once everyone agrees that the results are reasonable, the weights are fixed and cannot be changed. The matrix is then ready for use in the selection of future projects.

This is the preferred first step, as the calibration process is also an effective way to train people in the scoring matrix process. Once training is complete, and the weights established, the process can be put in place for the evaluation and selection of proposed (i.e., future) projects.

- *Selecting new projects:* The calibrated weights are fixed and used to select projects. Over time as more data become available, the process becomes more reliable.[11] The weights can be reviewed and adjusted to gradually improve the process.

Project selection should be done by an independent committee.[12] The project selection process typically begins with a widely distributed solicitation for new project ideas.

All ongoing projects should be included in the selection process, and compete for funds with the new projects. Existing projects are included to assess their progress, and to ensure that they still match the company mission and objectives. That is, funding is allocated on a year-to-year basis, and ongoing projects are not automatically funded.

Project managers should be called in to defend their projects in front of the committee, which then assigns the project scores.

In practice, once the matrix with winners and losers is produced, a great deal of negotiation takes place. Good projects naturally rise to the top, while poor ones sink to the bottom. Most of the discussion takes place in the middle, with several projects with similar scores competing for funds. At this point, a number of factors can be considered:

- The scoring model is based on opinions and future projections, so it is not an exact science. The scores must not be taken too literally. Projects whose scores do not differ by much should be considered as equal.

[11] Since you are forecasting the future, nothing is certain.

[12] Research data suggest that the president's pet project fails more often than most.

- Budgets are not sacred. The committee will often take funds from projects and reallocate the money to projects considered more worthwhile from a strategic perspective.

- Sometimes, the committee evaluating the projects sees synergy that the individual projects managers are not aware of. The committee can combine projects and reassign budgets to get two for the price of one.[13]

- Occasionally, a poorly scoring project is seen as a strategic necessity. Funding a low-scoring project sends a message to everyone in the company about priorities.[14]

The rankings are not absolute; the important idea is the overall strategy. After the scores have been analyzed, the budgets massaged, and the synergies exploited, there should be a coherence to the list of projects to be funded. When asked, you should have a simple, coherent answer the following question: *What was funded this year?*

A decent answer might be: *We funded growth projects this year, as membership has declined.* [15]

2.8   Financial Evaluation Criteria

Project managers must be able to calculate, evaluate, and most importantly, defend the financial implications of their projects. This is generally referred to as return on investment, (ROI). The following methods are typically used: Payback and Net Present Value (NPV).

2.8.1   Payback

Payback is a simple calculation of the time it will take to recover an investment. We propose a project that will cost $30,000, and estimate it will improve cash flow by $10,000 per year. The payback is:

$$Payback = \frac{Investment}{Cash\ Flow\ Improvement} = \frac{\$30,000}{\$10,000} = 3\ years. \qquad (2.2)$$

Shorter paybacks are obviously more desirable. Payback emphasizes cash flow, but ignores interest rates and profitability. Payback also depends on estimates of future cash flows, which are uncertain.

Payback is often used to determine if a project is viable or not and, sometimes, the answer is so clear that further analysis is unnecessary.

[13]Dear PM:
 We have good news and bad news. The bad news is that your project was not funded. The good news is that if you talk to the project manager for the fund-raiser project and combine your efforts, we believe that together you have an excellent chance of being funded.

[14]Next year, there will be a bunch of proposals in that area.

[15]Note the explicit link to the strategy. A poor answer is: Umm ... Joe's and Betsy's projects.

2.8.2 Net Present Value

Would you rather have $1 now, or wait a year for it?

If I give you $1 now, you can invest it and a year from now you will have more. Therefore, the *value* of cash is a function of time. When evaluating a project income received sooner is better, and to allow for this, we use the net present value (NPV) formula:

$$NPV = -I + \sum_{n=0}^{n=N} \frac{CF_n}{(1+i)^n},$$ (2.3)

where I is the amount invested in the project; N is the total number of years for which we will carry out the calculation; n is a quantity that indexes the years; CF_n is the net cash flow in year n; and i is the discount rate.

If the NPV is positive, then the project meets the minimum desired rate of return, and the project is eligible for consideration–at least from a financial perspective. A project with a negative NPV is rejected.

The following examples might help. First, we do an example that shows how to perform the mechanics of the calculation.

NPV Example #1

We invest $2 in a project. As a result, we expect that at the end of year 1, we will receive an **additional** $1. In years 2 and 3, we will receive an additional $2 and $3 respectively. We will use a discount rate of 10%.

$$
\begin{aligned}
NPV &= -2 + \frac{1}{(1+0.1)} + \frac{2}{(1+0.1)^2} + \frac{3}{(1+0.1)^3} \\
&= -2 + 0.909 + 1.653 + 2.254 \\
&= 2.81
\end{aligned}
$$ (2.4)

The project is financially viable, since the NPV is positive. Note that if we just added the cash flows we would have: $-2 + 1 + 2 + 3 = 4$. The fact that the NPV is less than 4 is because the future value of cash is considered less valuable.

NPV Example #2

A company is planning to purchase a machine that will improve productivity by 10%, resulting in a cost savings of $15,000 per year. The machine costs $30,000, and has a potential life of 3 years. The company demands that any investment should pay off significantly better than stock market returns, insisting on a discount rate of 20%. Should the company invest in the machine?

Table 2.7: NPV Example #2.

Year	Cash Flow	Rate		NPV	Net NPV
0	-30,000	1.0		-30,000	-30,000
1	15,000	$\frac{1}{1+0.2}$	$\frac{15,000}{1.2} = 12,500$		-17,500
2	15,000	$\frac{1}{(1+0.2)^2}$	$\frac{15,000}{1.44} = 10,417$		-7,084
3	15,000	$\frac{1}{(1+0.2)^3}$	$\frac{15,000}{1.728} = 8,681$		**1,598**

The NPV calculation is presented in Table 2.7, where we see that the project has a positive NPV, and so is financially viable (but only just!).

In any NPV calculation, one should examine the validity of all parameters: Are the cash flows realistic and sustainable? Is the discount rate reasonable? Has the calculation been carried out for an unreasonably long term?

In the above example, we should ask a number of questions. Is a 3-year life a reasonable assumption? Should we consider maintenance costs, which could negatively affect the cash flow?

Any extra costs will significantly reduce the attractiveness of the investment. For example, if the cash flow is reduced to $14,000 per year, the NPV turns negative ($NPV = -509$). The calculation is very sensitive to the estimate of the cash flow, and since we are attempting to predict the future, this does not look like a very promising investment.

2.8.3 NPV in PM

The standard interpretation of NPV in the finance world is that one should only invest in a project with a positive NPV. In the world of project management, this is an overly rigid interpretation:

- *Future uncertainty*: Since a project has not been done before, the projections of cash flow into the future are likely to be uncertain.

- *Compliance projects*: Changes to government or environmental regulations may require upgrades to a company's information system. These projects are mandatory, but are unlikely to have a positive impact on cash flow.

- *Bias*: A project manager estimating future cash flows for their own project introduces bias and optimism. Their job is at stake.[16]

[16]If management demands a 20% return for a project, guess what the PM will calculate?

2.8.4 I work at a Non-Profit!

Students who work for a non-profit agency often comment that their mission has little to do with cash flows and profits. NPV can still be applied; one just has to be creative about the quantity to measure.

One student worked for an agency whose mission was to help the homeless. She established the specific objective of helping more people (see SMARTO, section 2.5.3).

Just as it is preferable to have a dollar now rather than later, the student realized that it was also better to help someone now rather than to help them later. She applied the NPV formula to the *number of people helped*. Her revised NPV gave priority to projects that helped more people sooner. It was a brilliant adaptation of NPV.[17]

[17]We like this example because it breaks the obsession of measuring everything in dollars. Often, there are more natural units to measure the value of a project. Look at your projects and ask yourself, "What really measures the value of my project?" Then think about using that to report the true measure of progress.

CHAPTER

3

DELIVERABLES AND MILESTONES

Life isn't a matter of milestones but of moments.

Rose Fitzgerald Kennedy

Deliverables and milestones are so important they deserve their own chapter.

Projects begin with an end deliverable. That is, you'll know your project when you see it.[1] But how do you tell? More importantly, how will other people know it when they see it? The answer is *Deliverables*.

Also, the *date* on which the project is delivered is the most important *Milestone*.

When a project is complete, it is because the end result is delivered. No deliverable, no project. So a project is assessed and measured by its final deliverable, and when that occurs is the final *milestone*. It naturally follows that the ongoing status and progress of the project is measured by intermediate deliverables, both the quality of the deliverables and the timing of the milestones. Deliverables are the key to everything when it comes to assessing the project.[2]

3.1 Deliverables

The focus of most processes and tools is the development, completion, and assessment of the deliverables. e.g., the *Work Breakdown Structure* is a "deliverable-

[1] Just like love.

[2] If you think about this for a moment, you will realize that it is hard to measure anything else.

33

oriented hierarchy." Further, the entire theory of earned value depends on measuring the status of the project through the assessment of deliverables.

But what, exactly, are deliverables?

Deliverables are the tangible outputs of the project.

Deliverables are *tangible*, meaning you can see them and touch them.[3] It is important to recognize that deliverables are *outputs* of the project.

A project begins with an end-deliverable, which is the project itself. There are also intermediate deliverables, such as the design and deliveries of components. The project management process results in deliverables such as documentation and managerial reports. Examples of intermediary deliverables include:

- *The Scope.* This might actually consist of several, separate deliverables as the project proceeds: Preliminary Requirements, Conceptual Design, and Detailed Design.

- *Cost and Schedule Estimates.* These are required at major milestones to report on the status of the project.

- *Intermediate project components.* These might include early prototypes and partial project deliveries.

- *Project Management Reports.* These include monthly reports, containing cost and schedule data, project status, risk updates, stakeholder issues, etc.

Sometimes, items are delivered *to* the project, but these are not considered to be deliverables. For example, in a construction project, the delivery of 2x4s, paint, and cabinets are not examples of deliverables; they are *deliveries*.

3.1.1 Measuring Deliverables

A project manager spends a lot of time and effort assessing deliverables. Every deliverable must be checked for compliance with the scope, whether it is on-time or not, and if it is within its budget. All of these questions hinge on some kind of assessment or measurement of the quality and acceptability of the deliverable. Therefore, when the deliverables are proposed, the project manager must consider how they are to be assessed and measured.

Some deliverables are actually quite easy to measure. Examples of easily measured deliverables are:

[3]Even if they are electronic documents, we are still going to use the word *tangible*. We prefer the idea of a tangible deliverable, even if it is electronic.

- Miles of roadway completed.[4]

- Linear meters of steel girders erected.

- Square meters of wall painted.

- Pages of documentation written.

Let's examine the last item a little more closely. When you propose a document as a deliverable, someone knowledgeable about the project should be able to provide an outline, a decent estimate of the number of chapters, and maybe even a rough page count. This is essential because it provides a foundation for cost and schedule estimation, as most organizations have a good idea of how many pages per week a typical employee can produce.

When the activity of writing the document is assigned, you can communicate what is expected. After two weeks, you can reasonably measure the progress against expectations. If you expect 10 pages and you receive 5, you immediately know you have a problem and should investigate.

3.1.2 Small Deliverables

Suppose you assign Tom to write a 100-page technical document. From experience with similar documents, the company estimates the typical production rate at about 5 pages per day. Therefore, the document should take Tom (whom we assume is about average) about 20 days (4 weeks) to produce. After 4 weeks, Tom delivers only 50 pages, half of what you expected, with several major sections missing. You ask, "Tom! What happened?" Tom replies,

"The document was much more difficult than I anticipated!"

This is not Tom's fault. This is bad project management.

Deliverables should be divided into small, discrete, manageable pieces. The above document should have been divided into chapters (or sections) of 10-15 pages each. Then after the first week, you should ask Tom, *"How ya doin'?"*

If the document is more difficult than anticipated, you know immediately, not after four weeks. You still have the problem of a difficult-to-write document, but you know about it much earlier. You now have options: You can assign more people. You can assign different people. You can revise the table of contents. You can even ask the customer if any sections can be deleted.

The key is to divide all deliverables into small, discrete, manageable pieces. In fact, a good rule for the size of deliverables is:

[4] Drive by any road construction project, and you can measure for yourself the miles completed.

35

A deliverable should be able to be produced by one-to-two people in one-to-two weeks.

Break all the deliverables into pieces with the above rule. That way, you can manage them. If someone gets into trouble, you will know immediately.

When dividing up a deliverable, there are several things to consider:

- *Small.* The earlier you can tell if the deliverable is in trouble, the more options you have to fix it. Small deliverables make this possible.

- *Discrete.* The more separable the deliverable is into independent units, the less interaction there is among both the content and the staff. When building a house, one naturally divides deliverables between the plumber, electrician, carpenter, etc. The pieces are more manageable when divided into discrete technical sections that have little interaction.

- *Manageable.* Dividing the document into pieces also makes them manageable. It is easier to determine their cost and schedule, and to track them during production.

- *Parallel Development.* When it comes planning, dividing the deliverables into many smaller pieces gives the project manager the ability to work on the activities in parallel, which shortens the schedule. Also, smaller deliverables can often be assembled in different ways, which increases flexibility, e.g., in staff assignments.

3.1.3 Progressive Elaboration

Since a project has not been done before, you learn as you go and the project manager must expect changes, which must be managed with care. The gradual evolution of the project plan is called *progressive elaboration.*[5]

> *Progressive Elaboration is the continuous improvement and detailing of the plan as more specific information, and more accurate estimates, become available.*

The progressive detailing of the project management plan is also called *rolling wave planning.*[6]

Developing a prototype is an excellent way of obtaining planning data. A prototype will often solve technical problems, highlight risks, and lead to better estimates of the cost and schedule.

[5] Note that, technically, progressive elaboration applies to the project management plan.

[6] Both progressive elaboration and rolling wave planning apply to the plan, as distinct from *continuous improvement,* which is a part of quality improvement.

3.2 Milestones

It's a funny kind of month, October. For the really keen cricket fan
it's when you discover that your wife left you in May.

Denis Norden

Milestones allow you to track the status of the project. For example, the completion of the scope is a major milestone for all projects. Every milestone should have a date associated with it. During project planning the date is the planned milestone, and after successful execution, it becomes the actual completion date.

> *A milestone is a significant point or event in the project.*

For example, the completion of project planning is a major milestone for a project. The milestone is marked by the completion of the *Project Management Plan*, and its acceptance by the customer. It is appropriate, therefore, to create a milestone called *Planning Complete* when the plan is accepted by the customer.

A milestone is also considered to be:[1]

> *A milestone is an activity with zero duration.*

For example, in the PMA project, we could schedule an activity called *Design Complete*, and give it zero duration (which makes it a milestone). We can then link the milestone to end of the *Design* activity. That way, if the design is delayed, the completion milestone will automatically be delayed as well.

You can also create milestones for the planning events. For example, you might create a milestone called *Scope Planning Complete*. The difference between the scope planning and actual completion of the scope is useful information.

These milestone examples come from the New Kitchen project: As of June 1st:

- *Demolition Complete.* Planned: March 31st. Actually completed March 31st.

- *Gas line installed.* Planned: April 15th. Delayed by the gas company; completed May 15th.

- *Cabinet Delivery.* Planned: June 22nd. Not complete, on schedule.

Notice how the milestones accurately communicated the status of the project. In fact, project status meetings are usually all about milestones: Were they delivered on time?

Major milestones are associated with major deliverables. Since the *scope* is an important document, it is vital to track its status, and this would be reported through a major milestone called *Scope Complete*.

Consider the PMA web site project, the major milestones are: delivery and acceptance of the scope; completion of prototype user interface; completion of design; installation of web server; delivery of the major functional modules (there are several of these); delivery of documentation; integration complete; testing complete; user training conducted; and formal acceptance of the final project.

The status of the project at any point in time is clearly indicated by the completed milestones. Therefore, a project manager is expected to regularly report on the status of all deliverables during the execution of the project. If a milestone is late, the customer will immediately ask, "How late?" We leave the task of precisely determining the exact status of the cost and schedule of the deliverables to Chapter 12–Earned Value.

More milestones mean better project management. Since milestones usually denote completed deliverables, customers and stakeholders will be better able to judge what has been completed. But the milestones must make sense: They must be distributed appropriately throughout the project, and, at least, indicate the completion of major deliverables.

An excellent example of a well-planned milestone comes from the New Kitchen project. Mark listed in the contract several partial payments and one was *upon delivery of blue board.* Note that this payment was tied to a delivery, not a date. The partial payment allowed him to pay for the blue board, a major cash outlay, even if the schedule changed.

4

PROJECTS AND COMPANIES

There's no crying in baseball!

Tom Hanks, A League of Their Own

The project manager is *responsible* for the project. This means that project managers must do whatever it takes to get the job done and satisfy stakeholders. What happens when these ideas conflict with the goals or culture of the company?

This is an important issue for all project managers, because in most respects, companies and projects have completely different goals.

Both companies and projects must be successful: companies must flourish while project goals are achieved. The trick is to balance the needs of a project with the needs of the company.

The competition between projects and companies is inherent in their structures, and the stress created on project managers is a fundamental part of the job. If you wonder why organizations structure themselves in the complex ways discussed below, they are trying the balance the goals of the company and the goals of their projects.

But remember, as a project manager, you are responsible. No excuses.[1]

[1] Paraphrasing Tom Hanks, *There's no crying in project management!*

4.1 Projects Goals vs. Company Goals

Projects violate most of the ideas that companies consider as good management.[2] To be specific, projects and companies have completely different and competing goals. Project goals are almost always in direct conflict with those of the company that sponsors it.

The goal of a company is to manage efficiently, which implies repetitive actions that can be continuously improved. The Japanese have a word for it: *kaizen*.[3] A simple example is travel expenses: It doesn't make any sense to allow each department to have their own travel forms and procedures. Companies therefore, insist on a standardized, company-wide, travel reimbursement process.

On the other hand, by definition, projects are unique. How can you improve something if you only do it once?

Many of the key characteristics of projects are listed in Table 4.1, along with the opposite characteristic, which companies desire. We argue that for almost all project characteristics, the goals of the project (on the left) are completely opposite to the goals of the company (on the right).

Table 4.1: Project Goals vs. Company Goals.

Projects	Companies
Unique Creative, individualistic	Manage efficiently Routine, repetitive
Inter-Disciplinary Integration skills	Departments with expertise Technical expertise development
Project expertise Specific, narrow needs	Creation of subject matter experts Wide, general capabilities
PM in charge	Department managers in charge
Staff rewarded for project performance	Staff rewarded for company performance

[2]This is a strong statement, but we firmly believe it to be true in most instances.

[3]When considered as a philosophy, *kaizen* becomes the process of continuous improvement.

Projects are inherently interdisciplinary, while companies are organized into departments, usually with a single expertise. Departments are good for companies because they acquire and develop their expertise by investing in the skills of their employees, which generally enhances the capabilities of the company. Company departments stay current by investing in technology, staff training, etc.

On the other hand, projects are typically shortsighted because a project's technology may be static. Once the project team has learned enough about the technology to implement the current project, there is no incentive on the part of the project to invest in staff growth. In fact, projects are defined by their scope document, to which changes are actively discouraged. Therefore, it is not unusual for the skills of people working on long-term projects to become obsolete.

Departments are silos of expertise, and they have little or no incentive to become interdisciplinary. In fact, this is often discouraged as it dilutes their capabilities. An accounting department needs expertise in accounting, and doesn't really care about environmental regulations or web design. On the other hand, projects are inherently interdisciplinary, and a project manager may have to worry about accounting, environmental regulations, and web design.

4.1.1 The PM's Friend: The Technical Director

The role of the project manager (PM) is to manage the customer, the money, and the schedule. While the PM manages the deliverables' cost and schedule, who manages their content?[4]

For example: Do the deliverables meet customer requirements? Does the project actually work?[5]

In every project there is always a role for a person we call the *Technical Director* (TD) whose job it is to manage the technical aspects of the project.[6] There is a natural, and inherent, tension between the PM and the TD:

PM: Ship it on time on Friday!
TD: No! It's not ready!

Another word that describes the role of the TD is *architect*, in its most general sense. For example, on an IT project, there may be an architect, whose job it is to create the design, including the human interface, the database structures, etc.

In the movie industry, we suggest that the TD is the director, who controls the performance factors: directing, casting, camera angles, staging, lighting, etc. The producer controls the money, the schedule, and interfaces to the studio (the customer). The producer is fulfilling the role of the PM. What makes the movie case interesting is that it is one of the few cases where the TD often has more power than the PM.

On most projects, conflicts often arise when major deliverables are due. The situation typically evolves as follows: The project manager is pressing the team

[4] This entire topic is neglected in the PMBOK and most books. We happen to think it is really interesting and the subject of much discussion.

[5] We are deliberately staying away from the word *quality* here. Many organizations have a Quality Control group, but they work after the design and construction to check everything. What we are referring to is the responsibility for the creative design aspects and the idea that the project satisfies the mission and objectives.

[6] For small projects the PM and TD may be the same person, which leads to schizophrenia.

41

to meet the schedule for a major deliverable. The technical director is resisting, explaining:

- The performance is not up to the *spec*.

- To meet the required performance, extra time and money is required.

- Therefore, the deliverable is going to be late.

This is really bad project management!

It is not the team's fault, it is the fault of the project manager. A bad project manager will continue to insist that the team deliver on time, and more forcefully as the deadline approaches. Meanwhile, the PM assures the customer the project is on schedule and budget.

When the delivery date rolls around, lo and behold, the product is not ready, is over budget, and behind schedule.[7]

Let's roll the clock back and suggest a better approach. First, as soon as the TD is assigned, the project manager sets about getting to know the TD. They discuss the tasks, the budget, and the schedule. They discuss all of the estimates, and where problems might lie.[8]

The PM and TD jointly develop a workable project. The TD designs the approach, and the PM the cost and schedule, but they cooperate. The project manager sells the cost and schedule to the customer. The TD sells the product to the customer who agrees to the *spec*.

When technical issues arise, the TD meets with the PM and explains the problem. Together they work out the impacts and discuss options. When cost and schedule issues arise, the PM meets with the TD and explains the problem. Together they work out the impacts and discuss options.

In our view, if you are a project manager, it's your problem. Whatever it is.

Late? Your problem.

Over budget? Your problem.

TD whining? Your problem.

As the project manager it is your job to *induce* the team to perform, to *induce* the stakeholders to approve the project, and to *induce* the customer to pay for it.[9]

[7] Meanwhile, the team are all whispering, "We told you so!"

[8] Start now. Make sure the TD is your best friend.

[9] No exceptions. No excuses.

42

4.2 Cultures

A nation's culture resides in the hearts and in the soul of its people.

Mahatma Gandhi

You need to make sure your project does not infringe on cultural norms, which are the values, beliefs, and expectations that permeate the company. The team can either adopt or reject the organization's values, beliefs, and expectations, and their attitude will directly affect the project's success.[10]

The aspect of culture that we considering here is 'organizational culture,' and in particular, those aspects that apply to the project team. Cultures are defined by 'cultural norms.' [8]

Norms include the common knowledge regarding how to get the work done, what is acceptable, and who is influential. Organizational norms typically include:

1. Shared visions and beliefs: What makes your company good?

2. Unspoken company expectations: Is quality work expected? Can you slip a deadline to get it right?

3. Explicit policies and procedures: Every company has a P&P manual.

4. Views of authority and power: Can you easily approach the President?

5. Work hours: Are you expected to work extra hours to get the job done?

6. Ethics. What is considered right?

Often, there is a whole collection of unwritten rules that one has to learn when you join a new organization. For example, is the CEO a gregarious person who chats with everyone, or is the CEO a tyrant that nobody dares speak to?

Think about the culture of your own organization. What are the myths and stories that get passed down between employees? What are the first things you tell a new employee?[11] When you changed jobs, what was the first thing you noticed about the organization?

A project manager needs to understand the culture of the organization because it is very difficult to go against. For example, if the company allows and encourages flexibility in its working hours, then a project manager cannot arbitrarily impose a

[10] It can be empowering or destructive.

[11] Especially the off-the-record stuff.

43

regime of time-clock punching. In a flexible working situation, the project manager must insist on deliverables, and let the team figure out how to best deliver them.[12]

One of my favorite examples of a culture clash occurred when I was assigned to write a piece of a proposal teamed with another company. I had to work at their site and the assignment lasted several weeks. Near the end, we all had to work over a weekend. I was told that dress was informal for weekends and I could wear anything I wanted.

I showed up in jeans and a Red Sox T-shirt.[13] They all showed up identically dressed in khakis and polo shirts. I was not dressed correctly! Their khakis and polos were just another uniform, and I was definitely not regulation. This is a good example of an organizational norm: It was unwritten but very specific. Everyone eventually learns to comply with these unwritten expectations.

Research suggests that there are ten characteristics that capture the essence of an organization's culture and these are described in Table 4.2.[1]

Each of the characteristics in Table 4.2 has two extremes, which are defined in Table 4.3. Usually, the desires of projects and companies favor opposite extremes. For example, a project would probably prefer the team member to identify with the task at hand (i.e., the project), while the company might prefer identification with the organization.

The interesting question is: How do the above characteristics affect projects? Generally, projects tend to prefer the left hand extreme in Table 4.3.

4.2.1 The Abilene Paradox

It was a hot day in Coleman Texas, but Jerry Harvey was cool and enjoying lemonade on his back porch, playing dominoes with his wife and in-laws. Harvey's father-in-law was concerned that the others were bored, so he suggested that they all drive to Abilene for lunch. No one wanted to go, but nobody spoke up.

So they all drove 106 miles, ate really bad food, and then drove back.

Nobody wanted to leave the back porch, the fan, the lemonade, or the dominoes. But, no one spoke up. Nobody wanted to go to Abilene, but they all went anyway.

Harvey describes this as an inability to manage agreement. [9] However, the Abilene Paradox also includes the implications of speaking up. Does your organization encourage speaking up? If a project manager does not encourage people to speak up, then everyone will drive to Abilene!

---

[12]You can measure the progress of deliverables without asking what time people showed up for work.

[13]This was deliberate, because I was in Orioles country.

44

Table 4.2: Cultural Characteristics and Project vs. Company Goals.

Cultural Characteristic	Project vs. Company Goal
Member identity	Do you identify with the project or the company? In projectized organizations, the team tends to identify with the project, while in functional organizations they identify more with their department and company.
Group emphasis	Do you prefer to work in a group, or as an individual? Projects favor group work, although a project needs good technical skills to solve problems.
People focus	Do management decisions incorporate the views of the employees, or do they tend to strictly focus on projects, or even the bottom line?
Unit integration	Are departments structured to work independently, or are they encouraged to work together?
Control	Do rules, policies and procedures tend to dominate employee behavior? Does the company encourage independent thinking? Can PMs bend the rules?
Risk tolerance	Are employees encouraged to take risks, and even allowed to fail occasionally? Projects require innovation, which means voyaging into uncharted territory.
Reward criteria	Are salary increases and promotions awarded according to project or department performance, or other secret criteria?
Conflict tolerance	Are employees encouraged to speak out, and openly air their views? How does the company handle dissent?
Means-ends orientation	Does management focus on the outcomes and results or the processes to achieve them? Projects need to have discipline and procedures (means) but must deliver (ends).
Open focus	Does the organization encourage open discussion? Who is allowed to talk to customers?

Upper management's power to hire and fire can squelch speaking up. Does the company discourage a frank and outspoken discussion when safety is being compromised for profit? The Abilene paradox explains the inability of the participants to speak the truth when faced with policies they do not support. Discouraging dissent confuses telling the truth with disloyalty, and even betrayal.[14]

[14]Someone experiencing this conflict may be left with ethical and emotional challenges related to self-betrayal, shame, guilt, and even moral failure for not having acted upon his or her appraisal of the situation.

Table 4.3: Cultural Characteristics and their Extremes.

Project Dominance	Cultural Characteristic	Company Dominance
Task	1. Member Identity	Organization
Individual	2. Group Emphasis	Group
Task	3. People Focus	People
Independent	4. Unit Integration	Interdependent
Loose	5. Control	Tight
Low	6. Risk Tolerance	High
Project Performance	7. Reward Criteria	Department Performance
Low	8. Conflict Tolerance	High
End	9. Means-Ends Orientation	Means
Internal	10. Open Communications	External

4.2.2 A Cultural Clash

My son experienced a really good example of the clash of norms. He is an animator, and when the movie he was working on was close to its scheduled release date, everyone was forced to work 60 hours per week. Ok, so far. But every morning, the producer sent around junior assistant producers to see what time the animators arrived at their desks.

Animators are bunch of independent arty types, who usually don't respond well to authority.[15] One Friday morning in LA, there was a huge pile-up on the freeway, and everyone arrived late. Most had worked late the night before, so didn't appreciate reacted to junior assistant producers[16] yelling that they should be at their desks by 9 am.

4.2.3 Rewards

A second example from the same project illustrates the problem of attempting to reward productivity. The producer decided to reward the team that completed the most shots. (A reasonable goal.) The producer chose as the reward a free Sunday lunch at the animators' favorite watering hole.

My son's team connived to come in *second* every week. That way, they were seen as productive team players. But, as they were already working 6 days a week, the last

[15]The 'creatives,' as they refer to themselves.

[16]The 'suits'

46

thing they wanted was to give up a Sunday—their only day off!

This shows how problematical the use of rewards can be. People will manipulate the system in creative ways to achieve goals you would never have thought of.

If you insist on checking every detail, you cannot expect the team to take risks. If you curtail freedom, you cannot expect people to experiment. If you yell at people when they fail, they will never try anything new without checking with you first.

When the project manager does not understand the culture, the team will find ways around the system. We've seen many project failures from project managers trying to impose unreasonable discipline on creative types. The key is the "deliverable." If they deliver, who cares how they do it?[17]

4.3   Project Structures

> **Peace is a daily, a weekly, a monthly process, gradually changing opinions, slowly eroding old barriers, quietly building new structures.**
>
> *John F. Kennedy*

Companies set up three types of structures in which to execute projects: Functional, Matrix, and Projectized.

Each structure has different strengths and weaknesses. Rarely does the project manager get to choose the company structure, so it is important to understand the role of projects in the organization, and the challenges that will arise.

4.3.1   Functional Organizations

Departments, which have a specific mission, dominate a functional organization and the power of the project manager is weak. When a project arises, a team is assembled from the departments. Once the project is over, the team members return to their home departments. The managers of the departments are referred to as *functional managers*.

The functional approach is common in small organizations that do not want to create an expensive project structure. Management is handled through normal departmental channels. Table 4.4 describes the advantages and disadvantages of performing projects in functional organizations.

An example of a functional organization is a university, which is organized into academic departments. Occasionally, a project arises that needs an interdisciplinary

[17]Of course, we could just be explaining our personal philosophy here.

47

Table 4.4: The advantages and disadvantages of performing projects in *Functional Organizations*.

Advantages	Disadvantages
No organizational changes required	Unclear motivation for a project
Easy to create teams	Hard to prioritize projects
Departments build expertise	Staff are loyal to their department
Staff have expertise	Hard to coordinate interdisciplinary activities
Team returns to department when project is complete	Lack of ownership for the project

team, e.g., hiring staff, developing a marketing strategy, and rewriting the web site. Each of these requires expertise from many departments, and so a committee is formed to accomplish the project. The team members meet and work to accomplish the project, but do not leave their departments.

Suppose the Dean calls me up and asks me to chair a committee to hire a new Director for the student admissions department. I say 'OK.'[18] But I do not work directly for the Dean, I work for my department chair, who signs my pay raises.[19] In this example, the academic department manager is a *functional manager*.

But I still need to do a good job on the search committee. I can expect to get subject area expertise from the student admissions department. As chair, I am the project manager and responsible for the schedule (the person should start at the beginning of next semester), the budget (can I take the candidates to lunch at expensive restaurants?), and the resources (committee assignments). But I am a classic project manager in that I cannot order them around.[20]

While the project is important to the University, it is not my major priority. In a choice between answering emails from students and my committee assignment, which will I chose? Student emails.[21] In this example, we see many of the issues associated with performing projects in functional organizations.

4.3.2 Matrix Organizations

The matrix structure is a hybrid in which the project team is assembled from departmental assets. There are two chains of command: A project chain and a department (or functional) chain, and, as a result, team members report to two managers: The project manager on project matters, and their functional manager

[18]Because she is the Dean, and I have no real choice!

[19]So you can bet that I will want to keep him happy.

[20]I have to *induce* them to perform.

[21]Nothing makes a professor's life more miserable than a bunch of angry students.

48

on technical matters. This is a source of pressure for the team members, who must keep two bosses happy.

While complex, the matrix organization gives companies the best of both worlds. Projects get the advantage of a dedicated project manager, and a Program Management Office that invests in projects. The company realizes the long-term benefits and efficiencies of departmental structures, which are better at nurturing technical expertise and moving staff between projects. The advantages and disadvantages of performing projects in Matrix Organizations are summarized in Table 4.5.

Table 4.5: The advantages and disadvantages of performing projects in *Matrix* Organizations.

Advantages	Disadvantages
Clear project management Investment by PMO	Conflict between PM and TD
Easy to create teams	Team members have two bosses
Departments build expertise	Staff are loyal to their department
Departments provide resources to projects	Stressful, multiple bosses
Team members return to their department when project is complete	Department goals compete with project goals
Flexible assignment of staff to small and large projects	Can be slow and bureaucratic
Standard corporate policies and procedures for all projects	Corporate goals may conflict with project goals

Matrix organizations are classified as strong, balanced, or weak, where the adjective applies to the power of the project manager. A strong matrix behaves like a projectized organization (see below), while a weak matrix looks somewhat like a functional organization. The balanced matrix is the traditional form, where the project manager is responsible for the project and the functional managers have responsibility for its technical performance. Many large Defense Contractors are organized in a matrix structure.

The matrix structure is the most important one to understand:

1. It is a powerful way of accomplishing complex projects, while simultaneously balancing the needs of the organization and the needs of the project.

49

2. All of the managerial, staffing, and technical issues that occur in the matrix structure also occur in the other structures. The issues are much clearer in the matrix structure and easier to understand.[22]

4.3.3 Projectized Organizations

In a projectized organization, most of a company's work is performed in projects. Each project has its own independent team under the leadership of a project manager, who is usually dedicated to the project. The advantages and disadvantages of projectized organizations are summarized in Table 4.6.

Table 4.6: The advantages and disadvantages of performing in *Projectized* Organizations.

Advantages	Disadvantages
Teams are easily assembled	No standard policies
Clear authority–the PM	Resources may be duplicated
Responsive	Rivalries between project teams
Cohesive and committed	Limited technical expertise
Efficient communication	No place for staff when project is complete
Explicit staff expertise	No long-term growth plan for staff

An example of a projectized organization is a construction company. Each new building is a project, and teams are assembled as needed. When the project is complete, the team members all move on to other projects. That is a polite way of saying that either there is another project for the team to work on or they are unemployed. They also hire subcontractors as needed: steel workers, plumbers, carpenters, etc. Everyone is dedicated to the project.

Another example of a projectized organization is the movie business. The team for a movie is assembled from independent contractors: the director, scriptwriters, actors, lighting techs, grips, etc. When the project is over, they all move on, to the next movie or unemployment.

[22] If you understand the problems in matrix organizations, you will understand the issues wherever or whenever they occur.

5

PROJECT LIFE CYCLES

Life is what happens to you while you're busy making other plans.

John Lennon

All projects go through natural life cycle patterns or phases. The details differ from one industry to another, but all projects have an orderly sequence of phases and activities. We describe a few project life cycles from various industries to illustrate the diversity of patterns.

A simple, informal way to remember the project life cycle is by what we call the A-B-C-D-E-F stages:[1]

Alignment: of project goals with company strategy.
Business Case: the need and reason for the project's existence.
Charter the project: officially launch it and identify the project manager.
Develop the project: plan it.
Execute the project: do it!
Finish the project: close it down and learn its lessons.

Projects may have sub-projects, which also follow the same life cycle. The life cycle should seamlessly integrate the project management functions and processes with the technical aspects of the project. Life cycle activities include:

[1] At this point, we can get carried away with, G: evaluate goals, etc.

51

- *Organizing:* Determining the quality and quantity of resources needed and using communication skills to obtain and manage them.

- *Motivating:* Creating an environment that provides satisfaction to the team members and encourages them to do their best.

- *Directing:* Providing management and leadership to stakeholders and influencing them to achieve project goals

5.1   Products and Services Life Cycles

We first carefully distinguish between the *product* and *project* life cycles. The Product Life Cycle begins when a product is conceived and put into development. It is then introduced to the market, followed by a growth in sales, a sales peak, and a gradual decline. See Figure 5.1.

Profits follow a different curve. There is an early investment when the product is in development, and profits do not accrue until the product has been in the marketplace for a while. Eventually, if the product is successful, there is a period of profitability, called the mature stage, followed by a decline, and the product's withdrawal from the market.

The reality is complicated by many issues. Successful products rarely exist in isolation and often evolve through product lines, which enhances their life. Successful

Figure 5.1: The product life cycle

products engender competition and technological innovations may make products obsolete. Also, sales are not necessarily a good measure of the product health, since they are influenced by the economy, competitors, and customer whims.

The services life cycle also generally follows that of Figure 5.1, although many services are not designed to be profitable, e.g., renewal of a driver's license and computer telephone support. Other services are designed to be profitable, such as legal and accounting, restaurants, and bars. Many services are performed by large, non-profit organizations, such as universities and theaters.[2]

For new products and services, the development stage is typically a project. Once the product or service is introduced to the market, it is no longer a project, as the activities become routine: manufacturing, sales, distribution, etc. There may be occasional projects along the way, such as a product improvement, a new advertising campaign, or the implementation of a new supply chain.

5.2 The Project Life Cycle

Projects have their own life cycles (within the product life-cycle) with an orderly sequence of integrated activities.[3] There are three stages in the project life cycle:

1. *Pre-Project Phase*

   Activities in the pre-project phase include recognizing a business opportunity, creating a business case, and obtaining seed funding.

   The primary job of the pre-project phase is to ensure that there is a viable project, before one invests money in it. This is referred to as requirements definition, although design work is required to validate major technical issues. Also required at this stage are preliminary cost and schedule estimates.

   Building a prototype is often an efficient way to determine feasibility, estimate the cost and schedule, and analyze major risks. Of course, a prototype can be considered to be a separate project.

2. *Implementation Phase*

   During the project implementation phase, a project goes through a structured development life cycle, where the product or service is defined, designed, built, tested, and accepted by the sponsor.

   The products of this phase are the project deliverables, including the product or service itself, as well as intermediate deliverables such as the design. Outputs from this phase also include the project management process outputs.

[2]While most universities are 'non-profits,' they operate with all the same constraints as profit-making entities on sales, staff utilization, and overhead.

[3]Project life cycles are different from the project management *process groups*.

The deliverables in this phase are the outputs from the processes, e.g., *The Charter* is an output of the *Create Charter* PMBOK process; and the *Budget Forecast* is an output of the *Control Costs* process.

Each phase should have a clearly specified *Decision Gate*, which is a critical decision point, where the deliverables are carefully reviewed, along with the cost and schedule. At a decision gate, the team, customer, and stakeholders review the products and select among three possible outcomes: move to next phase; fix the products by revisiting activities; or kill the project.

3. *Post-Project Phase*

The post-project phase begins as soon as the product or service is commissioned and operational. The activities in this phase are typically not part of the project, consisting of such things as manufacturing, routine services, and maintenance activities.[4]

In some industries, the post-project phase is very expensive. For example, the decommissioning and retirement of a nuclear plant is extensive and rigorous, and can take several years.

They key idea is that each phase consists of activities with deliverables, and is concluded with a decision gate. Table 5.1 gives examples.

Table 5.1: Example of Activities, Deliverables, and Decision Gates.

Activities	Deliverables	Decision Gate Questions
Feasibility Study	Business Case Preliminary Plan Stakeholder Register	Customer support exists? Customers perceive value? Delivery dates acceptable? Cost & Schedule acceptable?
Requirements Analysis	Specification Scope Risk Register	Is the project feasible? Performance metrics acceptable? Risks acceptable? Contingency funds available?

[4]e.g, painting bridges when they rust.

[5]Despite the different vocabulary, the PM should still focus on scope, milestones and deliverables.

5.3 Industry Life Cycle Examples

Each industry has its own version of the project life cycle. Because the terminology and importance of deliverables is different, each industry has naturally evolved their own approach.[5]

5.3.1   The Software Development Life Cycle

The software development life cycles consists of:

1. *Definition phase:* During this phase the customer's problems are defined and the requirements elicited. The team conducts systems analyses and develops the project plan. The deliverable is the specification, which contains the user requirements, and a test plan to measure compliance.

2. *Design phase:* The software and business analysts design an acceptable solution for the customer. The deliverable is the design document. Also, the project manager finalizes the baseline cost and schedule.

3. *Construction phase:* The software is coded, and unit testing may occur here.

4. *Testing phase:* The product or service is tested against the specification.

5. *Acceptance phase:* The customer analyzes the acceptance test results and, if satisfactory, signs the acceptance agreement. Customer training may occur during this phase. The operation phase begins after customer acceptance.

The software development cycle is made up of four phases, but, depending on the size of the project, there may be additional phases or sub-phases. Each phase and sub-phase must have clear objectives, as well as achievable milestones and deliverables–see Table 5.2.

Table 5.2: Software life cycle: Major deliverables and milestones.

Phase	Deliverables	Milestone
Definition	Project Plan, Specification Acceptance criteria	Customer acceptance of plans & the specification
Design	Design Document Detail Design	Customer acceptance of design 40% complete point
Construction	The project	Successful Validation & Verification
Acceptance	Acceptance Test Results	Customer acceptance of project Contractual Close Out

5.3.2   The Pharmaceutical Industry Life Cycle

To contrast with the software development life cycle, we present a brief overview of a typical pharmaceutical life cycle, which consists of:[1]

- *Research and Development*: New potential drugs are identified.

- *Discovery and Screening*: Drugs are refined and tested.

- *Pre-clinical Development*: The effects on trial populations are determined.

- *Clinical Trial Phase*: The drug goes from laboratory sample to pilot production and, finally, to commercial production.

- *Registration Phase*: Government forms and compliance documentation are completed and, hopefully, the drug is approved.

- *Post Registration Phase*: Packaging and marketing occurs.

5.3.3   The Construction Industry Life Cycle

The key stages in the construction life cycle are:[2]

- *Apply for Permits.*

- *Site Work*: Clear ground, install temporary power and utilities. Inspection.

- *Foundation*: Excavate, concrete, basement walls, waterproof and insulate. Inspection.

- *Framing*: Install joists, frame walls. Inspection.

- *Dry In*: Sheathing, roof decking, shingles, doors and windows. Inspection.

- *Utilities*: Plumbing, electrical, HVAC, phone, cable, computers, alarms. Inspection.

- *Interior Finishing*: Insulating, dry wall, paint and wallpaper, cabinets, tile and appliances. Inspection.

- *Landscaping and Groundwork*: Driveway, sod, plantings. Inspection.

- *Final Acceptance*: Walk-through, inspection and complete punch list. Conduct final acceptance for Certificate of Occupancy.

Notice that in the construction life cycle, each phase explicitly ends with an inspection. This is a useful lesson for other industries.

5.4 Agile Project Management

The focus of this discussion is software projects, however, the basic principles hold true for all other industries as well. Agile software development processes are the most mature, and so represent the best state of the art.

5.4.1 The Old Way: The Waterfall

Historically, the *Waterfall* development cycle was the most widely used method for software development and is regarded as the classical approach. The waterfall approach is characterized by sequential steps. Once a process has been completed, it is not visited again. In this respect it is rather like a waterfall in that the water trickles down, and it only goes one way.

The characteristic aspect of the waterfall method is that the requirements are developed up-front and frozen. Then the software is designed and tested. The drawback is that the final software may arrive long after the requirements were developed. Often, the user requirements have evolved and the resulting system is obsolete.

It is widely acknowledged that the key strength of the waterfall is its strong managerial control over the process and, in particular, the schedule and costs.[6]

5.4.2 Evolutionary

To address the limitations of the waterfall model, researchers and practitioners introduced alternate methods, which we classify as *evolutionary*. One such model is rapid prototyping or rapid application development (RAD).[3] Widespread agreement on what this approach actually entails is difficult to achieve, however it typically involves:

- *Throwaway prototypes.* These are developed to clarify the user requirements and to test design approaches. The prototype is discarded and one subsequently moves to a more structured approach (perhaps even waterfall).

- *Built-upon development.* Development is iterative, designed to clarify user requirements and analyze the system design, continually delivering incremental improvements, and gradually refining the product.

- *Gathering requirements.* Focus groups are used to define requirements.

- *Reusing software components.* Previously tested components are used to enhances productivity and reduce errors.

[6]Since the requirements are nailed down, scope creep is minimized, and the cost should be relatively stable. Unless, of course, the problem is poorly defined, in which case, all bets are off.

57

- *Iterating the software design.* This ensures the system continues to meet performance requirements, even as the system loads and user base increase.

- *Deferring major improvements and enhancements to the next version.* Builders resist the urge to implement changes in the current iteration.

- *Less formality throughout the software development life cycle.* The focus is on the products and whether they satisfy the customer.[7]

- *Continuously evaluating the outcome with users.* To keep them happy.

5.4.3 Agile

An important and growing trend is that of *agile* project management.[8]

Agile development models are evolutionary in nature, the requirements evolve as the product is developed. There is flexibility in the development of components, as well as their cost and schedule. The model is particularly appropriate when the system requirements are vague or when the project feasibility is in doubt.

There are several variations of the agile development approach but they all share the following characteristics:

- The development process, the product, the cost, and the schedule all evolve.

- Proactive development of test cases and user scenarios ahead of time to analyze and test both the current and future iterations of the product.

- Periodic delivery and installation of product versions in the operational environment to ensure timely and increasingly effective functionality.

- Continuous evolution based on user input.

The agile approach has its roots in *The Agile Manifesto*, which contains 12 philosophical aspirations:[4]

1. Customer satisfaction by rapid delivery and integration of useful software.

2. Welcoming changing users requirements, even late in the development.

3. Working software is delivered in weeks rather than months.

4. Working software is the principal measure of progress.

[7]This appears to imply that formality is burdensome. We prefer to emphasize that the focus is on satisfying the customers by providing real products, rather than on attempting to define every detail in a document.

[8]In fact, agile is rapidly becoming the rage!

58

5. Sustainable development–maintaining a constant pace.

6. Daily co-operation between business people, users and developers.

7. Face-to-face conversation is strongly preferred.

8. Projects are built around motivated individuals, who should be trusted.

9. Continuous attention to technical excellence and good design.

10. Simplicity is the key in everything.

11. Self-organizing teams.

12. Regular adaptation to changing circumstances.

5.4.4 The Scrum Model

The "Scrum" model is another popular framework based on agile principles.[5] It is based on the Pareto Principle: The important realization that 20% of the product functionality can represent 80% of the business value.

The spirit of rugby is inherent in the methodology. In rugby there are planned "set" scrums and spontaneous "loose" scrums. The project is "set" by the Scrum Master who ensures that scrum practices are understood and followed. The Scrum Master also encourages the team to be self-directed, spontaneous and creative, in analogy with the "loose" scrum. The scrum model contains the following ideas:

- The customer is the Product Owner. The Project Manager is the Scrum Master. The software engineers are the Team.

- Development iterations are called *sprints*, which are typically less than 30 days in duration.

- The product features to be implemented in a sprint are determined during a sprint planning meeting.

- Brief 15 minute, stand-up meetings are held each day to review the previous day's work and to plan the current day's work.

- Daily meetings allow the Scrum Master to determine the productivity rate (and refine estimates and schedules) and to manage risks.

- A sprint ends with a *sprint retrospective* to review the work and plan for a future sprint.

59

The term "scrum" has its roots in the game of rugby and refers to the formation of players grouped together pushing each other with arms interlocked and heads down. The scrum metaphor helps us visualize what happens in the scrum model: A small team, determined to deliver a product or service, is grouped together (interlocked) to work (push) towards a goal.

The scrum methodology is generally based around sprints, which are 15 to 30 days in length and each sprint delivers a working piece of the product. That is, the system is developed incrementally.

The sponsor creates a rank-ordered list of requirements, called the "Product Backlog." The sponsor is an active and contributing player throughout, proposing the features to be implemented at the start of each sprint, reviewing the functionality at the end of each sprint, and, in between, constantly tuning the backlog by prioritizing features that provide the "best" value.

The Scrum Master's role is to coach and motivate the project team, to resolve issues, and to ensure the realization of the goals of each sprint. Therefore, the Scrum Master's role is very similar to that of a project manager, as she is responsible for the product content, the deliverables, the cost and the schedule.

The scrum methodology works as follows:

1. At the start of the scrum project, the sponsor defines the current requirements and creates the *Product Backlog*. It is important for the sponsor to prioritize the list of features so as to deliver maximum value.

2. Using the *Product Backlog*, the scrum team creates a *sprint* by defining the features it can complete in the first sprint iteration, usually 30 days.

3. The team is then left on its own to work during the *sprint*. No outside interference or influence is allowed from any source, including the sponsor, to impact the team's performance during the sprint.

4. The team meets for a "Daily Scrum," a 15 minute, stand-up meeting where each member of the team gives a brief report and answers the following key questions: What was accomplished since the last Daily Scrum? What is to be accomplished by the next meeting? What obstacles have come up?

5. *The Sprint Review.* Once the sprint ends, everyone gets together with the sponsor to evaluate the results. If the sponsor accepts the product, a new sprint begins with a list of prioritized tasks to be implemented from the backlog.

6. The above process continues, with a series of sprints, until there are no more items to implement in the *Product Backlog*.

5.5 Choosing a Development Model

We wrap up our discussion by presenting some considerations for selecting either the waterfall, evolutionary, or agile process. Your selection should be based on the characteristics of the project's requirements, the project team, and the commitment and availability of the user community. Table 5.3 is a guide.[6]

Table 5.3: Considerations for selecting either waterfall, evolutionary, or agile.

Considerations Based On	Project Attribute	Preferred Model
Stakeholders	Flexibility in approach needed	Agile
	Evolution of User Requirements	Evolutionary or Agile
	Extensive User involvement	Evolutionary or Agile
	Strict PM Control Required	Waterfall
	Flexibility in Development	Evolutionary or Agile
	Completion on schedule	Waterfall
Requirements	Well known, easily defined	Waterfall or Agile
	Defined during development	Waterfall
	Likely to change often	Evolutionary or Agile
	Demonstrations needed to develop the requirements	Evolutionary or Agile
	Proof of concept needed to determine feasibility	Evolutionary
Team	New to the problem domain	Evolutionary
	New to the technology domain	Evolutionary
	Might be reassigned	Waterfall or Evolutionary
Users	Limited availability	Waterfall or Evolutionary
	New to requirements definition	Evolutionary
	Want to be involved	Evolutionary or Agile
Risk	New area for organization	Evolutionary
	Involves system integration	Waterfall
	Involves Enhancements	Any
	Funding Is Unstable	Evolutionary or Agile
	Schedule Is Constrained	Waterfall or Agile

Part II

The Technical Skills

6

INTEGRATION

I'm not for integration and I'm not against it.

Richard Pryor

The *Integration Management* knowledge area is the least understood aspects of project management. Partly, this is because PMI keeps changing its mind about what is in it, and partly it is because it is hard to figure out what is actually meant by *Integration*.[1]

One way to understand this knowledge area is to view it as consisting of the activities that a project manager must perform in order to coordinate the project and keep an eye on the interactions between the various pieces. Integration, therefore, demands a global view of the project and strong communication skills.

For example, a technical change to the scope may impact the technical performance, introduce new risks, and require new team skills. It may also affect the project management, requiring: a new estimate of the cost and schedule; a modified communications plan if the change introduced new stakeholders; and possibly a sub-contract if the new work needs to be out-sourced. It is the project manager's responsibility to make sure that all technical aspects of the scope change are thoroughly analyzed and all impacts on the cost and schedule are considered.

[1] After you've said, "this is where you put all the parts together," it quickly gets fuzzy.

Processes are associated with both *knowledge areas* and *process groups*, and their relationship for the *Integration* knowledge area are shown in Table 23.1:

Each process produces deliverables. There are two major deliverables from the *Integration* knowledge area, the *Charter* and the *Project Management Plan*. During execution of the project, the major responsibility of *Integration* is to manage the *Change Requests*. The deliverables associated with the *Integration* knowledge area are shown in Table 23.2.

The major deliverables of the *Integration* knowledge area are the *Charter* and the *Project Management Plan* and the skills, tools and techniques that a project manager needs to produce these are discussed in the remainder of this chapter.

6.1 The Charter

The *Charter* is the document that formally authorizes the project. It is often developed as a partnership between the sponsor (who pays), the customer (who specifies performance), major stakeholders (users), and the performing organization. Usually, the project manager is specified very early in this process.

In section 23.1 we specified the inputs and outputs for the *Develop Charter* process. Here, we concentrate on the technical details: What goes into the *Charter*?

The charter is often a short document that kicks off the project.[2] The key is to make sure that the charter accurately represents the goals of the stakeholders.

As a first example, we present in Figure 6.1 a charter developed by one of our students for a party project.[1]

What we like about this charter is that while all of the information is there, it is also fun! As *fun* is an important theme and an attribute of the party, it is perfectly appropriate to feature it in the charter.

Don't be fooled by the presentation, there is a lot of important information here. The stylish format matches the stakeholder goals: "a vivid, imaginative ideology." There are cost and schedule details (a budget of $250,000 and completed for March 10th), but even the technical constraints match the party's philosophy: reduced paperwork, environmentally friendly products. (We present a more traditional charter for the PMA case in Table 23.4.)

The entire ethos of the party is clearly communicated throughout this innovative charter![3] The bright colors and graphics all communicate the ambiance and style of the party to the stakeholders.

[2]We once saw a one-page charter that authorized a $120 million dollar project.

[3]If you do not know how to proceed on this project, you are not paying attention. Read the charter again.

66

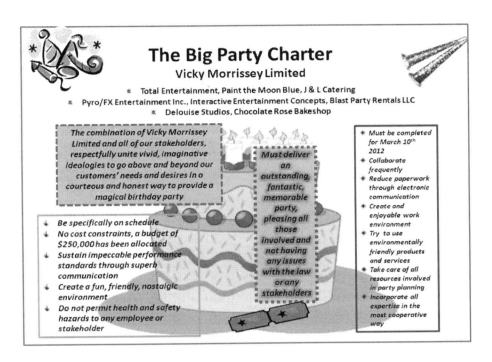

Figure 6.1: Vicky's Party Charter.

The charter identifies the project champion and the project manager. It also describes the project's purpose, description and goals, and they key requirements established by the stakeholders. Next comes the budget and primary milestones. Finally, the major stakeholders sign the charter to acknowledge their commitment to the project.

Some of the preliminary work on customer requirements may have been contracted out. This often happens on large projects where specific technical expertise is required to specify the performance. The data from such contracts are an input to the charter, and the Statement of Work (SOW) will be particularly useful, as it contains a concise summary of the project deliverables, the business need for the project, a preliminary scope, and the value of the project from a strategic perspective.

The charter usually specifies what the project will accomplish, the funding required, and an overall schedule. A good use for the charter is to focus agreement on the key features of the preliminary specification.

Many organizations require a *Business Case* to be completed before the charter is created. The Business Case identifies the needs or problems that the project will address. It should identify related projects undertaken in the past to resolve the same or similar business problem.

6.2 The Project Management Plan

The writing of the *Project Management Plan* is a massive undertaking, as it contains dozens of sections. The plan documents the actions necessary to define, prepare, integrate, and coordinate all subsidiary plans. In the *Integration Management* knowledge area, the focus is on making sure that all of the plans are coordinated and consistent.

The Project Management Plan has many sub-components:

- **Management:**

  - *Processes to be followed:* How much detail is required.[4]
  - *The Life Cycle:* The various phases.
  - *Tools and Techniques:* Company assets and references to existing documentation is appropriate.
  - *Change Control:* This is an important aspect of project management, and so it is important to explicitly lay out the rules and tools.

- **Cost and Schedule:**

  - *Earned Value Management:* This is a vital component of project management, and so it is important to explicitly lay out the approach to be followed and the tools to be used.
  - *Reviews:* Who and when? What information is distributed?

- **Sub-Plans:**

  - These include management plans for: Scope and requirements; schedule and cost; quality; human resources; communications; risks; and procurements.

[4]For small projects, a check-off of the issues might be all that is required.

SCOPE

**If you can't explain it simply,
you don't understand it well enough.**

Albert Einstein

The scope document describes both the project, as well as how it is to be accomplished. As such, it is by far the most important document in the entire project. Bar none.

> *The scope document is a complete description of all the products and services in the project.*

The scope has two functions. First, it describes the features and functions that define and characterize the project. We will reserve the word *specification* for the document that precisely defines what the project is supposed to do.

A good example of a *specification* is an architect's conceptual drawing, e.g., see Figure 20.2. Stakeholders can evaluate the proposed structure to determine if it satisfies their needs (The "What"). At this stage, it is quite normal for the discussion to include all sorts of non-construction issues, such as: Is there enough space for the way we live? Does its style match its surroundings? Is it energy efficient?

Once the conceptual requirements are agreed to, the architect creates the detailed design (the "How").[1] The specification is usually developed by asking stakeholders what they want. Unfortunately, and as the old saying goes, a user will tell you anything you ask about, but nothing more.

Second, the scope contains organizational and managerial information, such as milestones and deliverables, limits and constraints, the requirements for communicating with customers and stakeholders, and a Statement of Work (SOW).

The scope is the foundation document—it describes everything about the project, both the precise definition of what it is or will do, and how it will be executed. It therefore functions as the primary communication tool between the project team and the stakeholders. If you mess up the scope, the project is doomed.

The SOW describes *how* the project will be performed–the products and services–and in particular, who will perform which activity. The SOW is usually defined by the customer, who establishes the cost and schedule, the deliverables and milestones, and wants regular reports about the status of the project.

For completeness, we provide the PMBOK definition of the scope:

> *The project scope describes the deliverables and work required to create those deliverables.*

A problem with the PMBOK definition is that there is more to the scope than deliverables. The scope also includes *services*, such as monthly meetings with the customer. While there might be deliverables from such a meeting (e.g., the minutes), the actual entity being specified in the scope is the *meeting*, its frequency and attendees, not just the minutes.

7.1 Beginning the Scope

It is important to begin with an excellent understanding of the project's high-level goals and objectives. The following section helps to develop those ideas.

7.1.1 What? How? When? Who?

These questions are useful in determining what goes into the scope. For example, suppose our project is to build a web site that registers students for courses.

- *What?*

[1] Notice there is still no project management information here, e.g., no cost or schedule.

These are the requirements. For example, a web site that registers students would include details such as the response time, the number of students that can be handled simultaneously, the general look and feel of the site, testing criteria, etc. There would also be technical and legal requirements, e.g., there are legal privacy issues and parental rights associated with personal student data.

- *How?*

  This is the design for the project: For example, the details of how the above web site is to be constructed. One could expect to see the user interface defined (perhaps by screen mockups), the database design, and details about networking and communications with the server.

- *When?*

  This is the schedule for the project: For example, the web site should be up and running by the beginning of the next Fall semester.

- *Who?*

  Who will do what? The document that defines this is known as the Statement of Work (SOW), and for the web site project would consist of a list of tasks to be performed and the person responsible for each task.

7.1.2 The Theme

If you are planning a party, what is the theme? Suppose you specified the purpose (Mom's birthday), the time and place, as well as the guest list, budget, milestones and deliverables. You are still missing an important piece: The Theme!

What kind of party is it going to be? Establish the theme early on because it will tell you how to measure success.[2]

7.1.3 Complete and Precise

The scope must be both complete and precise. If you are building a new web page, the scope document defines exactly what the web page is supposed to do. If the scope does not include how to login, the scope document is incomplete—there is something missing. If the scope specifies that a user name is required, but not the number of allowed characters, then the scope is imprecise.

The scope should have only enough material to be complete and precise. Clear and precise writing is essential.[3] Tables, charts and diagrams accomplish this effectively. Resist the urge to describe a diagram, it duplicates information.

[2] For my Mom's party, there had better be dancing to 1940's Big Band music!

[3] We make no excuse for demanding excellent writing of project managers. Clear communication is an essential skill and good writing is paramount.

71

The scope must be complete. Forgetting to define the number of bathrooms will lead to a big problem later.

The scope must also be precise. Specifying 2 bathrooms is not precise enough. Do they include baths and/or showers?

One of the most useful phrases a project manager can use in meetings is "What does the scope say?" This immediately focuses energy on what is *required*, not what someone would like to implement. Also, there is no arguing with the scope, it is what the customer wants.[4]

7.2 Scope Contents

The are many topics that should be included in a scope document, but we emphasize that the contents of this section should be considered as a checklist, not an outline. The scope for each project is different and the information should be laid out in the format most appropriate to the particular project.

On small projects it is efficient to combine several sections. On the other hand, for large projects, many of the scope sections will be separated out into independently controlled documents. The Specification and the Statement of Work are the scope sections most often separated out into controlled documents.

7.2.1 The Specification

The specification, which is often referred to as the "spec," is the most important piece of the scope. The spec defines what the project is all about.

For a party project, the spec is where one defines all of the features of the party, such as invitations, food, drinks, and venue. However, you must also pay attention to the party's *theme*. These are the features that personalize the party and, most likely, will determine whether the party is a success.[5]

The formal definition of the specification is:

> *The specification completely and precisely defines the required features and functions that characterize the project.*

The spec defines the project and it is so important that it is often made into a separate document. This is a good idea even if the spec document is only a few pages long, because it is constantly being referenced by stakeholders. Also, a changes to a separate document are easier to control.

---

[4]Maybe it's not what they want, but at least it's what they agreed to.

[5]It is easy to get caught up in specifying venue contracts and food deliveries, and forget that the guests are supposed to have fun!

72

Let's examine some issues in the construction of the specification.

Design vs. Requirements

Sometimes I can't figure designers out.
It's as if they flunked human anatomy.

Erma Bombeck

The first thing to emphasize in the definition is the word *required*. The specification says *what* is required, not *how to do it*. Unfortunately, it is sometimes hard to distinguish the "what" from the "how."

In fact, it is naive to think that one can completely specify *what* is to be done without some notion of *how* it is to be accomplished. Suppose you ask a contractor to build a house. You can specify the requirements for the house: a kitchen, 3 bedrooms, 2 bathrooms, etc. However, the cost will certainly depend on how it is built: One floor or three?

Requirements cannot be specified without a context. Most projects have a requirements definition phase, and part of that work is preliminary design. This design work is not to define how to do the job, but to demonstrate the project's feasibility.[6]

"Feasibility" applies to a multitude of issues: Scope performance, cost and schedule. For example, the preliminary design might demonstrate: that performance requirements are achievable (a web site's response time, the span of a bridge); that the cost is appropriate (the design allowed you to conduct a parametric cost analysis); and that the schedule is achievable (a preliminary network diagram resulted in a reasonable schedule).

The primary responsibility of the requirements definition phase is to produce a *feasible* specification.[7]

As you try to refine the requirements, it becomes harder and harder without including design details. For example, suppose you require 25% more kitchen cabinet space in a new kitchen. This is a clear requirement. But it becomes difficult to specify it more precisely without explaining what the new kitchen will look like (i.e., you are specifying a design).

For example, suppose the specification said, "The new kitchen should have 25% more cabinet space." You have the responsibility to demonstrate that it is feasible both technically (in a suggested plan) and practically (via preliminary cost and schedule estimates). If the only way to get the 25% more space is to knock down

[6]The PMBOK defines this as *Collect Requirements.*

[7]It's easy to specify an unrealistic and impossible system with everything in it that you could possibly want. You just won't get it.

73

walls, then a cost estimate for that (very expensive) activity should be developed. You can then determine if the cost of knocking down walls is prohibitive or not.

7.2.2 The Project's Justification

Why are you doing the project? The project might be justified as a new business opportunity. Often, a project is required by changing regulations (tax, privacy, environmental, etc.). In this case, the motive is not profit, but compliance. Whatever the project's justification, it is important to demonstrate that the project is *essential* to the company's business goals.[8]

7.2.3 Deliverables and Milestones

For a complete discussion of deliverables and milestones, see Chapter 3. Examples of deliverables for a party are listed in Table 7.1. Note that we have divided them into the major milestones and intermediate milestones. We have also added dates, which might be considered information that goes in the schedule section. However, this is an example of combining information from different sections of the scope into one place. If a change occurs, you will only have to change the information once, eliminating a potential for errors.

Table 7.1: *Deliverables and Milestones* for a party.

Major Milestones	Date
Birthday Party	Aug 15, 2012
Planning Complete	June 30, 2012
Intermediate Milestones	**Date**
Select Venue	February 1, 2012
Contract with Venue	February 15, 2012
Invitations Designed	May 15, 2012
Invitations Sent	June 1, 2012

7.2.4 Budget

Customers almost always have a budget, or a target cost for the project, and so it is useful to identify this in the scope.

If possible, the cost drivers should be established, so that a range of costs can be considered. For example, when planning a party, you determine that the major factor driving the cost is the food and drink, estimated at $20 per person. You are

---

[8]Otherwise, why do it?

planning to invite 50 people, so you might establish a preliminary food and drink budget of $1,000, and an overall party budget of $1,500.

7.2.5 Acceptance Criteria

What will satisfy the stakeholders? How will you know when you are done?

Some thought about the acceptance criteria helps to clarify the scope. For example, for the PMA website, specifying response times will help to define ease of use.

7.2.6 Risks

While developing the scope, it is useful to list any major risks that are recognized at this stage. Risks are discussed in detail in Chapter 17—Risk.

7.2.7 Constraints

It is important to identify the constraints, so they can be analyzed and negotiated.

A constraint is any factor that limits the options for the project.

Some examples of constraints are:

- *Personnel Constraints:* The unavailability of a key technical person will hold things up. For example, in the kitchen project, the architect was the only one who had the skills to use the software program that analyzed beam loading. All changes to the structural design had to be checked by the architect. When he wasn't around, the project suffered a delay.

- *Equipment Constraints:* On construction projects, the availability of bulldozers and earth moving equipment is often a constraint, because they cannot be moved quickly from job to job.

- *Contractual Constraints:* The contract often contains provisions, such as the specification of a particular person by name. It is not unusual for the customer to demand a "right of approval" for the assignment of a new project manager.

- *Financial Constraints:* Cash flow and borrowing can impose financial constraints.

- *Schedule Constraints:* These may arise from several sources. For example, in the PMA web site, upgrades must be operational at the beginning of each semester. In the City of Boston, construction of roads cannot continue after October 31st.

Every constraint involves an associated risk because it limits one's options. Therefore, project managers should proactively manage constraints.

For example, suppose a deliverable must be available by a specific date. This is a schedule constraint and, if it proves problematic, the project manager may conduct a trade-off to analyze options.

The schedule might be accelerated by hiring an outside consultant, but at increased cost. Adding a consultant may also introduce new risks because an outsider may not be familiar with critical technical details. On the other hand, if the deliverable is a low priority, the project manager may propose to the customer that it be delayed or, perhaps even, deleted altogether.

These examples show how constraints affect projects and how trade-offs allow the project manager to examine carefully the different aspects of the issues and propose appropriate solutions.

7.2.8   Limits and Exclusions

It is useful to define what the project will *not do*. This often provokes interesting discussions with the customer.[9]

7.2.9   Assumptions

Project managers and teams must understand how assumptions affect the project.

An assumption is any factor considered to be true.

All projects contain assumptions, and they are sometimes hidden or not obvious. Assumptions can arise from diverse issues: The customer's desire to review documents; interactions with company management; technical issues; availability of personnel; and external events.

An example of a *Technical Assumption* is: The specification of a particular piece of hardware by the customer.

The project manager would then explicitly define the assumption in the scope document, along with relevant details: "The hardware shall be provided by the

[9]Particularly when they discover that their favorite requirement is excluded.

customer, and the selected model shall be sufficient to process all transactions in the required time frame."

We see immediately how important it is to have the assumption explicitly documented. In the above case, if the customer-provided hardware did not perform satisfactorily, the project manager may seek schedule relief or additional funds from the customer. If the assumption were not explicitly documented, it is not clear who would have to pay for the hardware upgrade.

If the hardware provided by the customer turns out not to meet the throughput requirement, the project manager may offer the following options to the customer:

1. The current throughput is close to the specified performance, and might be acceptable to the users, so the throughput requirement may be relaxed. Some minor modifications to the user manual and training may be required. This is low risk, and will incur no additional cost.

2. Upgrade the server at a cost of $5,000. This is considered a low risk solution that will work.

3. Redesign the database to speed up the transactions at a cost of $8,000. This is considered high risk, and may not accomplish the throughput goals.

Other examples of assumptions are:

- *Schedule Assumptions:* The approval date of permits by city or state governments; the availability of plans from an architect; the availability of hardware or software by certain dates.

- *Personnel Assumptions:* When redecorating, we all know how frustrating it can be to wait on plumbers, electricians, carpenters, and painters, who never seem to be available when you are, or when they were scheduled.

- *Financial Assumptions:* This may involve the availability of funds for equipment, or cash to pay people.

7.2.10 Technical Requirements

A project is usually subject to laws, regulations, and external standards, which are called *Technical Requirements*. Many technical requirements are found in industry standards, such as plumbing and electrical codes, environmental regulations, and tax laws. Other technical requirements are found in accounting standards and human resources regulations.

For example, if you decide to include fireworks in your party project, you must satisfy the local fire department regulations and maybe even have to pay for an on-duty fireman at the event. Another example example of technical constraints are the legal implications associated with serving alcohol at a party.

The details associated with Technical Constraints are not included in the scope, but are incorporated "by reference." That is, all applicable documents are formally referenced in the scope and all of their conditions must be upheld.

7.3 Statement of Work (SOW)

The SOW is the basis of the *contract* between the customer and the organization performing the project. The length and complexity of the SOW depends on the size of the project and it is usually a separate document from the scope. The SOW and the scope are closely linked, as the scope specifies what is to be done and the SOW specifies who will do it.

There may be several versions of the SOW as the project evolves: A short SOW for a request for proposal; the winning bidder may then develop a detailed SOW.

> *The statement of work (SOW) is a description of the products and services to be supplied during the project.*

Whatever the stage of the project, and whatever its size, the SOW contains the following type of information:

- Tasks to be performed, and by whom.

- Deliverables and Milestones (with dates).

- Schedule of reviews with customers and stakeholders.

- Cost and schedule reporting criteria.

- Payment terms and the payment schedule.

- Legalities, like cancellation clauses, Force Majeure,[10] etc.

An important part of the SOW is the *Customer Interface*. This specifies how often the project manager will meet with the customers and stakeholders, and what information will be reported. As a minimum, the project manager reports progress on deliverables, costs and the schedule.

[10]All contracts have one of these clauses, but few of us actually understand them.

The project manager must be careful not to introduce overlap and repetition between the sections of the scope. The SOW, in particular, is liable to contain duplicate information, such as task assignments and deliverable dates. We emphasize therefore, that the sections described here should be regarded as a checklist, not a document outline.

The job of the project manager is to find creative ways to include all the information without repetition. Tables are an excellent way to combine sections of the scope without repeating information. For example, combining Milestones, Deliverables, and Responsibilities into a table can avoid duplication and make the important information clear.

7.4 The Triple Constraints

Projects change, and so does the scope. A key to managing the scope is to realize that any change will induce ripples throughout the project, which is indicated in Figure 7.1, as the "Jell-O® Triangle."[11]

This is a visual device used to communicate the idea that changing any one of the three aspects of the project (scope, time, cost) will result in changes to the other two.

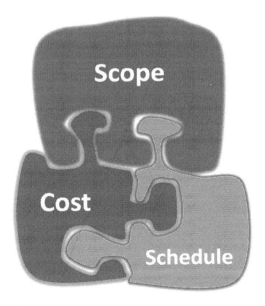

Figure 7.1: The Jell-O® Triangle: The triple constraints of scope, cost and schedule.

[11] This is sometimes referred to as the *Iron Triangle*, but we prefer to think of it as the *Jell-O* triangle. Frankly, we can't think of anything less like iron.

79

For example, if the customer suggests adding an activity to the project, then the cost will probably increase and the schedule will lengthen. Similarly, a reduction in cost can usually only be accommodated by a reduction in scope.

Sometimes, *quality* is inserted in the center of the triangle to indicate that quality is affected by the balancing the other three factors. In other words, quality is affected by changes in the scope, cost, and schedule. Actually, everything is affected by such changes, including risks, the team, contracts, etc. So why just quality in the middle?[12]

7.5   The Priority Matrix

Figure 7.1 illustrates that when a change is proposed, it is likely to affect the scope, cost and schedule. But which one has priority? Is holding the budget more important than keeping to the schedule? Complicating the decision is that different stakeholders will have conflicting views of priorities, making it difficult to impartially propose a uniformly acceptable approach.

The tool to help manage this issue is called the *priority matrix*, which is shown in Table 7.2. The *priority matrix* is created during scope development, but its real purpose is to manage changes during implementation. The idea is to establish the relative priorities between scope, cost, or schedule.

Table 7.2: The *Priority Matrix* for a fighter jet.

	Scope	Schedule	Cost
Constrain	■		
Enhance		■	
Accept			■

[12] Personally, we think this is dumb!

What is quality? The formal definition in the PMBOK is *conformance to requirements.* Requirements are in the specification, which is in the scope. But if quality is in the scope, why is it in the middle of the figure? That is just fuzzy thinking, and we hate fuzzy thinking.

To do that, we first pick either the scope or the cost or the schedule, and assign it to one of three categories:

- *Constrain:* If we constrain the scope, we are saying that maintaining the scope is more important than cost and schedule, and that we refuse to compromise on the performance characteristics.

  An example of this situation occurs when developing a military system, such as a fighter jet. The scope specifies the requirements for the jet, which are not negotiable. For example, the maximum speed may be defined by the requirement that the jet be faster than all potential adversaries. During the development of the jet, changes might be proposed, but they will be rejected if they compromise the speed requirement.

If changes are required to ensure the speed requirement is met, they will be implemented, even if they result in cost overruns or schedule delays.

- *Enhance:* Once we accept that the scope is constrained, we next chose between cost and schedule to enhance it as best we can, given that we cannot compromise the scope.

  Continuing the example of the jet, we might choose to enhance the schedule. That is, we take all opportunities to deliver early without compromising the scope.

- *Accept:* Once we accept that the scope is constrained, and that the schedule is enhanced, we must accept the cost implications.

  Continuing the example of the jet, when a change is proposed, we only accept it if it does not compromise the scope, and we will take all opportunities to enhance the schedule. We must also accept the cost (usually overrun!) implications.

This is documented in Table 7.2, where the bullet in the *constrain* row is in the scope column. This indicates that the scope is constrained—we accept no compromises on the performance. The bullet in the *enhance* row is in the schedule column, denoting that we will take all opportunities to enhance the schedule. The bullet in the *accept* row is in the cost column, denoting that we will accept the cost implications.

The *priority matrix* is filled out with exactly three bullets, with only one bullet in each row, and only one bullet in each column.

As another example, consider the project of organizing a party for my Dad's 85th birthday. The *priority matrix* is shown in Table 7.3. Here, we have stated that the schedule is constrained. That is, once we have fixed the date, it cannot change.[13] We decide that we are on a very firm budget, so we take all opportunities to save money. If that results in a slightly less fancy party, we will accept that.[14]

The project manager should establish the priority matrix during the development of the scope, and put it on the wall for everyone to see.[15] When changes are proposed, the project manager can look to the *priority matrix* to help referee between stakeholders.

[13] My Dad's 85th birthday is August 21st. We can save money by having the party in September. Ain't gonna happen!

[14] Dad will be so happy we are having a party, that he won't care where it is held.

[15] We suggest that there are two things that every project manager needs on the wall: The priority matrix and the network with the critical path.

81

Table 7.3: The *Priority Matrix* for my Dad's birthday party.

	Scope	Schedule	Cost
Constrain		■	
Enhance			■
Accept	■		

7.6 Scope Issues

7.6.1 Scope Creep

The customer comes first! Keep the customer happy!

Simply following these admonitions, leads to a serious problem: *scope creep.*

> *Scope creep is the tendency of the requirements to grow over time.*

Gold Plating is the phrase used to describe the process of adding things into the scope that are merely nice to have. The key is for the project manager to focus on *refining* the scope, not *embellishing* it.

Stakeholders and customers often try to add requirements to the scope, and the project manager must guard against this by carefully managing changes: Before implementing a proposed change, the project manager should evaluate the risks; develop the cost and schedule impact; and review all information with the customer and stakeholders. At that point, the customer can decide whether or not to approve the change, balancing the improvement in performance against the cost and schedule implications.

Most projects are under cost or schedule constraints and presenting the impact of changes will immediately force the customer to assess the true value of the changes and to prioritize them.

Most of the time scope creep results in cost overruns and delays. Despite this, scope creep is a common project affliction because there is relentless pressure on the project manager to satisfy the customer.

It is important to realize that changes are inevitable. Clarifications and refinements are OK, in fact are necessary. It is enhancements that must be ruthlessly rejected. Each proposed change should be analyzed to determine its impact on scope, cost, and schedule. This is the subject of *Integrated Change Control*—see Chapter 26.

A clear, well-defined specification immediately allows the project team to determine when extra work is being proposed. A clear specification is an insurance policy against scope creep. A specification that is broad and imprecise is an invitation for scope creep.

The tension between satisfying the customer and staying within cost and schedule is nicely illustrated by the practices of builders of super yachts.[1] A super yacht is a boat over 40 meters in length, and they are typically built under a fixed cost contract. A 40m power boat costs around $60 million!

When the customer asks for a change, it is hard to justify asking for an extra few thousand dollars, when the bill is already in the millions. Therefore, doing "small favors" for the customer is good business.

However, when a major change is requested, then the builder "opens up" the contract, and negotiates a major add-on.[16]

7.6.2 Avoiding Repeated Information

It is important that scope information not be repeated. If a piece of data occurs in two places in the scope, then when a change occurs[17] it is possible to miss the change to repeated data items. When it comes to implementation, a sub-contractor will select the easiest one to implement and then charge for an update to make the system consistent with the other one.[18]

Dates are excellent candidates for repeated information because they naturally occur in several scope sections, such as Milestones, Deliverables and Schedule. One way to deal with this is to place all dates in a single table. Then, when any date changes, only one place needs to be looked at. Also, relations between dates are all visible.

An example of the way in which a duplicate date can arise is as follows. A team is working on a party project and decides to survey the guests to see if they had a good time. The team proposes the survey should be sent out two days after the party, which is planned for May 11th. They can write this requirement as:

1. The survey will be sent out on May 13th.

2. The survey will be sent two days after the party.

The second way is the correct way to write the requirement. If the date of the party is changed, either during planning or if there is postponement due to rain, the date in #1 will be incorrect. However, #2 will be correct even if the party date changes.

[16]And attempts to make up for previous favors.

[17]Which it will.

[18]The one you probably wanted in the first place.

83

7.6.3 Plan, Scope & Spec

It is worth discussing the relation between the Plan, the Scope and the Specification. The Plan covers the *management* of the project, and, so, is about the *process*. The plan, therefore, covers *how (and when)* the project is to be developed (e.g., first the SOW, then the scope, etc.). Another item in the plan, for example, might be whether the process is to be agile or traditional.

As we have seen in this chapter, the scope is really a checklist of topics that need to be written before the project's implementation can begin. Included in the scope are sections such as the Justification (Business Case), Risks, Constraints, Assumptions, etc. Some of these documents should be independently maintained and controlled so that changes (e.g., a revised marketing assessment) don't need to be duplicated in the scope, which is an error prone process.

Finally, the most critical part of the scope is the specification, which details *what* is to be built (as distinct from the plan, which covers *how* it is to be built). The specification describes the project architecture (using the word in its most general sense), its components and their interfaces (internal and external).

While separate entities, the plan, scope and spec are all closely related. For example, the plan is linked to the specification and the scope through activities such as cost and schedule tracking. Earned value management (EVM) uses the costs and schedules of deliverables, which are architectural components in the specification. Based on these costs, EVM measures the actual progress against the plan.

A delay in the schedule also illustrates how these entities are related. Changes can be proposed to the plan (accept the late delivery), the scope (change the management process), or the specification (change the modules to be delivered).

7.6.4 Writing the Scope

> **The most essential gift for a good writer is a built-in, shock-proof sh**t-detector.**
>
> *Ernest Hemingway*

[19] I have only made this letter rather long because I have not had time to make it shorter— Blaise Pascal.

[20] There is but one art, to omit—Robert Louis Stevenson.
  An elegant commandment that I have disobeyed to get you to obey it. How ironic.

Good writing is essential in project management and nowhere is that more important than in the scope.

One might be tempted to think that the scope is always a long and complicated document. That would be wrong![19] While the scope must be complete and precise, one should ruthlessly cut it.[20] Clarity is the objective, not length.

The above scope sections should be regarded as a checklist, not an outline. If you include a table of deliverables, you can satisfy the milestone requirement by simply adding a date column to the table. This is an example of specifying information in exactly one place.[21] If a separate milestone table were included, when a deliverable changed, information would have to be changed in two places. This is inefficient, a source of errors, and to be avoided at all costs.

Many scope sections are interrelated. For example, a construction permit may involve an assumption (customer will obtain permit), a schedule constraint (permit in 30 days), and an exclusion (does not include environmental permit). All permit information should be one place, so that if anything about the permit changes, only one part of the scope need change. If the information were scattered among multiple sections, a change to the permit would require multiple changes to the scope, an error-prone process.

Finally, not all sections of the scope are equally important. Early on it is vital to establish the key ideas. For example, in party project it is crucial to establish the *style* of the party, e.g., a Spanish-costumed, dance party. It is easy to get caught up in the technical details and forget to provide the essential feel of the project: Spanish dancing.[22]

To become a good project manager, practice writing.[23]

> *Do not put statements in the negative form.*
> *And don't start sentences with a conjunction.*
> *If you reread your work, you will find on rereading that a*
> *great deal of repetition can be avoided by rereading and editing.*
> *Never use a long word when a diminutive one will do.*
> *Unqualified superlatives are the worst of all.*
> *De-accession euphemisms.*
> *If any word is improper at the end of a sentence, a linking verb is.*
> *Avoid trendy locutions that sound flaky.*
> *Last, but not least, avoid clichès like the plague.*

"Great Rules of Writing"—*William Safire.*

7.7 Sample Scope Statement

In Figure 7.2, we provide a sample scope statement for the kitchen project. Note that the scope references external documents such as building codes and the specification, which is described in Chapter 20—The New Kitchen.

[21]A friend of mine has a sign over his desk that says, **OHIO**—only handle it once.

[22]While leaving out the technical sections may be disastrous, failing to specify the Spanish costumes and dances will be much worse: A boring party.

[23]The difference between the right word and the almost right word is the difference between lightning and the lightning bug—Mark Twain

85

Scope Statement

Objective:
To renovate a kitchen within 6 months at cost not to exceed $63,000.

Justification:
Old cabinets and small workspace.
Unused spaces of little value.

Deliverables:
Conceptual Design and the Detailed Design.
Sheet rock (Partial Payment required).
Cabinets.

Milestones:
  Demolition Complete   Estimated March 31st.
  Gas line installed   Estimated April 15th.
  Cabinet Delivery   Estimated July 1st.

Specification:
See Figure 20.2 and associated discussion.

Cost Estimate:
See spreadsheet of the estimated costs. Cost estimate $63,000.

Risks:
  Cabinet Delivery: Schedule Risk.

Limits and Exclusions:
Contractor responsible for all construction permits.

Constraints:
Schedule: Work substantially complete for guests arriving September 1st.

Assumptions:
Contractor responsible for all subcontractors and their costs.
Painting not included in the bid.

Technical Requirements:
Architect responsible for all safety and loading requirements.
All construction to be consistent with local regulations and codes:
carpentry, safety, plumbing, electrical, environmental, etc.

Customer Reviews:
Monthly meetings with Joan Smith (PM) and John Smith (Sponsor).

Figure 7.2: Sample *Scope Statement* for the New Kitchen project.

THE WBS

Creating the Work Breakdown Structure (WBS) is part of the *Define Scope* process.

Once the scope is complete and approved, the next step is to create the Work Breakdown Structure (WBS), and it is the foundation for all the steps to follow, particularly the development of the cost and schedule.

8.1   The Work Breakdown Structure (WBS)

The WBS is a reorganization of the information in the scope, and we emphasize immediately that it is a *creative* process. There is no automated way to generate a good WBS.

Organizations often have templates for a WBS, which saves work and helps not to forget pieces. But a template is not the answer, as all projects are unique, and the WBS will require tweaking and tuning.

The WBS is a deliverable-oriented hierarchical decomposition of the work to be accomplished, with each descending level representing an increasingly detailed definition of the work.

Suppose we have a project to design invitations for a party. To begin the explanation, a simple WBS for this project is shown in Figure 8.1.

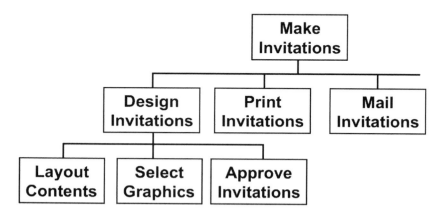

Figure 8.1: A portion of the WBS for a *Make Party Invitations* project.

The first thing to observe is that the WBS is hierarchical, which means that it is decomposed into in layers. At the top, we have a box, or node, that represents the entire project (Make Invitations). As one proceeds downwards, the layers contain more detail.

The second level contains three activities (Design Invitations, Print Invitations, and Mail Invitations). The Design Invitations box is decomposed further into Layout Contents, Select Graphics, and Approve Invitations.

Decomposition is the subdivision of project deliverables into smaller, more manageable deliverables, until the work is defined at the *work package* level.

Work packages are the lowest level items in the WBS, and represent the level at which cost and activity durations can be reliably estimated and managed.

8.2 WBS Construction Rules

There are several rules to follow in the construction of a WBS :

WBS Rule #1

Each WBS activity is derived explicitly from, and traceable back to, the scope.[1]

The traceability from Scope → WBS ensures that nothing is left out of the project.

WBS activities can come from many sources. Obviously, work is necessary to create the project deliverables. However, there are also project activities that have to do with the *process*, and these need to be in the WBS to ensure that all activities are in the Statement of Work.

For example, a scope *assumption* may define that the home owner will obtain the permit for construction. In which case, the WBS should contain an activity called *Get Permit*. The deliverable is clear (the Permit). Project management activities also go into the WBS, e.g., *Produce Monthly Reports*.

WBS Rule #2

WBS components are defined by active verbs.

Note that the top level box says *Make Invitations*. The verb "make" is important, it immediately expresses the idea that we are going to make the invitations—we are not going to purchase ready-made invitations. If we had decided to buy ready-made invitations, then the top level box would say *Buy Invitations*. Notice how important the verb is.[2]

As another example, consider *Pour Foundation*. The verb "pour" clarifies that the foundation is to be, well, poured, and not dropped in as a completed entity. Pouring also implies the need for a form to pour concrete into, the scheduling and arrival of a delivery truck, a time to harden, etc. All that derives just from the verb "pour." The WBS is enhanced by strong, active verbs.[3]

WBS Rule #3

The child components together make up the parent component, and only the parent component.

When decomposing a node, it is easy to add things into the project. You should take care to see that the decomposition only implements the contents of the parent, and no more.

For example, *Design Invitations* only involves *selecting* graphics. If someone proposes *creating* graphics, this is scope creep. If you feel the urge to add something into the WBS, you should first request a change to the scope. If the ruling is that the change is a clarification, then you can go ahead. If it is an addition, do not proceed.

WBS Rule #4

The WBS is deliverable-oriented: all of the components must produce a deliverable.

[1] Technically, the chunks of the WBS are components of the system and/or deliverables. They do not become activities until later in the project development cycle. However, since they will almost always turn into activities, we occasionally cheat and use the word here. It is clearer to talk about "activities" than components.

[2] The latest version of the PMBOK defines all activities in terms of verbs. We've been campaigning for verbs for years, and are delighted to see the world catch up with us.

[3] And unlike your English class, it is quite acceptable to repeat verbs. Always go for the precise and correct verb, even if you have to repeat it. For example, if you are planning a wedding, it is OK to *make invitations, make table settings*, etc.

89

In Figure 8.1, all of the nodes produce a deliverable, and it is easy to understand what they are. Even the *Approve Invitations* activity, which is not part of the design process, has a deliverable: The Letter of Approval from the customer.

We have continually emphasized the idea that deliverables are tangible. Consider the *Pour Foundation* example above, it is clear that the deliverable is tangible–the concrete foundation. By concentrating on deliverables and their verbs, you remove all ambiguity about the activity. You will easily be able to tell when the activity *Pour Foundation* is complete.[4]

WBS Rule #5

There is no time ordering in the WBS.[5]

When developing the WBS, you should never say things like "Printing comes *before* Mailing." Neither should you say "Mailing comes *after* Design." The WBS is just a list of activities. When designing the WBS, stay away from words like *before*, *after*, and *first*.[6]

WBS Rule #6

The 4 ± 2 *Components Rule.*

Psychologists tell us that we can only hold about 4-5 ideas in our heads simultaneously. Since all of the components of a layer are related, that means we should not have more than 5 or 6 nodes in a layer. If you have more than that, you should combine them into more manageable pieces.

When developing a WBS, it is not unusual in the early stages for some layers to sprawl across the page. This is where creative design is required. What nodes should be grouped together? Why should nodes be combined? What will be the result of combining nodes? There are reasonable answers to these questions, which we explore below when we talk about WBS design.

WBS Rule #7

The WBS is Progressively Elaborated.

[4]You won't be able to carve your initials in the concrete.

[5]Sequencing, as it is called, comes later; in the *Sequence Activities* process.

[6]It is quite acceptable, and even normal, to arrange the activities as we did in Figure 8.1, where the earlier stuff is on the left. It's just that you are not allowed to say it!

The first version of the WBS is at a high level. As project planning and project design proceed, more detail is added. Clarifying the design and detailing the deliverables as time goes on is called *progressive elaboration*. Clarifying the planning of schedules and costs as time goes on is also called *rolling wave planning*.

Excessive decomposition at inappropriate times or in low priority sections is unproductive. Therefore, not all levels need to be developed to the same level of detail—it is perfectly acceptable for the tree to be unbalanced.

In Figure 8.1, the node *Design Invitations* is decomposed, but *Mail Invitations* is not. This is perfectly acceptable, since the design step needs more clarification and definition, but mailing the invitations is pretty straightforward and needs no more explanation and, therefore, no decomposition.

The early work on the WBS tends to validate the requirements, finding spec errors and missing pieces. The later work on the WBS moves towards design, and begins to refine the project *performance*.

WBS Rule #8
Resist Obvious Details.

There is a temptation when developing the WBS to provide a lot of detail in areas that you know a lot about just because you know it. For example, when developing the WBS for a party project, novices often elaborate the food and drink in excruciating detail.

Once you have established that you are planning a "Beer and Pizza" party, it does not add value to the WBS to list the 12 kinds of beer and the 6 types of pizza, each with its own WBS number. This level of detail merely adds irrelevant pages to the WBS and makes the important information difficult to find.

When developing the WBS, focus on the important issues, particularly the parts that are uncertain.

8.3   Some Bad WBS Practices

In Figure 8.2, we have deliberately committed a number of WBS no-nos. First, there are no verbs. If we examine the *Software Applications* node, we know we need a word processor, spreadsheet and utilities (presumably because the scope required them). But we do not know whether we are to develop them or to buy them, which makes a huge difference! [7]

Another poor aspect of this WBS is that the *Software Applications* node is decomposed into too many child nodes.

Also, the child nodes mix up apples and oranges: What is the *Printer* doing there? Since there is no verb, we do not know if it is printer software (in which case it might belong), or the physical printer (in which case it does not belong in the *Software Applications* node).

We might consider dividing the *Software Applications* node into *Applications* and *Utilities*. Then we have to decide which software goes where. Suppose the applications are expensive and require a careful evaluation of features vs. cost. On the other hand, suppose the utilities are generally low cost and we just have to

[7]We have deliberately selected an information technology (IT) example here because the IT folks frequently suggest that their systems are different. For example, IT folks use an *object oriented* design paradigm, and as long as they include active verbs, it's OK by us. After all, it's a WBS, not a design.

91

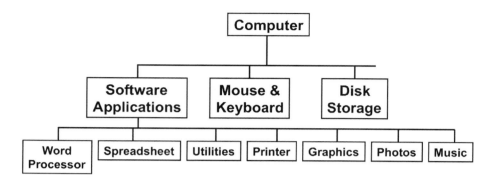

Figure 8.2: Some WBS No-Nos.

select which ones we want. In that case, it makes sense in the WBS to separate the applications from the utilities.

That separation also improves the management of the project because they are different types of activities requiring different expertise. Therefore, we would assign different people to the activities, since they require different skills: features and cost analysis for applications; simple selection for utilities. This separation is an example of a *design choice*. You should be careful with these, as they will haunt you for a long time.

This is an excellent example of how to go about the aggregating vs. decomposing process. It is about making the process easier to manage. Separating the complex software application evaluation from the simpler utilities acquisition puts like things together. Also, experts in applications may not be experts in utilities, so that is another reason to group them in separate entities.

We emphasize that the design of the WBS should facilitate the *management* of the project, not the design of the system.

8.4   Graphical vs. Outline WBS

There are two ways to present the WBS: graphical and outline. The graphical format is a good tool for the presentation of the status of the project to stakeholders and upper management. As details are added, the graphical format rapidly gets cumbersome and the outline format is preferable.

8.4.1 Graphical WBS

Figure 8.3 shows a first pass at a WBS for a kitchen remodeling project. In this form, it is called a *Graphical WBS*.

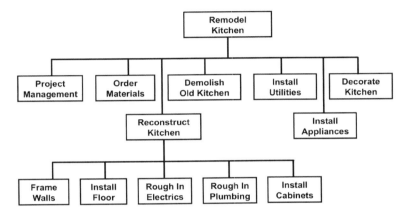

Figure 8.3: Preliminary WBS for the kitchen remodeling project.

We have the basics down, but it is now time to analyze it. The first step is to go back to the scope document and make sure that all of the requirements, features, and management processes are included in the WBS. Then we examine all of the other documentation (SOW, risk plans, etc.) and again ensure that all requirements are in the WBS.

If we did that, we would see that there is a large piece missing from the WBS. Can you figure what it is?[1]

The first layer decomposition has seven nodes. This is probably too many, so we should consider aggregating some.[8] There is no correct or right way to design a WBS, it is a creative process. So we will ask some questions and give suggestions as to how to proceed.

1. *Order Materials.* This has been separated out. This makes sense if one person orders everything; the project manager can determine the status of all orders by asking one person. On the other hand, if the appliances are to be ordered by the customer, and the plumber and electrician order their own materials, then it might not make sense to have a single ordering activity.

[8]Especially as there is a glaring omission.

93

2. *Utilities.* These are scattered throughout the WBS. We have *Install Utilities* at the top level, and plumbing and electrics at a lower level. We might consider moving the plumbing and electrics under utilities.

There are two questions:[9] Can the utilities be better managed if they are under one unified *Install Utilities* node? Or, is it better to leave them under *Reconstruct Kitchen* next to the walls and floor nodes. Since the plumbers and electricians will almost certainly be separate sub-contractors, with their own skills, schedule and deliverables, perhaps it makes more sense to manage them under an *Install Utilities* node.

The floor and framing are carpentry activities, and so belong together, and are probably OK where they are. Notice that we have learned something here: When we remove the plumbing and electric activities from the *Reconstruct Kitchen* node, what remains are activities for the carpenters. So a better name for the node might be *Do Carpentry.*[10]

As you start to add layers and nodes to the decomposition, the WBS quickly expands beyond the page. At this point, there are two approaches that help. First, separate pages can be developed for nodes that are relatively independent. For example, we could separate out the carpentry node, and place it on a separate page. Since this is an important piece of the project, this page will make managing much easier.

8.4.2 Outline WBS

When the WBS gets too complicated for a graphical representation, then there is another option that works much better for presenting the details: The Outline WBS Format. An example of this is shown in Figure 8.4.

To accomplish this, we need to add a numbering system to the WBS, so that when we view a subsystem, we know where it falls in the hierarchy.

There are several ways to number the WBS. The simplest is just to let *Microsoft Project* do it. Our preferred method is shown in Figure 8.4. Each major subsystem in numbered sequentially. Another method is to number the kitchen as 1.0, but then everything has a '1.' in front of it–see Figure 8.5.

You might object that the carpentry came after the utilities, which is illogical. However, we remind you that there is *no order* in a WBS. It is simply a list of activities.

One can also use letters for the major subsystems, which is useful when a large system is being developed, both because there are more letters than numbers and you can use meaningful letters for subsystems.

---

[9]At least two!

[10]We don't know the verb for *Carpentry,* so the boring "Do" will have to suffice

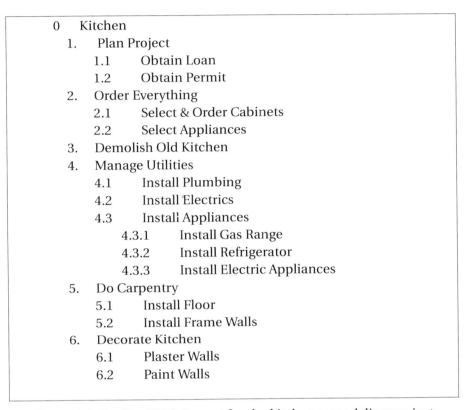

```
0    Kitchen
    1.    Plan Project
        1.1      Obtain Loan
        1.2      Obtain Permit
    2.    Order Everything
        2.1      Select & Order Cabinets
        2.2      Select Appliances
    3.    Demolish Old Kitchen
    4.    Manage Utilities
        4.1      Install Plumbing
        4.2      Install Electrics
        4.3      Install Appliances
            4.3.1      Install Gas Range
            4.3.2      Install Refrigerator
            4.3.3      Install Electric Appliances
    5.    Do Carpentry
        5.1      Install Floor
        5.2      Install Frame Walls
    6.    Decorate Kitchen
        6.1      Plaster Walls
        6.2      Paint Walls
```

Figure 8.4: Outline WBS Format for the kitchen remodeling project.

```
1.0    Kitchen
    1.1    Plan Project
        1.1.1      Obtain Loan
        1.1.2      Obtain Permit
    1.2    Order Everything
        1.2.1      Select & Order Cabinets
        1.2.2      Select Appliances
    1.3    Demolish Old Kitchen
    1.4    Manage Utilities
```

Figure 8.5: Outline WBS numbered starting with 1.0.

For example, in Figure 8.6, activities at the top system level are labeled with an 'A'. The software subsystem activities are labeled with an 'S', the radar activities with an 'R', etc. This has the advantage on a large system of immediately indicating the area of expertise. When a staff member calls and says, activity R.2.6.4.3 is going to be late, the project manager at least knows the radar subsystem is involved.

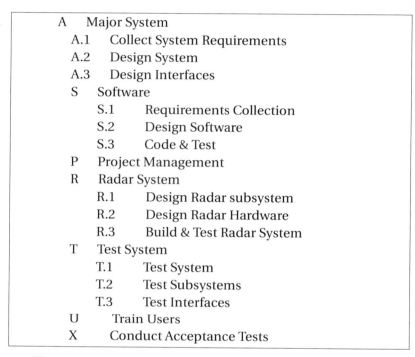

Figure 8.6: Outline WBS using letters for major subsystems.

8.5 WBS Design

In Figure 8.2, we provided some examples of the issues involved in the aggregating vs. decomposing process when designing a WBS. The decision to aggregate or separate is based on making the process easier to manage. That is separating the complex software application evaluation from the simpler utilities acquisition put like things together. Also, experts in applications may not be experts in utilities, so that is another reason to divide them into separate entities.

We emphasize that the design of the WBS should facilitate the *management* of the project. Note that we are not facilitating the design of the system, a subtle but important difference. The system designer has different goals from the project manager, and so the design may aggregate the software components for aesthetic design reasons, coherence (putting like things together), and de-coupling (reducing interdependencies).

The project manager structures the WBS completely differently from the design so as to make it easier to *manage* the project. The project manager focuses on deliverables, not design objects.[11]

Initially, one defines high-level deliverables, which give a broad overview of the project. In Figure 8.1, we established the high level actions of the Make Invitations project as Design Invitations, Print Invitations, and Mail Invitations. The completion of these activities (satisfactory acceptance of the quality of the delivberables) will define useful milestones and help communicate the status of the project to the stakeholders. Since the major activities are designing, printing, and mailing, it makes sense to represent them in the WBS.

8.5.1 Work Packages

The lowest level components in the WBS are called *work packages*; they are the leaves of the tree.

> *Work packages are the lowest level items in the WBS, and represent the level at which cost and activity durations can be reliably estimated and managed.*

In the Make Invitations project in Figure 8.1, *Select Graphics* and *Mail Invitations* are work packages, since they are not decomposed further.

Initially, when the WBS is first constructed, the work packages identify:

- The outputs required, i.e., the deliverables.

- The work with active verbs.

As project planning proceeds, and information becomes available, the WBS work packages accumulate more information:

- The time to complete or the completion date.

- A time-phased budget to complete the activity–the cost.

- The resources (personnel, time and equipment) required to complete the activity.

[11] This incidentally, is why we think a Process Breakdown Structure (a PBS instead of a WBS) is a bad idea. The PBS focuses on processes, whereas the WBS focuses on deliverables. Deliverables are the basis of project management, not processes, despite the fact that the PMBOK is process oriented–but that's another discussion.

97

- A single person who is responsible.

- Monitoring points (milestones) for measuring success.

- Quality requirements.

- Documentation, including scope references, technical requirements, etc.

- Relevant contract information.

8.5.2 Work Package Size

The WBS should be decomposed until the components are small enough to satisfy

The $1 \to 2$ **Rule:**
A work package should be finishable by $1-2$ people in $1-2$ weeks.

The rationale for this rule is that if something goes wrong, the project manager will learn about it quickly. The problem may still remain, but the project manager will have options, such as adding people, changing staff assignments, requesting clarification, etc.

8.5.3 Control Accounts

When people work on projects, their hours must be tracked.[12] To record the hours worked, a number or code is required to assign the work to.

For example, in the kitchen remodeling WBS (Figure 8.4), someone working on the *Install Refrigerator* activity may report their hours with the code: 4.3.2. Or, more likely, the company's information system will assign a number code that maps to the WBS item 4.3.2.

However the cost accounting is tracked, there is a direct relation between the WBS components and the costs incurred while working on the project. Later, we will see how this information is used to compare actual performance with planned performance using *earned value*.

Control accounts are designated after the WBS has been constructed, and are selected to give the best way to track and manage the deliverables.

[12] Usually, this is so that they can be paid, but in non-profits and many other organizations, one tracks hours, not dollars.

The WBS component used for the project cost accounting is called the Control Account (CA). Each control account is assigned a unique code or number that links directly to the company's accounting system.

Project costs are managed at the control account level. Control accounts may contain many work packages. For example, in Figure 8.4, the control accounts could be assigned at the level of *1. Plan Project, 2. Order Everything*, etc. Costs will be allocated to lower WBS levels, but this is the level at which they will be *controlled*.

Control accounts are often associated with departments, who are then held responsible for the work. Using Figure 8.4 as the example again, *1. Plan Project* is assigned to the project management department; *2. Order Everything* is assigned to the purchasing department, etc.

8.5.4 WBS Dictionary

The definition of the WBS Dictionary is:

The WBS Dictionary is a detailed description of the work and technical documentation for each WBS element.

For the PMA project, we provide an example of a *WBS Dictionary* element in Table 8.1.

Table 8.1: *WBS Dictionary Element* for PMA Case

WBS Code	WBS Element
2.1	Create a Data Entry Form to Register New Members
	WBS Element Description The entry form should consist of the following essential attributes, first name, last name and email address. Additional information that can be captured includes education, college of graduation, current job title. The form should have email validation for format of the email and should test if the first name and last name fields are not blank. The QA department will test the form after it has been tested by the project team. They will also test for ADA compliance.
Milestone	Should be completed by November 30th of the current year.
Responsible	Joe Smith
Cost	8 hours, $400
Test	Test the edit of all items. Test 'add new members.'

8.5.5   WBS and the Cost Estimate

The design of the WBS converts the scope into activities to be completed, and is the primary input to cost estimation process. The accuracy of the cost and schedule estimates depends directly on the quality of the WBS, because it is the foundation of the bottom-up cost estimation. Therefore, when designing the WBS, it is important to highlight, or separate out, items with a significant cost.

A good example of this is shown in the New Kitchen project, where the appliances are separated out—See Figure 20.7: *4.3 Install Appliances*. The appliances were a major cost item, and so appear prominently in the WBS. The actual installation of the appliances turned out to be a minor activity from the scheduling perspective, just a few days of work.

The selection of appliances was also a major planning issue, because we knew it would take a long time to select them. As it turned out, this activity was not on the critical path. The delivery of the kitchen units took so long (12 weeks), and the selection of appliances activity was in parallel with it, so there was plenty of time to select appliances.[13]

The WBS is also the document used to report the status of the project to the customer, management and stakeholders. The *monitoring and controlling* processes will measure the progress of the WBS components. The WBS is also the link from the project to the company accounting system, and allows the assignment of work to specific team members.

The WBS is, therefore, a critical document, as it is the foundation of all planning to follow. Finally, we again emphasize that the design of the WBS is a creative process and a good design will make planning better and the project go more smoothly. Templates help, but do not replace creative analysis.

---

[13]Which, incidentally, relieved a lot of pressure.

9

TIME

**Time is nature's way of keeping everything from happening at once.
Space is what prevents everything from happening to me.**

John Wheeler

Time Management is really all about the *schedule*,[1] and consists of:

1. *Define Activities.* The WBS work packages are turned into *activities*, which are the actions required to produce the deliverables.[2] High level WBS activities are decomposed in order to refine the deliverables to the point where their cost and schedule can be *estimated.*

2. *Sequence Activities.* This defines the order in which activities must be carried out and the relationships between them.

3. *Estimate Activity Resources.* Resources include people and materials, such as cash, equipment, or supplies. The types and quantities of resources required to complete the activity are estimated.

4. *Estimate Activity Durations.* The time required to complete each activity is estimated.[3]

[1] You can't really manage *time.* No one understands what time is, let alone explain how to manage it. But you can manage the schedule.

[2] An *activity* is anything that consumes time.

[3] The PMBOK defines this in terms of the rather cumbersome "number of work periods."

5. *Develop Schedule.* All of the above are combined to develop the project schedule. The schedule is an output of the network diagram, which is the focus of Chapter 10—Network. The critical path emerges.

6. *Control Schedule.* The project manager *monitors* the schedule as it evolves, and determines the true (vs. planned) schedule, and the impact of changes.

9.1 From WBS to Activities

The WBS is a deliverable-oriented list of activities. It is important to emphasize that there is no sequence to the activities in the WBS. The words "first" or "before" are not allowed when constructing the WBS. The order of activities is defined during the *Sequence Activities* process: Which activities need to be completed before others can start? Which activities can be completed in parallel?

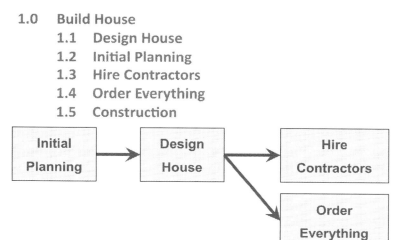

Figure 9.1: From WBS to ordered activities.

Figure 9.1 shows how to go from the WBS to an ordered collection of activities ready to enter into the network diagram.[4] It was decided that initial planning should come before the design. Also, once the design is in place, hiring contractors and ordering can be conducted in parallel.

[4]An estimate of the durations is also required, but is ignored here to concentrate on the ordering.

102

10

THE NETWORK DIAGRAM

**Even if you are on the right track,
you'll get run over if you just sit there.**

Will Rogers

The WBS is a deliverable-oriented list of activities and we have continually emphasized that there is no sequence to the activities in the WBS. During cost estimation,
the time to complete each of the activities (the duration) is estimated. With a list of
activities and their duration as inputs, we can now construct the network diagram.

The goal of the network diagram is to produce the schedule for the entire project.
The *critical path*, which is the most important concept in all of project management,
emerges from the network diagram.

10.1   A Simple Example

This example contains everything you need to know about network diagrams. No
matter what network you find yourself confronted with, no matter how large or
complicated it looks, it will not contain any concepts that are not in the simple
example presented here. If you understand this example, you need not be afraid of
any network.

It's dinnertime, and you decide to have chicken for dinner.[1] Some quick planning ensues, and you realize that you need to complete four activities, each with a time estimate (in minutes):

1. Marinate the chicken (15 min).

2. Cook chicken (20 min).

3. Microwave the vegetables (10 min).

4. Serve (5 min).

Next we must sequence the activities because they must be completed in the right order, e.g., cooking cannot happen before marinating. We also realize that cooking the chicken takes place in the oven, while the vegetables are microwaved. Therefore, these activities can happen in parallel. Finally, the 'serve' activity cannot take place until both the microwave and cooking activities are completed.

This is called activity sequencing, and the result is the determination of the *predecessor* activities. Predecessor activities are those that must be completed before an activity can start.

The next step is to create a table of activities, as shown in Table 10.1.

Table 10.1: Table of activities, durations, and predecessors.

ID	Name	Duration	Predecessors
A	Marinate	15	None
B	Cook Chicken	20	A
C	μWave	10	A
D	Serve	5	B, C

The first column identifies the activity, by giving it a label (or number), called the *activity identification* (ID). The *ID* is a unique number, and you can use any convenient system to identify the activities. For example, in a complex diagram with sub-activities, you may use 1.1, 1.2, etc.

The second column is the name of the activity, which was defined in the WBS, and the third lists its estimated duration. During the planning stage, which is where we still are in the project cycle, the durations are estimates. When the project moves into implementation, these will change to actual completion times.

[1]A student paying attention will say, "Hey! This is not a project, it's routine! Quite correct. However, we have selected a *simple* example to illustrate the network diagram, preferring clarity.

The fourth column lists the predecessor activities. For example, activity D (serving) cannot begin until activities B (cooking) and C (microwaving) are completed. Serving cannot happen until both microwaving and cooking are finished.

It is important to list only the *immediate* predecessors. For example, *marinate* is a predecessor to *serving* but is not listed in Table 10.1. When determining the predecessors to *serving*, we ask, "What must be complete before we can serve?" The answer is just cooking and microwaving.

10.1.1 Nodes

Using Table 10.1, we next construct a rough network diagram—see Figure 10.1. This is a useful step, as it allows you to lay out the diagram and arrange the activities on the page.[2] The circles in the diagram are called nodes.

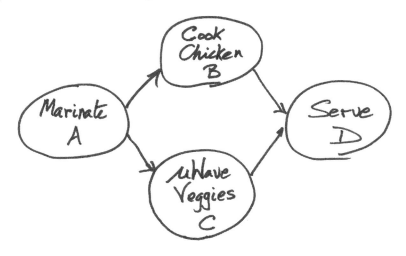

Figure 10.1: Rough Network Diagram.

10.1.2 Arrows and Predecessors

The arrows in Figure 10.1 have a well-defined meaning:

> *The arrow from A to B means that activity B cannot start until activity A is completed.*

A is said to be a *predecessor* of B. This definition of the predecessor is very precise. In fact, the entire network is constructed from this definition.

[2]We encourage you to draw this out first to figure out where the nodes go before attempting the forward pass.

105

Activity, A, the marinating activity, has no predecessors. Once we start the project, marinating starts.

As soon as marinating is completed, two more activities can start: cooking and microwaving. The arrows from A to B, and A to C have very specific, well-defined meanings: The arrow from A to B means that B cannot start until A has finished. The arrow from A to C means that C cannot start until A has finished.

The arrows from B to D, and C to D also have the same, very specific, well-defined meanings. The two arrows going into the node D mean that D cannot start until *both B and C have finished*. That is, D cannot start until both B and C are complete.

We emphasize that all this is contained in the definition of the arrows. In practical terms, the two arrows going into D mean that serving cannot take place until both the chicken is cooked and the vegetables come out of the microwave.

These predecessor (or ordering) relations are shown in Table 10.1. When the arrow is used in this way, it is called a finish-to-start constraint.

10.1.3 The Activity Properties Box

Each activity is described by an activity properties box—see Table 10.2.

Table 10.2: The activity properties box.

Earliest Start	ID	Earliest Finish
Slack	Description	Slack
Latest Start	Duration	Latest Finish

Let's fill in this box for activity 'A.' The identification (ID) is A, the description is "Marinate Chicken," and the duration is 15 minutes. The next box to be filled in is *Earliest Start*. A is the first activity in the project and so it starts at time zero. The earliest time that A can start is zero, so we put zero in the top left hand box.

We now ask the following question:

> *If the earliest start for A is zero, and A takes 15 minutes to complete, what is the earliest finish for A?*

It should be clear that the earliest finish for A is 15, which is shown in Table 10.3.

Table 10.3: Table of *earliest* properties for A.

0	A	15
	Marinate Chicken	
	15	

10.2 The Forward Pass

At what time will we serve dinner? Or, how long is our project?

This question is answered by completing what is known as the forward pass. The definition of the arrow from A to B means that activity B cannot start until A has finished. Therefore, the earliest that B can start is the same as the earliest finish for A. Therefore, the earliest start for B is 15.

We now ask the same question of B that we asked of A:

> *If the earliest start for B is 15, and B takes 20 minutes to complete, what is the earliest finish for B?*

It should be clear that the earliest finish for B is $35 = 20 + 15$, which is shown in Table 10.4.

Table 10.4: Table of *earliest* properties for B.

15	B	35
	Cook Chicken	
	20	

We now continue this *forward pass* process by completing the table for C, which is shown in Table 10.5.

A complication in the forward pass occurs when two arrows go into an activity, such as D—see Figure 10.2. The arrows from B to D and C to D mean that D cannot begin until both B and C have finished. In practical terms, the arrows represent the idea that serving cannot start until both cooking and microwaving have finished.

The earliest finish for B is 35, and the earliest finish for C is 25. Therefore, B finishes last at 35, and D has to wait around for that, so the earliest start for D is

Table 10.5: Table of *earliest* properties for C.

15	C	25
	μWave	
	Vegetables	
	10	

35. The earliest start for serving is the latest of the earliest finishes for cooking and microwaving, i.e., after whichever activity is the *last to finish.*

Since D takes 5, the earliest finish for D is 40. Since D is the last activity in the project, the earliest finish for the entire project is also 40.

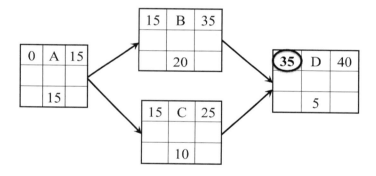

Figure 10.2: The completed *Forward Pass.*

We know the earliest finish date for the project!

When two arrows go into an activity, it is called a *merge activity.* A merge activity cannot start until both preceding activities are complete and, so, the earliest start time for a merge activity is the latest of the earliest finishes of its preceding activities.[3]

This completes the forward pass. The only issue is that, since B will take longer than

[3]This definition is almost impossible to remember, so when facing a test, we suggest you just draw Figure 10.4.

C, there is some spare time between the finish of C and the beginning of D—the vegetables are going to be sitting around for a while.

The power of the forward pass is that it determines the earliest finish for the entire project. If we start cooking at 6 pm, the earliest we can expect to finish serving is 40 minutes later.

10.3 The Backward Pass

Life can only be understood backward, but it must be lived forward.

Søren Kierkegaard

To start the backward pass, we go to the latest finish for the last activity in the network—serving, node D in Figure 10.3. Note that D is the last activity in the project, so the latest finish for D is the *latest finish for the entire project*. To fill in the correct value for this box, we ask a deceptively simple-looking question:

What is the latest finish for the project?

Actually, this is a trick question, and you might want to think about it before continuing. The answer is below.[4]

Assume we start cooking at 6 pm and suppose we want to watch a TV show that starts at 6:30 pm. Even if we are prepared to eat while watching TV, we will miss the start of the show because the earliest time the serving will finish is 6:40 pm. We estimated the activity durations and constructed the forward pass without knowing how long the project would take. The fact that we want to watch a show at 6:30 pm is now a problem.

In practice, this is not at all unusual. Customers always have a finish date in mind when they conceive the project. Sometime later, the earliest finish time emerges from the forward pass and, often, it is after the customer's preferred end date.

At this point, the project manager has several options, including doing some activities in parallel, reducing the time for activities by adding staff, and re-negotiating the end date with the customer, but these are topics for a later discussion. For now, we will proceed with the backward pass by inserting 40 as the latest finish for D. In section 10.5.1, we will show what happens when another value is used.

We ask the question:

[4]The end date for the project is .... *Whenever the customer wants it.*

If the latest finish for D is 40, and its duration is 5, what is the latest start?

It should be clear that the latest start for D is 35 (40 − 5 = 35), which allows us to complete the table for D—Table 10.6.

Table 10.6: Table of *latest* properties for D.

35	D	40
	Serve	
35	5	40

D can start as soon as both B and C have finished (this is the meaning of the arrows from B and C to D). Therefore, since the latest start for D is 35, the latest finish for both B and C is also 35.

For B, the duration is 20, and since the latest finish is 35, the latest start is 15 (35 − 20 = 15). Similarly, the latest start for C is 25 (35 − 10 = 25). The latest start for B is 15 and for C is 25.

The arrows from A to B and A to C mean that activities B and C can begin once A is completed. B has the earliest of the latest starts of B and C. Therefore, since the latest start for B is 15, the latest finish for A must also be 15. (If the latest start for C (25) were inserted as the latest finish for A, this would violate the condition that B's latest start is 15.

For A, the duration is 15 and, since the latest finish is 15, the latest start is 0 (15 − 15 = 0). Since A is the first activity, we have arrived at the latest start for the entire project. This completes the backward pass, which is shown in Figure 10.3.

A complication occurs in the backward pass when two arrows came out of an activity, which is called a burst activity. For the latest start time of a burst activity we used the earliest of the latest finish times as its latest start time.[5]

10.3.1 Finish-to-Start Constraints

The definition of the arrow is an example of a *finish-to-start* constraint. That is, we defined the arrow from A → B as meaning that B cannot start until A is complete. This is what is meant by the *finish-to-start* constraint.

[5]This definition is almost impossible to remember, so when facing a test, we suggest you just draw Figure 10.4.

There are other types of constraints, such as the *finish-to-finish* constraint. However, we believe that these other types of constraints are very difficult to understand and are a constant source of confusion. We suggest that you avoid them.

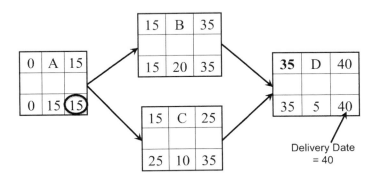

Figure 10.3: The completed *Backward Pass*.

10.4 Slack

The *slack*, which is also referred to as the *float*, is defined as:

$$Slack \quad = \quad Latest\ Finish\text{ - }Earliest\ Finish\ (LF - EF)$$
or
$$Slack \quad = \quad Latest\ Start\text{ - }Earliest\ Start\ (LS - ES)$$

The easy way to remember the above formula is indicated in Figure 10.4 by the vertical arrow to the left of the diagram: To calculate the slack, one subtracts the top number from the bottom number.[6]

The values for the slack are shown in Figure 10.4. For example, for activity C, the latest finish, LF, is 35 (bottom) and the earliest finish, EF, is 25 (top), so the slack is $LF - EF = 35 - 25 = 10$ (bottom - top). Similarly, the slack can be calculated from the latest start minus the earliest start, $LS - ES = 25 - 15 = 10$.[7]

[6] The PMBOK uses the term "total float," which we dislike for several reasons. First, *total* implies a sum, which it is not, it only applies to a single activity.

Also, *slack*, which means loose (like a rope), seems a better description, as in, "a slack schedule."

[7] We emphasize that you really should calculate both slacks, because when you make an error in the backward pass calculation (which is where most people err) the two slacks come out different. Making sure that the two slacks are the same eliminates a lot of errors.

111

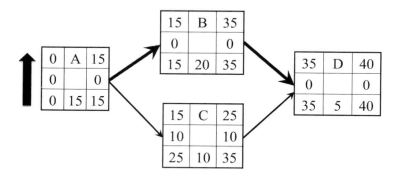

Figure 10.4: The network diagram, showing the *slack* and the *critical path*.

10.5   The Critical Path

If we look at Figure 10.4, we note that there is something special about the path: $A \rightarrow B \rightarrow D$. All of the activities on the path have the *least* slack (in this case, the slack is zero). If any of A, B, or D is delayed, the whole project will be delayed. There is slack in C, so if C finishes a little late, it will not delay the entire project.

The path $A \rightarrow B \rightarrow D$ is called the *critical path*.

The Critical Path is the most important concept in project management!

In Figure 10.4, the path $A \rightarrow B \rightarrow D$ has two very important properties:

- The critical path is the *longest path* through the network.

- The critical path is the *shortest time* in which the project can be completed.

The activities A, B, and D are *critical* because if anything delays any one of them, the entire project will be delayed. If the cooking takes 40 minutes, rather than the 30 that was planned, serving will finish 10 minutes later than scheduled.

Microwaving the vegetables does not lie on the critical path, and so it can be delayed without affecting the project schedule. If microwaving begins as soon as the marinating is done, and even if it takes an extra 8 minutes, it will still not delay the project. Activity C is said to have some slack.

The formal definition of the critical path is:

The critical path is the path that has the least slack in common.

Note that there may be more than one critical path. If the duration for activity C were 20 minutes, then there would be 2 critical paths: $A \rightarrow B \rightarrow D$ and $A \rightarrow C \rightarrow D$. This means that we should also allow the definition of the critical path to be ... *the path(s) that has (have) the least slack in common.*[8]

The microwaving activity has a slack = 10 minutes, and so it can be started up 10 minutes later and still not delay the serving activity. C can be started later or take longer, but as long as the combination does not exceed the 10 minutes of slack, the project will not be delayed.

Of course, if microwaving takes more than 10 minutes, it will now be on the critical path. If we forgot to turn on the microwave and only realized it after 15 minutes, then activity C ends up on the critical path and will delay the serving activity.

Warning:

A "task" is the word that MS Project uses for an activity. Tasks are essentially equivalent to *activities* as we have defined them.[9]

10.5.1 Please Finish Earlier!

> **The show doesn't go on because it's ready. It goes on at 11:30.**
>
> *Lorne Michaels*

Our project started at 6 pm, and we now know that the earliest finish is 40 minutes later. Let's now suppose we want to watch a TV program that starts at 6:30 pm. We simply insert 30 in the latest finish for D and repeat the process, i.e., we enter 30 into the latest finish for node D in Figure 10.5.

The latest finish for D is 30, and its duration is 5, so the latest start is 25.

Since the latest start for D is now 25, the latest finish for both B and C is also 25. For B, the duration is 20, and since the latest finish is 25, the latest start is 5 ($25 - 20 = 5$). Similarly, the latest start for C is 15 ($15 - 10 = 15$).

[8]The inclusion of the plural form, as in "path(s)", makes the definition of the critical path so ugly that we have left it out of our definition. We know it is formally correct that way, so just remember that it might be "paths."

[9]The word "task" is not used in the PMBOK.

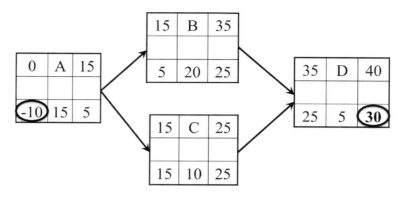

Figure 10.5: The completed backward pass with an earlier project finish date.

The latest start for B is 5 and for C is 15, so the latest finish for A is 5. For A, the duration is 15, and since the latest finish is 5, the latest start is -10 ($5 - 15 = -10$). The latest start for the project is at time *minus 10*

This simply says that to finish at 6:30 pm, we need to start 10 minutes earlier than 6 pm, i.e., at 5:50 pm. If the project has not started yet, then this is OK. If the project started at 6 pm, and you started the network diagram at 6 pm, then you are in trouble: You are going to miss the first 10 minutes of your TV show.[10]

10.5.2 Milestones

Milestones, or events, denote important points in time in the project schedule, such as the completion of an activity or a deliverable. Examples of milestones are: The receipt of planning permission for a construction project; the delivery of the scope; the acceptance by the customer of a deliverable.

Milestones are activities with zero duration.

Milestones can and should be indicated on the network diagram, where they appear as triangles with zero duration. Milestones do not affect the flow of a project, even though they may appear along the critical path. In our cooking example, we might create a milestone called *Finished Cooking*, at the point at which the serving activity starts. If cooking is delayed, then the milestone will be delayed.

Explanations of project status to customers and upper management are usually clearer when presented in terms of milestones. This is because milestones represent

[10]The PMBOK says that the critical path is "normally characterized by zero total float." This again introduces the confusion over the total float–the total path float or the individual activity floats. Also, in our experience, the earliest finish from forward pass rarely ends up at the same value as the desired customer finish date, the latest finish. In which case the critical path activities rarely have zero slack, or zero total float.

114

the completion of important activities and, so, are an excellent way to show the project status. Also, presenting milestones, rather than a complicated network diagram, is a much clearer way to present the status of a project.[11]

10.5.3 Managing the Critical Path

By far the most important feature of any network diagram is its critical path. It is not at all unusual for the activities to change during a project, and their delivery may occur either earlier or later than originally planned. As soon as any change occurs on the project, the project manager should immediately check the impact on the critical path.

Suppose your boss comes into your office and asks if he can borrow Mary for a few days. What do you do? *Check the critical path!*[12]

If Mary's assigned activity is not on the critical path, you can lend her out, and you gain credibility as a team player. If Mary's activity is critical, then you have an excellent excuse for declining to lend her out. On the other hand, you might suggest that Joe, whose activity is not on the critical path, would make a suitable substitute for Mary. You gain even more credibility as a smart team player.

Many project management decisions are made easier when viewed in terms of their impact on the critical path. Consider the following recommendations:

- *Assign the best people to critical activities.* Often, this is **not** the case. Companies usually assign difficult activities to the most senior staff. Personally, we suggest assigning senior staff to the critical activities, even if they are the simplest. That way, if they finish early you pick up some valuable time.

- *Prioritize critical activities.* Every day when you come in, check the status of critical path activities. Smooth their way.

- *Conduct risk assessment on critical activities.* Once you start making up risks, it is easy to get carried away. Assess the critical path risks first.

- *Regularly visit people working on critical activities.* Get them coffee. Keep them happy.

- *Assign the best computers and equipment to critical activities.* When a shiny, new, super-fast computer arrives, don't give it to the boss, give it to the person working on the critical path.

- *Roll up the non-critical activities.* An entire non-critical branch of the network can be lumped together as a single entity for management purposes. This

[11] The PMBOK actually says that since milestones are easier to understand, it is better to present to upper management this way!

[12] Actually, we say the correct response to any request is always, "I'll get back to you." Then check the critical path.

unclutters the network diagram, and makes it easy to quickly pass over non-issues. Management typically prefers only to deal with problems.[13]

All of these management actions depend on knowing and understanding the critical path. The critical path typically includes only a small fraction of the activities in a project.[1] This is useful, since it means the project manager can easily prioritize management decisions to ensure the critical path is not adversely affected.

10.5.4 Analyzing the Critical Path

The real work on the critical path begins once it is created. Some issues are discussed below:

- *Why is Microwave the Vegetables a successor of Marinate?*[14] We could actually start microwaving the vegetables as soon as the project starts, in parallel with marinating. While this does not make a lot of sense, it is a good example of the kinds of issues that arise when one conducts a detailed and thorough analysis of the critical path.

  Microwave the Vegetables need not necessarily have *Marinate* as a predecessor because one could perform both at the same time. This is another good example of careful analysis.

  To deal with this, one can add another constraint, such as, "The vegetables should be hot when served." This would delay the start of the microwaving.

- *Is the network sensitive?* When the majority of the activities fall on the critical path, the schedule is sensitive to any small delays. The project manager should decrease the sensitivity by moving activities around and breaking them up.[15]

- *A few long tasks dominate.* In this case, the long tasks should be divided into smaller activities. Many smaller activities can often be re-assembled in different ways and processed in parallel, shortening the schedule.

10.5.5 Time Reserves

The activity durations are estimates and the actual durations are likely to vary during execution.[16] Therefore, extra time may be added to the duration estimate to allow for a *schedule contingency*. These are called *time reserves*, or *time buffers*. *Time reserves* should be allocated to specific, identified risks.[17]

[13]Of course, if any of those noncritical activities are late enough to affect the CP, they can quickly turn into real problems. Their impact on the critical path must be carefully assessed. Many late activities on a noncritical path can quickly turn it into a critical path.

[14]We overlooked this interesting issue in the first edition and the students immediately caught it. Well done!

[15]See *Microwave Veggies* for an example of changing the constraints.

[16]Usually, they overrun.

[17]The schedule impact of the risks should be analyzed as part of the risk analysis.

116

Schedule reserves may be added to the activity duration either as a specific duration or as a percentage.[18] Contingencies are not usually included in the network diagram, but managed centrally by the project manager. As the project proceeds and more information becomes available, the schedule reserves may be used, reduced, or eliminated. The policy for using the schedule reserves should be clearly documented in the schedule section of the project management plan.

10.6 *Free* Slack

We now make a small change to the network diagram: We divide activity C into two parts (C1 and C2)—see Figure 10.6. This small change has a huge impact.

We have not changed the critical path, so we have not changed the project schedule. Nevertheless, there is now something very special about activity, C2. The key idea is that:

> Activity C2 can be delayed without affecting *any other activity* in the network.

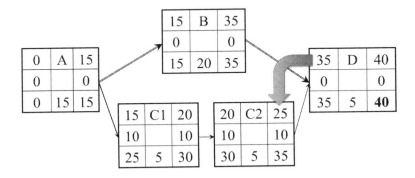

Figure 10.6: A network diagram with *Free Slack*: $ES(D) - EF(C2)$.

[18]Adding time "in case" is unnecessary padding.

117

This is an incredibly useful property of C2, and it is called *free slack*.[19]

It is true that C1 can be delayed and not affect the project schedule, but a delay in C1 will delay the start of C2. Therefore, if C1 is delayed, the people and resources associated with C2 will be affected.

For example, suppose that activity C2 is *Pour Foundation* and requires the delivery of concrete by an expensive and carefully scheduled truck. If C1 is delayed, the concrete truck will have to be postponed, perhaps causing further delays and expensive penalties.[20]

On the other hand, C2 can be delayed without affecting any other activity. For example, if activity, D, requires the expensive concrete truck, a delay in C2 will not impact the concrete truck.

10.6.1 Definition of Free Slack

There are two ways to define *free slack*. The practical method that can be used when analyzing a network diagram is:

> *An activity has free slack if it occurs at the end of a non-critical chain in the network diagram.*

A more technical definition of free slack is:[21]

> **Free** *slack occurs in the last activity in a non-critical chain and is the difference between the ES of the activity that follows it and the EF of the activity, i.e.,*

$$FS = ES^+ - EF. \tag{10.1}$$

10.6.2 The Value of Free Slack

A theme that emerged from the analysis of the network diagram and, particularly, the critical path was the idea that, during the project, changes are inevitable. When your boss calls asking to use Alice on another project, your immediate response should be, "I'll get back to you."

You look at the critical path. If Alice is working on activity C2, an activity with free slack, you call back and say "Sure."[22] On the other hand, if Alice is working on a critical activity, you have several options:

---

[19] It is also called *free float*, but we have the same reservations as expressed earlier about the use of the word 'float.'

[20] C1 is not on the critical path but it is a very important activity. Note the distinction: C1 is important, but not critical.

[21] This is another definition that's hard to remember. Just remember where the arrow is in Figure 10.6: From the EF of the activity at the end of the chain to the ES of the next one.

[22] You are a team player.

118

1. Say, 'No.'

2. Let Alice go and move someone from C2 to Alice's activity.

3. Let Alice go, but explain to your boss that there will be a schedule slip.[23]

4. Let Alice go, but explain to your boss that there will be a cost overrun.[24]

Free Slack is the project manager's friend. Once a network diagram is completed, the project manager should identify all the activities with *free slack*.[25]

10.7 Activity Sequence Relationships

Identifying the activity sequence relationships defines the logical flow of work. Predecessor and successor activities are constraints on the sequence in which activities must be performed. They dictate the order of activities.

- *Predecessor Activities.* These must finish before any following activities can begin. (A is the predecessor to B in figure 10.4.)

- *Successor Activities.* These follow immediately after other activities. (B is the successor to A in figure 10.4.)

- *Concurrent, or parallel, activities.* These can be worked on at the same time, which shortens the schedule. (In Figure 10.4, activities B and C can be performed in parallel—cooking the chicken and microwaving the vegetables can be performed at the same time.

- *Merge Activities.* These have at least two preceding activities on which they depend. In Figure 10.4, activity D is a merge activity (B and C merge into D).

- *Burst Activities.* These have at least two succeeding activities on which they depend. In Figure 10.4, activity A is a burst activity (B and C burst from A).

Dependencies dictate when or how an activity must be performed, and there are three types:

- *Mandatory Dependencies.* These are restrictions specific to one or more activities. Mandatory dependencies never change. Sometimes, mandatory dependencies are referred to as *hard logic*.

  For example, a mandatory dependency occurs in our cooking example, because we specified that marinating must be completed before cooking can

[23]Yawn.

[24]What?!

[25]Put them in your pocket, and save them for a rainy day.

119

begin. Many examples arise when building a house: The permit must be obtained before construction can start; the foundation must be finished before the walls can be started.

- *Discretionary Dependencies*. These are *preferred* ways of doing the project. Because they are *discretionary*, they may change as priorities change.[26]

  For example, in our cooking example, we may choose to complete the microwaving the vegetables activity after the chicken finished cooking. That way, the vegetables are still hot. We may equally well decide that the vegetables need to be cooked as quickly as possible, and so we would start them as soon as the chicken is marinated.

- *External Dependencies*. These are restrictions that result from activities outside the project itself. Usually, neither the project manager nor team members can control external dependencies. External dependencies may be either mandatory or discretionary.

  For example, obtaining a construction permit is an external, mandatory dependency. It is external, since the regulation comes from the town, and it is mandatory before construction can start.

Both mandatory and discretionary dependencies should be used with care, since they can affect the sequence of activities. Often there are assumptions involved, and these should be clarified and documented because the justification for the assumptions may change as the project evolves.

An example of an internal discretionary dependency is to insist that the vegetables and the chicken finish at the same time, so that they are hot.

10.8 Network Issues

There are a number of issues that affect networks.

10.8.1 Lags

The classic situation where a lag is used is in purchasing an item. Suppose you decide to buy a computer part and the delivery time is ten working days. The time estimate for the *Order Part* activity might be one day (the time it would take to fill out the purchase request form, get signatures, etc.). Therefore the duration for the *Order Part* activity should be 1 day.

[26]Discretion is the better part of valor, and so the best way to perform the task is often the way that keeps the stakeholders happy.

120

Then you sit around for 10 days, waiting for the part. If you put 11 days in the network (1 to purchase the part and 10 for delivery), then the system will compute the cost of 11 days of work, when only one is really required. The 10 days of waiting should not be charged as a labor cost.

What is also important when adding up the costs is that the *Order Part* activity only consumes one day's worth of labor, the waiting activity costs nothing.

However, waiting for the delivery takes 10 days, during which time no work is being performed. To properly handle this in the network diagram, you introduce a lag into the buying activity—see Figure 10.7.

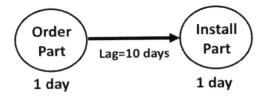

Figure 10.7: A classic lag: Ordering takes one day, but waiting for the part to arrive takes another 10 days.

The definition of a lag is:

> *In a finish-to-start dependency, a lag is the time between the finish of a predecessor activity in a network diagram and the start of its successor activity.*

Our preference is not to use lags, but to explicitly put some sort of *Wait* activity in the network diagram. This clarifies the delay, and explicitly presents it to everyone. Especially if it is a significant item on the critical path, you would want everyone to know what the delay is. Also, you might not be able to affect the delay (e.g., manufacturing and shipping times), and so need to highlight it in the discussions.

10.8.2 Leads

A *lead* says that an activity can begin early. (It can be thought of as a negative lag.) For example, in the preparation of a document, you might allow editors in the proofing department to start work a week before the document is complete and formally delivered. This is a risky action. The benefit is that some schedule compression might accrue because activities are being done in parallel. This must

121

be balanced against the risk that the document might change substantially before delivery, and the editors might have to edit the document twice.

Leads and lags affect the timing of activities and, therefore, the critical path. In fact, they make the calculation of a critical path a bit tricky. Software packages usually bury leads and lags inside tasks, which makes the resulting critical path difficult to understand.[27]

10.8.3 Loops and Conditional Branches

A document that requires multiple drafts might be considered as an example of activities that could use loops in their sequencing. This might be described by Figure 10.8 as follows: Suppose Chapter #1 is written and delivered, so that the activity is complete.

The next activity is *Edit Chapter #1* and create a second draft. This might be considered as a loop in the network diagram because *Write Chapter #1* is being re-executed. Such loops are not allowed in network diagrams. The arrow from *Edit → Write* in Figure 10.8 is considered an illegal construct.

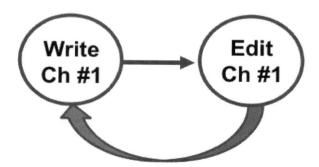

Figure 10.8: An illegal loop in a network diagram.

A much better way to describe the activities is by the following sequence of activities: *Write Chapter #1*, *Edit Chapter #1*, and *Re-write Chapter #1*.

Since the activities of writing, editing and even re-writing, require different skills, they can (and probably should) be assigned to different staff members. The initial writing may require an expert, but editing skills are quite different. After that, the re-write might be accomplished by a junior staff member. By not writing the activities in a loop, we more clearly define the work required and retain flexibility in assigning staff. So it is probably a much better option not to use a loop.

[27]We try to stay away from leads all together.

122

A conditional branch is one that has an "if" statement in it. An activity is completed "If something happens." Both loops and conditional branches tend to complicate the network. If you really want to include looping and branches, a technique called *Graphical Evaluation and Review Technique* (GERT) can be used.[28]

10.8.4   AOA and AON

Two approaches are used to describe project networks, and the one we have used so far is called *Activity on Node* (AON). AON is also called the *precedence diagramming method* (PDM), and is used by most project management software packages. In practice, AON has come to dominate most projects.

The diagrams in this chapter all used AON. Each activity is associated with a node, and represented by a circle in the diagram. The activities consume time, which is represented by the nodes.[29]

There is another method called *Activity-on-Arrow*, (AOA) in which activities are denoted by arrows, so that if Figure 10.1 is rewritten in terms of AOA, it becomes:

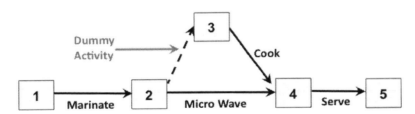

Figure 10.9: An *activity on arrow* (AOA) diagram, equivalent to Figure 10.1.

In an AOA diagram, the activities (and therefore, time) are denoted as arrows and are labeled by the numbers of the nodes they connect. In the AOA diagram, the nodes consume no time. For example, the activity *Marinate* is represented by the arrow from $1 \rightarrow 2$, as it goes from node 1 to node 2. The activity *Cook* is $3 \rightarrow 4$.

The complication that occurs in an AOA diagram is the need for *dummy* activities. In order to designate that *Cook* cannot start until *Marinate* is finished, the dummy activity $2 \rightarrow 3$ (the dotted line in Figure 10.9) must be added to the network.

Some analysts claim that the AOA form is easier to read and draw. We believe that the addition of the dummy activities tends to make AOA more difficult to understand and construct.[30] What is true, however, is that AON has come to dominate the world of project management.

[28] Typically, both loops and conditional branches complicate the reading of network diagrams and confuse the readers more than they help. We avoid them like the plague.

[29] Remember, the definition of an activity is that it consumes time.

[30] Personally, we think that any system that requires adding something called a *Dummy* is pretty dumb! On the other hand, one of my colleagues thinks that AOA is the *only* thing to use. You decide.

123

10.9   An Example

We present a more complex network to illustrate the concepts presented in this chapter. The table of predecessors and durations is in Table 10.7.[31]

Table 10.7: Network Example: Table of activities, durations, and predecessors.

ID	Predecessors	Duration
A	None	10
B	A	6
C	A	8
D	None	17
E	B, C	5
F	C	3
G	B	4
H	D, E, F, G	2

10.9.1   Network Analysis

Once a network diagram is produced, the job of the project manager is to *analyze* it. The network diagram is shown in Figure 10.10. We note the following issues:

- We have inserted start and end nodes, which all projects should have. Sometimes an activity can be started at any time, but without a start node, it cannot be linked to the network. An activity without an input arrow or an output arrow is called a 'dangling' activity.

  Activity D has no predecessor and, so, can be started at any time. Therefore, we connected D to the *Start* node, otherwise it would be dangling.[32]

- Start and stop nodes allow us to create milestones for the start and end of the project, so they are important planning tools. All projects need both a start date and an end date, and the start and end nodes are a convenient place to put them.

- We explicitly include two boxes for calculations of the slack. It may seem redundant because the two slack values should indeed be the same. However, a mistake in the backward pass often shows up as a difference in the two slack values.

[31] Students are encouraged to develop the network diagram from Table 10.7 without looking at Figure 10.10.

[32] Every activity must be connected at both ends.

124

- Arrows may cross. This is allowed.[33]

- The critical path is highlighted with thick arrows, which makes it obvious and easier to manage.

- The critical path has four activities out of a total of eight, so it contains only 50% of the activities. Although this is only a small network, we begin to see that the critical path contains only a fraction of the activities.[34]

- Activities with shaded boxes have *free slack*. Activity D has free slack, even though it is the only activity in the non-critical chain, i.e., between Start and activity H.

- Activity G has free slack because it is at the end of the non-critical B → G chain.

- The network is somewhat *sensitive*, because the path B → G has a small amount of slack. Therefore, small delay in either B or G will turn that path into a critical path.

- Although it is not explicitly stated, activity D represents a roll-up of a collection of non-critical activities. That is, there is an entire sub-network represented by D with a total time of 17. When presenting the project status to stakeholders, this helps to clarify the important schedule issues because all the clutter of the D subnetwork is hidden.

- Activity G is the *lag* in activity B. For example, suppose activity B is the selection and purchase of an item, and G represents the delivery time of 4 days. By explicitly adding the activity G we see the delay when waiting for the item to arrive.[35] Since G is not on the critical path, a small delay in the delivery time is not a problem.

[33]It is difficult to draw this diagram without having some arrows cross. Make it clear rather than obsessing about crossing arrows.

[34]Worry about these and then go home early.

[35]We much prefer this approach to burying the lag in activity B.

125

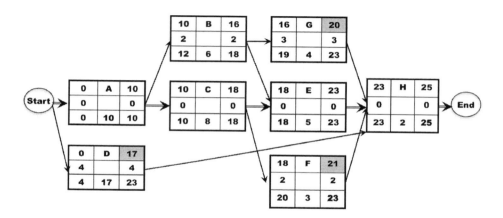

Figure 10.10: The example network diagram.

CHAPTER 11

COST ESTIMATION

The first 90% of the job took the first 90% of the money.
The remaining 10% of the job took the other 90% of the money!

Anonymous

Cost estimation is one of the hardest things to do on a project, for many reasons. First, it is technically challenging and quite difficult in its own right, but we will postpone this discussion until later in the chapter. Meanwhile, let's discuss the *perceptions* of a cost estimate.

11.1   Cost Politics

Yes, politics!

11.1.1   It's an Estimate!

One of the problems that make a discussion of cost difficult for the project manager is that once you have told the customer what the project cost is, that's it! No matter how many times you told them the number was "just a preliminary estimate," that number haunts you forever.

We all behave the same way, no matter how enlightened we think we are. Does the following anecdote sound familiar? You ask the plumber for an estimate to unblock your sink drain. "About $150" the plumber says. Then plumber opens up the pipes under the sink and groans. Eventually, you get the bill: $250!

"But you said it would cost $150!" you cry.

Now magnify that by a thousand, and that is how your customer feels.[1]

In our experience, many people do not understand the concept of a draft document. Often people insist on correcting minor grammatical errors in something you clearly explained was a *Draft*. What you were hoping for was a high-level conceptual review of the ideas, you wanted to know if the project was feasible. They came back and said, "You should have asked if the project *were* feasible—it's subjunctive you know."

The same is often true of a cost estimate. Once people hear the dollars, they conveniently forget you said it was "within ±25%." If they heard anything, they only heard the *minus* 25%.

11.1.2   It's about the Future

> **If I had asked people what they wanted,**
> **they would have said faster horses.**
>
> *Henry Ford*

Another issue that makes cost estimation difficult is that it is inherently a prediction about the future. Since projects have not been done before, there is little data to go on, and the more innovative the project, the less reliable the prediction. Some of the most famously innovative projects also have infamously incorrect price tags: Our two top personal favorites are the Sydney Opera House and Boston's "Big Dig."

11.1.3   The Dream Factor

The scope represents the customer's dreams and aspirations, which crash against the hard realities of cost and schedule. Figure 11.1 shows the spirit of this.

The new project is always the shiny new idea without any apparent blemishes. The old project is slow, buggy, obsolete and dirty.[2]

[1]Remember, in this book, you are the project manager. That tiny change to the scope document that hardly anyone noticed is now estimated to add thousands to the project. Imagine how your customer feels.

[2]And when the new project is finished, it often feels a lot like the old one.

128

Figure 11.1: Scope dreams often crash on the reality rocks of cost and schedule.

11.1.4 The Optimism Factor

People want to please, and when it comes to giving a cost estimate to a customer, even more so. We want to give a low number. A mature project manager will distinguish between doing what's right for the project, and the desire to please.

11.1.5 Cost Estimation Errors

The accuracy of a project estimate is a function of where you are in the project. Early on, a macro estimate maybe off by 100%! Suppose you estimate the project cost as $10,000. A 100% error means that the project might cost $20,000. Of course, the error cannot be −100%, because then the cost estimate would be zero. Also, over-runs are much more likely than under-runs. In fact, this is a well-known property of projects, which we describe as follows:

A project that starts to overrun stubbornly stays overrun!

11.1.6 Marketing vs. Technical Estimates

There is an inherent tension between the marketing and technical departments over the budget. Often, marketing has a good estimate what the customer is willing to spend. This may be completely different from the cost estimate derived from the scope by the technical team. Both organizations will appeal to the project manager:

Marketing: The technical bid is too high. We can't win with their number.
Technical: We can't deliver if we use the marketing bid.

Target costs should be distinguished from cost estimates. Typically, a target cost is proposed by the Marketing department, and is often based on information about the customer's desires, or goals. If marketing knows that the customer has allocated $100,000 for the project, they will press for the estimate to come in at $100,000 (or less). The cost estimate made from the specification may not bear any relation to the customer's needs and wants, as the specification may include a long list of customer wishes, which force the cost well over $10,000.

One way to deal with this situation is for the technical team to estimate the cost of a minimum system, and then propose a series of optional add-ons. The customers can then select which options they can afford, according to their priorities.

11.1.7 Will it get canceled?

Large public sector projects often experience enormous cost growth. One of the contributing factors is that politicians sometimes believe that if they tell the truth about the cost, the public will not support it, and the project will be canceled.

This is a "failure of nerve" combined with a lousy cost justification argument. A good project manager should be able to make a financially compelling case for the project, and to convince a variety of stakeholders.[3]

11.1.8 Protect the Valuables!

Customers are understandably curious about how you came up with the cost estimate. It's their money, and they feel entitled to investigate if you are taking advantage of them. It is a reasonable request.

[3]A good PM can even convince politicians.

On the other hand, if you hand over your carefully calibrated cost estimation formula, you risk giving away your competitive edge.

We recommend you educate your customer in *general* cost estimation, especially industry standards if they exist. That way, the customer can work from the scope to determine a reasonable cost estimate. This will be an independent estimate, and if it is close to the one you have submitted, then everyone should be happy.

11.2 Cost Estimation

> **It's tough to make predictions, especially about the future.**
>
> *Yogi Berra*

There are two types of cost estimates: high-level and low-level. High-level estimates are created early on in the planning cycle, while low-level estimates require more detail and so are generated later. Any of the techniques of cost estimation described below can be used at any stage, the real difference is their purpose.

The first estimate for a project is not likely to be very accurate and is often referred to as a rough order of magnitude, or ROM. The goal of the ROM estimate is often to decide on the feasibility of the project. If the estimate and the budget are out of line, then adjustments can be made, either to the budget, or more likely, to the project content. The project manager can also begin lining up the cash-flow needs: Will it be necessary to borrow funds? When?

The early estimates establish the *budget* (the cost baseline) for the project, which is defined as the Budget at Completion (BAC). As soon as the project gets underway, costs will be reported, and progress is measured against the budget. If the budget is not well thought out, the project manager will have to continually ask for more money from the customer, which is not a good situation to be in.

An early, high-level estimate is also referred to as a macro or a top-down estimate. Such estimates are made from the *scope* document.

> *Estimation is the process of forecasting the time and cost of completing project deliverables.*[4]

The question of how long and how much are intimately related. Usually, one estimates in person hours, not dollars. Estimates in person hours are independent of hourly rates (and inflation) and, so, are more reliable. For example, if it takes 8 hours to paint my office today, it will still take 8 hours to paint it next year. Next year, however, the painter's rates may increase and the job will cost more.

[4] The PMBOK also adds "while balancing stakeholder expectations and the need for control." This is typical of junk added to definitions in the PMBOK. Balancing stakeholder expectations is a good idea, but technically irrelevant to the development of the cost estimate. The cost estimate is defined in terms of project parameters and the stakeholder needs come later in the negotiation about the cost.

131

We wish to estimate in terms of some sort of constant productivity rate that is predictable. That is why almost all estimates are in terms of person-hours, not dollars. Dollars change, hours don't.[5]

11.2.1 Estimation Accuracy

Figure 11.2 shows the accuracy of the cost estimation process as the project proceeds. During the concept phase, the macro estimate is typically within $+75\% \rightarrow -25\%$.

During planning, the micro estimate from the WBS is $+25\% \rightarrow -10\%$. By the time the project is 30%-40% complete, the cost estimate is an excellent representation of the actual, final cost.[6]

Notice the asymmetry: The project is more likely to overrun than under run.

[5]One of the more interesting estimates I learned many years ago (sorry, I don't remember where) is that the cost of a man's tailored suit is approximately equal to the price of an ounce of gold, and has been for over 700 years! That is a great example of a time-independent cost estimate!

[6]There are many projects for which the estimate is consistently incorrect. For example, the estimate for Boston's Big Dig was initially $2.6B in 1984, then $6.4B in 1992. The actual cost of $14.6B was not owned up to until 2002. However, the politicians were not telling the public the truth. The engineers always knew it was a $12-$14B program.

[7]Note that the estimate is made from the *scope*, but it will be dominated by *spec*, which specifies the project content.

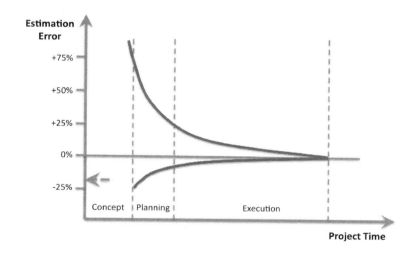

Figure 11.2: The accuracy of cost estimation during the project life cycle.

11.3 Types of Cost Estimates

There are two types of cost estimates:

1. Top-down (macro) estimate:

    The top-down estimate is made early on in the project, typically from the scope.[7] The estimate is typically derived using a mathematical relationship between the scope items (parameters) and historical cost data. However, many other aspects of the *scope*, such as the schedule or assumptions, will affect the cost estimate. The estimate may be refined by analogy with other projects. Sometimes, a group of experts confer to reach a consensus.

There are several methods for performing a top-down cost estimate: A Parametric equation, section 11.5; The Delphi Technique, section 11.5.1; and reasoning by analogy, section 11.5.2.

2. Bottom-up (micro) estimate:

The bottom-up estimate is typically derived by estimating the cost of the individual activities in the WBS. Each element of the WBS (at some appropriate level) is independently estimated, and the layers summed to derive a total cost for the project. The estimates may be derived through a mathematical relationship, even at the lowest levels of the WBS.

The bottom-up estimation technique is discussed in section 11.5.3.

An important rule about cost estimates is that they are always made for the "average" situation, the most likely case. You should never add contingencies into a cost estimate, because that is handled in the risk analysis. It is tempting to add some rainy day funds into the cost estimate, but if you do, you will be adding unnecessary cost.[8]

First, we show the general approach with some examples.

11.4   Cost Estimate Examples

Go get some pizza!

One of our favorite cost estimation formulas is the one that tells us how many pizzas to order:

$$N = 1 + \frac{3G}{8}, \tag{11.1}$$

where G is the number of guests. With 10 guests, I need 4.75 pizzas, so rounding up, I order 5. I just have to multiply by the cost per pizza, and I have the cost.[9]

This is a quick and simple formula that does the job. It contains a parameter from the scope (number of guests) and is calibrated, i.e. it works in practice.[10]

Every industry has a standardized set of estimation parameters. You can't do business without them. Here's another example, which, despite its simplicity, also has all the features we need.[1]

[8] Besides, when your boss reviews your bid, she will invariably uncover your rainy-day funds, and immediately delete them.

[9] I am indebted to one of my students, Grant MacElhiney for telling me about this formula.

[10] Grant also said that it has worked for him for years, so it is calibrated. What more can you ask of a cost estimation formula?

133

I want a Super-Yacht!

A super-yacht is defined as a yacht whose length is greater than 40 meters (>130 feet) long. The cost estimate is:

Sail: $1 million per meter
Power: £1 million per meter

How is this used? Someone saunters into the boat yard, and casually remarks that they just saw a yacht they rather liked. It was about 150 feet long, and they'd like to know how much it would cost to build one. You listen, rub your chin thoughtfully, and ask, *Power or sail?*[11]

Listen carefully to the accent, because the cost depends on the currency. *Sail*, they say in an American accent. You quickly divide the 150 feet by 3 to get 50 meters, and say,

"In which case, it's about $50 million."

Obviously, the eventual cost of the yacht will depend on a lot of factors, but for now you have established the ballpark. Assuming your client did not faint at the price, it is now probably a good idea to hedge that number, *"But, of course, the actual cost will depend on the quality of the outfitting."*

This simple cost estimate formula actually has all the necessary features:

- *Parameters.* In this case there are two parameters: the length of the yacht, and whether it is power or sail. These two parameters are the major determinants of the eventual cost.

- *Accurate.* Accuracy depends on the situation, obviously, and there will be a lot of variation in super yacht costs. But this estimate is good enough to begin negotiations.[12]

- *Easy to use.* A good cost estimate is practical. You need to be able to be able to immediately give the client a decent answer.

- *Calibrated.* Somebody plotted a chart of super yacht costs vs. length.[13] Then they noticed that the line representing *$1 million per meter* was a decent fit to the data for sail.[14] This rule must be derived by an expert in the field; someone with credibility and access to a decent sized data sample.

- *Uncertain.* An "exact estimate" is an oxymoron. Estimates have uncertainties, which are important to understand.

[11] Power yachts are about 50% more per meter than sail yachts.

[12] And, not incidentally, like all good "quick and dirty" estimates, it will immediately sort out the serious buyers.

[13] Actually, in this case, our colleague, Steve Leybourne– see [10]

[14] A good analyst would also list the standard deviation and the major factors that increase or decrease the estimate.

While few of us will get to purchase such a yacht, the same process is repeated for every project. If someone gives you an estimate for a project, you are entitled to ask, "On what basis did you estimate that?"

Cost estimates that are created during the planning phase are used in strategic planning and feasibility studies. As the scope evolves (progressive elaboration), the cost estimate is refined (rolling wave planning), becoming more accurate. The basic process has three steps:

1. Estimate the size of the product, e.g., the *length* of the super yacht.

2. Estimate the effort (person-months) and convert to a cost, e.g., a 50m yacht will cost $50 million.

3. Estimate the schedule, e.g., a 50m yacht takes 3 years to build.

11.5 Parametric Estimates

A dollar per horse per mile.

Paul Parnegoli

The above quotation by Paul Parnegoli was his cost estimation rule for transporting horses in his special truck, from Kentucky Downs to places as far as California and Boston. As we shall learn, it is a parametric estimate.

> *A parametric estimate is a mathematical relationship between the cost (or schedule) of an element of the project and the project's parameters.*

Most cost estimating tools have a parametric model inside. Parametric techniques are mathematical models that use project characteristics to compute project estimates. The estimates are usually for the cost, but may also be for the schedule. For example, a painter may use a parametric relation between the number of square feet to be painted and the hours required to do the job.

Parametric estimates consist of equations, constants and parameters. The equation links the end result (e.g., the cost) to the constants and parameters. The values of the constants are determined by calibration using historical data. The parameters are system characteristics usually available in the specification or scope.

Equation 11.1 is an example of a parametric estimate. It is an equation that links the estimate (the number of pizzas required) to one parameter (the number of guests, *G*) and one constant, 3/8. This constant was determined by calibration: The equation was used in many different situations and the number of pizzas that showed up usually seemed to be about right.

It is important to realize that parametric estimates are used in both macro and micro cost estimates.

Parametric techniques can be used as a fast and reliable way to obtain a cost estimate in the early stages of a project. Early on, the project parameters are usually determined from the specification.

However, parametric estimates are not confined to the early stages of a project. Even when performing a micro cost estimate deep down in the layers of the WBS, one still uses the parametric technique. For example, at the lowest level of the WBS, you may be asked to estimate the cost of a party project work package: *Mail Invitations.* You would multiply the cost of mailing an invitation by the number of guests, which is a parameter.[15]

When facing an estimation task, the estimator should always have a particular model in mind. Most, if not all, estimation models use predictors. According to De Marco, "A predictor is an early-noted metric that has a strong correlation to some later results." [11]

Drinks and Hors D'Oeuvres

Here's an excellent example of a parametric cost estimate.[16] It demonstrates the idea that all industries need a cost estimation model for their business.[2]

At a reception, the cost of drinks is:

$$C = n \times h \times \$6.75. \tag{11.2}$$

The two parameters are *n*, which is the number of people at the event, and *h*, which is the number of hours the bar will be open. The constant, \$6.75, is determined in two parts: \$4.50 is the average cost of a drink and is multiplied by 1.5, which is the average number of drinks each person consumes per hour.

The cost of hors d'oeuvres is:

$$C = n \times h \times \$6.75. \tag{11.3}$$

The two parameters are *n*, which is the number of people at the event, and *h*, which is the number of hors d'oeuvres that will be served. The constant, \$6.75, is determined in two parts: \$1.50 is the average cost of an hors d'oeuvre and is

[15]We think there is really only one way to estimate anything, and that is using the parametric technique. If someone uses an analogous estimate, you are entitled to ask, "How analogous?" Any satisfying answer will have to use some parameters to compare the two cases.

[16]This example was provided by Andrew Korda, one of our undergraduate students.

multiplied by 4.5, which is the average number of hors d'oeuvres each person consumes per hour.[17]

Therefore, the cost of drinks plus hors d'oeuvres is:

$$C = 2 \times n \times h \times \$6.75. \tag{11.4}$$

Elegant!

Vijay's Parametric Model

In an excellent and quite sophisticated example, the author (Vijay Kanabar) designed and implemented a parametric model called a 4GT Model. But what is 4GT? According to Pressman, the term fourth generation technique (4GT) encompasses a broad array of tools that have one thing in common: each enables the software developer to specify some characteristic of software at a high level. [12] The tool then automatically generates source code based on the developer's specification. There is little debate that the higher the level at which the software can be specified, the faster a program can be built.

Here is Kanabar's formula to estimate the cost of a 4GT software project. The programming effort, PE, in person-hours, is.

$$\begin{aligned} PE \quad = \quad & 10.2 \times \#Forms \\ & +7.9 \times \#Reports \\ & +4.9 \times \#Entities. \end{aligned} \tag{11.5}$$

This is the programming effort only. The total effort, TE, for the project is:

$$TE \quad = \quad 3.1 \times PE. \tag{11.6}$$

The formula consists of several pieces. The parameters are the *number of forms*, the *number of reports*, and the *number of entities* (the data items). These can be estimated by examining the *spec*. The formula also contains several constants: 10.2, 7.9, and 4.9. These are determined by calibration using historical data.

The 4GT model only estimates the Programming effort, which is estimated as 32% of the total effort. This data leads us to recommend a multiplier of 3.1 in the 4GT Model to obtain the total effort for a project.

There were three steps in the development of this parametric cost estimate formula:

1. The parametric formula itself. The formula must be in terms of useful *spec* entities that can be counted (e.g., the number of screens).

[17]We find it fascinating that the same constant arises in both cases, but for completely different reasons. The symmetry is charming.

137

2. The formula must be calibrated to determine the constants. This requires company data from similar projects.

3. Finally, the assumptions that apply to the model's use must be listed, e.g., it applies to 4GT software developments only.

PMA Cost Estimate

Suppose we want to add capabilities to the PMA web site to allow referees to register and examine the conference papers they have been assigned to review. The scope would contain information about logging in; presenting screens for referees to enter their data; listing the titles of papers; and allowing the referees to select and reject papers. (The scope would have more specific detail, but this is enough for now.)

We analyze the scope and decide we need 2 login forms for name and addresses; 2 forms for the referee's background and expertise; and 2 forms to select the papers, a total of 6 forms. We have one form to print out the paper titles when the referee has completed her assignment. As to data entities, we estimate 50 are associated with the referee's name and address, 20 with their qualifications, and 20 with each paper (title, author data, subject area, accepted/rejected, etc.), for a total of 90 data entities.[18]

The cost estimate for the programming effort, PE, is:

$$\begin{aligned} PE &= 10.2 \times 6 + 7.9 \times 1 + 4.9 \times 90 \\ &= 61.2 + 7.9 + 441 = 510 \\ TE &= 3.1 \times PE = 1{,}581 \; person \; hours = 39.5 \; person \; weeks. \end{aligned}$$
(11.7)

We immediately see the largest item in the cost is the data. Therefore, we should be very careful with our estimate of the number of data entities. We say that the number of data entities is *cost driver* for the project.

At this point we should go back and carefully re-estimate the number of data entities, because the accuracy of our cost estimate is very sensitive to the number of data entities. Do we really need 50 entities for the referee's name and address? After drawing some rough pictures of the screens, we may decide that we could cut that to 20 entities, and re-estimate the cost of the project.

This is an example of a *sensitivity analysis*.

When the stakeholders scrutinize your bid during a review, they will pick up on the fact that the number of data entities drives the cost. They will immediately try to cut the number of data entities, which will lower the bid. At that point, you will need to be able to defend your count of the data items.[19]

[18]Notice that there may be hundreds of papers, but that is not what is being counted. We are only to estimate the number of different data items.

[19]Since you almost always have to cut the bid, this is also a useful, practical skill.

138

At this point we have the cost estimate in person hours, but we have said nothing about either the dollar amount, or the schedule. Usually, the customer has a schedule in mind, and here we'll assume it is six weeks. If we put 4 people on the job, it will take 39.5/4 = 9.9 weeks, while if we use 6 people, it will take 39.5/6 = 6.6 weeks.[20]

We now convert to dollars by multiplying by the rates for the proposed mix of people to be employed on the job. Many organizations have a standard job mix of people they use to bid on jobs—see Table 11.1. Small organizations may simply bid the rate of the people who will be actually assigned to the project.[21]

Table 11.1: Sample job mix cost rates .

Job Title	Percent	Rate	Cost
Principal Engineer	10%	$100,000	$10,000
Senior Engineer	20%	$80,000	$16,000
Engineer	40%	$50,000	$20,000
Junior Engineer	10%	$30,000	$3,000
Clerical Support	10%	$20,000	$2,000
Total Person Year Cost			**$51,000**

Therefore, the cost of the job is estimated to be 39.5 person weeks at $51,000/52 per week = $38,740. We would probably quote this as "around $39,000," since this is, after all, an estimate.

Detailed Parametric Estimating

Parametric estimation techniques can be used at all levels of the estimation process. Here is an example in which the method is used at a very detailed level of the WBS.

In this example, a form in the PMA web site has been assigned to a programmer. During the detail design stage, the total number of data elements on the form, and their properties are completely specified. The *Adjusted Specification Effort*, ASE, is the development effort for the whole form. It consists of the number of data element *specifications* multiplied by the complexity of the elements. The specification of each data element is classified as follows:

- *Simple Element (SE)*. These are simple screen elements that do not have any specification complexity beyond just data entry, e.g., a field that represents a

[20] Of course that assumes that adding more people actually shortens the job. At some point, when you add people they just get in each other's way.

[21] Of course, all these parameters can be manipulated to get the bid to the desired number.

139

zip code, but with no implied retrieving of the town and state when the zip code is entered.

- *Basic Elements (BE)*. These are data elements that require some validation, and/or some simple additional processing. For example: checking the ZIP code for numeric values, and looking up and automatically populating the city and state fields.

- *Detailed Elements (DE)*. Such screen fields require implementation of a trigger or a stored procedure. For example: when the zip code is entered, the system accesses a shipping company's web site, and sends some data to calculate the cost of shipping.

The cost estimation formula for the form is:

$$
\begin{aligned}
ASE \quad = \quad & \textit{No. of SE elements} \times 10 \\
& + \textit{ No. BE elements} \times 24 \\
& + \textit{ No. DE elements} \times 250.
\end{aligned}
\tag{11.8}
$$

For example: You are implementing a form in the PMA web site with the following data elements: 20 simple (SE), 5 basic (BE), and one form-function (DE). The application development effort is:

$$
ASE = 20 \times 10 + 5 \times 24 + 1 \times 250 = 570 \; \textit{person-hours.}
\tag{11.9}
$$

This particular form will take about $570/40 \sim 14$ weeks of work.

When the programming department is called upon to write the form, the project manager will send over the specification of the form and request a quotation for the work. The programming department manager will carry out the above calculation, and explain to the project manager that the job will take about 14 weeks of work. This is a simple form, and so perhaps a junior programmer will be assigned. The project manager thus knows the form's estimated cost and schedule.

These examples show how the parametric technique is used at all levels of the project WBS—it is not confined to the higher levels.[22]

11.5.1 The Delphi Technique

Wideband Delphi is an expertise-based process that a team can use to generate any kind of estimate. Delphi is an anonymous, group approach to estimation, based on the theory that:

[22] By the way, the *Practice standard for Project Estimating* says that parametric techniques are useful at "level one and level two" of the WBS. Actually, as you can see from this example, parametric models are actually used at *all levels* of the WBS.

140

- Group opinions are fairly reliable.

- Extreme views get annulled.

- Informal one-on-one conversations are susceptible to bias and intimidation.

- An individual might not estimate frankly in the presence of managers, customers or other stakeholders.

To begin the Delphi technique, the project manager chooses an estimation team, and asks each person (or small sub-team) to estimate a series of quantities (costs or schedules). The teams are then informed about the other teams' estimates, and the process is repeated. The Delphi technique can be used when no historical data exists, and is useful when estimating a unique product or a project with no history.

Somewhat amazingly, the Delphi technique seems to converge to the right answer!

11.5.2 The Analogous Estimation Technique

In this case, one reasons by analogy with similar projects. One uses the values of parameters from a previous project for the scope, cost, or schedule as the basis for estimating the same parameter for the current project.

The analogous estimate is often one of the first estimates to be performed, early on, as a rough guide. It is generally considered to be the least accurate method of estimating.

We all use this idea constantly when we estimate how long it will take to drive somewhere that we have driven to before. We know the previous estimate for the length of the trip and modify our estimate to allow for the things that might crop up.

For example, driving to New York to visit our children takes about 4 hours.[23] But that 4-hour trip can change depending on: Random events (accidents in Southern Connecticut); Friday and Sunday night traffic is always much worse; and

An interesting analogous estimate is the average cost-per-pound to launch something into space: [3]

| Low Earth Orbit: | $3,600 | $\rightarrow$ | $4,600 |
| Geosynchronous Orbit | $9,200 | $\rightarrow$ | $11,000 |

Notice that an analogous estimate is a lot like a very rough, preliminary parametric estimate. Also, it is only as good as the degree to which it is *analogous*. Not only must the new project be similar to the baseline project, but the parameters used

[23] Both authors have children living in New York, so we know this trip well, satisfying the constraint that only experienced people should estimate.

141

for comparison must be appropriate. The parameters should be those that actually drive the cost.

11.5.3 Bottom-Up Cost Estimate

This is sometimes referred to as a Micro Cost Estimate. Bottom-up estimation is typically carried out using the WBS. The more detailed the WBS level that is used for the estimate, the more accurate will be the cost estimate. When performed on work packages, which are at the lowest level of the WBS, the estimate is about as accurate as possible.

In bottom-up WBS estimation you focus on individual project activities, which requires a detailed breakdown, and requires the project manager and team members to precisely estimate individual activities and work packages. Once they are estimated, you roll up the costs of the lower level activities to come up with an estimate for the entire project.

Bottom-up estimation is generally considered to be more accurate than top-down estimation because it is based on the WBS, which is a refined version of the scope. The major risk is that the project manager is so focused on the details that he or she might overlook the fact that the WBS is missing some key features.

Therefore, the bottom-up estimate should be compared to the top-down estimate as a consistency check. When the two estimates disagree, the usual explanation is that items are missing or incorrectly represented, either in the WBS or the parametric estimate (i.e., from the scope).

In Fig. 11.3 we show a summary level snap shot of an estimate for the PMA Project. (All details of the WBS view will not fit in the figure.) The total estimated effort for the PMA Conference Management System project is 522 work-hours.

The final step of the bottom up estimation stage is to compare the results with the top-down (macro) analysis. While the bottom-up estimate is more precise, it is possible to make systematic errors, such as leaving out pieces of the project. Resolution of any discrepancies between the two estimates provides confidence that the final estimate is not only precise, but also correct.[24]

Table 11.2 summarizes the situations when you might use the top-down approach, and when the bottom-up. If you need speed, and you only have a preliminary scope, use top-down. If you need accuracy, have the time, and there is a detailed WBS, then use bottom-up.

[24]The precision of the estimate is the number of figures, e.g., $10,271.25 is a very *precise* estimate. However, if a major piece of the project is left out, then it may not be *accurate*.

142

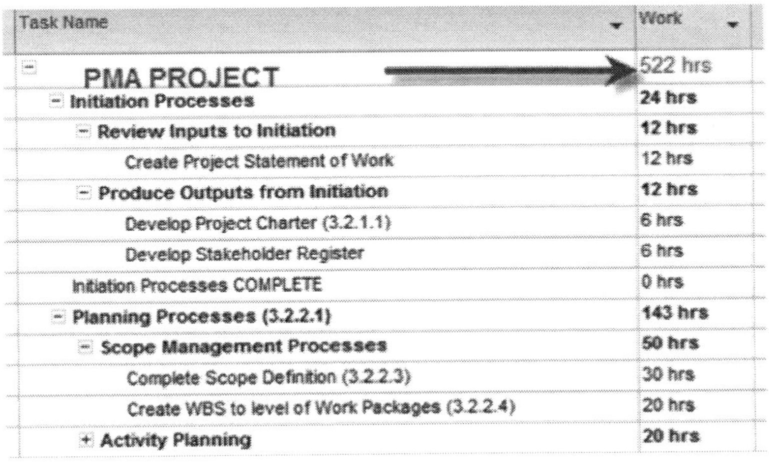

Task Name	Work
PMA PROJECT	522 hrs
− **Initiation Processes**	24 hrs
− **Review Inputs to Initiation**	12 hrs
Create Project Statement of Work	12 hrs
− **Produce Outputs from Initiation**	12 hrs
Develop Project Charter (3.2.1.1)	6 hrs
Develop Stakeholder Register	6 hrs
Initiation Processes COMPLETE	0 hrs
− **Planning Processes (3.2.2.1)**	143 hrs
− **Scope Management Processes**	50 hrs
Complete Scope Definition (3.2.2.3)	30 hrs
Create WBS to level of Work Packages (3.2.2.4)	20 hrs
+ **Activity Planning**	20 hrs

Figure 11.3: A portion of the micro (or, bottom-up) estimate for the PMA project derived using Microsoft Project.

Table 11.2: When to use Top-Down vs. Bottom-up Cost Estimates.

Situation	Top Down Macro	Bottom Up Micro
Strategic planning	X	
Speed important	X	
Accuracy important		X
Customer needs options	X	
Poor scope		X

11.6 The Budget

The budget includes all funds required to execute the project. A budget requires the cost estimate as the starting point, and adds the times of the cash flow events: When will outgoing costs be paid? When will incoming payments be received?

A cost estimate is a budget when it is time-phased.

Time-phased budgets show the project's cash needs over time. The budget details

143

the expected cash flows, both in and out. Budget variances occur when actual and forecast cash flows do not coincide. Also, see *Estimate Costs*, section 24.3.5.

The *cost baseline* is:

> *The cost baseline is the approved time-phased budget.*

It is interesting to note that the cost baseline does not include the *management reserve*–see 11.6.2.

11.6.1 Subcontractors

A question that often arises is, "Do I need to estimate the cost of work I have assigned to subcontractors?"

Yes! *Absolutely.*

You may think that since the subcontractor will perform the work, they should develop the cost and schedule estimates. While that may be a reasonable approach, it does not relieve the project manager of the necessity to perform his or her own cost estimate.

There are two reasons to perform your own estimate. First, you will need to develop a budget to get project approval. This likely to occur well before you have enough information to write a subcontract bid request. And second, how do you know if the subcontractor's cost is reasonable? Are you being taken for a ride? The only way to answer these questions satisfactorily is to perform an independent cost estimate. A macro (parametric) estimate may be sufficient to determine if the subcontractor's bid is reasonable.

11.6.2 Contingencies and Management Reserves

Cost estimates may include *contingency reserves* or *contingency allowances*. Like the *time reserves*, they should be allocated to specific, identified risks. The cost impact of the risks should be analyzed as part of the quantitative risk analysis, e.g., a Decision Tree Analysis.

Cost contingency reserves may be added to an activity or managed centrally for the entire project.[25] As the project proceeds and more information becomes available, the reserves may be used, reduced, or eliminated. The policy for using cost contingencies should be clearly documented in the project management plan.

The *Management Reserve* is a cost that is typically *not* included in the cost baseline. It is withheld and managed by the project manager to be applied to unforeseen

[25]Adding cost "in case" is unnecessary padding.

work that is within scope.[26] Since the *Management Reserve* is assigned to "unknown unknowns," it is difficult to estimate. When the project manager decides to use some of the *Management Reserve*, since it is not included in the cost baseline, the request should go through the formal change control process.

It is important to distinguish between contingencies and management reserves. Contingencies are included in the cost baseline because they are specifically allocated to risks. While not all risks will materialize, if the likelihoods and impacts have been reasonably analyzed, the contingency funds should cover the risks that do occur. On the other hand, management reserves are not included in the cost baseline because they are to cover unknown events, which are hard to estimate with any accuracy.[27]

11.6.3 Cost Estimation Summary

We summarize the cost estimation process as follows:

- People familiar with the project make the estimate.

- Use several people to make independent estimates.

- Use normal conditions, efficient methods, and standard resources.

- Don't make allowances for contingencies.

- Use consistent time units.

- Treat each task as independent.

11.7 PERT

How do we estimate things when there is uncertainty? Usually, we use the concept of the standard deviation, which measures the likely spread in a sample of numbers. For example, if we toss a coin 100 times, we expect *on average* that we will get 50 heads. Of course in reality, we also know that we may get 46 heads, but we would be surprised to get 100 heads.

Unfortunately, the Normal distribution doesn't work for project management because once projects start to be late, they stay late. So project management costs and schedules are *not* symmetric. Since the normal distribution is symmetric, we cannot use it. Instead we use something called the β distribution.

[26] For those "unknown unknowns."

[27] Management will often eliminate reserves, on principal, as they raise the cost without adequate justification.

145

To estimate an effort, a cost, or a schedule, a project manager can use the three-point technique, also called the PERT Weighted Average (or simply, PERT).[28]

We begin by assuming that each activity duration has a range of values, and that these durations statistically follow a beta distribution—see Figure 11.4

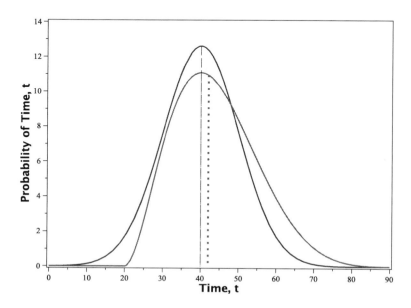

Figure 11.4: A comparison of the β and normal distributions for projects with the same total cost. β is asymmetric, with less likelihood of being early, and more likely to take longer.

In the PERT technique we use three data points. For example, if we are estimating an activity duration, then:

- *Pessimistic estimate, p.* The pessimistic estimate is used to come up with a worst-case scenario–if all the risks materialize and everything that could go wrong did go wrong. If the project were repeated, 1% of the time this pessimistic estimate of the activity duration would be realized.[29]

- *Most likely estimate, m.* If the project were repeated, this would be the activity duration that occurred the most often. (In statistics, it is called the mode.)

- *Optimistic estimate, o.* The optimistic estimate is defined as the shortest activity duration one has had, or might expect to experience. If the project

[28]PERT is an acronym for Program Evaluation and Review Technique, and was developed as a quick estimating strategy in the 1950s for the Polaris Missile System. One of its main advantages is that it uses very simple mathematics—this was long before electronic calculators.

[29]This is the Murphy's Law estimate.

146

were repeated, this would occur 1% of the time.[30]

The formula to calculate the Pert Mean is:

$$\mu = \frac{o + 4m + p}{6}. \qquad (11.10)$$

The variability in the activity duration estimates is represented by the standard deviation, σ:

$$\sigma = \frac{p - o}{6}. \qquad (11.11)$$

The standard deviation, σ is used with the PERT Mean to determine how diverse the range in the estimate is likely to be, and allows the assignment of a degree of confidence to the estimate of the mean.[31]

The confidence intervals for the σ are as follows:

1σ	$\rightarrow$	68%.	The actual schedule has a 68% chance to be within $\pm 1\sigma$.
2σ	$\rightarrow$	95%.	The actual schedule has a 95% chance to be within $\pm 2\sigma$.
3σ	$\rightarrow$	99.7%.	The actual schedule has a 99.7% chance to be within $\pm 3\sigma$.

PERT Example 1

Suppose we are going for an interview. We estimate the drive is most likely to take 60 minutes. Then we consider the worst case, and decide that if there is snow, it might take 120 minutes. On the other hand, if there is no traffic, we could possibly do it in 45 minutes. These values are shown in table 11.3.

Table 11.3: Driving to the interview: The PERT optimistic, pessimistic, and most likely estimates.

Optimistic	o	1% chance	45 min
Pessimistic	p	1% chance	120 min
Most Likely	m		60 min

[30] This is the wishful thinking estimate.

[31] Both the PERT mean and standard deviation formulae are approximations to a *Beta Distribution*, which is more appropriate for projects, in that once a project starts to be late, it stays late. The two PERT formulae are accurate enough for practical work, and their simplicity makes them useful.

The PERT Mean is:

$$\mu = \frac{o + 4m + p}{6} = \frac{45 + 4 \times 60 + 120}{6} = 67.5 \qquad (11.12)$$

The variability in the driving times is represented by the standard deviation, σ:

$$\sigma = \frac{p - o}{6} = \frac{120 - 45}{6} = 12.5 \qquad (11.13)$$

Our best guess for the time to drive to the job interview is 68 ± 13 minutes. But that only gives us a 66% chance of arriving on time. However, this is a job interview and we want to reduce the chance that we arrive late, so we might chose a 95% confidence level. Therefore, we would use 2σ: $68 + 26$ minutes, i.e., we should allow 94 minutes.[32]

Table 11.4: PERT interview chances of being on time.

1 σ	$68 + 13 = 81$ min.	66% chance of being on time.
2 σ	$68 + 2 \times 13 = 94$ min.	95% chance of being on time.
3 σ	$68 + 3 \times 13 = 107$ min.	99.5% chance of being on time.

Personally, if I really were going to a job interview, I'd leave 1 hour and 47 minutes for the trip (3σ, 99.5%); show up early; and walk around outside if need be.[33]

PERT applies to many different types of estimates, not just activity durations. It can be used to estimate costs, schedules, or personnel requirements.[34]

PERT Example for the PMA Case Study

The team estimates the time to develop a new system as follows: Most likely, the prototype will take 2 months. Pessimistically, if things go wrong, we estimate that development will take 5 months. Optimistically, the prototype can be completed in one month. Substituting the above numbers in the PERT Mean equation gives:

$$\mu = \frac{o + 4m + p}{6} = \frac{1 + 4 \times 2 + 5}{6} = 2.3 \ months. \qquad (11.14)$$

The variability in the activity duration estimates is σ:

$$\sigma = \frac{p - o}{6} = \frac{5 - 1}{6} = 0.66 \ months. \qquad (11.15)$$

[32] One of the characteristics of PERT estimation is that schedule accelerations are much more unlikely than delays. This is shown in the above example, which shows how the schedule a acceleration tends to become unreliable for more than 1 or 2 σ. This is one of the limitations of the beta distribution.

[33] My best friend's father gave me some useful advice when I was a teenager going to meet girls: "If you can't be there on time, be there a few minutes early. Never arrive after the girl!"

[34] Vijay is famous for teaching PERT in the classroom by having students estimate the weight of an Indian elephant. Amazingly, it works, even though the students do not know much about elephants. The key is to spread out the o and p values.

148

Therefore, we would quote our estimate for the schedule as:

$$Project\ Schedule\ Estimate = 2.3 \pm 0.7\ months. \qquad (11.16)$$

For the PMA project, we would like to have a 95% confidence estimate for the project schedule, i.e., 2σ. We therefore quote the following schedule estimate: The project schedule estimate is 4 months, with 95% confidence.[35]

PMA Project Function Point Analysis

Table 11.5 is an example of a function point analysis.

Table 11.5: PMA Function Point Analysis.

Measurement Parameter	Number	Weighting Factor
Number of User Inputs	3	Simple
Number of User Outputs	1	Simple
Number of User Inquiries	1	Simple
Number of Files	5	Average
Number of External Interfaces	6	Average
Total	**90**	**Function Points**
Estimated Effort	**180**	**person-hours**

In Table 11.5, the function points score of 90 considered Complexity Adjustment Factors for attributes like the operational environment, performance constraints, and distributed processing. Assuming that each Function Point may take 20 Person Hours to implement, the worksheet estimates that for the PMA project we have an estimate of 180 person-hours.

Depending upon the industry, worksheets and templates may be available to help the project team estimate the costs of specific activities. For example, the City of Boston has comprehensive worksheets for construction projects.[4]

11.8 Overhead Costs

Beware of the little expenses; a small leak will sink a great ship.

Benjamin Franklin

Overhead costs are the costs of running the business. A team member needs a desk, a computer and a place to work, which require utilities (heat and light). Also, if a

[35] If the customer insists, it is 2.3 months with a standard deviation of 1.4 months, i.e. 2σ.

149

team member works on several projects, the company needs a way to divide up the expenses fairly. If someone works 90% on project A, and 10% on project B, then project B should only pay for 10% of the heating bill.

The sum of all the company's expenses is called the *total overhead*. The process of allocating charges fairly across projects is to calculate a percentage overhead that is applied to the direct labor for each project. To do this, we need to calculate the total expenses and figure out what percentage they are of the direct labor. The largest overhead cost is almost always the occupancy (mortgage or rent, utilities, supplies, etc.).[36]

It all begins with the direct labor, which are the salary payments to the staff. When you pay a staff member $1, what does it cost the customer? Somewhat surprisingly, usually between $2 and $3.

Direct labor (DL) is the cost to pay the staff.

Charges for work directly associated with the project are called direct costs.

Direct Costs are items that are chargeable to a specific work package.

Direct costs come in two categories: labor (i.e., staff work), and materials and equipment. Only labor directly performed actually working on the project can be charged to the project. The same applies to materials and equipment: only equipment used directly on the project can be charged to the project. For example, the cost of renting a backhoe used to dig a hole for a construction project is a legitimate cost and will be paid for by the project. Expenses that can be legitimately charged to the project are called *allowable expenses.*

Not all staff time is chargeable to the project. Sometimes, team members perform non-project related work, such as company assignments, attending professional development conferences, and even the dreaded committee work. This is called *indirect labor* and the customer will not pay for it.[37]

11.8.1   What Does $1 Cost?

The *total overhead rate* is the sum of all the costs other than direct labor: benefits (vacation, sick time, and health insurance), office costs (rent, utilities, and computers), the company bureaucracy (payroll, accounting, legal, and human resources), and profit. The total overhead rate is defined as the multiplier from $1 of direct labor to the final amount charged to the customer.

[36]A mentor once told me that 90% of companies fail, not because of profitability, but because of cash flow, and 90% of cash flow problems are due to occupancy.

[37]The PM must understand the categories of allowable and non-allowable expenses.

Suppose the *total overhead rate* is quoted as 2.2. For every dollar of direct labor applied to the project, the customer is billed $2.20. For example, if you make $17.00 per hour and work 40 hours, the bill to the customer is $40 \times 17 \times 2.2 = \$1,496$. In this section, we show you how to calculate that important number, the 2.2.[38]

The *total overhead rate* is a unique characteristic of every company. For companies that deal with federal, state and local governments, it is an official, audited number that applies to everything the company does. The *total overhead rate* is often public because it is an integral part of both the bidding and billing processes. The *total overhead rate* is audited to ensure that only legitimate costs are included, but the details are not made public because they contain sensitive information and are a competitive advantage.

Even if you do not work on a government contract, every company must still know its overhead rate, if for no other reason than to know when it is making a profit. Even non-profits and charities need to clearly understand the details of overhead calculations. The overhead is calculated each year before the fiscal year starts. The costs for the previous year are audited and the proposed costs for the upcoming year are estimated and the overhead rate established.

11.8.2 Calculating the Overhead Rate

> **The real problem is not the overhead.**
> **What is really stifling is the underfoot.**
>
> *Bill Carlson*

The process for calculating the overhead rate is the same in all organizations. Suppose you are thinking of starting the Small Beer Company, and want to determine if you should quit your job. Here's how you would go about it.

The first step is to make a cost budget for the entire year. The Small Beer Company has estimated they need the following staff: 3 senior partners, who will make $40,000 per year; and 4 semi-skilled brewers who will make $20,000 per year.

Everyone is allocated 2 weeks' vacation, 8 holidays and 5 sick days. All employees have a pension plan that costs the company 6% of the labor cost and a medical plan that costs 25% of the labor cost.

The partners estimate they need to borrow $250,000 for the beer making equipment and they plan to pay off the loan in 5 years. They require 20,000 square feet of space, rented at $0.50 per square foot per year. Utilities are estimated at 33% of the space

[38]This is also referred to as the *fully burdened* or *fully loaded* rate.

151

rental. Office supplies, computers, etc., are estimated at $10,000 per year. Payroll, legal, and other corporate expenses are estimated at 5% per year—the G&A.

Table 11.6: The overhead calculation for the Small Beer Company.

Direct Labor					
	Partners	3	$40,000	$120,000	
	Labor	4	$20,000	$80,000	
Total DL					**$200,000**
Fringe Benefits					
	Vacation	10 days	3.8%	$7,692	
	Holidays	8 days	3.1%	$6,154	
	Sick Pay	5 days	1.9%	$3,846	
	Medical		25%	$50,000	
	Pension		6%	$12,000	
	DL+Fr % =	79.69/200	39.8%	$79,692	
DL + Fringe					**$279,692**
Overhead					
	Equipment			$50,000	
	Interest	8%		$4,000	
	20K sq ft	$0.5 / sqft		$10,000	
	Utilities	33% of Rent		$3,300	
	Office Supplies			$10,000	
	Total OH			$77,300	
Total	OH% =	77.3/279.6	27.6%		**$356,992**
G& A	1.05*(DL+Fr+OH) Payroll, etc.		5.0%	$17,850	**$374,842**
Total Cost					**$374,842**
Sales					
	Plan	20,000 cas.	$30.00	$600,000	
	Cost of Goods	Ingred.	$10/cas.	$200,000	
Gross Profit					**$400,000**
Net Profit			6.3%	$25,158	
Planned Profit			25%	$100,000	

One of the partners performed a preliminary marketing study and believes their specialty beer will be competitive at $30.00 per case. Each case of beer contains $10 worth of ingredients. The preliminary marketing study also suggests that, initially, they can sell around 20,000 cases per year. To be worth the effort and sacrifice, the partners plan for a profit margin of 25%.

The overhead calculation is shown in Table 11.6 and we begin with the direct labor: The yearly direct labor for the partners is $3 \times \$40,000 = \$120,000$. The direct labor for the brewers is $4 \times \$20,000 = \$80,000$, so the total direct labor is $200,000.

Next, we add all the fringe benefits, such as vacation time and sick pay. For example, the employees receive 10 days' vacation. They work 52 weeks, 5 days per week, so the percentage vacation time is $10/(52 * 5) * 100 = 3.8\%$. Similar calculations are performed for the holidays and sick pay.

We can now calculate the *fringe percentage*. The total cost of the fringe package is $79,692 and, as a percentage of the direct labor, is: $79,692/$200,000 = 39.8%. For every dollar paid to an employee, there is a cost of $0.398 for the fringe benefits.

Next we calculate the *overhead rate*.[39] The major occupancy items are the equipment, rent, and supplies. The total overhead adds to $77,300, which, as a percentage, is:[40]

$$\textbf{Overhead Percentage} = \frac{Overhead\ Expenses}{Direct\ Labor} = \frac{77,300}{279,692} = 27.6\%. \qquad (11.17)$$

The General and Administrative Costs (G&A) are the central corporate expenses, such as payroll, accounting, human resources, and legal. Typically, these are expressed as a percentage of the Direct Labor plus Fringe plus Overhead. The Small Beer Company allocated 5%, i.e., 5% of DL+Fr+OH = 5% × $356,992 = $17,850.

We now have the total costs to run the Small Beer Company for a year.[41] To pay these costs, the company needs sales. The marketing study suggested that they could sell 20,000 cases at $30.00 each, for gross sales of $600,000. Subtracting the cost of making that beer ($200,000) leaves a gross profit of $400,000.

The net profit is the gross profit minus the total costs:

$$\textbf{Net Profit} = \$400,000 - \$374,482 = \$25,158. \qquad (11.18)$$

The percentage profit is $25,158/400,000 = 6.3\%$. This is the best estimate of the profit for the first year. It is a lot less than the planned 25%![42]

If the overhead costs go up (e.g., the landlord demands a rent increase), the profit will fall. Also, if the sales do not meet their target while the costs remain the same, the profit will be reduced. Thus, the overhead calculation is a critical component of planning.

We now have the overhead percentages, which are summarized in Table 11.7.

[39] This is distinct from the *total overhead rate*.

[40] Notice that the overhead rate is calculated as a percentage of the Direct Labor **plus** Fringe.

[41] A sharp-eyed student will again notice that we have used a non-project example; it's another manufacturing case. That is because this case has all the pieces that go into an overhead calculation. Your project might not have a Cost-of-Goods, but if it does, at least you'll know where to put it.

[42] This is quite typical. In fact, the first pass often indicates a loss, never mind a smaller than desired profit. This is where the work really begins: how to get more sales at less cost.

Table 11.7: The overhead summary for the Small Beer Company.

Direct Labor			$1.00
Fringe	39.8%	DL*1.398	$1.40
Overhead	27.6%	1.276*(DL+Fr)	$1.79
G&A	5%	1.05*(DL+Fr+OH)	$1.88
Total Cost			$1.88
Profit	25%	1.25*(DL+Fr+OH+G&A)	$2.35

11.8.3 Cost vs. Price

Price is what you pay. Value is what you get.

Warren Buffett

Suppose a friend calls you up and asks you to create a special brew for a party.[43]
We estimate the labor cost for the special run as $10,000 and the total project cost
immediately follows from the overhead calculation—see Table 11.8.

Table 11.8: The bid for the special brew from the Small Beer Company.

Direct Labor		$10,000
Fringe	39.8%	$13,980
Overhead	27.6%	$17,838
G&A	5.0%	$18,730

[43]A sharp-eyed student will
notice that this is (finally!) a
project–a unique brew, never
been done before, one time,
etc.

[44]Assuming, of course, the
labor estimate is correct.

We emphasize that the *cost* of the special brew is $18,730, which is different from
the **price**. What we charge the customer, *the price*, can vary considerably.

For example, this special brew might be a lot of bother and interfere with normal
operations. In which case, we might inflate the price to make it worthwhile: We
explain to our friend that the price is $30,000. On the other hand, if we see this as
an opportunity to get into an exciting new area, we might price the brew below cost
at $15,000. We are planning to lose $3,730.[44]

This highlights the important distinction between the cost and the price. The cost is fixed, while the price can be any number at all.[45] As the project manager, you should be quite willing to do the job for $15,000, but you should make it absolutely clear that the company stands to lose $3,730.

Unfortunately, what often happens is that upper management says, "We'll do the special brew project, just try to do it for $15,000." This is a nasty trap, because you might think that it is OK to go ahead with an $18,730 project with company investing $3,730. In fact, a more correct reading of upper management's position is *We expect you to complete the project for $15,000."*

At this point, our recommendation is for the project manager to write a charter for the unique brew project, explaining the new venture and its excellent potential for increasing sales. Then sneak into the charter that the company will invest $3,730. Circulate the charter and ask everyone to sign it.[46] Then stand back and wait for the sparks to fly!

11.9 PMI and Estimating

The Project Management Institute released a *Practice Standard for Project Estimating* in 2011. [13] This standard provides guidance for sound estimating principles for the life of a project and treats estimating as a living process.[47]

---

[45]The Marketing department often wants to win the job by bidding low.

[46]Remember, it is perfectly standard for everyone to sign the charter; you are not asking anything unusual.

[47]This is the first edition, and like many first attempts, it is a bit weak. In our opinion, the estimation examples are not very insightful. For a detailed analysis of the standard, see [14].

155

12

Earned Value Management

The more education a woman has, the wider the gap between men's and women's earnings for the same work.

Sandra Day O'Connor

Earned value management (EVM) is such an important topic that we dedicate an entire chapter to it. Normally, EVM is covered as part of the *Cost Management* knowledge area.[1]

12.1 How ya doin'?

This is the question everyone wants the answer to. Customers, upper management, stakeholders, and the project team all want to know the true status of the project. By which they mean they want to know about the cost and schedule. How do you determine that? Earned Value.

While the details of earned value management can get quite complicated, the basic idea is simple.

Suppose I am asked to write a 50 page document. I look at the requirements, and estimate that I can deliver 5 pages per day for 10 days.

[1] We believe that the two most important technical concepts in project management are the critical path and earned value.

157

I explain to the customer that I earn $10 per hour, and I agree to work 10 hours per day.[2] However, I am paid for all the hours I work and I report the number of pages I write each day, the hours worked, and the cost.

Here's what happened:

Day #1   I worked 10 hours and wrote 5 pages. The customer accepted the pages and paid me the agreed amount for my day's work: $100. I am clearly on budget and on schedule.

Day #2   I again worked 10 hours and produced the planned 5 pages. The customer paid me $100. I am still on budget and schedule.

Day #3   I ran into a problem and only delivered 2 pages. Also, I worked an extra 2 hours trying to fix the problem. (I worked 12 hours.) Since I get paid $10 per hour, I submit a bill for 12 hours: $120.

I am over budget!

But is my cost overrun significant? Should I be worried? Can I fix it?

So far, the total cost of the project is $320, but I have only delivered 12 of the planned 15 pages. How can I measure my *true* progress? Can I determine the *value* of the 12 delivered pages?

We go back and carefully analyze the *plan*: I estimated I could deliver 5 pages per day, and get paid $100. Therefore each page has a *planned value* of $20. After 3 days, I planned to deliver 15 pages, so the value of the work I planned to deliver is 15x$20 =$300. We refer to this as the *Planned Value* on day #3, $PV(3) = \$300$.

Now let's look at the *Actual Cost, AC*: I have actually spent $320. There is no arguing with this, it is simply the invoiced amount: $AC(3) = \$320$.

I only produced 12 of the planned 15 pages, so the actual cost applies to the 12 pages delivered, not the planned 15 pages. Therefore, I need to determine the *value* of the delivered work.

We noted above that in the plan, each page was worth $20. I have delivered 12 pages, so the value of the completed work is 12x$20 = $240. We call this the *earned value* on day #3, $EV(3)$. It is the value of the work I have actually delivered.

The value of the work accomplished (the earned value) is $240, but the actual cost for that work is $320. That is, I have done $240 worth of work (12 pages), but it has cost $320. Therefore, my cost efficiency is: $240/$320 = 75%.

From the cost perspective, at the end of day #3, I am working at an efficiency of 75%.

[2]We are keeping the numbers as simple as possible.

158

This simple example has all the features of an earned value calculation:

1. A planned value for the work over time. This was the budget estimate over time, which 5 pages per day and $10 per hour: $100 per day.

2. A time at which we wish to estimate the progress. In this case, we decided to measure the progress on day #3.

3. On day #3, we used a *cumulative* measure of progress. I reported the total number of pages delivered (12), and the total cost ($320). I did not report that on day #3, I spent $120 to produce 2 pages.

4. A physical measure of progress. I measured progress in terms of completed deliverables (in this case, pages). This is the important feature of earned value. Every deliverable must be measured in some way to actually determine the real progress. This is discussed in detail in section 12.2.9.

We emphasize that earned value calculations use a *cumulative* measure of cost progress. This makes sense, because I did 2 days of work, which was on budget, and it was only on day #3 that I ran into problems. I should get credit for the on-budget work in the first 2 days. Therefore, a reasonable measure of my cost progress is 75% ($240 worth of completed deliverables which cost $320).

Now let's examine the schedule.

At the end of day #3, I was supposed to have completed 15 pages, and I have only delivered 12. Obviously, it will take more time to finish the work I am supposed to have completed by now.

I am behind schedule!

But how much am I behind schedule? I was supposed to complete 15 pages (my planned deliverables), but I have only completed 12 (my actual deliverables). So a measure of my schedule progress is that I have completed only 12/15 = 80% of the planned deliverables due on day #3, i.e., I have actually completed 80% of the planned work.

My schedule efficiency is 80%.

This simple schedule example also has all the features we need, and they are the same as for the cost example above.

There are some technical details, such as: What is the quality of my work in the first 2 days? I should not get credit for completing pages if the customer rejects by them and they have to be re-written.

Also, we measured progress in pages, establishing that we measure progress in terms of the physical deliverables. We can also measure the progress in dollars, which can confuse things. In general, it is much easier to understand progress in terms of a physical measure of the deliverables. This is discussed in detail in section 12.2.9.

12.1.1 Earned Value

We now cover the same example as above only this time we will carefully define all of the quantities involved. First, it is important to stress that you can only measure deliverables.[3]

We first specify the time, t, at which all measurements are made. In this case, we are reporting the status of the project on Day #3. The data are typically presented in table form, see Table 12.1.

On Day #1, we planned to complete $100 worth of work. We actually completed that work, and so we *earn* 100% of the value of the planned work. i.e., we earn 100% of $100. The same is true on Day #2. In Table 12.1, the *PV* column lists the cumulative planned value, which is $200.

The *Planned Value* is the budget of the work that is planned to be complete at time, t. Note that this is value of the *total* work to date, i.e., the cumulative total.

Now we come to day #3, when we planned to have completed another $100 worth of work for a total planned value, *PV = $300*.[4]

Table 12.1: The EVM Data for the Simple Example.

Day	Planned	Daily Earned	Actual	Cumulative Planned PV	Earned EV	Actual AC	CPI	SPI
1	$100	$100	$100	$100	$100	$100	1.00	1.00
2	$100	$100	$100	$200	$200	$200	1.00	1.00
3	$100	$40	$120	$300	$240	$320	0.75	0.80

[3]After a little thought, you will realize that until it is delivered, to the project manager, it does not exist.

On Day #3, I ran into a problem, and only delivered 2 of the planned 5 pages. I only delivered 2/5 of the planned work and so I only *earned 2/5 = 40%* of the planned value, which is *40% of $100 = $40*. Therefore, the cumulative total *earned value*, up to and including Day #3, is *EV = $240*.

[4]Notice this is the cumulative planned value.

On Day #3, I ran into a problem, and worked an extra 2 hours trying to fix the problem. I worked 12 hours, and since I get paid $10 per hour, I submitted a bill to the customer for 12 hours: $120. Therefore the actual cost for Day #3 is $120, and the total actual cost is, $AC = \$320$.

We can now calculate the schedule and cost efficiencies for the project:

- *Schedule Efficiency:* At the end of day #3, I have completed 12 of 15 planned pages, which is 80%. I can interpret this as: My schedule efficiency is 80%.

  In dollar terms, I have completed 12x$20 = $240 worth of work, compared to the planned work I was supposed to have completed at the end of day #3, which was 15x$20 = 300. So again, my cumulative schedule efficiency is, $240/$300 = 80%.

  On day #3, I completed 2 out of 5 pages, so my instantaneous schedule efficiency is 40%. This is distinct from my *cumulative* schedule efficiency, which is 80%.

- *Cost Efficiency:* At the end of day #3, I have spent $320, and I have completed $240 worth of work (12 of 15 pages). I can interpret this as: My cost efficiency is $240/$320 = 75%. My cumulative cost efficiency is, $240/$320 = 75%.

  On day #3, I completed 2 out of 5 pages, which was worth $40. I actually spent $120, so my instantaneous cost efficiency is: $40/$120 = 33%. This is distinct from my *cumulative* cost efficiency, which is 75%.

The most important quantity is the **Earned Value**.[5]

The power of EV is that it provides measures of efficiency for the work accomplished: EV provides a measure of the efficiency with which I am completing the project. We will make this more formal with the concepts of cost and schedule variance, and cost and schedule performance indexes.

To calculate this measure of efficiency, we only needed three quantities, PV, AC, and EV. A little thought shows that these are the minimum data that the project manager reports to the customer. The plan was agreed to upon contract signing, and so the planned value is readily available. Table 12.1 is the minimum information that a project manager should present to the stakeholders: What you planned, what you delivered, and what it cost.

The project begins with a plan. The cost is always regularly reported to the customer, because otherwise the team does not get paid. So the customer also has the actual cost. Finally, the project manager reports progress on deliverables, which is nothing more than the earned value.

Therefore, the customer has all the data needed to calculate all of the earned value quantities.[6]

[5] We emphasize that Earned Value Management uses *cumulative* quantities. We added the instantaneous quantities in this discussion to clarify the distinction.

[6] This is why we say that when customers learn to use *Earned Value*, we will no longer be able to hide the true project status!

12.2   Formal Definitions

The formal definitions of the *Earned Value* quantities are as follows:

12.2.1   Planned Value, PV

The Planned Value, PV, is the cumulative time-phased budget.[7]

In the above example, the planned value of the work is $20 per page, or $100 per day for 5 days.

The PV at the end of the project is called the Budget at Completion (BAC).

In the above example, the budget at completion is the total planned budget for the project, $500.

12.2.2   Earned Value, EV

The Earned Value, EV, is the cumulative value of work performed.

We emphasize that in the standard definition, EV is the *cumulative* value of the work completed to date.

[7]The PMBOK definition also includes the idea that the budget is authorized, and allocated over the life of the project. All that just clutters the definition. Somewhat strangely, the word cumulative is left out of the PMBOK definition.

EV can be measured both instantaneously and cumulatively.[8] An instantaneous EV measurement would be: On day #3, I completed 2 planned pages. In dollar terms, I actually completed $40 worth of work on day #3.

12.2.3   Actual Cost, AC

The Actual Cost, AC, is the total cost incurred to date.

[8]The PMBOK uses the word *incrementally*, rather than *instantaneously*. We believe that an *instantaneous* measurement is a more correct description of what is being performed, since we are measuring the *EV* at that instant. An *increment* is a change, which is not what we are measuring, unless you regard day #3 as the increment.

AC includes all expenditures, including labor costs, overhead costs, equipment rentals, purchases, and subcontractor costs. While AC is a cumulative measure, it can also be measured instantaneously. An instantaneous measurement of the cost is: On day #3, I spent $120.

12.2.4   Cost Variance, CV

The cost variance is the earned value minus the actual cost.

$$CV = EV - AC. \tag{12.1}$$

The cost variance is a measure of the cost performance of the project. When the value of the work actually completed (i.e., work earned, EV) is less than the actual cost spent, AC, the project is over budget. Simply put, you have spent more than you were supposed to on the work you have actually completed. Therefore, when $EV < AC$, the project is over budget and CV is negative.

In the above example, at the end of day #3, I have spent $320, and I have completed $240 worth of work (12 of 15 pages). Therefore, the CV is negative:

$$CV = EV - AC = 240 - 320 = -80. \tag{12.2}$$

When the project is complete, CV measures the total cost overrun or under run. At the end of the project,

$$CV_{end} = Budget - AC_{end}. \tag{12.3}$$

Suppose that the budget for the project was $1,000 (the BAC). If at the end of the project you have spent $1,200, the *Cost Variance* is:

$$CV_{end} = BAC - AC_{end} = 1,000 - 1,200 = -200. \tag{12.4}$$

12.2.5 Schedule Variance, SV

The schedule variance is defined as the earned value minus the planned value.

$$SV = EV - PV. \tag{12.5}$$

The schedule variance is a measure of the schedule performance of the project. When the work actually completed (i.e., the earned work, EV) is less than what was planned (PV), the project is behind schedule. Simply put, you have not done what you were contracted to have done, so you are behind schedule.

Therefore, when $EV < PV$, the project is behind schedule and SV is negative.[9]

In the above example, at the end of day #3, I was supposed to have completed $300 worth of work, and I have completed $240 worth of work (12 of 15 pages). Therefore, the SV is negative:

$$SV = EV - PV = \$240 - \$300 = -\$60. \tag{12.6}$$

Notice the weird set of units here. Your boss calls and says, "I hear you are behind schedule. How much are you behind?"

You answer, "I am $60 behind schedule."

[9] We feel obliged to point out that there are problems with the SV concept. First, it is not actually a variance in the statistical sense. It is really a difference. Also, it is measured in dollars, which is a strange set of units for a schedule delay. You say to your boss, "I am $40 behind schedule." Shouldn't a schedule difference be measured in days or weeks?

Your boss is perfectly entitled to ask, "How can you be $60 behind schedule? How much is that in days?"[10]

When the project is complete, all deliverables will be complete: All planned work is finished. Therefore, at the end of the project $EV = PV$, and $SV = 0$. If the project is behind schedule, this may happen after the planned delivery date.

12.2.6   Cost Performance Index, CPI

The cost performance index (CPI) is a measure of the cost efficiency with which the money is being spent on the project. It is one of the most important concepts in all of project management. The CPI is:

$$CPI = \frac{\text{Earned Value}}{\text{Actual Cost}} = \frac{EV}{AC}. \tag{12.7}$$

When $CPI < 1$, the project is over budget, when $CPI > 1$, the project is under budget, and when $CPI = 1$, the project is exactly on budget.

In the above example, on day #3 I have actually spent $320. There is no arguing with this, it is simply the invoiced amount. $AC(3) = \$320$. The value of the work accomplished (the earned value) is $240. Therefore, CPI is:

$$CPI = \frac{EV}{AC} = \frac{240}{320} = 0.75. \tag{12.8}$$

From a cost perspective, after day #3 I am working at an efficiency of 75% and I am over budget ($CPI < 1$).

12.2.7   Schedule Performance Index, SPI

The *schedule performance index* measures the efficiency with which the schedule is progressing. It compares the actual to the planned schedule.

$$SPI = \frac{\text{Earned Value}}{\text{Planned Value}} = \frac{EV}{PV}. \tag{12.9}$$

When $SPI < 1$, the project is behind schedule, when $SPI > 1$, the project is ahead of schedule, and when $SPI = 1$, the project is exactly on schedule.[11]

In the above example, on day #3 I planned $300 worth of work. The value of the work accomplished (the earned value) is $240. Therefore, SPI is:

$$SPI = \frac{EV}{PV} = \frac{240}{300} = 0.80. \tag{12.10}$$

[10]And you do not know, because SV is measured in dollars, not days!

[11]At the end of a project, the $SPI \to 1$, always, so the SPI inevitably rises towards the end of the project. This does not actually mean the efficiency is improving; it is just an inherent property of the SPI. This makes the use of SPI problematic after about the 50% point.

From a schedule perspective, after day #3, I am working at an efficiency of 80%.

At the end of the project, the earned value is equal to the planned value. This is most easily seen in a simple example.

Suppose I plan to deliver 4 pages, one per day, and each page costs $1 ($BAC = \$4$). Suppose I deliver 1 page every two days, instead of the planned 1 page per day. It will take me 8 days to complete the 4 pages. The planned and earned values are calculated in Table 12.2. The SPI is plotted in Figure 12.1.

Table 12.2: The SPI for the 4 page project.

Day	Daily Planned	Earned	Cumulative Planned	Earned	SPI
1	$1.00	$0.00	$1.00	$0.00	0.00
2	$1.00	$1.00	$2.00	$1.00	0.50
3	$1.00	$0.00	$3.00	$1.00	0.33
4	$0.00	$1.00	$4.00	$2.00	0.50
5	$0.00	$0.00	$4.00	$2.00	0.50
6	$0.00	$1.00	$4.00	$3.00	0.75
7	$0.00	$0.00	$4.00	$3.00	0.75
8	$0.00	$1.00	$4.00	$4.00	1.00

Once I have delivered all the pages, my total earned value is $4: I earn the value of the completed deliverables, and when I have delivered them all, I earn the planned value. Therefore, at the end of the project, $EV = PV$, and $SPI = 1$.

However, this occurs after the planned end of the project, which here is not until day #8. Also, in a real sense, my schedule efficiency was 50% *at all times*, because I was completing 0.5 pages per day. However, the shape of the SPI curve does not reflect a constant page delivery rate of 50%, it rises towards the end of the project.

Figure 12.1 illustrates some of the pitfalls in the use of SPI curves.[1] The project manager cannot take any credit for the "improving" SPI in Figure 12.1, it is an artifact of the definition of the SPI.

12.2.8   The Estimate at Completion, EAC

What every customer wants to know is: *How much is it going to cost?*

165

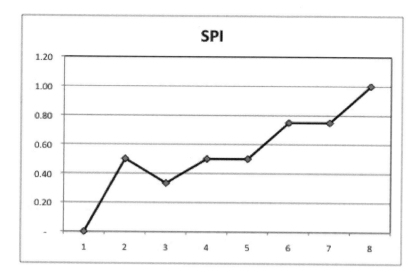

Figure 12.1: *SPI* for the 4 page project. The *SPI* → 1 at the end of the project, which, here, is on day #8.

When you are in the middle of the project, and have some cost data, you can estimate the final cost, which is called the estimate at completion (*EAC*). There are several ways to estimate the *EAC*.

The Average CPI Method

A quick and easy way to estimate the final cost is to estimate the average *CPI* for the project, and then,

$$EAC = \frac{BAC}{\langle CPI \rangle},$$ (12.11)

where $\langle CPI \rangle$ denotes the average *CPI* for the project. If you think you have a decent estimate of this, then equation 12.11 provides a decent estimate for the final cost of the project.

However, equation 12.11 assumes that the average *CPI* is constant and that the average value is a reasonable representation of the *CPI* for the life of the project.

Consider another book project. I agree to write 10 chapters, each with an estimated cost of $100. The Budget at Completion, $BAC = \$1,000$. Suppose I immediately run into problems, and deliver the first chapter on time, but at a cost of $133. I also deliver the second chapter on time, but at a cost of $138.

The planned value after month 2 is $PV = \$200$. The actual cost is $AC = \$135 + \$138 = \$271$. After two months, my $CPI = \$200/\$271 = 0.74$. I can now estimate the EAC:

$$EAC = \frac{BAC}{\langle CPI \rangle} = \frac{1,000}{0.74} = \$1,351. \tag{12.12}$$

I am working at roughly at a $CPI = 74\%$. Therefore, I should increase my original budget by dividing by my CPI. If, as the project manager, I believe that the team can increase its efficiency, then perhaps I can convince the customer that we will do better than the above estimate.[12]

The EAC Formula

A more careful analysis proceeds as follows: The expenses to date cannot be argued with, they are what they are, and have probably been invoiced. Therefore, what is needed is the *Estimate to Complete* the project, ETC. To calculate the ETC, we estimate the remaining work and then assume that it will be completed at the current efficiency. That is,

$$ETC(t) = \frac{BAC - EV(t)}{CPI(t)}. \tag{12.13}$$

The remaining work is the numerator in equation 12.13: the budget (for the entire project) minus the work completed to date, which is represented by the earned value.[13] Therefore, the *estimate at completion* is the actual cost to date plus the estimate to complete:

$$EAC(t) = AC(t) + \frac{BAC - EV(t)}{CPI(t)}. \tag{12.14}$$

At any time, t, we can estimate the final project cost as follows: First, at the current time, we have spent a specific amount, indicated in equation 12.14 as $AC(t)$. One cannot argue with this amount, it is the actual amount spent (and presumably invoiced) to date.

Next we have to estimate the cost to complete the project. The remaining work is the total work to be done, BAC, minus the work completed, which is defined as the earned value to date, $EV(t)$. So the remaining work is: $BAC - EV(t)$. This is the numerator in equation 12.14.

Next we note that our cost efficiency to date is measured by the current $CPI(t)$. If the $CPI = 1$, then we are on budget, and we can expect to complete the work at that rate in the future.

[12] But you'd better have a really good , credible reason. Remember, the customer probably has the same data you have.

[13] Remember, EV is the percentage of the plan completed.

On the other hand, suppose the $CPI = 0.5$, which says we are only performing at a 50% efficiency rate on the cost. For the remaining work, therefore, we should double the estimate of the cost to complete it. This is accomplished in equation 12.14 by dividing the work remaining by the current CPI.

This is perfectly fine, as long as the current value of the CPI is a good representation of the efficiency we can expect on the remaining work. If so, then equation 12.14 will give a good value for the EAC. On the other hand, if the CPI is declining, as it often is, the estimate in equation 12.14 goes up. Therefore, if the CPI is declining, equation 12.14 gives an *optimistic* estimate of the cost.[14]

We should note that there are two formulas for the Budget at Completion, BAC: 12.11 and 12.14. However, they are algebraically identical and give exactly the same answer.[2] Equation 12.11 is easier to use, while equation 12.14 provides a detailed look at how the EAC is arrived at and the assumptions involved.[15]

12.2.9 Measuring Progress

The CPI formula has two terms, AC and EV. The actual cost can only be measured in dollars,[16] and so to calculate the CPI, the earned must also be measured in dollars—we need all quantities in the same units. Therefore, EV must be converted into dollars.

Sometimes, EV is presented as if the deliverable value is only measured in dollars.[17] It is not! Progress is measured in physical units.

Suppose I hire a painter to paint a room, then the progress is easily measured in square feet actually painted. Suppose the wall is 10' tall by 10' long (area = 100 square feet). The painter discovers that he cannot reach above 8', and needs to borrow a ladder to complete the work. At the end of the day, he has only completed the lower 8' by 10' = 80, which is 80/100 of the area = 80%.

Therefore, the value of the work earned is only 80% of the planned work. It is hard to argue with such a simple measure of progress, and here it is the square feet of wall actually painted.

The painter might argue that his efficiency is actually better, and he could have finished the wall if he had a ladder. He might argue that it is 'unfair' to say his efficiency only 80%. As a project manager, however, we are only interested in *actual progress*. It really does not matter how fast the painter *might* have finished the work, the *actual* progress was only 80% of planned.

The painter may say that tomorrow, he will 'make it up' because now he has the ladder. However, he is currently over budget and behind schedule.

[14] A declining CPI means that the estimate is as low as it will get; it's an optimistic estimate. The situation, however, is pessimistic.

[15] The PM should always be aware of the assumptions involved in any calculation.

[16] Assuming you get paid in dollars and not euros.

[17] For example, the PMBOK says that EV is the "value of work performed expressed in terms of the approved budget," i.e., it is assumed to be measured in dollars.

If the painter agreed to a fixed price contract, he may be motivated to catch up and finish on time. Alternatively, he may say that the ladder was not his responsibility, and that he expects to receive more money because the delay was not his fault. If the painter is working on a Time and Materials contract, he has no incentive to work harder to catch up.

The point is that it is pretty easy to see that the painter has only accomplished 80% of the planned work. He is behind schedule and over budget.

Mathematically, the CPI is simply a ratio—there is not much to it. However, even in the simple painting example, we see immediately that the CPI can be interpreted and used in different ways. We refer to this as the 'political' aspect of earned value, and it complicates the discussion.

Some manuals on the use of the earned value are hundreds of pages thick, and propose a process involving dozens of steps. Much of the complication and bureaucracy is intended to define carefully how to collect data, and how to interpret the results, i.e., they attempt to remove the political aspects.[18]

We claim that on any project, if you give it a little thought, the deliverables can be measured in physical units. Some examples of physical units of measure for deliverables are:

- Miles of roadway completed.

- Number of steel girders erected.

- Cubic yards of tunnel dug out. Cubic yards of concrete poured.

- Software modules designed, tested, documented, or delivered. Web pages operational.

- Scope pages delivered.

- Book chapters delivered to the publisher.[19]

12.3 EV Example: The Re-Paving Project

Data is what distinguishes the dilettante from the artist.

George V. Higgins

We now work through an example of using EVM to determine the true status of a project. The state has decided to repave a road, which is 7.7 miles long. The plan

[18] In our opinion, such unwieldy documents have given *EVM* a bad name.

[19] In our experience, usually with an $SPI \sim 0.4$!

169

is to complete the job in 10 months. The estimated cost of the whole project is $1,470,000.

12.3.1 Month Three

The following table represents the status of the project in month three:

Table 12.3: The status of the repaving project after month 3.

Month	Miles Completed		Costs	
	Planned	Actual	Planned	Actual
1	0.77	0.77	$147,000	$147,000
2	0.77	0.62	$147,000	$161,711
3	0.77	0.64	$147,000	$158,492

We claim that this table is the minimum that any project manager would report to the client on a monthly basis. It consists of the work completed (in miles) and the costs incurred.[20]

From this data we can calculate the earned value as follows: The planned amount to be paved each month is 0.77 miles, and the planned cost for this is $147,000. The planned cost per mile is therefore:

$$\text{Planned Cost per mile} = \frac{\$147,000}{0.77} = \$190,909. \qquad (12.15)$$

In month one, we complete all of the planned 0.77 miles on time and on budget. Our earned value in month one is, therefore, $EV(1) = 0.77$ miles, or in dollars, $EV(1) = \$147,000$.

In month two, we only completed 0.62 miles. So our earned value for month two is $EV(2) = 0.62 \times 190,909 = \$118,364$. The actual cost is $161,711, so we have spent more than was planned to accomplish less than was planned. Let's augment the above table with earned value. Remember: EV requires cumulative data.

From this we can now compute the CPI, SPI, and EAC–see Table 12.5. Remember, the formula for EAC is equation 12.14.

For example, the month two calculation for $EAC(2)$ is:

$$EAC(2) = 308,711 + \frac{1,470,000 - 265,364}{0.86} = 1,710,126. \qquad (12.16)$$

[20]We immediately see that unlike its bad press, EVM actually does not require any extra bookkeeping.

Table 12.4: The repaving project after month 3 with cumulative costs.

	Costs			Cumulative Costs		
Month	Planned	Actual	Earned	PV	AC	EV
1	$147,000	$147,000	$147,000	$147,000	$147,000	$147,000
2	$147,000	$161,711	$118,364	$294,000	$308,711	$265,364
3	$147,000	$158,492	$122,182	$441,000	$467,203	$387,546

Table 12.5: CPI, SPI, and EAC for the repaving project after month 2.

Month	CPI	SPI	EAC
1	1.00	1.00	$1,470,000
2	0.86	0.90	$1,710,126
3	0.83	0.88	$1,772,149

In month 2, the best estimate for the final cost, based on the expenditures and the efficiency to date, is: $1,710,126. The variance at completion is:

$$VAC(2) = BAC - EAC(2) = \$1,470,000 - \$1,710,126 = -\$240,126. \qquad (12.17)$$

We are already two hundred and forty thousand dollars over budget!

It is interesting at this stage to plot the CPI and SPI, which are shown in Figure 12.2. We have selected the current CPI as the one to use in the formula for EAC. But an interesting question to ask is: What value of CPI should we really use?

A quick look at Figure 12.2 shows that the CPI is declining. We are entitled to ask, therefore, if the current $CPI(3)$ is, in fact, a good representation of the overall CPI of the project. One might argue that because the CPI is declining, the current value is an *optimistic* estimate. In which case, our estimate of the final cost could be higher.[21]

If the customer plotted this chart, the project manager will have some explaining to do.[22] The customer might well ask how you intend to get back on track.

Here we see the importance of earned value management. Using a few simple concepts, we have in month three, an estimate of the final cost, and it is problematic. The only good news is that it may be early enough for the project manager to take corrective action.

[21] And immediately introducing the idea that the cost estimate is *political*. Which CPI should the PM chose?

[22] Remember, this chart is easy to plot. If the project manager reported the miles completed and the costs to date, the customer has everything necessary to plot the chart!

171

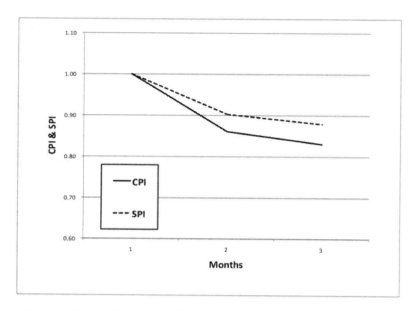

Figure 12.2: CPI and SPI in month 2 for the repaving project.

12.3.2 Plot Everything

To carefully analyze the project status, we recommend that the project manager plot all quantities because plots explain what is happening far better than do tables. In the next few figures, we show the data for the entire 10 month project.

Figure 12.3 shows the actual miles completed, and it pretty quickly reaches a value of around 0.6 miles per month. We can quickly determine that we are not going to achieve the planned 0.77 miles per month.

Figure 12.4 shows that in the first few months, the CPI and SPI fall and then level off. After a few months, the CPI is pretty well established. This means that the final cost estimate, the EAC, quickly converged to a reasonable value, which is shown in Figure 12.5.

In fact, data from thousands of projects shows that the EAC is an excellent approximation of the true cost after about 25% of the project. When it is a poor estimate, it is an underestimate! This is because the CPI is often seen to decline over the life of a project, making the EAC a lower bound on the cost.[3]

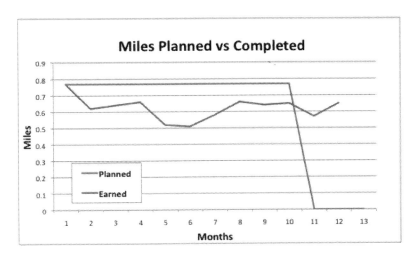

Figure 12.3: Miles (planned and completed) for the repaving project.

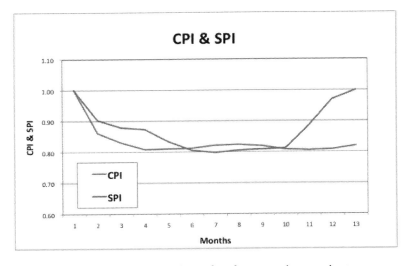

Figure 12.4: CPI and SPI for the repaving project.

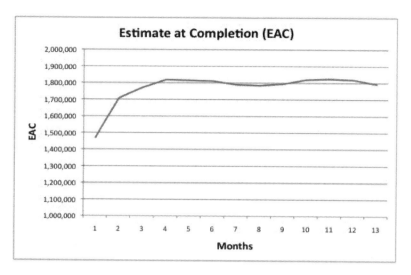

Figure 12.5: EAC for the repaving project.

12.4 Using Earned Value

The only way to enjoy anything in this life is to earn it first.

Ginger Rogers

Earned value management (EVM) is designed to address an issue that is sometimes known as the *work-in-process measurement problem.* EVM has been established as a valuable, but much neglected tool. It provides early warning signals of project trouble, and its predictions are reliable as early as 15% into the project.[4]

So why doesn't everyone use it? There are many excuses, for example: [15]

- "It is not needed on small projects."

  OK, so let me get this straight. Just because you are working on a small project, you do not want to know if your project is late or over budget. Hmm.

- "It is too hard to use."

  You have to report the cost and completed deliverables to your customer every month. Why not divide the cost of the deliverables by the actual cost to determine the CPI? That doesn't sound too hard.

- "The terminology is complex and the rules are overly restrictive."

  There are two quantities, the CPI and the SPI, and they are nothing more than percentages. Reporting those every month doesn't seem to be very complex at all. Since you have to report those to the customer anyway, why is this so "restrictive?"

We suspect the real reason that people don't want to report the CPI and SPI is that their customers will discover the truth about their projects.[23]

12.4.1 Using Hours

Many companies and organizations do not track dollars spent, but only "hours worked." In this case, it is still possible to use Earned Value, one simply calculates everything in hours. A project must be defined in terms of deliverables, and each has a number of *planned hours* over time. As the project proceeds, the hours spent define the *actual cost*. As deliverables are completed, they *earn* the planned value of the deliverable in *hours*.

12.4.2 No Progress

Figure 12.6 shows what happens when a project does not start well. The project was supposed to complete many small deliverables at a constant rate. In the early stages, a small fraction of the deliverables was completed, and each one was completed on budget. Therefore, $AC = EV$, and $CPI = 1.0$, as shown in Figure 12.6.

The project is on budget!

Where are the trouble signs? The problem is that there is not much progress, and this is indicated in the SPI curve in Figure 12.6, where the $SPI = 0.4$. Only 40% of the deliverables are being completed in the early stages of the project. (The $PV = 100$, but the $EV = 40$.) In fact, this project continued at the 40% completion rate all along, right up until week 24 when the project was completed.

Notice that the SPI eventually begins to increase, which has nothing to do with the actual progress. Actually, the productivity is constant: 40% of the deliverables are completed each week. Nevertheless, the SPI is useful, particularly early on, when the lack of progress is shown in the SPI, not the CPI.[24]

12.4.3 Throw Money At It

Figure 12.7 shows what happens when a project gets into schedule trouble and the project manager decides to throw money at it to get it back on schedule. This

[23]We have repeatedly suggested, both here and in talks, that the real problem with EVM is that our customers will find out the truth!

[24]One should not allow the project manager on such a project to claim that the rising SPI means progress!

175

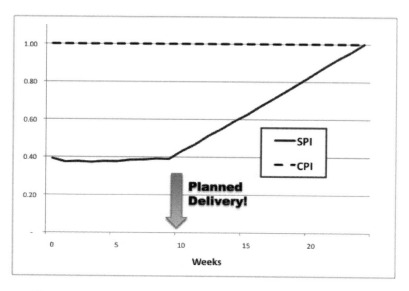

Figure 12.6: CPI and SPI when there is not much progress.

project was *schedule dominated*, meaning that the stakeholders would not tolerate a delay. In the early stages, the project is on schedule, but slightly over budget, which can be seen in Figure 12.7: $SPI \sim 1.0$, and $CPI \sim 0.96$.

The project is on schedule.

Around week 8, the project runs into trouble and a few deliverables are late. The SPI falls to around 0.96. The project manager immediately recognizes the trouble, and spends extra money to get the project back on schedule. This is shown in Figure 12.7, where the SPI climbs back to 1.0, and the CPI falls to around 0.88.

This is a useful combination to recognize. The SPI falls and then climbs back to where it was. Meanwhile the CPI falls to a new average level. The decline in the CPI shows that money was thrown at the project to get it back on schedule.[25]

12.4.4 Rotten Quality

Finally, we note that Earned Value will not help with the *quality* of the deliverables. It not unusual for the first few deliverables to be completed on time and on budget, but for a thorough review to uncover errors and missing pieces. The $CPI = 1.0$ (on budget!), and the $SPI = 1.0$ (on schedule!), but the quality stinks.

In this case, one has not actually *earned* the value of the planned deliverable. A

[25]Whether the money is well spent, we leave to the reader to decide when they uncover such a pattern.

176

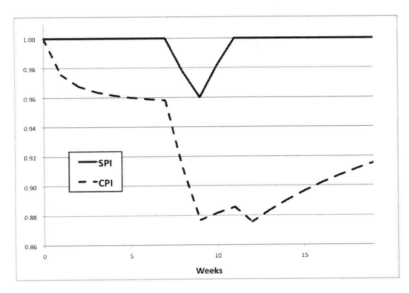

Figure 12.7: CPI and SPI when the project manager throws money at it to get back on schedule.

good project manager assigns the value of the deliverable only after a thorough review of the quality of the deliverable and its acceptance by the customer.

Earned Value does not tell you what is wrong, or what is causing the problem. Neither does it tell you how to fix it. Think of Earned Value as a Thermometer, it merely *indicates* when there is a problem. The project manager needs to investigate the *cause* of the problem.

12.4.5 Important at Major Milestones

Earned Value is particularly important at major milestones. Customers will want to see a measure of progress at these important events. At major milestones, the discussion is not going to be about the money spent, but the accomplishment of something useful.[26]

12.4.6 Non-Profits

You might get lulled into the idea that earned value is only about dollars. It is not, it is really about deliverables. While the easiest way to measure deliverables is indeed in dollars, it is not the only way.

[26] Earned Value doesn't deliver a project, people do!

177

Suppose you are working on a non-profit project and the staff is all volunteers. You are not paying them and, because you cannot measure their actual labor costs, you might assume that you cannot use earned value. This is not so, as the following example illustrates.

You decide to hold a golf charity event with the goal of raising $5,000.[27] The plan is for each sponsor to donate $50.

In the first week, you get 9 sponsors. Are you ahead or behind schedule?

You do not actually know because it depends on how many volunteers showed up.[28] You need a project management plan.

Let's provide some details. You decide to use volunteers who will work on Saturday mornings to call sponsors and solicit pledges of $50. You need 100 sponsors and your project schedule allows ten weeks to get them. Therefore, you plan on using five volunteers each week who are assigned the goal of obtaining two sponsors each per week.

The first week only three volunteers show up and they exact pledges from nine sponsors. You can now perform the earned value calculation, as follows: The plan was for 5 volunteers to show up and entice 2 sponsors each for a planned 10 sponsors. The sponsors are the deliverables, so we can assign the planned value $PV = 10$. The number of sponsors actually obtained was 9, so the number of sponsors earned on the first week was $EV = 9$.

The actual cost is a little tricky, but think of it as follows: Only 3 volunteers showed up, so they consumed only 3 people's worth of the sponsors (the deliverables). That is, they consumed 6 sponsors (3 volunteers × two sponsors each = 6), so the "actual cost" is $AC = 6$. Table 12.6 summarizes the results.

Table 12.6: The status of the non-profit golf fund-raiser project after week 1.

Week	PV	EV	AC	CPI	SPI
1	10	9	6	1.5	0.9

[27]A real project from one of our students who wrote an excellent paper on the use of earned value to track his volunteers.

[28]This is the non-profit version of the "How ya doin'?" problem.

At the end of week 1, the CPI is significantly greater than 1. This makes sense because the earned work (9 sponsors) was accomplished by only 3 people. Three people are supposed to obtain 6 sponsors, so the fact that they actually obtained 9 is a 50% improvement, as shown by the $CPI = 1.5$. The $SPI = 0.9$, which shows the project behind schedule. This also makes sense because at the end of week 1, the plan was to have 10 sponsors.

This simple example shows that by tracking deliverables (in this case, sponsors), non-profits can use earned value to track a project that doesn't use money.[29]

12.5   Implementing Earned Value

What is the best way to implement EV? *Excel.*[30]

All the project management tools support EV, including *Microsoft Project.* However, they tend to make the EV process very complicated and unwieldy. In our opinion, it is much more practical to use *Excel.* Tables 12.4 and 12.5 can form the basis of a clear presentation, see Figure 12.8, which shows an effective layout. It is easy to add the interesting quantities to the right of the data, such as the Estimate at Completion (EAC), TCPI, etc. Also, you can produce beautiful charts quite easily that show the interesting features of the project, e.g., Figure 12.9.

		Weekly			Cumulative						
	Week	Plan	EV	Actual Cost	C Plan	C Earned	C Actual	CPI	SPI	EAC	TCPI
13	0	-	-	-	-	-	-				
14	1	0.7	1.0	0.5	0.7	1.0	0.5	2.00	1.47	$600	1.00
15	2	1.4	1.0	0.8	2.0	2.0	1.3	1.54	0.98	$780	1.00
16	3	2.0	1.0	0.6	4.1	2.0	1.9	1.05	0.49	$1,140	1.00
17	4	2.7	2.0	0.5	6.8	3.0	2.4	1.25	0.44	$960	1.00
18	5	3.4	1.0	1.0	10.2	3.0	3.4	0.88	0.30	$1,360	1.00
19	6	4.0	2.0	2.0	14.2	5.0	5.4	0.93	0.35	$1,296	1.00
20	7	4.7	2.0	3.0	18.9	7.0	8.4	0.83	0.37	$1,440	1.00
21	8	5.3	4.0	4.0	24.2	11.0	12.4	0.89	0.45	$1,353	1.00
22	9	6.0	4.0	5.0	30.2	15.0	17.4	0.86	0.50	$1,392	1.00
23	10	6.6	4.0	6.0	36.8	19.0	23.4	0.81	0.52	$1,478	1.00
24	11	7.2	6.0	7.0	44.1	25.0	30.4	0.82	0.57	$1,459	1.00
25	12	7.8	6.0	8.0	51.9	31.0	38.4	0.81	0.60	$1,486	1.01

Figure 12.8: Column layout of Earned Value quantities in Excel.

[29]Supporting our claim that there is no excuse for not using earned value.

[30]While Microsoft Project can do earned value, it is very difficult to implement. Excel is much easier to use.

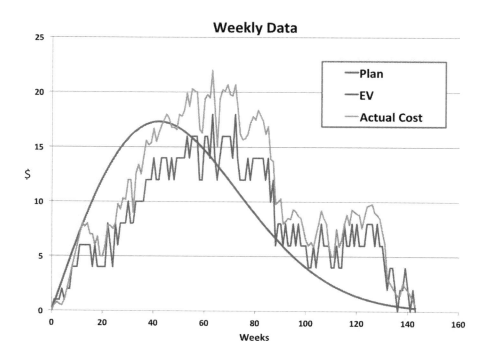

Figure 12.9: Interesting project data in Excel.

12.6 Further Reading

For a gentle introduction to earned value management, see the book by Fleming and Koppelman, who basically invented its modern formulation. [16] Fleming & Koppelman are also a good source of materials on what works in EVM. [17]

Frank Anbari wrote the definitive summary of the state of the art of EVM. [18]

Christensen & Heise found that EVM provides reliable early warning signals of project trouble as early as 15% into a project. Contracts from the Defense Acquisition Executive Database (DAES) indicate that *without exception, the cumulative CPI does not significantly improve during the period of 15% through 85% of the contract performance; in fact it tends to decline.* [19]

Christensen summarizes this succinctly by saying, "Usually, on a project, things will only get worse!"

For one solution to the *SPI* time-dependence, see [20].

13

EXPLAINING IT TO THE STAKEHOLDERS

**If you guys were women, you'd all be pregnant.
You just can't say no.**

Congresswoman Pat Schroeder

Everyone wants to know what it will cost and how long it will take. Your job, as the project manager, is to figure that out and to explain it to anyone who will listen.[1] While this chapter introduces two new skills (TCPI and Schedule Estimation), the focus is on analyzing the cost and schedule data, understanding what it means and communicating that to the stakeholders.[2] To do that, we:

- explain what data you will need to collect,

- demonstrate the use of the relevant tools and techniques, their shortcomings and applicabilities,

- show how to forecast the actual cost and schedule,

- explain the ambiguities, risks and uncertainties[3] associated with making projections, and

- show how to communicate effectively both the current status and the future estimates.

[1] And to some who won't listen.

[2] In this chapter, we are explicitly ignoring the technical status, which is covered in Chapters 14 and 17.

[3] Because a lot of this is guesswork.

181

13.1 TCPI

**Once our customers start using earned value,
we will no longer be able to fudge the cost!**

Roger Warburton

The fourth edition of the PMBOK added a simple idea that could change the world. The new topic carries an unwieldy name: The *To-Complete Performance Index*, or *TCPI*. While *TCPI* sounds very similar to *CPI*, it is, actually, a very different idea:

- *CPI* is about *your* view of your project and describes the *past*.

- *TCPI* is about the *customer's* view of your project and describes the *future*.

When you present the status of your project to your customer, you typically report three things: what you planned to do; what you actually did; and what it cost. In the technical language of Earned Value Management, you report the planned value, the earned value, and the actual cost. Therefore, your customer can calculate your *CPI* and *SPI*.[4] However, as more customers become smarter in project management techniques, they will also calculate the *TCPI*, which will tell them how much trouble your project is in.

TCPI is defined as follows:

> *TCPI is the projection of cost performance that must be achieved on the remaining work to meet a specified management goal, such as the planned budget—the BAC.*

The equation for the *TCPI*, using the *BAC*, is:

$$TCPI = \frac{\text{Work Remaining}}{\text{Funds Remaining}} = \frac{BAC - EV(t)}{BAC - AC(t)}. \tag{13.1}$$

[4] From your data and without your help.

What is the point of this formula?

[5] The ethical issue is whether you have the responsibility to tell the customer the truth.

We already have *CPI* and *SPI*, so what else do we need? *TCPI* is not yet another formula to measure the status of a project, it is a revolution waiting to happen, but, surprisingly, it's a political and ethical revolution.[5]

Here's an illustration of the problem: You're a couple of months into a project, the first few deliverables have been completed and you diligently calculate the $CPI = 0.9$. Noticing that the $CPI < 1.0$, your customer asks about your plans to deal with the cost overrun.

"No problem, we'll make it up," you say.

Unfortunately, once your customer computes the *TCPI*, that answer is not going to work anymore. Let us show you why.

13.1.1 TCPI Example

Suppose we are writing a book and we propose 10 chapters (the scope). We estimate the cost and negotiate the following deal with the customer: The planned cost of each chapter is $100 and we promise to deliver one chapter per week for 10 weeks. Therefore, the *Budget at Completion, BAC*, is the planned (estimated) cost of the book, which is $1,000.

We started the project and dutifully delivered the first 3 chapters on time. While we kept to the schedule, we had to put in some over-time to complete each chapter and this added some extra cost. Table 13.1 shows the status of the project at the end of month three.

Table 13.1: The status of the book project after month 3.

Month	1	2	3
Planned Value	$100	$100	$100
Earned Value	$100	$100	$100
Actual Cost	$125	$125	$125
Cumulative Earned Value (EV)	$100	$200	$300
Cumulative Actual Cost (AC)	$125	$250	$375
CPI = EV/AC	0.80	0.80	0.80

Line 1 of Table 13.1 shows the planned costs for the first three months. We delivered the first 3 chapters on time and, so, according to the standard earned value approach, we *earn* the planned value for those deliverables (the second line of the table). Line 3 of the table shows the actual costs incurred, which are larger than the planned costs because of the extra work performed.

We dutifully calculated the $CPI = 0.8$, which showed we ran a little over budget, but at this stage we might just shrug it off... no problem, we'll make it up later.

13.1.2 Hints of Trouble Ahead: The TCPI Calculation

There are some people who have trouble recognizing a mess.

Bill Cosby

Now let's add the *TCPI* calculation. The work remaining is the total work minus the work accomplished to date:

$$BAC - EV(3) = \$1,000 - \$300 = \$700. \tag{13.2}$$

It is important to note that the work remaining is the *earned value remaining*. The total earned value for the project is \$1,000 (the *BAC*) and we have completed three deliverables, so the earned value *remaining* is, $EV = \$300.$[6]

The funds remaining are simply the total budget minus the actual costs expended:

$$BAC - AC(3) = \$1,000 - \$375 = \$625. \tag{13.3}$$

We now calculate the *TCPI* at month 3 according to equation 13.1:

$$TCPI(3) = \frac{1,000 - 300}{1,000 - 375} = \frac{700}{625} = 1.12. \tag{13.4}$$

The interpretation of the *TCPI* is as follows: To complete the project within budget, you have to work at a rate of 1.12 times your plan, which is 112% of your plan.[7]

We just need a 12% improvement? No big deal, we'll make it up later.[8]

[6]Remember, when a deliverable is complete, you earn the *planned* value, not the actual cost.

However, we should not be quite so casual. So far, we are working at an 80% rate (remember, our $CPI = 0.80$) and we need to get our production rate up to 112%. Therefore, to deliver on budget, we need a 32% improvement in productivity (from 80% to 112%). Maybe we should worry!

[7]That is, your productivity needs to be 12% greater than you had planned.

13.1.3 Two Months Later

[8]Isn't that what we tell the customer?

Let's now consider the situation at the end of month 5. We delivered 2 more chapters on time and at the same cost. The status is shown in Table 13.2.

Table 13.2: The status of the book project after month 5.

Month	1	2	3	4	5
Planned Value	$100	$100	$100	$100	$100
Earned Value	$100	$100	$100	$100	$100
Actual Cost	$125	$125	$125	$125	$125
Cumulative Earned Value (EV)	$100	$200	$300	$400	$500
Cumulative Actual Cost (AC)	$125	$250	$375	$500	$625
CPI = EV/AC	0.80	0.80	0.80	0.80	0.80

We delivered chapters 4 and 5 on time, so we again *earn* the planned value for those (the second line of the table). Our $CPI = 0.8$, which says that our cost efficiency is constant.[9]

Let's now perform the *TCPI* calculation at the end of month 5. The work remaining is: $BAC - EV(5) = \$1,000 - \$500 = \$500$. The funds remaining are: $BAC - AC(5) = \$1,000 - \$625 = \$375$. The *TCPI*, according to equation 13.1, is:

$$TCPI(5) = \frac{1,000 - 500}{1,000 - 625} = \frac{500}{375} = 1.33. \tag{13.5}$$

To complete the project within budget, we must work at a rate of 133% of our plan, i.e., 33% greater than we planned. Since our actual production rate is only 80% of what we planned, we need to raise our production from our current performance rate of 80% to the necessary rate of 133%.

We need a 53% improvement in our production rate!

At this point, it is getting extremely difficult to justify our position: "No big deal, we'll make it up." If our customer computes the *TCPI*, she will have every reason to be concerned.

13.1.4 The TCPI does not lie

I cannot help it–in spite of myself, infinity torments me.

Alfred De Musset

[9] In reality, this is not an uncommon occurrence. There is ample data showing that projects tend to perform at a constant rate. "A project that starts late, stays late." [21]

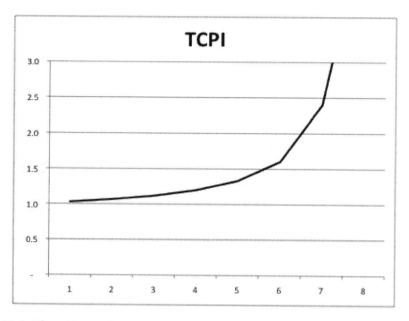

Figure 13.1: The *TCPI* is the cost performance required to complete the rest of the project on budget. The *TCPI* rises dramatically and goes to infinity in month 8.

In fact, things get rapidly much worse. In month 6, the *TCPI* reaches the value, $TCPI(6) = 1.6$, suggesting we need an 80% improvement to meet the planned budget. The point is that *TCPI* continues to rise, and very rapidly.

The story does not end here—it gets even more interesting. Figure 13.1 shows a plot of the *TCPI* for the book project if things continue at the same production rate. The *TCPI* goes to infinity in month 8!

No matter how optimistic you are, no matter what miracle you think you have up your sleeve, and no matter how great an improvement you think you can induce from your team, the *TCPI* will eventually overtake that performance. The *TCPI* will show your customer that your project will inevitably reach a point where you just cannot deliver on budget. You can't fight infinity.[10]

[10]We actually think it is rather cool that a well-defined project management quantity legitimately approaches infinity.

13.1.5 PMBOK to the Rescue

At this point, the PMBOK suggests a fix. Buried in the *TCPI* paragraph is the apparently innocuous comment:

If it becomes obvious that the BAC is no longer viable, the project manager develops a forecast estimate at completion (EAC). Once approved, the EAC effectively supersedes the BAC as the cost performance goal.

This is a fancy way of saying that the *TCPI* formula changes to:

$$TCPI = \frac{BAC - EV(t)}{BAC - AC(t)} \rightarrow \frac{BAC - EV(t)}{EAC - AC(t)}. \tag{13.6}$$

The subtle change is that *EAC* replaces *BAC* in the denominator and this is referred to as the *EAC version* of the *TCPI* formula. Let's see what happens when we use it. First, we need to determine the *EAC* and using the average *CPI* formula gives:

$$EAC = \frac{BAC}{\langle CPI \rangle} = \frac{\$1,000}{0.80} = \$1,250. \tag{13.7}$$

We can now calculate the new *TCPI* using the right hand version of equation 13.6. At the end of month 5, we get:

$$TCPI(5) = \frac{BAC - EV(5)}{EAC - AC(5)} = \frac{1,000 - 500}{1,250 - 675} = \frac{500}{625} = 0.80. \tag{13.8}$$

The new *TCPI* is equal to the *CPI*. Remember, the *TCPI* is the "performance that must be achieved on the remaining work to meet a specified management goal." Equation 13.8 simply says that our remaining performance need only be at the rate of *TCPI = 0.8* to meet our cost goal, which is the newly revised budget of $1,250.

In other words, we have been forced to admit that our productivity is really at the level of the *CPI* (80% of our plan) and that the project will really cost $1,250. Therefore, if we continue to produce at our past rate, we will meet the revised EAC goal.[11]

Let's review the process. We calculated the *TCPI* over time and its rapid and relentless rise meant that, eventually, we were *forced* to admit that the original budget was no longer viable. We then calculated the new estimate at completion using our ongoing, established *CPI*, and this brought our *TCPI* and *CPI* into agreement.

All of this comes down to a relatively simple idea: As a project manager, you will eventually have to admit that your productivity is really at the level of the *CPI* and, that if you produce at that rate, the project cost will be the revised *EAC*.

[11] Somewhat ironically, we could actually have determined this value for the overrun in month *one* from the *EAC* formula, equation 13.7.

13.1.6 TCPI = CPI?

When we admitted that the *BAC* was no longer a viable goal, we used the *EAC* version of the *TCPI*, which turned out to be equal to the *CPI*. Is this a coincidence? Actually, no, it is a direct consequence of the *EAC* version of the *TCPI* formula.[1]

This reinforces the idea that if we own up to the cost overrun, the efficiency that is required for the rest of the project (the *TCPI*) is simply our current performance level, which is the *CPI*. That is, the *TCPI* has the remarkable property that if we own up to the cost overrun, we can proceed at our current efficiency (defined by our current *CPI*) and hit the new cost target—the *EAC*.

13.1.7 Oh-Oh. The customer knows

One of Albert Einstein's oft-quoted sayings was "insanity is doing the same thing over and over and expecting a different result."[2] As project managers, we are often guilty of this kind of insanity when we measure a few values for *CPI* < 1, and then convince ourselves (and even worse, our customers) that all will be well.

> **PM:** *We've run into some problems and our CPI = 0.9.*
> *Nevertheless, we still believe that we can deliver on budget.*
> **Customer:** *Oh Yeah? I've computed your TCPI = 1.2.*
> *How are you going to get 30% increase in productivity?*

See what we mean? If your customers start computing the *TCPI*, it's going to change the world. *TCPI* makes your customers tougher and smarter.[12]

13.1.8 Advice on Overruns

In our experience, project managers are often reluctant to accept the reality of an overrun. When the *CPI* calculation consistently predicts a significant overrun, it is advisable to let everyone adjust gradually to the new reality. The following modification of the Kübler-Ross model, which deals with grief, might help. [22]

The Stages of Grief:

1. *Denial*: The reality of the overrun is hard to face. People tend to ignore the data and develop a false, preferable reality in which the project is on budget.

2. *Anger*: Why my project? It's not fair! Because the anger gets in the way, no one wants to talk about it.

[12]We keep insisting that your customer can calculate the *TCPI*, and all other EVM quantities, from your monthly reports of deliverables and costs. You cannot hide.

188

3. *Bargaining*: We'll do anything. There must be something we can do. Perhaps we can buy more time.

4. *Depression*: Things are really bad on the project, so why bother doing anything? The overrun is certain and there is not much we can do about it.[13]

5. *Acceptance*: Maybe it's going to be okay. We can't fight it, so we may as well prepare for it. We have to come to terms with the reality of the overrun.[14]

Once the team has gone through the grief stages, there is another roadblock: The customer, who is often even more reluctant than the team to deal with the overrun. After all, it's not the customer's fault. The project manager should plan to give the customer some time to go through the same stages of denial, anger, etc.[15]

13.2 Schedule Estimation

**I am definitely going to take a course on time management
... just as soon as I can work it into my schedule.**

Louis E. Boone

In chapter 12, we defined the schedule variance, *SV*, and the schedule performance index, *SPI*, both of which are advertised as indicating whether the project is on schedule or not. While both *indicate* a delay, neither *SV* nor *SPI* can be used to estimate the size of a schedule overrun.[16]

Also, many people are confused by the completely non-intuitive measurement of a schedule delay, represented by the *schedule variance*, as:

$$SV = EV - PV = \$10,000 - \$12,000 = -\$2,000. \qquad (13.9)$$

This says that, because *SV* is negative, the project is "$2,000 behind schedule."[17]

Therefore, we need a way to estimate the future schedule and the technique to do that is called *Earned Schedule, ES*.[3] [23]

13.2.1 Defining Earned Schedule

**We've been running a little behind schedule,
but only by about 15 years or so.**

Matt Groening

[13] There is often some progress at this stage, as the team begins to accept the situation.

[14] This stage often comes with a calm, more stable mindset.

[15] It is also unreasonable to expect the stakeholders to accept the overrun in the first discussion.

[16] We did not present a formula equivalent to the cost estimate at completion because there isn't one.

[17] Shouldn't schedule overruns really be measured in time units (days, weeks, or months), not dollars?

189

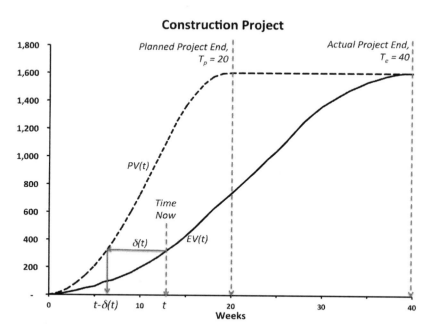

Figure 13.2: The *Earned Schedule* construction: The schedule delay at time, t, is $\delta(t)$, which is determined by the arrow from $EV(t)$ to $PV(t - \delta(t))$. The earned schedule, $ES(t)$, is defined as $t - \delta(t)$.

Given some early project data, we want to determine if the project is on schedule or not. To do that, we have to estimate the final schedule[18] and the method is based on a concept called *earned schedule, ES,* which can be calculated by using a graphical construction procedure. However, what is important is that *ES* is directly related to the estimate of the final schedule. Therefore, *ES* is just a way to get to the revised schedule estimate.

We first plot the cumulative planned value, $PV(t)$, and the cumulative earned value, $EV(t)$—see Figure 13.2.[19] The earned schedule, *ES*, is defined using the following graphical construction:

[18]Just as we did for the final cost by using the EAC.

[19]We add the '(t)' to the quantities to remind the reader which ones are functions of time.

At any given time, ES corresponds to the project duration at which the current earned value, $EV(t)$, is projected back to meet the planned value curve, which is at $PV(t - \delta(t))$.

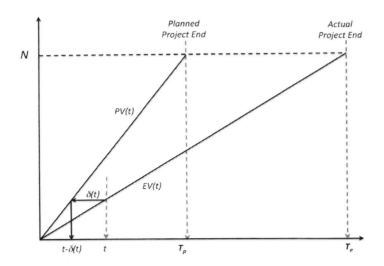

Figure 13.3: Linear cumulative labor profiles. The schedule delay at time, t, is $\delta(t)$ and is denoted by the arrow from $EV(t)$ to $PV(t - \delta(t))$. The earned schedule is, $ES(t) = t - \delta(t)$.

The schedule delay at time, t, is $\delta(t)$ and the *earned schedule* is the point, $t - \delta(t)$, on the time axis. [4]

13.2.2 Deriving the Earned Schedule Formula

It is straightforward to derive the earned schedule formula for the case of linear cumulative labor profiles.[20] Linear labor profiles occur in a project for which the number of people planned to work on the project is a constant for the life of the project and they work a constant number of hours in each time period.[21]

For example, if they work 10 units in each time period, the cumulative planned values are, $PV(1) = 10$, $PV(2) = 20$, $PV(3) = 30$, etc. This is shown in Figure 13.3.

At the planned end of the project, which is at time, T_p, the total cost is the budget, N, and the cumulative planned value is given by:

$$PV(t) = N \frac{t}{T_p}.$$ (13.10)

[20]Students may skip this derivation and proceed directly to the next section, where we show how to use the formula.

[21]The earned schedule formula turns out to be the same, but the mathematics is easier in this linear case.

191

We can easily see this makes sense by substituting a couple of values: For $t = 0$, $PV(t) = 0$, and at the end of the project, where $t = T_p$, $PV(T_p) = NT_p/T_p = N$.

During execution, we assume that the project is delayed and that the actual end point of the project is at time, T_e, where, $T_e > T_p$. At the end of a successful project, all of the value that was planned has been earned, so the total earned value equals the total planned value. Therefore, the cumulative earned value is:

$$EV(t) = N\frac{t}{T_e}. \tag{13.11}$$

We can now mathematically define the earned schedule, $ES(t)$, at time, t, as the intersection of the projection back from the current time in the project, t, on the earned value curve, to the planned value curve:

$$EV(t) = PV(t - \delta(t)). \tag{13.12}$$

Using the planned and earned values, from 13.10 and 13.11, gives,

$$N\frac{t}{T_e} = N\frac{(t-\delta)}{T_p} \qquad \frac{T_p}{T_e} = \frac{(t-\delta)}{t} = 1 - \frac{\delta}{t}. \tag{13.13}$$

Therefore, the delay in the project at time, t, is,

$$\delta(t) = t\left(1 - \frac{T_p}{T_e}\right). \tag{13.14}$$

This equation says that $\delta(t)$ is a function of time, which can be seen in Figure 13.3, where the distance from $EV(t)$ curve to the $PV(t)$ curve increases over time. The *earned schedule* is:

$$ES(t) = t - \delta(t) = t\left(\frac{T_p}{T_e}\right). \tag{13.15}$$

This is the formula for *earned schedule* and it contains the quantity, T_e, which is the estimate of the final schedule. Therefore, this formula will allow us to calculate an estimate for the final schedule.

The SPI for Linear Profiles

For project with a constant level of effort, the planned and earned values are given in equations 13.10 and 13.11. Therefore, the *SPI* at time, t, is:

$$SPI = \frac{EV(t)}{PV(t)} = \frac{Nt}{T_e}\frac{T_p}{Nt} = \frac{T_p}{T_e}. \tag{13.16}$$

The *SPI* is a constant at all times. However, a constant *SPI* is only a property of a project for which the labor rate is constant and, therefore, the cumulative labor is a linear function of time. For such a project, we can estimate the final schedule from an early estimate of the *SPI* by using equation 13.16.

13.2.3 Using Earned Schedule

The formula for the *earned schedule* is:

$$ES(t) = t\left(\frac{T_p}{T_e}\right), \tag{13.17}$$

where, t, is the current time, T_p, is the planned schedule, and T_e is the revised estimate of the final schedule. Therefore, once we calculate the *earned schedule*, $ES(t)$, we have all of the quantities that we need in equation 13.17 to calculate T_e. The *earned schedule*, $ES(t)$, is determined by using the graphical construction shown in Figures 13.2 and 13.3.

By rearranging equation 13.17, we find the formula for the revised final schedule, T_e, which is what we really want:

$$T_e = \frac{tT_p}{ES(t)}. \tag{13.18}$$

Note that all quantities in equation 13.18 are in time units. In particular, the final schedule estimate, T_e, is time units, so we have eliminated the confusion about SV being in currency units. Also, the derivation presented in section 13.2.2 shows that the equation for T_e is exact.[22] Finally, we note that the estimate of the final schedule, T_e, is legitimate because, unlike $ES(t)$ and $\delta(t)$, it is a constant.

We now show how to use equation 13.18 to estimate the revised final schedule. Suppose the planned schedule for the project is, $T_p = 20$, the project is now at time $t = 4$, and we do the intersection to measure $ES(t) = t - \delta(t) = 3$. The revised schedule, T_e, is:

$$T_e = \frac{tT_p}{ES(t)} = \frac{4 \times 20}{3} = 26.6. \tag{13.19}$$

Our new schedule is 27 weeks, so we are estimating that we will be 7 weeks late.[23]

While the reader need not remember all of the theoretical details, there are a number of important lessons for a project manager:

- The *SPI* is only a constant for a project with a constant level of effort. In general, the *SPI* varies over time and so measuring it will tell you nothing about the final schedule estimate.

- Both the earned schedule and the schedule delay are functions of time and, so, measuring them at one point does not determine them. We must use the time-dependent formula, equation 13.18, to determine the new schedule estimate, T_e.

[22] No approximations were required.

[23] There is no point in using the decimal, just round up. There is likely to be lots of scatter in the data.

193

- The T_e equation is pretty easy to use and, in practice, gives a good estimate of the final schedule.[24]

13.2.4 Presenting the Data: An Example

> **What's here? The portrait of a blinking idiot.**
> **Presenting me a schedule!**
>
> *William Shakespeare, The Merchant Of Venice*

The analysis of the project's schedule begins by collecting the data for the current period, which consists of what was planned, what was accomplished and how much it cost. The data are usually presented in dollars, but the calculations are perfectly valid in any set of units.[25] The weekly data are presented in Table 13.3 and the current time is week 10. Note that the time (weeks) is in column B and the last value in column B is the current time, week = 10.

The budget for this project is 1,600 and the planned schedule is $T_p = 20$ weeks. The cumulative data are calculated as follows: The cumulative planned value for week 3 is, $PV(3) = 87$, which is the sum of the weekly planned values: 14+28+45.[26]

Table 13.3: The project data up to week 10.

		Weekly			Cumulative			
Row	Week	Planned	Actual	Earned	Planned	Actual	Earned	$t - \delta(t)$
A	B	C	D	E	F	G	H	I
5	0	0	0	0	0	0	0	0
6	1	14	5	5	14	5	5	0
7	2	28	13	13	42	18	18	1
8	3	45	17	14	87	35	32	1
9	4	56	18	18	143	53	50	2
10	5	67	25	18	→ 210	78	68	2
11	6	82	31	22	292	109	90	3
12	7	94	35	24	386	144	114	3
13	8	102	35	30	488	179	144	3
14	9	118	40	32	606	219	176	3
15	10	122	44	34	728	263	← 210	5

[24] Just like the EAC equation gives a good estimate for the final cost.

[25] Students are encouraged to interpret the units in Table 13.3 in creative ways. Our favorite: The number of windows installed.

[26] The data for this project is taken from a famous construction project, see [24].

It is useful to plot the data and the cumulative planned and earned values are shown in Figure 13.4. Because the earned value data lags the planned value, we see that the project is delayed and, so, we need to estimate the new schedule.

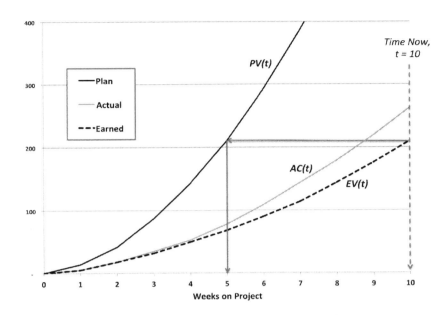

Figure 13.4: A plot of the cumulative planned and earned value data in Table 13.3 showing the *earned schedule* construction at time, $t = 10$.

We are in week 10, so $t = 10$. The *earned schedule* construction for week 10 is shown in Figure 13.4: The line is projected back from $EV(10) = 210$ to the planned value curve and the intersection occurs at $PV(5) = 210$.[27] The time at which the intersection occurs is $t - \delta(t) = 5$. We can now estimate the revised schedule using the *earned schedule*, equation 13.18:

$$T_e = \frac{tT_p}{ES(t)} = \frac{10 \times 20}{5} = 40. \qquad (13.20)$$

The estimate of the schedule has grown from $T_p = 20$ to $T_e = 40$ weeks.[28] It turns out that for this real project, the final schedule was indeed $T_e = 40$ weeks, confirming the accuracy of the technique.

Once we have the cumulative values, we can calculate the other interesting project quantities, such as *CPI*, *SPI*, *TCPI*, and *EAC*—see Table 13.4.

We plot the *CPI* and *SPI* in Figure 13.5 and the cost estimate at completion, *EAC* in Figure 13.6. We also present the estimate of the final schedule, T_e, in Figure 13.7,

[27] In general, the planned value will not be exactly equal to the earned value. In which case, one selects the week with the nearest value.

[28] And we know this in week 10.

195

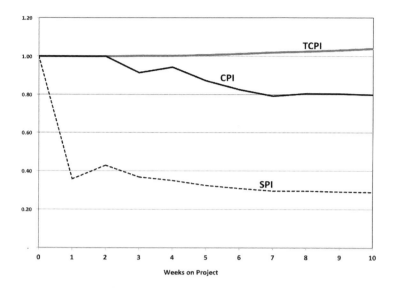

Figure 13.5: The CPI, SPI and TCPI.

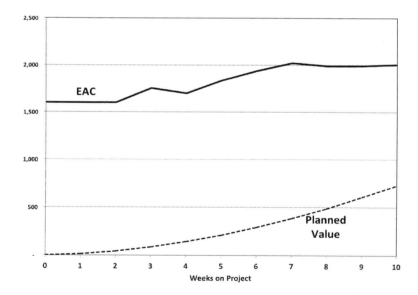

Figure 13.6: The Estimate at Completion (EAC).

Table 13.4: Project estimates for week 10.

Week	t - δ	T_e	CPI	SPI	BAC	TCPI	EAC
0	0	20	1.00	1.00	1,600	1.00	1,600
1	0	20	1.00	0.36	1,600	1.00	1,600
2	1	40	1.00	0.43	1,600	1.00	1,600
3	1	60	0.91	0.37	1,750	1.00	1,750
4	2	40	0.94	0.35	1,696	1.00	1,696
5	2	50	0.87	0.32	1,835	1.01	1,835
6	3	40	0.83	0.31	1,938	1.01	1,938
7	3	47	0.79	0.30	2,021	1.02	2,021
8	4	40	0.80	0.30	1,989	1.02	1,989
9	4	45	0.80	0.29	1,991	1.03	1,991
10	5	40	0.80	0.29	2,004	1.04	2,004

which shows how it evolves over time. Early on, there is considerable scatter in the estimate, but it settles down and converges to the correct value.

The general rule of thumb about the final schedule estimate is that it is within about 10% of the correct answer about 15%–20% into the project. In this regard, T_e is similar to *EAC*, both of which have considerable scatter early on, but quickly settle down and converge to their correct final values. The cumulative aspect of the planned and earned value data tends to smooth things out over time as more values contribute. Both schedule and cost estimates are available early on in the project and are quite accurate.

Automating the Excel Calculation of ES

The first column (A) in Table 13.3 gives the row number in the spreadsheet. The cumulative PV is in column F and the cumulative EV is column H. Column I gives the values of $t - \delta(t)$. It is slightly tricky to implement this in Excel, but the method is as follows: The Excel formula in column I, labeled $t - \delta$, is (in row 15):

=INDEX($B$5:$B$15,MATCH(H15,$F$5:$F$15))

The MATCH function looks for the row where H15 occurs (*EV=210*) in the PV column, which is specified by F5:F15. Therefore, the MATCH function looks for where the value 210 occurs in the cumulative planned value column (F) and the answer is, row 5. Therefore, the MATCH function returns '5'. The INDEX function then returns the value in the weeks column, defined by B5:B15, for row 5. The result is that this calculation returns '5'.

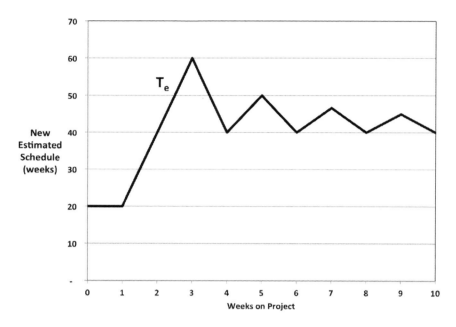

Figure 13.7: The estimated schedule, T_e, over time.

This process is indicated in Table 13.3 by the arrows. Once the value of $ES = t - \delta(t)$ is known, we calculate T_e from equation 13.18–e.g., see equation 13.20.

13.3 Writing the Report

We now have all the data necessary to write a report to the customer or any other stakeholder. There are several ways to do this and, if our students are any indication, there is considerable debate about the best way to do it. Therefore, we will present the two extremes and let the reader decide on the style that best fits their taste and situation.[29]

The Short Letter

The idea behind this approach is that your report status is probably going to a senior executive who only wants the minimum, essential information. For example, you are working on resurfacing a major highway through the center of Boston and your report must be sent to the mayor. The mayor only wants a short summary of the key facts and then he will send it to his staff to check it out.

[29]Even the authors disagree on the best way to do this.

In this case, the approach is to write a short letter (about one page) that presents the progress to date, lists the essential data (the cost and schedule overrun), and briefly explains the key issues (why it is late and over budget). Then, one should attach an appendix that presents the data in all its glory.[30] A sample short-form letter is shown in Figure 13.8.

ABC Properties, Inc.
Boston, MA

May 30, 2014
Re: Door Upgrade Project report:

Dear Customer:

Two and a half months ago we embarked on the ambitious project of upgrading all the doors in your building at a cost of $1,000 each. We planned to complete the project within 20 weeks and with a Budget at Completion of $1.6 million.

The strategy was to start upgrading the doors at a rate of 14 for the first week and then quickly increasing the pace every week until we reached the apex of 134 doors per week during the winter months. Please refer to the Appendix for all the data used in this report.

Technical Performance

After ten weeks of work we should have completed 728 doors; however the team only completed a disappointing 200 doors. The inspection confirmed that all of the doors were installed according to the highest standards. In fact, the building occupants liked the new doors and the building guards were particularly impressed with the security and safety features.

Cost

Using the concepts of Earned Value Management I would like to present the cost data. To date, we have only spent $263,000, against our plan of $728,000. Therefore, our Cumulative Earned Value is only $200,000 and we are $63,000 over budget (about a 31% overun). The $CPI = 0.76$, which implies a less than desirable 76% cost efficiency.

The planned Budget at Completion is $1,600,000. However, based on the current data, the new Estimate at Completion is a very concerning $2,105,100.

I'd like to be able to tell you that a mere 5% improvement in our cost efficiency, calculated using the To-Complete Performance Index, TCPI, would get us back on track. However, I also know that the people on your team will remind me that, because our CPI is 0.76, the improvement in efficiency we would actually need is closer to 29%.

Schedule

The indicators confirm that, unfortunately, we have an extremely poor schedule efficiency. The $SPI = 0.27$, which indicates that we are advancing at a dismal 27% efficiency in the production schedule. Even more concerning is that at the current rate, using the new Earned Schedule method, I predict the project will take 40 weeks to complete.

So this is the sad state of this affair. We have an issue of cost and an even bigger one of schedule. I suggest that we meet soon to discuss how we might proceed to move forward with this project
Sincerely,
    Michel Laflamme,
Project Manager, ABC Properties

Figure 13.8: Sample short-form letter.

[30]Charts, data, problems, excuses and mea culpas, which is Latin for "It's the project manager's fault."

The Long Report

Many people prefer to lay it all out in a continuous narrative. Their rationale is that this allows them to present the situation more carefully, with each topic backed up with the appropriate level of detail and with its own charts and data. In this case, the document is typically of a *formal* report with sections addressing the technical issues; the cost and schedule; risks; and potential solutions.[31]

Comments

Whether you select the short or long form, there are several issues to consider.

- *Should the chart go in the letter?*

  We think so.[32] Presenting one really powerful chart with all the data demonstrates competence on the part of the project manager.

  An example of a chart that we like for this purpose is shown in Figure 13.9. It clearly indicates that the earned values are well behind the planned values. The inclusion of the *EAC* shows where the project is relative to its end point (we are not very far along) and that the estimate of the final cost is well above the budget. Finally, *ES* shows the significant delay in the schedule estimate.

- *Fix it.*

  The customer's first reaction might be that the letter is a demand for more money and more time.[33] Once the customer sees the new cost estimate, he may not see much of anything else.

  Therefore, a genuine reason for presenting the data early is to mitigate its negative impacts by suggesting different approaches for the completion of the project. If the customer has a limited budget, you should investigate ways to reduce the cost: Maybe you can use some less expensive doors or even leave some doors as they are. Are there backstairs or basement doors that the tenants do not use and that don't need upgrading? There is probably not a lot you can do about the doubling of the schedule, but adding people might reduce it somewhat.

- *Why wait until week 10?*

  Given the early *EAC* and *ES* data, we might actually have determined that the project was in trouble much earlier. For example, we can see from Table 13.4, that at week 5 we could have easily predicted that the schedule might double and that the cost overrun might be greater than 15%.

[31] In which case, you are going to need an executive summary, which is going to look a lot like the short form.

[32] We also admit that, again, not everyone agrees.

[33] Which it usually is.

200

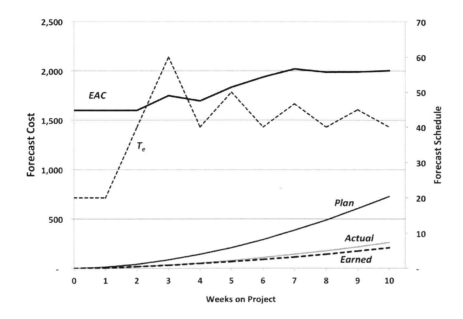

Figure 13.9: The project status at week 10.

Figure 13.10 shows the same chart as Figure 13.9, except that it only includes the data up to week 5. There is a lot of scatter in the week 5 data, but, nevertheless, it clearly shows a schedule delay and a cost overrun. Therefore, should we have presented these preliminary conclusions to the customer?

How confident would you be about the predictions in week 5? Are they sufficiently reliable? Would it be unnecessarily alarming to present these tentative conclusions? On the other hand, the earlier you present the bad news, the more options you have to make adjustments and to solve problems.

- *The Ethical Dilemma*

Finally, is informing the customer at week 5 the correct ethical choice? The Project Management Institute (PMI) continually stresses that ethics is an integral part of the profession and has defined a rigorous *Code of Ethics and Professional Conduct*. [25] (See Chapter 19.) The code says that practitioners will "provide accurate information in a timely manner."

This seems to mandate that the project manager report the delay and the overrun in week 5. On the other hand, do you believe the data from week 5 is

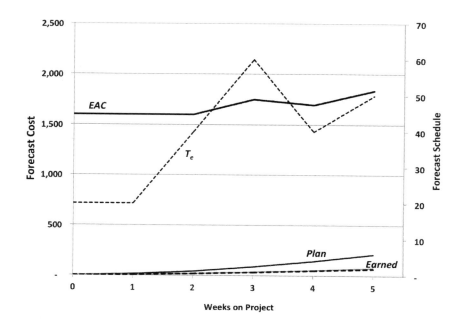

Figure 13.10: The project status at week 5. Should we tell the customer?

reliable? Perhaps you feel that it only *indicates* trouble.[34] Are you ethically obligated to report an *indication* of trouble?

You might decide to wait for more data. However, by waiting, you introduce another risk: The customer might respond, "You knew this in week 5?!"

Collecting, analyzing and plotting the cost and schedule data is an essential part of the project manager's job. The much more intriguing and challenging task is to understand the implications, for both the cost and schedule, and to communicate them to the stakeholders.

[34]We actually believe that the week 5 data is pretty clear: The project schedule is in serious trouble. But, we allow that you might disagree.

14

QUALITY

Be a yardstick of quality. Some people aren't used to an environment where excellence is expected.

Steve Jobs

While delivering the project on time and within budget is critical, meeting the customer's requirements and quality expectations is even more important because they will probably have to use the project for a long time. When planning the project, we must clearly define the customer's needs and quality expectations for the final product. This is a challenging task, as a project team might define and interpret quality differently from the stakeholders. However, since the customer is the ultimate custodian of the final product, the definition of quality must come from the customer, and not the project team, and this must be well understood and communicated throughout the project life cycle.

In this chapter we focus on the technical concepts, as well as tools and techniques, associated with the *Quality Management* knowledge area. Project quality management consists of three processes: *Plan Quality, Perform Quality Assurance*, and *Perform Quality Control.* The goal of these processes and the activities associated with them, is to assure the stakeholders that the project meets their needs. This is embodied in the definition of quality:

Quality is the degree to which a set of inherent characteristics fulfills requirements.

While this is the international standard definition of quality (*ISO 5000*), *meeting requirements* is a complex issue. For example, meeting stakeholder requirements (their wants and needs) is vastly different from meeting performance goals (e.g., speed and throughput).

Also, quality applies to both the product and the management of the project. For example good quality project management would ensure that the project was delivered within the cost and schedule goals, that changes were all approved jointly with the stakeholder, and that the process for managing deliverables was transparent and efficient. All of this might be accomplished with excellent quality, but is of little value if the product itself has low quality.

Process quality does not guarantee product quality, and vice versa.

Mathematically speaking, quality is equal to conformance to requirements plus fitness for use.[1]

Grade is also different from quality. ISO defines grade as a category assigned to products or services having the same functional use but different technical characteristics.

For example, international grade specifications for sugar range from very high to low. White refined sugar, which has a minimum purity of 99.8%, is considered to be the highest grade. In comparison, crystal sugar has a minimum purity of 99.6%. Brown sugar, which has a purity in the range of 94% to 97%, is classified as lower grade sugar.[2]

However, from a quality perspective all the above three grades of sugar meet the internationally accepted quality standards for human consumption.[3]

14.1 Key Concepts

[1] This says nothing about the quality of the development process!

[2] But you might prefer it in your muffins.

[3] Sugar specifications can be found at genesisny.net.

Before we begin our discussion of tools and techniques, we review some basic approaches to quality management and some terminology.

The International Standards Organization (ISO) is widely known to provide resources pertaining to quality standards. The PMBOK approach is compatible with a variety of approaches, such as Total Quality Management (TQM), Six Sigma, and Continuous Improvement, as well as approaches from quality theorists such as

Deming, Juran, Crosby and others. Here is a quick overview of some of the above concepts.

TQM is a quality management philosophy from the noted expert Dr. W. Edwards Deming. It is uses statistical analysis to measure whether a process is in control. More importantly, Dr. Deming introduced the concept that quality should be planned in, not inspected in, and that investing in quality saves money.

Six Sigma is a methodology also rooted in statistics. The focus of the Six Sigma Quality standard is to reduce process output variation, for instance, focusing on processes continuously over time to reduce the defect rate to no more than 3.4 defects per million opportunities. In terms of standard deviation, for instance, Six Sigma translates to being 99.99966% defect free.[4]

Continuous Improvement, which is also known by its Japanese name *Kaizen*, is a proactive approach to quality management. It focuses on not being content with things the way they are, but instead seeking continuous process improvement.

Zero Defects is a quality management philosophy from Philip Crosby. As the name suggests, its basic approach is to do something right the very first time. Investing money up front will minimize the need for rework and further expenses down the road to fix defects.

Fitness for Use was designed by Joseph Juran, and focuses on identifying and meeting the real needs of stakeholders.

Gold plating is the practice of providing more features than the customer asked for. From a project management perspective, gold plating can result in a project that is risky and expensive.

An example of gold plating is when a programmer implements a digital clock on the website of a North American business, assuming that it adds value. Something like this could create complexity and additional cost down the road when the product is used in multiple time zones, or when users want to see the clock in a 24-hour format.

Gold plating might even be unethical if the customer was not informed of the add-ons and is later compelled to pay for them.

14.2 Quality Planning

The quality plan defines the standards that the project should achieve. The team can either adopt existing, well-defined quality standards or create new standards by defining quality metrics for the deliverables. A good quality plan guides the project

[4]It is worth pointing out that a project is *unique*, so the idea of defects per million does not apply, as there would need to be a million copies of the project.

team by identifying procedures for both quality assurance and quality control and provides a means to confirm that quality objectives are being met.

In a software development project the quality plan might include an existing quality metric such as one that measures code defects per thousand Lines of Code (LOC). Such a metric would also define the maximum tolerance, or acceptable number of defects, such as: no more than six defects per thousand LOC.

The major inputs to the quality planning process are the scope, stakeholder register, and the cost and schedule estimates. The major output is the *Quality Management Plan*, along with quality metrics, the quality checklist, and a process improvement plan—see Table 24.21.

The following sections describes tools and techniques the project team uses to generate these outputs:

Cost-Benefit Analysis

The concept of a quality cost-benefit analysis is similar to a traditional cost-benefit analysis. The team focuses on creating a business scenario for several quality activities and compares the investment in such activities with the perceived benefits, such as higher productivity, less rework, lower-cost and better reputation.

Cost of Quality

This refers to determining the total cost of quality over the life of a project, and includes:

- *Cost of Conformance*, which is the money spent to avoid problems and to build a quality product or service. Investing in cost of conformance is money well spent as it reduces failure costs.[5] Examples include:

  - *Prevention Costs*: Investment in quality through testing and inspection; training or acquisition of automated equipment; investment in time and effort to document processes properly; and creating checklists to communicate the correct way to do things.

  - *Appraisal Costs*: The costs associated with determining the appropriate level of quality required, such as inspections, testing and stakeholder product evaluation.

- *Cost of Non-Conformance*, which is the money spent to fix problems and is a result of failures or quality expectations not being met.

[5]We have already explained that defects found after delivery by the users are the most expensive to fix.

206

- *Internal Costs*: Costs identified with the scope of the project, such as scrap or thrown-away pieces, i.e., work that was not judged worthy of inclusion and that had to be re-done.

- *External Failure Costs*: The costs associated repairing a project after it was delivered, i.e., warranty fulfillment and liability costs.

Control Charts

These graphically describe performance data and include upper and lower limits within which a healthy process runs. Such a chart is usually used to reveal if equipment is producing products outside the defined specifications.[6] Control charts can be used both to establish standards and to monitor various types of output variables.[1]

Figure 14.1 gives an example of a control chart. The goal, or target, which is usually the mean of the process, is the solid line in the middle. The goal is 10 errors per week and the upper limit is 13 and the lower limit is 7. We see in the chart that one data point is outside the upper control limit, and we conclude therefore the *entire process* is out of control. The point outside of the control limits should be investigated.

A process can also be out of control if too many data points are all on the same side of the mean. The "rule of seven" declares that an entire process out of control if seven data points lie on the same side of the mean, even if the points are within the limits—see Figure 14.2.[2] Even though all points are within the control limits, the process is still *out of control*.

Benchmarking

This refers to comparing a project's internal production process with industry standards with the idea that the comparison will result in establishing a viable quality standard for the project at hand.

Design of Experiments (DOE)

This is a statistical method for identifying the factors influence specific variables of a product or process under development or in production. From a quality planning perspective, it is used to determine the number and type of tests, and their impact on quality. An example given in the PMBOK guide describes automotive designers using DOE to determine which combination of suspension and tires will produce the most comfortable ride at a reasonable cost.[7]

[6]Many of the examples of Control Charts are non-projects and routine manufacturing.

[7]Another non-project!

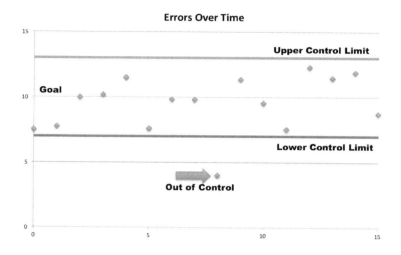

Figure 14.1: A simple control chart with one data point outside the control limits.

Statistical Sampling

This is the study of a population of interest, and it involves gathering information from the sample domain and then analyzing it. As a tool, knowledge about various statistical sampling techniques is very helpful to a project manager. For example, during the project, many choices may be made during the design phase, and selecting the right representative data sample is critical if the project outcome is to produce the right results. A type of statistical sampling that is commonly used is random sampling. An example would be to use a random number generator function to select 20 data points from a population of 1,000.

Flowcharting

This is a graphical depiction of a process flow—see Figure 14.3. It consists of rectangles, which represent processes, and a diamond, which represent decision points. A review of a visual flowchart during quality planning can help identify stumbling points.

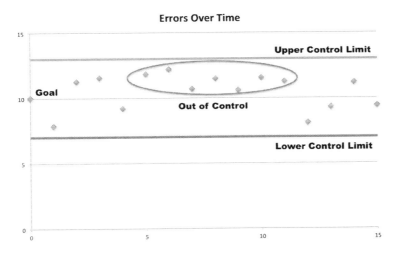

Figure 14.2: The rule of seven. A control chart showing an out of control process: more than seven data points on the same side of the mean.

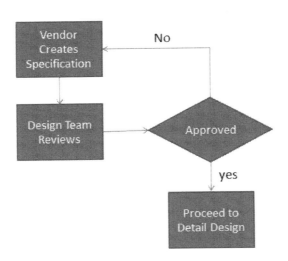

Figure 14.3: A simple flow chart.

14.3 Quality Assurance

Here, the team ensures that the project is meeting the quality standards established during the quality planning phase. Quality Assurance (QA) is a prevention-driven process that proactively corrects problems during the execution phase.[8] The process also provides anxious stakeholders some confidence that the final project will be free of defects and of good quality.

Many organizations invest in mechanisms to conduct credible QA and the team conducting such assurance is usually independent of the development organization. The goal of the QA group is to work cooperatively with the project team to review deliverables. The key outputs are change requests, project management plan updates, and process asset updates.

QA tools are described in the following sections.

Quality Audits

A quality audit should confirm if the quality processes are functioning correctly and deliverables are meeting the project's objectives. If the benchmark cannot be achieved then a comprehensive review is undertaken to see if the initial goals were appropriate. Steps are taken to get the project to the expected level of quality.

Quality audits are formal reviews and should be scheduled at key intervals during the project. They can also be conducted randomly as needed. The internal QA department is involved along with experts from outside as required. The lessons learned from a quality audit should be documented so that both shortcomings and strengths are evident to stakeholders.

Process Analysis

The current processes are analyzed to determine if improvements are needed. For example, a process analysis may reveal an opportunity to reduce waste or save time, in which case the project manager might recommend a new process be implemented. Process analysis may include a root cause analysis.

14.4 Quality Control

[8]Finding mistakes at the end of the life cycle can be expensive to fix.

Several tools play an important role in evaluating the quality of deliverables.

Cause and Effect Diagrams

These are also called Ishikawa diagrams or fishbone diagrams, and are a useful tool for getting to the root cause of a problem. They are used in general problem solving, discovering bottlenecks and uncovering process issues. In team meetings, Ishikawa diagrams are an excellent communication tool.

The source of a problem is uncovered by asking the 'Why?' question three times. For example, suppose it is observed that pizza delivery is more likely to be late on weekends. The analysis of this problem begins by asking the following question:

- *Why is pizza delivery late on weekends?*

  Assume the response is that there are employee issues, resource issues, and quality issues. Brainstorming continues with a second round of 'Why?'

- *Why are employees inadequate on weekends?*

  The second 'Why?' is trying to uncover possible *causes*. Suppose the causes are: Weekend employees are unhappy and quit frequently. Therefore, adequately trained staff is not available on weekends.

- *Why are employees unhappy?*

  Brainstorming continues with a third 'Why?' The answers include: Wages are low and benefits non-existent. Also, funding is not available for training and instructors are not available to train the weekend crew.

These issues are documented in an Ishikawa Diagram—see Figure 14.4. The problem (late delivery of pizza on weekends) is shown in the box on the right. The diagonal arrows represent *issues* that are identified, e.g., staffing. The horizontal arrows represent *causes* of the issue. For example, one *cause* of the *resource* issue is, *"Frequently running out of pizza boxes."*

We now have a potential root cause for the problem: Employees are inadequately trained with poor pay. We may even have a solution: If it is not possible to raise wages, then, at least, we should consider providing better training.

An Ishikawa diagram with a more complete analysis of the pizza delivery problem is shown in Figure 14.4. Other issues can also be analyzed using the same technique, e.g., resource issues.

211

Figure 14.4: *Ishikawa Diagram* for late pizza delivery on weekends.

Pareto Chart

> **A small fraction of participants produce a large fraction of the accomplishments.**
> **A small fraction of participants also produce a large fraction of the problems.**

Augustine's Corollary to Pareto

A Pareto chart is a histogram (bar chart) ordered by frequency of occurrence that shows which issues you should really worry about. The key idea is most of the problems are concentrated in a few issues.[9]

As an example, suppose PMA implemented a new web site and collected data on the number of complaints they received. The website support group analyzed the complaints and assigned them to general categories, such as slow response, poor technical support, broken links, missing features, etc. They then organized the data as shown in Table 14.1.

The first column contains the number of complaints, the second column the cumulative number, and the third column the cumulative percentage. For example, in row 2, there were 55 complaints about slow response, which makes the cumulative total, 66+55 = 121. The total number of complaints was 164, so the cumulative percentage was 121/164 = 74%. The data are plotted in Figure 14.5.

[9]This is commonly known as the "80-20" rule, because, typically, 80% of the defects are due to 20% of the causes.

Table 14.1: Pareto chart for complaints about the PMA website .

Complaint	Number	Cumulative Count	Cumulative Percent
Broken links	66	66	40%
Slow response	55	121	74%
Poor tech support	18	139	85%
Missing feature	11	150	91%
Confusing	6	156	95%
Poor help	4	160	98%
Site unavailable	2	162	99%
Poor English	2	164	100%
Total	164		

A Pareto chart is useful when there are many issues and you need to concentrate on those that are most significant. The technique is even more useful when followed up with an Ishikawa diagram to address the causes of the problems.

In projects, stakeholders may perceive the quality of the products as poor. Collecting all of the comments and analyzing them in a Pareto chart can help to explain the issues and prioritize the order in which they are addressed.

Fixing the troublesome few may quickly result in a significant improvement in quality.

Inspection

This is a technique for examining product quality and goes by names such as reviews, audits, and walks-through. Inspections occur in different formats and at multiple project stages.

Control Charts

These give a picture of the process outputs over time.[10]

---

[10] These were described in the *Plan Quality* process.

213

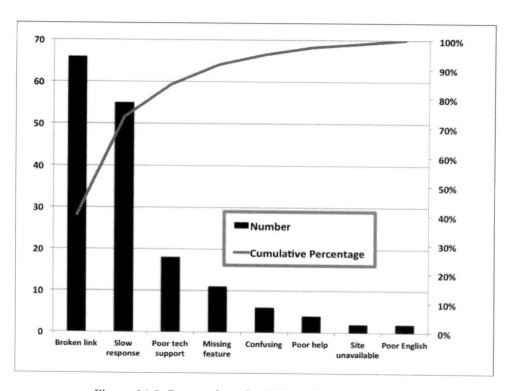

Figure 14.5: Pareto chart for PMA website complaints.

15

HUMAN RESOURCES

**Never hire anyone you wouldn't want to run into
in the hallway at three in the morning.**

Tina Fey

Human Resources (HR) management is one of the areas where project management borrows heavily from general management principals. In this chapter we will cover some of the traditional HR theory and wrap up with the tools and techniques that are associated with HR management as it applies to projects.

A project manager must possess a wide variety of skills, including leadership, communication, negotiation, influence, and conflict resolution. A project manager must be a mentor, and be able to motivate and manage the project team after the initial excitement of project kick-off has faded. A project manager also needs strong skills in delegating and follow-up.

15.1 Develop Human Resource (HR) Plan

This is the process of organizing, managing, and leading the project team, and it is documented in the *HR Plan*. To assemble the HR Plan, the project manager uses company organization charts and position descriptions to define the positions. To acquire the team requires soft skills, such as networking.

Organization charts are classified under the following types: Hierarchical; Matrix, RACI; and Text-Oriented formats.[1]

Hierarchical Charts. These are the organizational charts that most organizations publish. They are hierarchical and show titles, positions, and reporting relationships, and are easy to understand—see Figure 15.1.

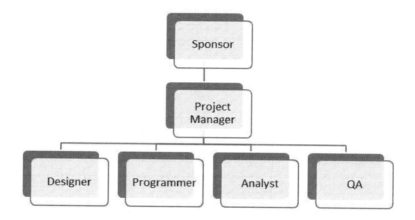

Figure 15.1: A simple organization chart.

Matrix Charts. These are useful tools that associate a resource name with a work package and project responsibility. One such chart frequently used during the planning stages is the Responsible, Accountable, Consult, Inform (RACI) chart.

Typically, only one resource is assigned the Responsibility (R) label. The person accountable for the work is given the (A) label. Of course, there might be sharing or delegation involved. Typically, the sponsor is given the Inform (I) label as they need to be kept up-to-date on progress. Staff members who are consulted are designated with the Consult (C) label.

You should try to avoid giving a person more than one label. Someone is either responsible, accountable, consulted, or informed. An example is shown in Figure 15.2.

[1]Note: Organization charts should not be confused with organizational structures: functional, matrix (weak, balanced, strong), and projectized.

Work Package	Analyst	Designer	Programmer	QA
Analysis	R	C	C	A
Design	C	R	C	I
Build	C	C	R	I

Figure 15.2: An RACI Chart.

15.2 Acquire Project Team

During the execution phase, the project manager assembles the team. The project manager develops staff assignments and *resource calendars*, which explain who is assigned to what activity and when. In acquiring the team, the project manager makes sure that it is a balanced and effective mix.

When assigning resources, the project manager considers previous experience, matches skills with activity requirements, and assesses leadership and communication styles. The personal desires and interests of a team member should not be overlooked.

The key concepts in acquiring a team are:

Pre-Assignment: This refers to the fact that some project team members may be selected in advance.

Negotiation: In a matrix structure, the functional manager controls resources. The project manager has to influence the functional manager to obtain the best mix of resources.

Acquisition: This is the procurement of resources from outside the project.

Virtual teams: This refers to teams that are not co-located and have very little opportunity for face-to-face contact. Some of the team members could be in another city or even another country.

Since distributed project development occurs in many large organizations, the project manager must be able to assure an effective pattern of communication, and develop a team where the members trust each other.

15.3 Develop Project Team

After the project staff assignments have been completed and calendars created for the resources, the next step is to *Develop Project Team*. The following skills, tools and techniques are used during this process:

Soft skills: Project managers that have good soft skills can ensure smooth running of projects by sincere communication with project team members and true empathy. Such skills are vital in negotiation with, and influence of, stakeholders.[2]

Training: This is essential to ensure that the team members are well prepared to accomplish their tasks, preferably before they start working on them. Scheduling training proactively can mitigate quality risks and reduce costs.

Team-Building Activities: Good team building activities help teams to perform synergistically. Early team building activities may include simple introductions (which help through communicating previous experience and hobbies), clarifying roles and expectations, and describing the management process.

More significant team building may include comprehensive off-site, facilitated, workshops focusing on bonding and integration of diverse personality types.[3]

Phases of Working Teams: The project manager must understand the classic stages that teams go through. Dr. Bruce Tuckman published a classic model in 1965, which explains the typical phases that teams go through: [26]

- *Forming:* The team is formed and they look to the project manager for guidance and direction.

- *Storming:* Team members compete for position, as they establish their relation to other team members. The project manager might be challenged at this stage. The project manager must intervene proactively, before conflicts get out of hand. If a project manager has defined clear roles and responsibilities, the storming stage will be brief.

- *Norming:* Agreement and consensus occurs in the norming phase and the team works well under the direction of a project manager.

- *Performing:* The team is "strategically aware" and motivated, knows what it is doing, and where it is going.[4]

- *Adjourning:* The team breaks up, which occurs during the closing stage.

[2]Do not forget that project team members are stakeholders.

[3]All of these activities need a line item in the budget.

[4]The plane is on autopilot and the project manager can relax.

218

15.3.1 Recognition and Rewards

Motivation recognizes and promotes desirable behavior and is effective when carried out by the management team and the project manager. This is an important skill for the project manager: Encouraging the required behavior from the team. To develop teams requires understanding of the following theoretical concepts:

Maslow's Hierarchy of Needs

Dr. Abraham Maslow proposed that a person's needs must be satisfied in the following hierarchy: Physiological, Safety, Social, Self-esteem, and Self-actualization. See Figure 15.3. [27]

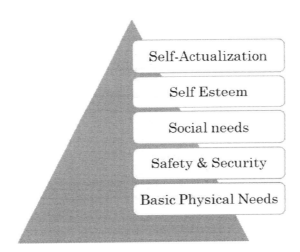

Figure 15.3: Maslow's hierarchy of needs.

The primary motivation for an individual is to satisfy their basic physical needs, such as food, drink, shelter and warmth. Only when these needs are satisfied can a person begin to deal with the higher level needs.

The next level deals with safety, and applies to needs such as protection, law and order, and stability. Social needs deal with the desire to belong to a group and involves family, affection and relationships.

The next level in the hierarchy is where individuals are motivated by self-esteem, which includes achievement, status, responsibility, and reputation.

Finally, when all of the needs in the lower end of the hierarchy have been fulfilled, a person can begin to deal with self-actualization. Such an individual is motivated by personal growth and fulfillment.

A project manager must realize that team members are usually motivated by personal growth and fulfillment and so must take time to identify each member's interests and how to achieve them.

McGregor: Theory X and Theory Y

Douglas McGregor defined two models of worker behavior: Theory X and Theory Y. Theory X managers believe that team members will not perform their duties unless threatened or closely supervised.

On the other hand, Theory Y managers believe the team will perform well if given the right motivating environment and appropriate expectations.

Managers that practice *Theory Y* behavior are much more likely to succeed in a project environment because, as we learned from Maslow's Hierarchy, project team members tend to be motivated by personal growth and fulfillment.

Herzberg's Theory of Motivation

Herzberg's "motivation-hygiene" theory proposes that certain motivator and hygiene factors affect job satisfaction and dissatisfaction. The *hygiene factors* merely prevent dissatisfaction. Examples are pay, benefits, the conditions of the work environment, and relationships with peers and managers.

The *motivation factors* are those that lead to satisfaction and deal with the substance of the work itself. These include the ability to advance and the opportunity to learn new things.

According to Herzberg, pay (a hygiene factor) will not motivate project teams, but new responsibilities (a motivation factor) might.

Expectancy Theory

Expectancy theory deals with how the expectation of a positive outcome can motivate people to perform and drive outcomes. People will behave in certain ways if they think there will be positive rewards for doing so.

[5] We expect our students to succeed!

If a project manager expects the team to succeed, they will. If the project manager believes they will fail, they will not be motivated and just might fail![5]

15.4 Manage Project Team

During the project, the project manager tracks each team member's performance, provides feedback to his or her manager, manages resources, and resolves conflicts. The following tools and techniques are used when managing project teams:

Observation and Conversation: A simple example of communication with team members is inquiring about their work and the issues they face.

Project Performance Appraisals: Periodic feedback can help team members, especially if constructively given.

Use of Issue Logs: The project manager should keep a written log of issues with target dates for them to be resolved.

Interpersonal Skills: This involves an appreciation of:

- *Leadership:* Varying leadership styles exist, such as, directing, facilitating, coaching, supporting, autocratic, consultative, and consensus.

- *Influencing skills:* This requires good listening skills, the ability to persuade and articulate points and positions, and building trust.

- *Effective decision-making:* This requires clearly understanding the project goals, having a well-defined process to follow, consideration of risks and opportunities, and the ability to come up with creative solutions.

Conflict Management: Conflict and frustration occurs in most projects. Conflict is natural in all organizations due to different values. The modern theory is that conflict is good as it can create deeper understanding and respect. Two skills that a project manager must develop are:

- *Encouraging functional conflict:* The project manager encourages dissent by asking tough questions, encouraging different points of view, and even asking the team to consider an unthinkable, or even unpopular, alternative.

- *Managing dysfunctional conflict:* This involves working through the natural stages of a conflict: mediate, arbitrate, control, accept, and closure.

The following techniques are methods for resolving conflict:

- *Withdraw:* Avoid or retreat from an actual or potential conflict scenario.

- *Smooth:* This is also called "accommodate," and involves emphasizing areas of agreement, rather than the conflict at hand.

- *Compromise:* This involves concession and conciliation. Neither party involved in the conflict gets what they value the most. This is generally considered to be a *lose-lose* strategy!

- *Force:* One of the parties involved in the conflict imposes their view point at the expense of the others. This is a *win-lose* scenario!

- *Collaborate:* This leads to consensus and commitment and involves consideration of multiple viewpoints.

- *Confront:* This is also known as "problem solving," and involves facing the conflict boldly, and brainstorming to come up with a *win-win* alternative. This takes more effort than *collaborate* or *compromise*, but is generally considered to be the best approach for resolving conflicts.

If good team building has occurred early on in the project, the project manager can avoid conflicts that are destructive and harmful.

Project managers generally do not have formal, legitimate power. Team members often report to functional managers, so project managers rarely have direct authority over them, and cannot order them around. It is important, therefore, to use soft skills to motivate and lead a project to a successful completion.

A key concern for managers in many organizations, and certainly for project managers, is motivating employees and teams, and this problem is more acute for a project manager as limited financial resources are available at his or her disposal. In such situations, an effective form of power is *expert power*, where the project manager leverages "technical expertise" to drive the project towards success.

We also note that good project managers trust their teams, while poor manager tend to exhibit "Theory X" behavior, where they constantly intervene and micro-manage. This can result in frustration and dissatisfaction, and drives down productivity.

16

COMMUNICATIONS

It is better to keep your mouth closed and let people think you are a fool than to open it and remove all doubt.

Mark Twain.

Communications Management is all about keeping upper management, stake-holders, and the project team in the loop throughout the life of a project. In large projects, communications can become a very complex because the number of communication paths rises rapidly as the number of people increases. Projects led by project managers with strong communication skills have a much better chance of success.[1]

Examples of communications skills include listening and understanding people, in all modes of communication, speaking, writing, and presenting. Communication management skills also include communication planning, information distribution, performance reporting, and stakeholder management. We introduce some communications theory as well tools and techniques to assist the project manager in these activities.

[1] It is often said, especially by Vijay Kanabar, that project management is 80% communications.

16.1 Identify Stakeholders

Very early on in the project, the project manager must identify stakeholders and categorize them according to their influence, identify their needs, as well as understand their perceived threats. An easy way to identify the stakeholders is to ask "Who will be impacted by this project?"

It is necessary to consider stakeholders who are both internal and external to the project. Examples of external stakeholders include the project sponsor,[2] upper management, government agencies, customers, and users of the product. Internal stakeholders include functional managers, and the project team.

One should also consider people impacted by the process. For example, a construction project might be disruptive to businesses in the neighborhood.

To identify stakeholders, the first activity is the performance of a stakeholder analysis, which first identifies them, and then classifies them as to their influence on the project.

Once the project manager has identified the stakeholders, the next step is to create a *stakeholder register*, which lists the attributes for each stakeholder, such as name, role, expectations, and potential influence.

For the PMA case study, Table 16.1 provides example illustrating stakeholder roles, expectations, and influence.

---

[2]Remember, the sponsor is paying!

Table 16.1: Stakeholder identification for the PMA web site.

Role	Expectations	Influence (IL = 1-5)
Executive Sponsor	**Key Stakeholder.** Provide direction and ground-rules for the project. Guidance by request.	IL = 4. Defines project success and adjudicates rewards for accomplishments.
Project Sponsor	**Key Stakeholder.** Provides guidance for the project in a weekly review of the website and develops recommendations.	IL = 4. Defines project success and adjudicates rewards for accomplishments.
Steering & Guidance	**Key Stakeholder.** Provides guidance for the project in a weekly review of the website and develops recommendations.	IL = 4. Provides direction for the team.
Project Manager	**Key Stakeholder.** Management oversight of all activities.	IL = 5. Handles all status reporting to upper management.
Designer & Architect	**Key Stakeholder.** Implement website design.	IL = 5. Website design experience.
Lead Developer	**Key Stakeholder.** Implement website.	IL = 5. Website development experience.
Business Analyst	**Key Stakeholder.** Provide direction to maximize the effectiveness of the website.	IL = 3. Knowledge of markets.
PMA Members IT Dept.	**Key Stakeholders.** End Users. Consumers expected to be the most active users of the website. **Medium Stakeholders.** Website maintainer upon completion.	IL = 3. Will dictate the success of the project by frequency of visitation. IL = 3. The quality and timeliness of website maintenance will influence end users' perception of the quality.
Prospective Employers	**Medium Stakeholders.** End Users. Prospective employers will use the website to locate PMs.	IL = 2. Use by employers could contribute to success.
Alumni	**Minor Stakeholders.** Alumni may visit website.	IL = 1.
Prospective Students	**Minor Stakeholders.** End Users. Masters and certificate students may use site for networking. Students may add content.	IL = 1.

16.2 Communications Planning

Inexperienced project managers often spend too little time planning their project communications. This should be a big concern, however, as project managers spend a substantial fraction of their time communicating. It is less glamorous and more challenging to identify communication requirements and to create a communications management plan than to analyze risks.

There are four main types of communication and, generally, a combination of all four occurs in all projects. The four types of communication are: formal, informal, written, and verbal. They are used in the following combinations:

Formal Written:	Used to communicate specifications, product requirements and change control.
Formal Verbal:	Used in official presentations such as status reviews.
Informal Verbal:	This includes project team meetings.
Informal Written:	This includes non-legal documents and general notes.

The *Communication Management Plan* is the primary output of the *communications planning* process, and becomes part of the project plan. It informs all stakeholders how and in what form communications will be handled on the project. An example of a portion of a communications plan is given in Figure 16.1.

Steering Committee

A project steering committee will be created. It includes faculty, the executive sponsor, the team, a member of the IT Infrastructure and one alumni.

Project steering committee meetings will be held weekly, at 9:00AM Friday to allow issues to be raised and addressed without spanning the weekend. The role of the committee will be to make decisions on outstanding items, address issues, and review change requests and resource utilization.

Issues Tracking

Unplanned issues that occur will be collected and tracked by the PM. Any issues that cannot be resolved will be presented to the steering committee. All reported issues will have an owner and a resolution date.

All issues will be captured and tracked in an issues database, managed by the PM, and reviewed during weekly project team meetings. The issues will be assigned a severity based on potential impact to the project.

Figure 16.1: A portion of the *Communications Plan* for the PMA web site

16.3 Techniques to Identify Communication Requirements

The following resources are helpful in identifying communication requirements: organization charts, project structures, the stakeholder register, and data on the functional departments involved with the project.

Communication complexity and communication channels increase rapidly as the number of people on the project rises. For example, the number of interactions between n people is $n(n-1)/2$. For example if a project has two stakeholders $n = 2$ and the number of communication channels is $2(2-1)/2 = 1$.

If the project has four stakeholders the project has $4(4-1)/2 = 6$ communication channels. If a project has 12 stakeholders there would be 66 communication channels indicating a challenging communication problem if the project manager needs to manage them all.

A theoretical communication model is helpful in understanding the communication process. This model is shown in Figure 16.2, and consists of the following components: Encode and decode; message and feedback; and medium and noise. The *message* refers to the verbal (spoken or written) symbols, as well as nonverbal signs, which also represent information that the sender attempts to convey.

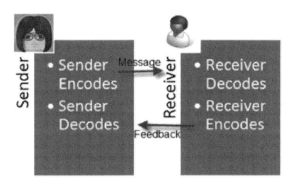

Figure 16.2: The communications model.

The first issue in the above simple model is that unless the sender receives feedback of the message just communicated (e.g., via parroting), the sender cannot be sure that the message was properly received (let alone understood). The model also indicates that both the sender and the receiver have to be good listeners, otherwise

227

the message cannot be decoded properly.

Adding to the complexity of the basic communication model is that many things can interfere with the transmission of the message. We classify such barriers as filters and noise, and list some examples below:

- Distance, unfamiliar technology, lack of background information.

- Different spoken languages or use of unfamiliar technical jargon; physical separation; different cultural, educational, or social backgrounds.

- Sabotage also hinders communication and could include hidden agendas, and power plays.

- Having a pre-determined mind-set or a self-fulfilling philosophy, can result in miscommunication.

- Historical considerations, such as the manner in which a task was "always done in the past," can also jeopardize communication.

A project manager facing the challenges described above must create a communication plan that clearly specifies the appropriate format, duration and frequency of communications to mitigate the risk of communication failure.

16.4   Tools & Techniques to Distribute Information

The goal of *Distribute Information* is to share information with the team, project sponsors, and stakeholders. Examples used to distribute information include individual and group meetings, video and audio conferences, and computer chats.

Examples of information distribution *tools* include electronic communication and conferencing tools, such as e-mail, telephone and web conferencing, as well as web portals and project management software.

16.5   Tools and Techniques to Manage Stakeholder Expectations

**Everyone is entitled to his own opinion,
but not to his own facts.**

Sen. Pat Moynihan.

Interpersonal skills and management skills fall in this category. Examples of interpersonal skills include building trust, resolving conflict, active listening, and overcoming resistance to change. Examples of management skills include presentation, negotiation, writing, and public speaking.

Project managers can learn from Steven Covey's *Seven Habits of Highly Effective People* to communicate more effectively and manage stakeholder expectations. [28] The steps are pretty self-explanatory and are listed below:

1. Be proactive

2. Begin with the end in mind

3. Put first things first

4. Think win/win

5. Seek first to understand, then to be understood

6. Achieve synergy

7. Sharpen the saw

16.5.1 Report Performance Tools & Techniques

Four tools and techniques are covered here: Variance analysis, forecasting methods, communication methods, and reporting systems.

Variance analysis is a tool to analyze the difference between what was planned and the actual performance. An example is Earned Value Management, which is used to calculate cost and schedule variances. The following steps are performed during a variance analysis:

- Verify the quality of the information collected to ensure that it is complete and credible.

- Determine variances and document if they are favorable or unfavorable to the project's outcome.

- Determine the impact on project cost and schedule, as well as the impact on quality and scope.

- Analyze the trends of the variances and note the sources of variation.

Forecasting method: On the basis of the actual performance, a project manager may have to predict the future project performance. For example, Earned Value Management contains a technique for predicting the estimated cost at completion (*EAC*).

Communication methods: The project manager conducts periodic status review meetings to gather and exchange information about the project progress and performance. The project manager can use electronic methods to distribute status updates and reports.

Reporting systems: A project management information system (PMIS) helps the project manager to capture, store, and distribute information to stakeholders. Examples of such reporting systems are Microsoft Project and Primavera.

Table 16.2 shows an example of a reporting system, completed for an issue that arose during the PMA project.

Table 16.2: Issues tracking for the PMA web site.

Project Issue	Severity (H, M, L)	Owner	Resolution Due Date
Need to sign a release form from PMI to get certain content to be utilized by the site.	H	PM	07/01/2012

17

RISKS

Risk?! Risk is our business!

Captain James T. Kirk

Risk Management is the art and science of dealing with risks. During planning this involves defining a comprehensive approach to risks: identifying them, quantifying them, and creating a risk response plan. During execution, the project manager monitors and controls risks.

Historically, risk management was considered an optional, add-on process, as distinct from activities such as project scheduling or cost estimating, which were always considered to be an essential part of project management.[1] However, the reality is that every project faces risks and, inevitably, some will materialize.

Starting in the mid-1980s project management standards, such as early versions of the PMBOK, formally began to recognize that comprehensive and integrated risk management is fundamental to project success. Today, managing risk is considered an indispensable and integral part of every stage of project management, and that it must be practiced diligently throughout the life of the project.[1]

Risk management is a proactive attempt to recognize what can go wrong and to plan ahead. Just as in medicine, prevention is better than cure. Here are some questions

[1] Greg Ballesteros, the former CEO of PMI, says "Risk Management is PM for grown-ups."

231

the project manager should ask: What can go wrong? How can we minimize the impact? What can be done in advance? What will our response be?

17.1 Risks

We begin with the definition of a risk:

> *A risk is an uncertain event or condition that, if it occurs, has a positive or negative effect on the project.*

It often comes as a surprise that the definition of a risk includes the idea that a risk can be *positive*. People usually assume that a risk has only negative consequences, and that risk management consists of mitigating the impact of the things that can go wrong. However, it is as important to enhance the effects of the positive risks as it is to mitigate the impact of negative risks.

Consider the following examples of risks:

1. *The staff does not have the required technical skills.*

   This is a negative risk, and the job of the project manager is to develop a strategy either to prevent the risk from occurring (e.g., by changing staff assignments), or mitigating the risk (e.g., by implementing a training plan).

2. *The subcontractor can provide the deliverable earlier than planned.*

   This is a positive risk. If the deliverable is on the critical path, this may result in accelerating the schedule. The project manager should work to maximize the positive impact of the subcontractor's early delivery, perhaps by providing extra staff to help with delivery documentation.

Project managers should diligently investigate all risks and apply the correct tactic: Preventing and mitigating negative risks, and enhancing positive risks.

17.1.1 Risk Causes and Consequences

Risks have *causes*: For example, people get sick, the scope changes, a construction permit takes longer than anticipated.

Risks also have *consequences*: For example, some consequences associated with the above risks are:

Risk	Consequences
People get sick	Inexperienced, replacement personnel make mistakes.
The scope changes	The change in scope increases the cost.
Permit delayed	The completion date is delayed.

Notice that the cost increase is a *consequence*, not a risk. Technically, it is incorrect to say there is a *cost risk*. It is also incorrect to speak about a *schedule risk*. Instead, the project manager should explain that there are risk causes that may have schedule consequences, i.e., a delay in the schedule.

There are many sources of risks:

- Scope creep.[2]

- Insufficient or poor resources. An expert may be needed simultaneously in two places.

- Pressure to compress the schedule from customers or management.

- Pressure to reduce the cost from customers or management.

- Lack of a formal project management process. Uncontrolled changes are a major source of confusion and delay.

- Stakeholder friction. Stakeholders can hold up approvals if they feel their particular interests are not being satisfactorily addressed.

- Poor communications. Team members will not know what to work on, or how to prioritize their time. Customers will not understand the status of the project. Stakeholders will not know what is going on.

Examples of risks on a plumbing project are shown in Table 17.1. The consequences were that each one contributed to an increase in the cost.

17.1.2 Known Unknowns and Unknown Unknowns

When trying to identify risks, one is always looking into the future, so it is an uncertain business. For a risk, its degree of uncertainty can be classified as follows:

- *Known unknowns*: These are risks that can be *identified*. A good way to identify risks is by reviewing similar projects. An example from the New Kitchen project is:

[2] Can you make this small change for me?

233

Table 17.1: Sources of risk on the Kitchen project.

Risks in Cost Estimate	Source of Risk
Unforeseen circumstances.	When the plumber opened the cabinet to replace the faucets, he found rusted pipes that had to be replaced.
Use of wrong estimation parameter.	The estimator used the parameter for a new house, instead of a renovation.
Formula inaccuracy.	The estimation formula is only good to $\pm 20\%$.
Optimistic estimate.	The PM knew the customer's budget, and agreed to do the project for that amount.
Junior plumber assigned.	The estimate assumed an experienced plumber.
The estimate was made by "analogy."	The project turned out not to be "analogous," it was completely different.
It took longer.	Sometimes, this just happens.

We have to install a gas line in the kitchen and on the last project the permitting process was delayed by 6 weeks.

Known unknowns are risks that we can "kind-of-anticipate." According to David Logan,[2] "much of the scientific research .... (about risks) .... is based on investigating known unknowns." That is, we tend to allow for the things we expect.

- *Unknown unknowns:* These are the events we did not expect, things we had no idea about, as in:

What?! You can't quit, you're our best programmer!

Technically, unknown unknowns are the risks that could not be identified. NASA space exploration missions provide fascinating examples of things that went wrong that no one could possibly have anticipated. On a more mundane level, it is just not humanly possible to anticipate all risks.[3]

The general process is as follows: First, the risks are *identified*, e.g., in a brainstorming session. It is quite easy to make a very long list of the things that can go wrong. Therefore, once you've identified the risks, you need a way to prioritize them and to decide which ones should be actively addressed. This is accomplished by performing a *qualitative* assessment in which risks are classified according to both their likelihood and their impact.

[3]And if experience is anything to go by, we are not very good at this. Unknown unknowns constantly catch us by surprise.

Next, the risks that are both likely to occur and that may have a significant impact must be assessed in more detail. This is called a *quantitative* assessment and the goal is to estimate specific *contingency* amounts. Contingencies are additions to the cost and to the schedule.[4]

Finally, you should make an allowance for things that you just can't anticipate—the unknown unknowns. The allowance for these unexpected events is called the *management reserve.*[5]

The lesson for project managers is serious: Risks will materialize, so plan ahead.[6]

17.2 Risk Strategies

The approach to dealing with risks is to formulate a strategy for both negative and positive risks.

17.2.1 Strategies for negative risks

The negative risk strategies are: avoid, transfer, mitigate and accept.

- *Avoid:* If possible, this risk *prevention* strategy should be the first choice.

  A technique of risk avoidance is to change the scope, which changes the project's functionality so that the risk cannot occur. For example, if the kitchen does not have gas, and the installation of a gas stove introduces an unacceptable delay, then propose an electric stove.[7] Another avoidance strategy is to defer risky parts of the specification to a future delivery.

  The advantage of *avoid* is that you do not need any contingency funds or schedule buffers. You have eliminated the risk.

- *Mitigate:* In this approach, one attempts to reduce either the likelihood of the event occurring or its impact, or both. This can result in lowering the ranking of the risk from high to medium, or even low. In practice, it is unlikely that a risk can be entirely prevented from occurring.

  An example of *mitigation* is as follows: Assume that an information technology project plans to use a new, sophisticated development system, and the organization does not have any previous experience with it. One *mitigation* strategy is to send the inexperienced staff members for training.

  Notice that *mitigation* almost always involves extra cost. In the above case, training funds will be required to mitigate the risk of inexperienced staff.

[4]Identified risks (known unknowns) result in contingencies: additional funds and schedule buffers.

[5]There is considerable debate over the management reserve. Some organizations require it (e.g., The Federal Highway Administration), while in a competitive situation many companies automatically delete the reserve to lower their bid.

[6]You can't anticipate all eventualities. Plan to bury some funds and schedule some slack. You never know when you will need them.

[7]Of course, the customer may say "No way!" But at that point, she may also be willing to accept the delay.

235

- *Transfer:* In this strategy, we outsource the risk to a third party. Often, risk *transfer* involves investing in insurance, performance bonds, or warranties.

  An example of risk *transfer* is the hiring an expert consultant to build a difficult piece of the project. The transfer of risk usually involves extra funds.[8]

- *Accept:* In this strategy, we accept the reality that the risk can neither be avoided, mitigated, nor transferred. The project team then decides to take a chance and *accept* the risk. The team recognizes that they will have to deal with this risk if, and when, it occurs. To allow for the risk, the project manager should set aside contingency reserves of time, money and staff.

  An example of *accepting* a risk is: A deliverable is to be supplied by an unreliable subcontractor who holds a monopoly on the technology and there are no alternatives. The only option is to accept the risk.[9]

17.2.2 Strategies for Positive Risks

Positive risks can enhance the performance on a project. As there were with negative risks, there are four strategies for dealing with positive risks: Exploit, enhance, share, and accept. These strategies parallel those for negative risks.

- *Exploit:* Here we leverage our strengths and attempt to take advantage of the risk. For example, the company might have talented programmers and assigning them to critical deliverables may result in early completion at a lower cost.

- *Enhance:* In this strategy, we attempt to increase either the likelihood or the impact of the risk occurring. An example of risk enhancement is as follows: If an activity is finished early freeing up staff, then they can be assigned to activities on the critical path to shorten the schedule.

- *Share:* Here, we enhance the opportunity for project success by teaming with a third party and delegate to them pieces they are better equipped to perform. Large projects usually share risks among several companies, each with their own expertise. For example, Boeing subcontracts the design and development of jet engines to third parties.

- *Accept*: Here we acknowledge that we cannot construct a viable strategy for maximizing the benefits of the positive risk, so we accept the status quo.

[8]Do you want to add travel insurance for your trip?

[9]Note that almost all risk strategies involve adding costs and time–the contingencies. You did put those in your budget and schedule, didn't you?

17.2.3 Risk Response

Despite the team's best efforts to mitigate them, some risks will actually occur, and often in unexpected ways. Therefore, the final piece of the strategy is to *respond.*

We emphasize that one should not sit around waiting to respond to a risk materializing. The project manager creates a *Contingency Plan,* which defines how the team will react to the risks *before* they materialize. The plan should include responses for both positive and negative risks.

17.3 Planning Risk Management

The purpose of the *Plan Risk Management* process is to create the overall management approach to risks. Since this is a plan, the most appropriate tool is a template, the key components of which are:

- Risk management scope and objectives.

- The methodology to be used for risk identification, assessment, quantification, and response, as well as for monitoring and control.

- The participants in the risk analysis process.

- The risk analysis tools to be used, and identification of helpful templates and other organizational process assets.

- Risk prioritization, e.g., risks impacting cost take priority over schedule. Risk weights, labels, and selection guidelines.

- The communications approach for risks when distributing status reports, including protocols for elevating risks to sponsors and senior management.

17.4 Identify Risks

The goal of the *Identify Risks* process is to create the *Risk Register,* which contains a list of risks, and evolves to include their assessment and ranking in importance.

PMI introduced a *Practice Standard for Risk Management* [29], which contains a comprehensive description of risk analysis tools and techniques, their strengths and weaknesses, as well as critical success factors for their effective application. The standard suggests that a useful method of identifying risks is to continually repeat the following mantra:

Because of **<one or more causes>**, **<risk>** might occur, which would lead to **<one or more effects>**.

The following is a list of risk identification techniques:

- *Assumptions and Constraints Analysis:* Each assumption and constraint in the project scope statement represents a risk. This can be used as a starting point to identify risks during the planning stage.[10]

- *Brainstorming:* The project team, and other stakeholders, should be encouraged to generate a list of risks in a facilitated process.

- *Cause-and-effect (Ishikawa) diagrams:* This visual diagram promotes brainstorming, clarifies root causes, and helps develop mitigation strategies.

- *Checklists:* By examining historical data from similar projects, a list of relevant issues can be developed. Project lessons are sometimes available in industry databases, and are a great source for risk identification.

- *Delphi Technique:* This is similar to brainstorming, but is a structured and formal process that requires formal facilitation and anonymity.

- *Influence Diagrams:* Risks can be inferred from this diagram, which shows the main project entities and decision points, uncertainties and outcomes, and the relationships among them.

- *Interviewing:* This is similar to brainstorming in that expert consultants are interviewed to help identify and understand risks.

- *Historical information:* Organizations with good project management assets have a repository of lessons learned—an invaluable resource for identifying risks.

- *Questionnaires and Software:* Software that prompts the project team or stimulates creativity can help with risk identification.

- *Risk Breakdown Structure (RBS):* The RBS is a valuable tool for identifying and classifying risks. An example of an RBS is shown in Figure 17.1

- *SWOT analysis:* A SWOT analysis might be available, since it is often part of the business case. If not, the team can perform a SWOT analysis, focusing on threats and weaknesses.

[10]Assumption: The permit will be available in 30 days ... Risk: Permit schedule delay.

238

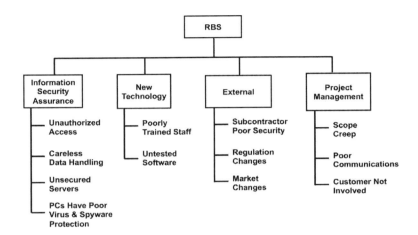

Figure 17.1: A *Risk Breakdown Structure.*

- *WBS:* This provides a comprehensive overview of all activities and can act as a starting point for brainstorming another source of risks.

The *Risk Identification* process results in a *risk register*, in which each risk has the following attributes: ID, Name, Description, Impact (area and at what stage), Type (positive or negative), Likelihood, and Estimated Severity.

17.5 Risk Assessment

Given a list of risks in the *Risk Register*, the next step is to assess them, and there are two steps: qualitative and quantitative. The *qualitative assessment* considers all risks and calibrates them in terms of their likelihood of occurring and potential impact. The risk data are updated in the risk register by adding both their likelihood and impact, which, at this stage, are usually just in terms of high, medium, and low. Unlikely risks and those with little impact may be placed on a "watch list."

The goal of the *qualitative* assessment is to develop a list of risks with the potential to significantly affect project outcomes, either negatively or positively. These significant risks are then further investigated in a *quantitative* analysis, the goal of which is to estimate the required contingencies (cost and schedule).

239

17.5.1 Techniques for Qualitative Risk Assessment

In a qualitative risk analysis, each risk is analyzed to determine its likelihood of occurring and its impact. Tables 17.2 and 17.3 provide examples of how the likelihood and impact might be defined for a project. Risks are scored on a scale from 1 to 5 in both likelihood and impact, with 5 being 'high.'

Table 17.2: Definition of risk *Likelihood* values.

Rating	Likelihood	Definition
1	Rare	Occurs in exceptional circumstances
2	Unlikely	Could occur at some time
3	Possible	Might occur at some time
4	Likely	Will probably occur in the project
5	Very Likely	Expected to occur in most situations

Table 17.3: Definition of risk *Impact* values.

Rating	Impact	Definition
1	Insignificant	No Damage or Loss
		No cost or schedule impact
2	Minor	Minor damage or loss
		Minor cost or schedule impact
3	Moderate	Some damage and/or loss
		Significant cost or schedule impact
4	Major	Extensive loss and damage
		Extensive cost and/or schedule impact
5	Catastrophic	Damage to reputation
		Huge financial loss
		Unrecoverable cost and/or schedule impact

Table 17.4 shows an example of a risk assessment for the PMA project, it lists all risks as well as their likelihood and potential impact.

These scores are then used as coordinates on the *Risk Assessment Matrix*, which is a useful visual aid—see Figure 17.2. Likelihood is plotted on the *y-axis* and impact on the *x-axis*. In the *Risk Assessment Matrix*, bands of color help to categorize the risks. The top right hand corner is red, and risks in this area have *high likelihood* of occurring and *high impact* if they occur. Many risks in this area is a sign of trouble. The middle band represents medium risks, while the bottom left corner represents *low likelihood* and *low impact*.

Table 17.4: The *Risk Assessment* for the PMA web site.

Risk ID	Category	Risk	Impact	Likeli-hood	Mitigation Action
1	Infra-structure	Not set up in time.	3	2	Select highly recommended VAR for servers.
2	Design	PMA Data may be hacked.	5	5	Select developer skilled in tools. Backup: Alternate tools.
3	PM	Aggressive schedule. Schedule fixed, possible delays.	3	5	Accept the risk. Monitor progress closely . Re-assess if slip occurs.
4	Skills	Key resources part time.	4	3	Tool easy to learn. Conduct training sessions.
5	Technology	Fixed price, contract. Added content may need to be purchased.	1	2	Include contingency $2,500 for unforeseen expenses.

17.5.2 Tools for Quantitative Risk Analysis

The risks in the upper right quadrant of the *Risk Assessment Matrix* are classified as significant candidates for further investigation, which is accomplished using a *quantitative* analysis. When a risk occurs, it affects (usually negatively) the cost and the schedule and the goal of the quantitative assessment is to *numerically* estimate its impacts.

Not all identified risks will materialize. Therefore, to fund the risks that actually occur, one assigns contingency funds and time buffers. There should be a contingency for cost (in dollars) and a contingency for schedule (in weeks), which is often called a time buffer.

The following analysis tools can be used to estimate contingencies.

Expected Monetary Value (EMV)

EMV is a technique used to calculate a weighted average, or expected cost, when the outcomes are uncertain. We illustrate the EMV technique with three examples:

241

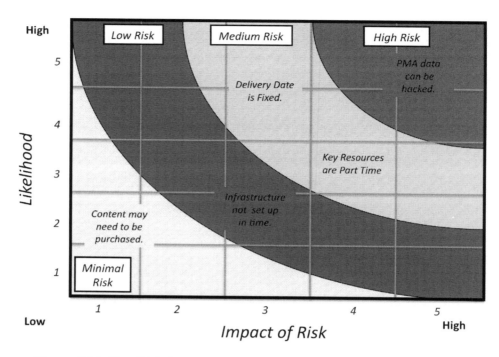

Figure 17.2: The *Risk Assessment Matrix* tool for *Qualitative Assessment.*

1. *Rank Ordering Risks:*

   EMV is a good tool to prioritize and rank order risks. Suppose that all the risks in the risk register are negative. First, we express the risks in monetary form, e.g., *The cost of a one-week delay is $10,000.*

   Next we assign a probability to each risk, e.g., *The probability of the risk is 50%.* Finally, we multiply the monetary impact by the probability to determine the expected value of this event:

$$Expected\ Value\ of\ Risk = \$10,000\ x\ 0.50 = \$5,000. \qquad (17.1)$$

   One can then rank order all of the risks by their expected monetary value to reveal which ones are most important and require more attention.

2. *Calculating Contingency Amounts:*

   The contingency budget is the amount allocated to cover the cost of the risks. (There should be a similar allowance for the schedule.) The contingency budget can allow for the fact that some risks are positive and some negative, as shown in Table 17.5.

Table 17.5: Calculation of the contingency budget.

Risk Event	Amount at Stake	Probability	Contingency (EMV)
Project will incur cost overrun resulting in financial penalty	-$50,000 (Loss)	0.80	-$40, 000
Vendor supplies component early. Early completion of project	+$10,000 (Gain)	0.50	+$5,000
Potential Project Impact			**-$35,000**

Table 17.5 suggests the project manager should set aside around $35,000 to cover the losses associated with identified risks.[11] The probabilities, gains, and losses are all *estimates*. A wise project manager will conduct a sensitivity analysis in which the amounts and probabilities are varied, and a range of values determined for the contingency funds.

3. *Alternative Outcomes:*

   When calculating the contingency budget, several alternate outcomes for risk events might have to be considered. To show how this is accomplished, we expand the EMV calculation to include several possible events. We then weight the outcomes by their probability of occurrence.

   To the above case, we add the idea that the 'reward' can be either high or low. We assess that the probability of the reward being high is 0.6, and of being low is 0.4. We multiply the Amounts at Stake by the probabilities to obtain the total Potential Project Impact—see Table 17.6.

Decision Tree Analysis

A decision implies there are several alternative approaches, each with different potential outcomes. The *decision tree* is a tool for evaluating decisions, and showing which alternative provides the highest payoff.

We illustrate a decision tree with an example from the PMA case. The PMA board proposed a campaign to increase membership, and the team thinks the quality of the web site will be a significant factor in the success of the campaign. Therefore,

[11] This does not guarantee that this is the right amount, it is simply the best guess. Both (or neither!) of the risks might occur.

243

Table 17.6: Calculation of the contingency budget using multiple outcomes.

Outcome	Amount at Stake	Probability	Contingency (EMV)
When reward is High: Demand for new software results in financial penalty	$40,000	0.6	-$24,000
If reward is Low: No financial penalty	$10,000	0.4	-$4,000
Potential Project Impact			**$20,000**

the team proposed investing in a development environment, which would cost around $50,000.

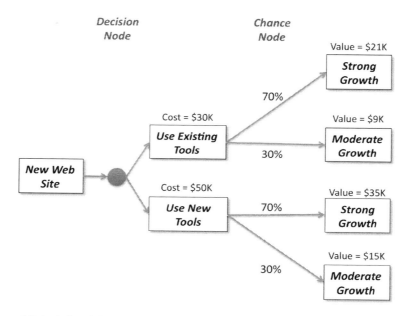

Figure 17.3: A *Decision Tree* analyzing the investment in new web site tools.

Figure 17.3 shows the way in which a decision tree is structured. The decision node, which is represented on the diagram by a small circle, has two options:

1. *Use Existing Tools:* In this option, the investment is $30,000, which is the estimated cost of upgrading the existing tools. This should include staff costs to implement the upgrades, training, and any new hardware.

2. *Use New Tools:* In this option, the investment is $50,000, which is the investment amount for new tools, including staff, training, and hardware.

Next we allow for multiple outcomes, which is accomplished by assessing and evaluating the potential of the campaign to increase membership. After some analysis, the team proposes that there are two likely outcomes:

1. *Strong Growth. Likelihood: 70%:* The team believes that the campaign is very likely to succeed, and they propose that there is a 70% chance that the membership growth campaign will be successful.

2. *Moderate Growth. Likelihood: 30%:* Since nothing is certain, the team admits that there is a 30% chance that the membership campaign will be only moderately successful.

We now calculate the payoff for each outcome. The team estimated that each new member is worth around $1,000 to the organization. Therefore, to determine the payoff, we must estimate the increase in membership for each branch of the tree.

When the team uses the existing tools and the growth is strong, they estimate an increase of 21,000 members. However, when new tools are used, that number should increase to 35,000, as the new tools will allow the team to reach a wider audience and process potential new members more efficiently. For moderate growth, the corresponding numbers are 9,000 for existing tools, and 15,000 for new tools.

The final analysis step is to determine which is the most effective option. To do this, we calculate the *Expected Monetary Value* of each branch of the tree:

Existing Tools   = -$30,000 + $21,000 x 0.7 + $9,000 x 0.3   = -$12,600.
New Tools   = -$50,000 + $35,000 x 0.7 + $15,000 x 0.3   = -$21,000.

The decision with the highest payoff is *"Existing Tools"*.[12]

Because both options have negative payoff, one may reasonably ask what happens if the team decides to do nothing. That is, what is the impact of conducting the campaign with no upgrade of web tools at all?

In that case, we can add a third decision, *Do Nothing*, with an investment of zero. Further, suppose we estimate that the growth in membership for the two scenarios are *Strong = 2,000* and *Moderate = 1,000*. If we add the *Do Nothing* decision node to the diagram, we will get the following EMV for that branch:

$$Do\ Nothing = -\$0 + \$2,000 \times 0.7 + \$1,000 \times 0.3 = +\$1,700. \qquad (17.2)$$

[12]It has the smaller negative number.

245

This option produces a positive payoff, and is actually the best option.

This is an example of a sensitivity analysis. After constructing the decision tree, the project manager should present it to a variety of stakeholders. Their feedback will help calibrate the data and evaluate which parameters drive the decision. In this case it was the investment amounts, which are large. Therefore, the natural question to ask was, "What happens if we eliminate the investment?" This led to a third decision option, *Do Nothing*, which turned out to be the best option.[13]

Using Decision Trees

A major problem with decision trees is the so-called, "Myth of Analysis," which covers a variety of issues:[3]

- *All options are included.* Not all of the decisions may be included or, even, analyzable. In the first version of the decision tree, we omitted the *Do Nothing* option, and that turned out to be the best approach.

- *All consequences are included.* We can easily add a third outcome: *Weak Growth*. If the economy declines, such an option may be important.

- *The data are valid.* The costs and probabilities are fundamental in assessing the usefulness of the decision. Questions that might be asked in a sensitivity analysis, include: Do small changes in either probabilities or payoff change the decision? If so, all outcomes should be considered to be equally valid.

- *The tree rapidly gets complicated.* It is confusing to analyze multiple decisions with multiple outcomes. A useful approach here is to prune obviously bad branches.

- *Belief in impartiality.* A fallacy is that the data, because they are probabilities, are somehow impartially developed. They are not. Analysts bring their biases and preconceptions to the assignment of probabilities and costs.

- *It is not about the cost.* Making a decision based solely on the estimated future costs is a poor approach.[14]

- *Intermediate decisions.* Sometimes, a branch of the tree may have a decision point built in. For example, when pursuing the option of a new development environment, there may be an initial investment in a prototype followed by optional add-ons. If the membership growth is going well, the team may decide to purchase the options.

[13]Only by conducting the sensitivity analysis did we uncover the best option. If we had blindly followed the "best" decision tree outcome, we would have lost a lot of money.

[14]In Chapter 2 we learned that the most important critical success factor for new products is a "unique differentiated product." A better question than "What is the lowest cost?" is, "What strategy delivers the most unique product?"

Such conditional decisions make the decision tree very complex. The best approach is often to wait until the decision is imminent, at which time one will have better data on the costs and income.

On the other hand, there are definite benefits in the use of decision trees:

- *There is a decision!* The first and most important aspect is that it informs everyone that there is indeed a decision to be made. The tool formalizes the process and allows stakeholders a chance to give input.

- *Open analysis.* The assumptions, data, and decisions are open to everyone.

- *Team discussion.* The process generates an informative discussion. In particular, a sensitivity analysis will strengthen the confidence of the stakeholders that the decision is correct.

17.6 Risk Monitoring and Control

This is where risks are tracked and responded to. Different risk categories warrant different approaches.

- *High Risk:* These must be continuously monitored. Throughout the project, high risks should be analyzed to determine if there are actions that might reduce the likelihood of occurrence and the impact if it occurs. If possible, risks should be *prevented* from occurring, e.g., change the scope.

- *Medium Risks:* These should be monitored closely and continuous mitigation should attempt to contain their effects, and to ensure that they do not escalate to high impact risks.

- *Low Risks:* These should be routinely monitored at regular meetings to ensure their status remains as 'low.'

17.6.1 Tools for Risk Response

This is where the project manager *responds* to the risks when they arise. If significant planning has occurred, and a response strategy is in place, then this is where the contingency plan is implemented.[15]

There are several tools and techniques to help the project manager to respond to risks, including brainstorming and scenario analysis. In both, participants suggest solutions and analyze their effects.

[15]If there is no contingency plan, then the strategy becomes: *Dig Out!*

247

17.6.2   Tools to Monitor and Control Project Risk

During execution, the project manager monitors and controls risks. This occurs throughout the life cycle of the project by regularly reassessing and updating the *risk register*. Status meetings and periodic team meetings are an excellent opportunity to review the risks, which should be an agenda item.

Other tools and techniques that can be used during execution include risk audits, variance and trend analysis, technical performance measurement, and reserve analysis. Table 17.7 lists some potential responses to risks when they occur.

Table 17.7: Risk events and some potential responses.

Risk Event	Risk Response
Personnel shortfall	Hire subcontractors. Enhance productivity through training.
Scope unclear	Develop prototype with user input.
Subcontractor not performing adequately	Conduct frequent site visits. Co-locate with team. Invoke performance clauses in contract.

17.6.3   Risk Occurrence Over Time

The PMBOK suggests the probability of risks occurring is high initially and then declines throughout the project's life. We claim that this only applies to the known risks.[16]

We are not convinced that the likelihood of occurrence of "unknown unknowns" declines over time, as the following examples from the kitchen project illustrate:

- When the refrigerator arrived, it did not fit in the cabinet opening. The contractor, Mark, immediately measured the opening size, which was correct according to the specification.

  Mark then measured the refrigerator and found that it was 1.2 inches higher than the specification. Mark was furious and called the refrigerator manufacturer. There was a lot of yelling and screaming, which came to a head when the refrigerator manufacturer said, "Standard practice is to allow an extra inch."

  "I allowed two inches!" Mark yelled back.

[16]Probably because the project manager is looking at them and containing them.

Fortunately, the refrigerator had leveling screws on the bottom, and some careful adjustments allowed the refrigerator to *just* fit in the opening. This is an example of a specification error that could have been expensive to fix.[17]

- Hurricane Irene barreled through town and ripped the roof off the finish carpenter's house. Only less skilled carpenters were available, and the finish work was delayed. This is an example of a personnel risk.

- The ceiling was scheduled to be insulated with foam. The insulation contractor told us that we could not sleep in the house the night the foam was installed. We planned to stay with friends.

  However, when the insulation contractor showed up, he said that nobody could stay in the house while the foam was being blown in.[18] That happened to be a day when the plumber, painter, and carpenters were all scheduled to work! This is an example of a communication risk.

- Peter, the electrician, suffered an accident that cut his hand rather badly. He was out of commission for a week. His assistant filled in, but could only do low level electrical work and the project was delayed. This is another example of a personnel risk.

Hurricanes, injuries, and specification errors were all "unknown unknowns," and completely unanticipated. They are all examples of high-impact, low-probability events, and most risk analytical models fail miserably in predicting and allowing for such situations.

17.6.4   Risks, Contingencies and Reserves

Finally, we remind the reader that the results of the risk analysis are amounts (costs and/or schedules) to be included in the *contingency reserves*. Contingency reserves are explicitly assigned to identified risks. On the other hand, *management reserves*, which are allocated to cover unidentified risks, are *not* included in the cost baseline, i.e., reserves are for *unknown unknowns*.

[17]This is also a good example of Mark's planning ahead. When everyone had calmed down, Mark drolly observed, "This is why we add tolerances."

[18]He actually said this at 8:30 am when Eileen not had a chance even to dry her hair. The insulation contractor was less than popular! The project manager was not happy.

249

18

PROCUREMENT MANAGEMENT

**I wish to be cremated. One tenth of my ashes shall
be given to my agent, as written in our contract.**

Groucho Marx

Procurement management defines how the project manager purchases products or services from sellers outside the project. This is accomplished by developing and awarding a contract. There are many types of contracts, and the project manager selects the type that assigns to the seller both a reasonable risk and the greatest incentive for efficient and cost-effective performance.

We begin with the definition of a contract:

> *A contract is a mutually binding agreement that binds the seller to provide specified products and services, and also obligates the buyer to provide monetary or other valuable consideration.*

For a project, the contract will usually reference the scope document as the definition of what is to be provided. We note here that the scope not only includes the specification (the definition of the project), but also major milestones, schedule constraints, etc. Thus the scope becomes the fundamental basis of the contract, and every statement carries legal implications.

The above definition is a simplified version of that found in legal books.[1] The project manager is considered to be the *buyer* of the services and the contractor providing the goods or services is called the *seller*.

There are two contracts that the project manager must be aware of. The first is the contract for the project itself. That is, the project manager is probably working on a contract to deliver the project to the buyer. This contract defines what it is that the project manager must do. In this case, the project manager is the seller.

The second type of contract occurs during the execution of the project, when the project manager decides it is necessary to employ a third party to perform some of the work. This is called a subcontract, and the project manager is the buyer.

The fact that the project manager is both a seller and a buyer means the project manager has to understand all aspects of contracting, its terminology, and the different types of contracts. For the rest of this chapter, we will assume that the project manager is the buyer.

In order to pursue a subcontract, the project manager must have a clear description of the physical product or service to be delivered. Therefore, the project manager begins the subcontracting process by separating out a well-defined piece of the scope. Next, the project manager creates a Statement of Work (SOW), which is the most important contracting document.

When developing a subcontract, the project manager must answer the following questions:

1. What should we procure and how?

2. When should we procure it?

3. What type of contract will we use?

4. What metrics will we use to measure completion and success?

5. How will we administer the contract?

[1] Legal definitions add phrases such as "often in writing." We believe a PM needs practical guidance on contracts and we leave the legal technicalities to the lawyers.

The work to be completed may not be well specified. This occurs when someone is asked to analyze a problem where the answer is not known. In that case, the SOW should define the problem to be solved, along with goals and objectives and success criteria. The document that defines the goals is called a Statement of Objectives (SOO).

18.1 Contract Types

There are three broad categories of contracts:

1. *Fixed Price:* The contractor is awarded a total sum as payment for performing the project, no matter how much time, effort, and money it took to deliver the project.[2]

2. *Cost Reimbursable:* All legitimate project costs for performing the work of the project are reimbursed to the contractor. A fee (or profit) may also be added. This is also known as cost-plus contract.[3]

3. *Time and Materials:* The buyer pays a fixed hourly rate for the labor spent working on the project and also reimburses the contractor for all the materials and expenses associated with the project work.

A major theme of modern contracting involves the movement to *performance-based* contracting (PBC), where the project manager defines the desired results or outcomes. This is in contrast to *cost-plus* contracts, where one looks for best effort. When a contract is performance-based, the project manager must carefully define both the desired outcomes and the criteria for assessing the performance. Contract incentives (positive or negative, or both) are also included.

There are two major advantages of performance-based contracts. The first is that the seller can determine the best technical alternatives and the most cost effective approach. The second is that the buyer is relieved of detailed contract administration and can focus on helping the seller to achieve the specified goals. Incentive and award contracts are a good compromise for risky projects, which has accelerated the trend towards performance-based contracts.

Contractors may be awarded extra fees, i.e., incentives, for completing the project early, or for controlling costs. If the contractor finishes a project at a cost less than specified in the contract, the buyer and seller may split the savings. The opposite of incentives is *penalties*, which are imposed on the seller for poor performance.

Many variations and combinations of the basic three types are possible. The most frequent types of contracts a project manager will encounter are:

- *Firm Fixed Price (FFP) Contract:* The amount to be paid for the project is determined at the time the contract is signed. In this type of contract, the contractor bears all the risk. It is a very common contract type, because both the buyer and the seller want relative certainty as far as costs are concerned.

[2]While the total amount is fixed, it may be paid out over time.

[3]The key word here is *legitimate.* There are strict accounting and government rules and regulations for what is *legitimate.*

253

The buyer must be willing to put significant effort into providing a clear, well-defined specification. The seller must be willing to deliver the entire project for a firm fixed price.

FFP contracts work well when the project is well-defined and the specification is clear.

- *Fixed Price Plus Incentive Fee (FPIF) Contract:* This is similar to the FFP contract in that the conditions are determined at the time of signing the contract. However, the buyer is willing to give a bonus to the seller based on some clearly identified superior project performance. Performance criteria may include delivering ahead of the defined schedule or under the defined budget. Penalty clauses may be imposed for late delivery or cost overruns.

- *Costs Plus Fixed Fee (CPFF) Contract:* This provides for the reimbursement of all *allowable costs* plus the award of a fixed fee upon completion. This type of contract is common with projects in which the scope is uncertain, such as research and development contracts and many Department of Defense contracts.

- *Costs Plus Award Fee (CPAF) Contract:* This is also a cost-plus contract, except that instead of paying a fee, the buyer pays an award based on the buyer's evaluation of the seller's performance. The award amount is earned based on defined criteria, such as completion time, cost effectiveness, quality of work, or technical ingenuity.

  An important issue in a CPAF contract is: Who decides the amount of the award? If the criteria are subjective, the award fee may be determined by an independent external board. The award amount may also be based upon objective performance metrics, e.g., the range of a battery powered car or a web site response time with 1,000 users accessing it simultaneously.

- *Costs Plus Incentive Fee (CPIF) Contract:* This also provides for the reimbursement of contract costs, but the buyer is willing to award a fee if well-defined performance goals are met. For example, if the final cost of the project is less than the budgeted cost, the buyer and seller may share the savings based on a predetermined, legally documented incentive arrangement.

- *Cost Plus Percentage of Cost (CPPC) Contract:* This provides for the full reimbursement of allowable costs. The seller is also given a fee, which is an agreed percentage of the allowed project cost. In this type of contract, the buyer bears all the risk. It is used only when there is major uncertainty associated with the project.

The CPPC type of contract is banned in U.S. Federal Contracting and you can understand why.[1] There is no incentive for the contractor to hold down costs because the more they spend, the more money they receive.

CPPC is used only occasionally in the commercial sector. For example, in the pharmaceutical industry, there is so much uncertainty and risk when searching for a new drug that only the CPPC contract type provides the appropriate motivation for contractors to take on the work.

18.2 Selecting a Contract

When selecting a contract, the project manager must balance the risks versus the available information.

18.2.1 Fixed Price Contracts

In a *Fixed Price* contract, the seller agrees to pay a fixed amount to the seller. Usually the seller requests a certain percentage at the start (or award) of the contract and progress payments tied to major deliverables. The buyer will usually hold back a certain amount until the job is successfully completed.

For large contracts, a third party may be employed to define when the seller's work is satisfactorily complete. This is called a Validation and Verification contractor.

The installment payments are often driven by the seller's cash flow. For example, in the New Kitchen contract, Mark requested major payments when he was facing expensive purchases. One such contract condition was: *$3,000 at delivery of blueboard.* Since the purchase of blueboard was a major expense, Mark inserted a provision for a payment at that time.[4]

Table 18.1 shows the positive and negative incentives of a fixed price contract from both the buyer's and seller's perspectives. For the project manager, an FP contract is a good choice when there is an excellent specification.

18.2.2 Cost-Plus Contracts

In a *cost-plus* contract, the seller is reimbursed for all allowable costs, which include labor, materials, and travel. The seller must have an audited overhead rate, which determines the rate at which overhead costs are reimbursed by the buyer. The seller also receives an additional prior-negotiated fee, which is often set as a percentage of the initially specified contract cost.

[4]Notice Mark did not specify a date, but tied the payment to a deliverable. If Mark accelerated the schedule, he would still receive a payment when he needed to pay for the blueboard.

Table 18.1: The positive and negative aspects of a fixed price contract.

Buyer's Perspective	
Advantages	**Disadvantages**
Predictable, known cost	More costly to prepare
Incentives for lower cost	Requires a good spec & knowledge of needs
	Mistakes in the spec are costly
	Incentive for fast completion at lowest cost
	May require contingency costs
Seller's Perspective	
Advantages	**Disadvantages**
Potentially larger fee	Underestimated costs mean a loss

For example, suppose you negotiate a CPFF contract with a cost of $100,000 and a $6,000 fee (6%). The total contract cost is $106,000. You successfully perform the project and your costs are $90,000. The buyer audits your project, and your overhead rate, and agrees that these are all legitimate costs. You receive $90,000 for the costs, plus your fixed fee of $6,000. Since the fee was "fixed," your fee rate is actually: $6K/$90K = 6.7%.[5]

On the other hand, suppose you successfully perform the project but your costs are $200,000. The buyer audits your project and your overhead rate and agrees that these are all legitimate costs. You receive $200,000 for the costs, plus your fee of $6,000. In this case, you do not lose money, but your boss will probably be unhappy that your fee rate is down to 3% ($6,000/200,000 = 3\%$).

The major disadvantage with cost plus contracts is that the buyer must rely on the seller's best efforts to contain costs. Table 18.2 shows the positive and negative incentives of a cost plus contract from both the buyer's and seller's perspectives.

18.2.3 Incentive Fee Contract Example

The best way to understand an incentive fee contract is through an example.

The project manager of the PMA website decides to subcontract out the work of building the web site. The project manager prepares a detailed scope document, including a Statement of Work. The project manager uses a macro estimation formula to determine a cost of $10,000. The project manager then assesses all the risks and decides that a creative subcontractor might get the job done for less. But the project manager also needs to be able to establish a firm budget, which will not exceed $13,000.

[5]You need to check the contract carefully to determine if what was "fixed" was the fee in dollars or the percentage.

Table 18.2: The positive and negative aspects of a cost plus contract.

Buyer's Perspective	
Advantages	**Disadvantages**
Maximum Flexibility	Relies on seller's best efforts to contain costs
Minimizes early negotiation costs	No assurances of actual cost
Eases selection of best-qualified rather than lowest bid	
Allows use of same contractor for design and implementation	
Seller's Perspective	
Advantages	**Disadvantages**
Can undertake risky efforts	High costs reduce profitability & fee percent
Can undertake long projects	

The project manager therefore selects a CPIF contract with a 70%/30% sharing of the savings. The budgeted cost is $10,000 and the project manager proposes that a profit of 10% will be a sufficient incentive for sellers to take on this small job. The contract summary is shown below.

Target Price:	$11,000
Target Cost:	$10,000
Target Fee (or Profit):	$1,000
Contract Ceiling:	$13,000
Profit / Loss Sharing:	Seller Share: 30%
	Buyer Share: 70%

We now explore what happens in the following scenarios:

Case 1: Under Run

The subcontractor completes the contract at a cost of $8,000, i.e., less than the originally budgeted cost of $10,000. The fee, or profit, calculation is:

Seller Cost:	$8,000
Cost Savings:	$2,000
Profit / Loss Sharing:	Seller Share: 30% of $2,000 = $600
	Buyer Share: 70% of $2,000 = $1,400
Seller Profit:	$1,000 + $600 = $1,600
Contract Price:	$8,000 + $1,400 = $9,400

We note that incentive fee contract calculations are based on the costs, since these are always auditable and verifiable. In this case, the seller made an additional profit of $600, while the buyer's total cost is $9,400. Notice that the seller receives the agreed fee ($1,000) as well as a share of the cost saings, which in this case was $600.

Case 2: Over Run

The subcontractor completes the contract at a cost of $11,000, i.e., more than the originally budgeted cost of $10,000. The fee, or profit, calculation is as follows:

Seller Cost:	$11,000
Cost Savings:	-$1,000
Profit / Loss Sharing:	
	Seller Share: 30% of -$1,000 = -$300
	Buyer Share: 70% of -$1,000 = -$700
Seller Profit:	$1,000 - $300 = $700
Contract Price:	$11,000 + $700 = $11,700

In this case, the seller made a slightly smaller profit of $700. The buyer's total cost is $11,700, which consists of the costs ($11,000) plus the reduced profit.

Case 3: Exceeding the Ceiling!

The seller's cost is $15,000. The buyer informs the seller that the contract ceiling is $13,000 and so the buyer receives only $13,000. The seller has lost $2,000 on the contract, and these costs will have to be paid by the seller's company.

Case 4: Low Risk

If the project were not very risky, then the percentage share of the profit might be adjusted. For a low risk project, the buyer might adjust the share to a 30%/70% ratio, so that the contractor gets less in the case of an overrun. Using a 30%/70%, Case 2 becomes:

Seller Cost:	$11,000
Cost Savings:	-$1,000
Profit / Loss Sharing:	
	Seller Share: 70% of -$1,000 = -$700
	Buyer Share: 30% of -$1,000 = -$300
Seller Profit:	$1,000 - $700 = $300
Contract Price:	$11,000 + $300 = $11,300

The seller's profit is reduced significantly.

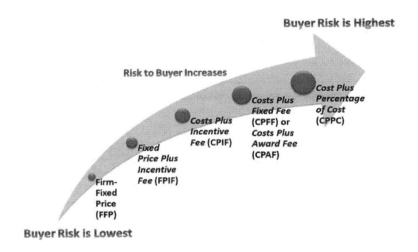

Figure 18.1: Buyer risk versus contract type.

18.2.4 The Scope and Contract Types

There is direct relationship between the quality of the project scope (and particularly the specification) and the type of contract that should be employed. The specification defines what is to be produced, so when the specification is well-defined, the buyer is in a position to request a fixed price contract. If the specification is incomplete, or is or risky, the buyer should move towards a cost-plus contract.

The buyer risk versus contract type is shown in Figure 18.1. Buyer risk is lowest for fixed price contracts, because the cost is known in advance. The buyer risk increases for cost plus contracts because the seller's costs are not known, and may increase as the specification is refined.

The seller's risks are shown in Figure 18.2. Sellers have more risk on a fixed price contract because they must specify the bid in advance, with only the scope document to go on. Seller risk is lower for a cost-plus contract, because they will be reimbursed for all contract costs.

18.2.5 Statement of Work

The major effort in preparing a contract is the preparation of the Statement of Work (SOW). It contains the tasks to be completed and who is to perform them. The SOW usually defines the milestones and deliverables, as well as the reporting procedures.

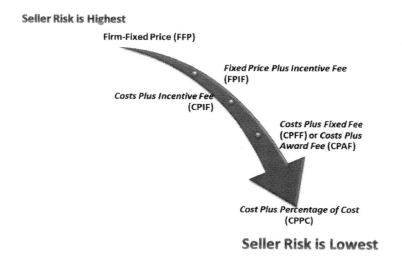

Figure 18.2: Seller risk versus contract type.

Another important piece of the SOW is the payment schedule, as this defines the cash flow needs.

Table 18.3 shows an example of a Statement of Work for the PMA contract.

Table 18.3: Statement of Work for the PMA contract.

Statement of Work for the PMA Project
Project Manager: Dr. Vijay Kanabar Project Start Date: March 10th, 2010 Projected Finish Date: April 25th, 2010

Project Objectives:

The PMA web site is a social network site dedicated to all BU students interested in project management, including alumni. The primary stakeholders are students interested in becoming certified as PMPs, as well as those wishing to maintain their certification status. The website provides a channel for PMPs to earn PDU's to maintain their certification. Other stakeholders include any students interested in PM who will benefit from the website.

It is conceivable that a non-BU audience interested in the field of project management will access the site. Therefore, the website will have resources that anyone can use, such as templates, links to project management websites, and links to interesting research.

Only the following personal information will be captured and maintained: First name, last name, email address. The email address will act as proof of a current or past BU association. MailChimp will be used to store all student names and email addresses, because it comes with a built-in database. Students with data in the system will be considered to be *registered*.

The web site will have a designated *Director*, who will email to registered students: the newsletter and special information such as job postings and internships. Students will be requested to link to resources such as Facebook, Wordpress, and Linkedin. Jobs and internships will also be posted.

While we are not dictating functionality, Social Networking site features that will be useful to members are: A News and Announcements Section; User Blogs and Forums; a Reading Room (document repository); an Event Calendar; BU TV PM related videos; Resource Links – split into two PM and IT PM categories; a link to the Project Management in Practice Conference website; Job tips and opportunities; PMP Certification links and resources; PM templates and papers; and an "Ask the Expert" feature, for users to post questions about their projects and receive advice from other PMA members.

Budget Information:

Hosting investment has already been made for this site to the tune of $200 per year. The majority of costs for this project will be internal labor. An initial estimate provides a total of 40 hours per week per team. Other proposed budget items will be considered.

19

ETHICS

Relativity applies to physics, not ethics

Albert Einstein

Ethics plays an important role in project management. The Project Management Institute (PMI) continually stresses that ethics is an integral part of the project management profession and has defined a rigorous *Code of Ethics and Professional Conduct*, which we will refer to as the *code*. [25]

PMI has emphasized their position by including questions about ethics in the PMP exam. In addition, PMPs are continually held accountable to the *code*.

The *code* defines the rules for the professional practice of project management. More important from a practical perspective is that it communicates to stakeholders the values and standards that project management professionals will bring to their work. Values that the PMI community defined as most important were responsibility, respect, fairness, and honesty. [30]

Some of the more interesting aspects of the *code*, at least to us, are:

- We do what we say we will do.[1]

- When we make errors, we own up promptly, accept responsibility, and make amends.

[1] Since we are both PMPs, the word "we" applies to us, too.

- We listen to others' points of view.

- We negotiate in good faith.

- We provide accurate information in a timely manner.[2]

- We disclose conflicts of interest of stakeholders.

- We report unethical or illegal conduct.[3]

In a 2010 PMI Member survey, awareness of the *code* rose to 83%, and virtually everyone found it useful in helping to resolve ethical issues. Ethics is not just a theoretical concept. The practical implications are illustrated by the fact that 'loss of trust' was cited as a major reason motivating workers to seek new jobs.

19.1 An Example of an Ethical Issue

You are the project manager holding a team staff meeting. In last week's meeting, the Technical Director (TD) reported that his design group had run into technical difficulties, which had resulted in a delay of a deliverable. You assigned the Assistant Project Manager (APM) the task of determining the impact on the cost and schedule.

In this week's staff meeting, the TD said that the design issues were now resolved. The APM reported that the because of the delays, the new $CPI = 0.93$. The APM projected a small, but significant, overrun in both the budget and the schedule.

In a staff meeting, the following conversation took place between the TD and the APM:

TD: The technical issues are resolved and we will be able to get back on track. I don't foresee this as a problem.

APM: The issue was an error in the spec. The $CPI = 0.93$, which reflects the true productivity. We should not assume that was the only spec error. We should inform the customer.

TD: It is way too early to go to the customer. We have fixed the only error.

APM: We owe it to the customer to explain the situation.

TD: We don't want to bother the customer yet. It will work out.

As the project manager, what do you do?[4]

First, let's discuss some of the surrounding issues:

[2]Emphasizing, once again, the political overtones of the cost and schedule.

[3]The real challenge is not just to behave ethically yourself, but to report unethical conduct. What do you do if your good friend is behaving unethically?

[4]*Beware! This is not an easy question.*

264

- *Legal vs. Ethical:* We should immediately remove any legal issues. Nobody in this meeting is suggesting that the team should deliberately hide data, pad estimates, or engage in dubious behavior. If that were to happen, the approach of the project manager is clear: Call the police!

- *Difficult vs. Ethical:* Not all difficult decisions involve ethical issues. For example, a really difficult decision that project managers often face is to lay someone off (perhaps their task is complete, and there is no more work). This would indeed be difficult for anyone, but if there is no money to hire someone, it is inevitable. Although difficult, we would not consider this an ethical dilemma.[5]

- *Competence:* We assume that all of the actors are well qualified and that their conclusions are based on reasonable data and informed opinion.

- *Integrity:* All actors are behaving well and genuinely believe in their respective positions.

Project management is complicated and invariably involves many gray areas of judgment and interpretation. For example, let's examine the claim of the TD that he can make up the cost and schedule. Consider the following alternatives:

1. The TD is deliberately falsifying his estimate.

2. The TD has made an error in his estimate.

3. The TD is exaggerating his estimate due to optimism.

4. The TD believes that he can complete the project within his estimate.

We suggest the first three interpretations of the TD's behavior are: illegal (#1), incompetent (#2), and dumb (#3). The fourth is legitimate, but creates an ethical dilemma. How does the project manager proceed? At this point, some terminology is required. First, we define an ethical dilemma as:

> *An ethical dilemma is one in which it is difficult to decide on the right outcome.*

An ethical dilemma is usually a complex situation that involves a choice. Often however, the issue is not resolved by the selection of *any* of the alternatives. Part of

[5]We often say that laying off good people is the hardest thing we've ever had to do.

265

the complication is that your ethics are your own *personal* standards of right and wrong.[6]

It's not just about opinions and personal differences, and here's at least one reason why: There are two approaches to ethical decisions that philosophers use in handling ethical dilemmas:[7]

1. *Deontology:*

   Deontology is from the Greek "deon" meaning duty, and "logos" meaning logic. Deontology is therefore the study of ethics based on *duty*. You do it because you think it is "right." The basic duties are usually considered to be:

Fidelity	Keeping promises
Reparation	Righting the wrongs you've done
Justice	Distributing goods equitably
Beneficence	Improving the lot of others
Self-Improvement	Improving one's own intelligence and virtue
Gratitude	Exhibiting when appropriate
Non-injury	Avoiding injury to others

2. *Teleology:*

   Teleology is from the Greek "telos" meaning end, and "logos" meaning logic. Teleology is therefore the study of ethics based on *the end result*. This is often summarized as "The end justifies the means." You evaluate whether the decision is a good one by examining the consequences or outcomes. Correct actions produce the most good, while wrong actions do not contribute to the general good. Outcomes are usually classified as:

Egoism	Focusing on self-interest goals, and asking if the action benefits oneself.
Utilitarianism	Operating in the public interest rather than for personal benefit.
Altruism	Maximizing the benefits of some, even at the expense of oneself.

[6]And, of course, quite different from everyone else's.

[7]Our intent is not to debate philosophy, but to provide practical guidance.

Altruism is generally regarded as the highest moral virtue. Notice that Deontology and Teleology are alternative views, and that neither is right nor wrong. They are different approaches to an issue.

266

A project manager must be able to recognize and understand these different world views in order to understand conflicts within the team. If two people are arguing from two different sets of ideals, then it is difficult for them to compromise—they both think they are right.[8]

19.2 More Ethical Examples

A student was explaining to the class that his company had not reported their earnings correctly. He was carefully explaining the rationale for dealing with the failure by updating the latest reports and explaining the legal and political issues.

Suddenly, another student yelled, "That's just wrong!"

Everyone immediately took sides and chaos ensued. This is a classic example of an ethical issue.

The students were approaching the problem from two different ethical points of view. The first student was going through the *teleological* argument: Justifying company actions by the idea that it would be OK in the end. Meanwhile, the second student reacted from the *deontological* viewpoint: It's just not right!

This is a good example of the dilemma faced by a project manager. The project manager (in this case the teacher) needs to understand that the two students have completely different world views and it is unlikely they will agree. Proposing a compromise is unlikely to work in this situation.

In our experience, progress can only be made when everyone understands the difference between Deontology and Teleology, and that there are two legitimate, but different, points of view.[9] Notice that we are not presenting an easy fix. All we can say is that when people understand the different ethical approaches, they can begin to work on the practical issue: Shall we tell the customer?

Here's an approach that produces interesting discussions and helps to resolve the issue: The deontological camp tends to take a righteous stand and refuse to compromise. Therefore, pick a member of the other—the teleological—camp and try to modify the issue gradually until they reach the point of saying, 'That would be wrong!' At that point they have reached a deontological truth, and often begin to understand the other point of view.

Then, take the opposite approach: Move the deontologists until they are in the teleology camp. Once the camps begin understand each other, the project manager can get back to discussing the cost and schedule!

[8]And they both will be right!

[9]The next time someone asks you what you learned in your project management class, you can say 'I learned the difference between deontology and teleology!'

Here's another example from a classroom discussion. Students were asked to list things they thought were of personal importance. Nestor[1] said:

"I always call my mother on Sundays."

How do we classify this? Deontology or Teleology? I asked Nestor why he did that and he quietly said, "It's the right thing to do." He clearly regarded it as his *duty* to call his Mom on Sundays. Nestor was practicing Deontology.

Suppose you tried to convince Nestor to go out and get some Pizza and that he really doesn't need to call his Mom this week. You might suggest that his Mom won't mind if he misses a week and that his Mom will understand that he's busy.

In fact, when I tried this in class, Nestor just sighed, looked down, and politely shook his head. "I have to," he said. When someone is motivated by duty they will (strongly!) resist attempts to make them change their behavior, especially if you are using an *end-justifies-the-means* argument.

Here's another example: Julie said:

"I always do my homework."

I asked Julie, "Why?" She said, "I want to get a good grade." Julie was not doing her homework because she thought it was her duty to do so, she was doing it because of the end result—a good grade. Julie was practicing Teleology.

It is important to realize that the same action can result from different ethical perspectives. Two different students said:

"I am always good to my classmates."

When asked, "Why?" one student said, "It is the right thing to do." (Deontology) The other student said, "Because they will be good to me in return." (Teleology) Here we have two students with the same action, but motivated by completely different ethical perspectives.

19.2.1 TD vs. PM Revisited

We now have the vocabulary to discuss the debate between the APM and the TD. Table 19.1 provides a summary of the ethical positions on whether to inform the customer about a possible schedule slip.

Both actors are approaching the issue from a sound ethical position. The project manager must recognize when team members believe that they are operating ethically, because an attempt at compromise might be viewed as an attack on their integrity.

Table 19.1: An *Ethical* Summary of the TD and APM positions.

Role	Argument	Ethical Position
TD	I don't expect any more issues. We will get back on track	The outcome justifies the position —Teleology
APM	We owe it to the customer to explain the situation.	It is our duty —Deontology

It might be impossible for the project manager to resolve this issue.[10]

19.2.2 Ethical Situations Test

Look at Table 19.2. Decide on whether the issue in the left hand column is an "ethical dilemma" or not.

Hint: When analyzing you need to pay very careful attention to the words and think about them. Don't rush in.

We emphasize that in Table 19.2, we are giving our *opinion*. It is guidance and there may be situations where you disagree.[11]

Answering questions on ethics, more than any other topic, involves a very careful inspection of the precise words used and an understanding of terminology. Complicating the situation is the fact that the audience may come from different cultural perspectives.[12]

Ethical issues require a subtle and patient approach on the part of the project manager, as emotions can run high on questions of integrity. A calm, unemotional presentation usually works best.

19.2.3 Sleeping at Night

As a final comment, we note that making the right ethical decision is a personal issue. At some point in your career, you will be confronted with a very difficult choice, such as:[13]

- Should you quit a good job and risk your family's well being because you are uncomfortable with management?

- Should you tell what you know and risk censure or, even, being fired?

The only advice we can offer is that you are the one who has to sleep at night. Only you can make this decision. Only you will know whether you sleep peacefully.

[10] This is one of the few times when we freely admit that we do not have an answer. All the project manager can do is to make everyone aware of the issues and the ethical choices. People will have great difficulty compromising on these types of issues.

[11] As always, you can disagree, but you have to back up your claim.

[12] PMI is often accused of imposing U.S. ethics on the world, a criticism with which we sympathize.

[13] Beware! Fate has a way of constructing the exact situation guaranteed to give you the most discomfort.

Table 19.2: Ethical Issues Test.

Issue	Ethical Dilemma?
Padding a cost estimate because you know the customer can afford it.	Not really–this is basically lying. You have a responsibility to make money. The key word here is "padding," implying a deliberate act, hence lying.
Report an environmental violation by your own company.	Yes. A classic ethical dilemma. You have a conflict: 1) Company loyalty, which may even be protected by legal non-disclosure agreements. 2) A desire to do the right and honorable thing.
You discover confidential information in the copier. Do you report it?	This is not an ethical dilemma. The right thing to do is to report it. It may be your own salary review (tricky!), but using the information is wrong.
Approving sub-standard work to shorten the schedule.	No. This is a difficult decision, but not an ethical dilemma. Do not approve the work. Take the cost and schedule hit.
Changing the schedule due to pressure from your boss.	This is an ethical dilemma that depends on circumstances. You and your boss disagreed, but she insisted you report her version to the client—a genuine ethical dilemma. If your boss pressures you, then the path is clear: Tell the truth!
Assuring customers the project is on track when you suspect it's not	Trick Question! We deliberately added the word "suspect." The answer depends on why you *suspect* the project is late. A "gut feeling" you do not have to report. If it is based on earned value, you should report it.
Falsifying the schedule data.	No! This is not an ethical dilemma. It is just plain unethical, and maybe even illegal.
You listen to your team about the schedule and report the optimistic case to your boss.	Yes. This is an ethical dilemma. If you lie, then it's not an ethical dilemma. If there is genuine disagreement among the team, and you believe you can accelerate the schedule (for valid reasons!), it might be OK to report the optimistic version.
Firing a problem employee.	This may be an ethical dilemma, depending on the "problem." If he is simply annoying, it is wrong to fire him, and the right path is to work with him. If he disrupts the team, it might be best to remove him.
An employee tests positive for an illegal drug. Do you fire them?	Not an ethical dilemma. Nasty perhaps, but not ethical. The company policy should be clear on this. Unless you discover the test results accidentally, then you have ethical issues.
Accelerating progress by ignoring standards.	Not an ethical dilemma. Probably illegal.

Part III

The Examples

20

A New Kitchen

> You're not using that project management stuff on me, are you?
>
> *Eileen Warburton*

In this chapter we follow a project through all its phases, and give examples of the essential project management tools and techniques.

20.1 Conceptual Development

Like many projects in our house, it all started with a book: *The Not So Big House*, by Sarah Susanka.[1] [31] Sarah is a brilliant architect, who suggests that most people do not need a bigger house, they need to examine the way they live, and how they use their existing space. The key idea is that many houses have "dead spaces," and rethinking their use can lead to innovative redesign. That proved true.

In the summer of 2009, we began reading Sarah's books and discussing the kitchen project. Except that at this stage, it was not yet a project. It would take a year to get to preliminary planning.[1]

Figure 20.1 shows a plan of the house before construction. The kitchen had old units and appliances and Eileen had been campaigning for a while to redo it.[2] We never used the 'fireplace room,' which looked over the street and was dark. The

[1] Projects do not spring fully formed from nothing. They begin with an idea, which is explored and worked on until it begins to look like a project.

[2] *The Not So Big House* inspired her

273

living room looked over the garden and was a much nicer room in all respects. Eileen's key realization was that the fireplace room was dead space and could go![3]

Figure 20.1: Conceptual plan. The dotted lines show the proposed new position of the kitchen and closet walls. The arrow indicates the goal of creating a sight line from the front door through to the garden.

The second key idea emerged when we admitted that the garage was really a *1.8 car garage*. It was never going to hold two cars! The chimney was awkwardly placed and so Eileen proposed to expand the kitchen in two directions: Into the garage to create a pantry; and, into the fireplace room to generate more space. We needed an architect.

20.1.1 The Requirements Analysis Phase

We knew that we did not yet have a project. We did not know enough to define the project—we needed to develop the requirements: What did we want?[4]

We needed to answer the following questions: Is a new kitchen design possible? Can the chimney be eliminated? Will the new garage space reasonably hold one car? Also, we needed a rough cost estimate.[5]

Therefore, in late September 2010 we selected an architect, Scott, who had re-designed several rooms in a friend's house, and we liked what we saw. Thus began

[3]Of course, this plan did not exist back then. It is used here to explain the problem.

[4]One of the first mistakes that people often make, is that they assume they have one project, when they really have two or more. In this case, there are at least two projects. The first project is to answer the question, 'What is the kitchen project?'

[5]Requirements analysis requires preliminary design work because the purpose of the requirements phase is to produce a *feasible* project.
    The project must be both technically and financially feasible: the design must resolve all (or most) of the issues; and the cost must be affordable. You cannot simply list a series of wants and desires, the resulting project will almost certainly be unaffordable.

the pre-kitchen project, which we refer to here as *Pre-K.*

The goal of *pre-K* was to specify the kitchen project.[6] We invited Scott to look around and discuss the project. We liked him immediately. Scott did not freak out at the over-stuffed bookcases everywhere. He also indicated that he "liked the challenge" of our particular problem. Scott sent us a contract and we signed it.

We then had a requirements session. We discussed everything we thought we might want, the idea being that Scott should design everything. We could eliminate things later if the cost was too high (which of course, it was!). However, it would be much harder to add to the design later. We also discussed planning issues, such as breaking the work into phases, the cost, and the schedule.

We ran into our first problem: Scott explained that he did not do cost estimates or schedules, and neither was he good at detailed kitchen layout. We would need a kitchen designer to do that. This required a new plan for the *pre-K* project. Scott would produce a preliminary design, which we would discuss and evaluate. Then we would put the kitchen project out to bid to three contractors. After we had selected the contractor, all of us together would modify the plans and produce a complete specification for the job.[7]

The immediate impact was that the *pre-K* project had just become much longer. Scott's design would take 4-6 weeks, and the bidding process would take another month. That put us into December, 2010. Nothing much happens in December, so a realistic date for contractor selection was January, 2011. The next step was that we would all meet and revise the plans; probably have to go through a bid modification; develop new plans; and get the loan.

In October 2010, we realized that the kitchen project would not start before March, 2011. Scott went ahead and produced the preliminary design, Figure 20.2. While we made some major changes, we were thrilled.[8] Scott had several new ideas, which we thought were excellent, but the "lav" in the middle of the kitchen had to go. However, Scott's proposal to move the front door to get a clear line of sight all the way to the rear windows was an excellent idea.

20.1.2 The Bidding Cycle

We invited three contractors to bid. Scott recommended someone from up-state and we contacted two locals that we knew.

The up-state guy was the first to visit and a week later delivered an outrageously expensive bid. We eliminated him.[9] His bid was simply a one-page statement of the cost. While not very useful for our purposes, it was interesting from a project

[6] You have to iterate. In fancy project management language, the project is progressively elaborated. You produce a rough design and estimate the cost and schedule. You modify the design (usually to reduce the cost!), and try again.

[7] I would get to referee a bidding cycle. Cool!

[8] Our fantasy of a new upper-floor bedroom was quickly eliminated by the cost!

[9] The bidding process is not just about cost, it is also about evaluating potential bidders. Can you work with them? In the case of the up-state guy, the answer was a comfortable, 'No'.

275

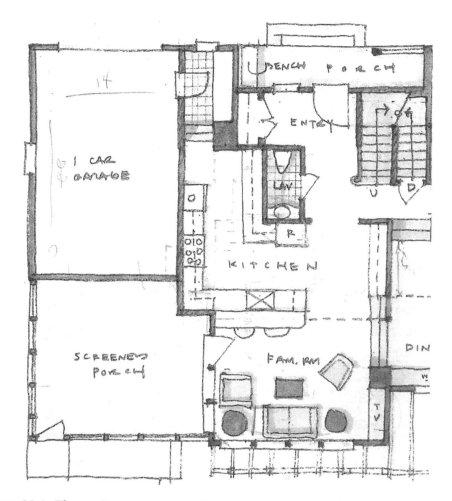

Figure 20.2: The preliminary design for the new kitchen, which was used for the bidding cycle. The lav in the middle of the kitchen had to go!

management perspective, it was a classic macro estimate: He simply measured the square footage of the job and multiplied by $200 per square foot.

The two local contractors walked through the house, discussed the project, and examined the plans. Both were pleasant, eager for the work, and had creative suggestions. Joe had done a large addition for a friend of ours and was well thought of around town. Mark had done some work for us before and his finish work is excellent. He is smart, courteous and a great planner. We thought it was going to be a tough decision and felt bad that we would have to choose.

Two weeks after the walk through, Mark produced a 10-page bid, carefully laid out with multiple options. Each piece was clearly explained and estimated. Mark also suggested several cost saving measures, and proposed a kitchen designer he had used in the past for the detailed kitchen layout. It was a well thought out bid.

Joe did not get back to us, so we called him again. He said he was working on it. A week later, we had still not heard from Joe, and with the holidays approaching, we decided to go with Mark. We called Mark, he came over and we congratulated him. We also felt good about the whole process.[10]

The next step was the production of a detailed design, which would involve the architect, the contractor, and us. Scott estimated that it would take a couple of months. From Scott's design, Mark would produce a detailed cost estimate, to be followed by the bank financing activity, which would take 4-6 weeks.

We had all the elements: The detail design provided the scope; Mark had produced a rough cost estimate, which was within our budget; and the schedule was realistic.

We now had a project!

20.1.3 The Charter

The charter is the next step, it grants authority to the project manager to spend money and assign resources. [11] The Charter for the new kitchen project is shown in Figure 20.3.

---

1. Increase the kitchen size by moving the garage wall and the fireplace room wall.
2. Create a walk-in pantry.
3. Create a one-car garage.
4. Re-purpose little used spaces.
5. Create lines of sight from the front door through the kitchen.
6. New doors and windows to let in more light as appropriate.
7. Investigate more efficient utilities.
8. Cost: Budget $60,000 plus appliances.
9. Schedule: Begin indoor work around March 1st. Outdoor work as weather permits. Work essentially complete within 6 months to comply with city permit restrictions.

Figure 20.3: *Charter* for the New Kitchen project.

[10] One of the key ideas of the bidding cycle is that you end up comfortable with the contractor you have selected. It is not just about the cost.

[11] Before a project can formally begin, a *Charter* must be created and a project manager assigned. This is the preferred order, but few projects follow it.

20.2 The Scope

Few things are harder to put up with than the annoyance of a good example.

Mark Twain

In Figure 7.2, we provided a scope statement for the kitchen project. For convenience, we duplicate it here as Figure 20.4.

Figure 20.2 showed a part of the preliminary design for the kitchen. The diagram showed a new screened in porch, which was eliminated as too expensive during cost estimation.[12] The detailed design, which is shown in Figure 20.5, is part of the detailed specification of the project.

Here we see an example of the scope being refined—progressive elaboration. The scope evolved from concept design, through preliminary design and, finally, detailed design. Note that there is little scope creep (the project did not grow in scale), it was merely refined.

20.2.1 Deliverables

Deliverables include:

- The Scope. This actually consisted of three separate deliverables: The Concept Design, the Preliminary Design, and the Detailed Design.

- Cost Estimate. A multi-page spreadsheet of the estimated costs.

- Cabinets.[13] The cabinets turned out to have the longest delivery time, so determined the critical path, i.e., the schedule.

20.2.2 Milestones

Milestones included:

- Demolition Complete. Estimated March 31st.

- Gas line installed. Estimated April 15th.

- Cabinet Delivery. Estimated July 1st.

[12] This is a good example of a *Technical Requirement:* The existing deck was sound, but not within the new code, which required that any small change would require an entirely new deck.

[13] These turned out to be a big deal.

New Kitchen Scope Statement

Objective:
To renovate a kitchen within 6 months at cost not to exceed $63,000.

Justification:
Old cabinets and small workspace.
Unused spaces of little value.

Deliverables:
Conceptual Design and the Detailed Design.
Sheet rock (Partial Payment required).
Cabinets.

Milestones:
Demolition Complete	Estimated March 31st.
Gas line installed	Estimated April 15th.
Cabinet Delivery	Estimated July 1st.

Specification:
See Figure 20.2 and associated discussion.

Cost Estimate:
See spreadsheet of the estimated costs. Cost estimate $63,000.

Risks:
   Cabinet Delivery: Schedule Risk.

Limits and Exclusions:
Contractor responsible for all construction permits.

Constraints:
Schedule: Work substantially complete for guests arriving September 1st.

Assumptions:
Contractor responsible for all subcontractors and their costs.
Painting not included in the bid.

Technical Requirements:
Architect responsible for all safety and loading requirements.
All construction to be consistent with local regulations and codes: carpentry, plumbing, electrical, safety, environmental, etc.

Customer Reviews:
Monthly meetings with Joan Smith (PM) and John Smith (Sponsor).

Figure 20.4: *Scope Statement* for the New Kitchen project.

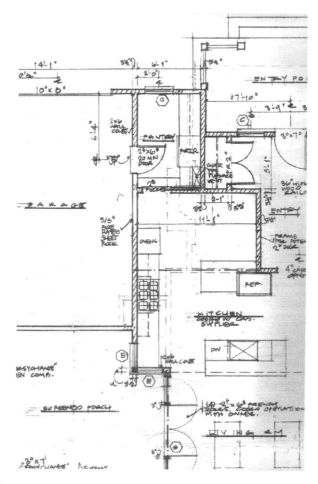

Figure 20.5: The detailed design—the specification—shows the new entry room closet, pantry, and kitchen island.

20.3 WBS

The high level WBS is given in graphical form in Figure 20.6. This is suitable for managing the project and estimating the costs.

The low level WBS is given in outline form in Figure 20.7. This is suitable for managing the project and estimating the costs.

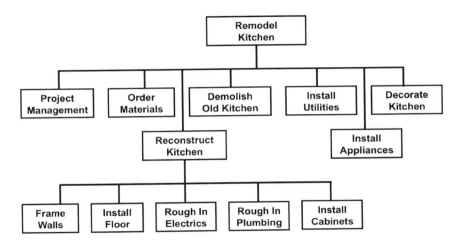

Figure 20.6: The graphical form of the WBS.

```
0    Kitchen
   1.    Plan Project
         1.1    Obtain Loan
         1.2    Obtain Permit
         1.3    Detailed Architectural Plan
         1.4    Detailed Cost Estimate
   2.    Order Everything
         2.1    Select & Order Cabinets
         2.2    Select & Appliances
   3.    Demolish Old Kitchen
   4.    Manage Utilities
         4.1    Install Rough Plumbing
         4.2    Install Rough Electrics
         4.3    Install Appliances
                4.3.1    Install Gas Range
                4.3.2    Install Refrigerator
                4.3.3    Install Appliances
                         4.3.3.1    Install Dishwasher
                         4.3.3.2    Install Garbage Disposal
         4.4    Finalize Utilities
                4.4.1    Install Lights
                4.4.2    Install Refrigerator
                4.4.3    Install Electric Appliances
   5.    Do Carpentry
         5.1    Install Floor
         5.2    Install Frame Walls
         5.3    Install Blueboard
         5.4    Install Under Floor Heating
   6.    Decorate Kitchen
         6.1    Plaster Walls
         6.2    Paint Walls
         6.3    Install Floor
         6.4    Install Counter Tops
```

Figure 20.7: WBS in outline format for the New Kitchen project.

20.4 Cost Estimate

The cost estimate is shown in Table 20.1.

Table 20.1: The cost estimate for the new kitchen

Code	Item	Cost
1.0	Plan Project	
1.1	Obtain Loan	
1.2	Obtain Permit	$3,000
1.3	Architectural Plan	$5,000
1.4	Cost Estimate	$35,000
2.0	Order Everything	
2.1	Select & Order Cabinets	$10,000
2.2	Select & Order Appliances	$7,500
3.	Demolish Old Kitchen	
4.	Manage Utilities	
4.1	Install Rough Plumbing	
4.2	Install Rough Electrics	
4.3	Install Appliances	
4.4	Finalize Utilities	
5.	Carpentry	
6.	Decorate Kitchen	
6.3	Install Floor	$1,500
6.4	Install Counter Tops	$1,000
	Total Cost	**$63,000**

We were already over budget.

20.5 The Network Diagram

The first step in the creation of the network diagram is the development of the Table of Activity Times and Predecessors—Table 20.2. The most important aspect of the table is the estimated activity times. The predecessors are the first pass in the design of the schedule and will change as the schedule evolves.

From Table 20.2, we developed the network diagram using Microsoft Project®. The overall look of the Gantt chart is shown in Figure 20.8.

In Figure 20.9, the Gantt chart for the end of the project is blown up to show the interaction of the activities. Microsoft Project can also output a network diagram, and examples of this are shown in Figures 20.10 and 20.11.

Table 20.2: The time estimates for the activities in the new kitchen

Code	Item	Predecessors	Time (days)
1.0	Plan Project	None	
1.1	Obtain Loan	None	30
1.2	Obtain Permit	1.3	30
1.3	Architectural Plan	None	30
1.4	Cost Estimate	1.3	14
1.5	Project Approval	1.1, 1.2, 1.3, 1.4	0
2.0	Order Everything		
2.1	Select & Order Cabinets	5.2	60
2.2	Select & Order Appliances	1.5	10
2.3	Select & Order Counter	1.5	60
3.	Demolish Old Kitchen	1.5	10
4.	Manage Utilities		
4.1	Install Rough Plumbing	3.0	5
4.2	Install Rough Electrics	3.0	3
4.3	Install Cabinets	4.1, 4.2	4
4.4	Install Appliances	5.1, 6.1	2
4.4.1	Install Gas Range	5.1, 6.1	1
4.4.2	Install Refrigerator	5.1, 6.1	1
4.4.3	Install Appliances		
4.4.3.1	Install Dishwasher	5.1, 6.1	1
4.4.3.2	Install Garbage Disposal	5.1, 6.1	1
4.4.4	Appliances Complete	4.3, 4.4	0
5.0	Do Carpentry		
5.1	Install Floor		3
5.2	Install Frame Walls	3.0	10
5.3	Install Blueboard	5.2, 4.1, 4.2	5
5.4	Install Under Floor Heating	5.2, 4.1, 4.2	2
6.0	Decorate Kitchen		
6.1	Plaster Walls	4.1, 4.2	2
6.2	Paint Walls	6.1, 4.4.4	4
6.3	Install Floor	5.3	2
6.4	Install Counter Tops	4.3	2

20.5.1   Designing the Schedule

A careful look at the network diagram in Figure 20.12 will reveal that the list of tasks and their predecessors is different from the activities in Table 20.2. This is because the predecessors in the table are used to create the first pass at the network diagram. Once you get into it, you will quickly find yourself moving tasks around to clarify the schedule. This is perfectly normal and acceptable.

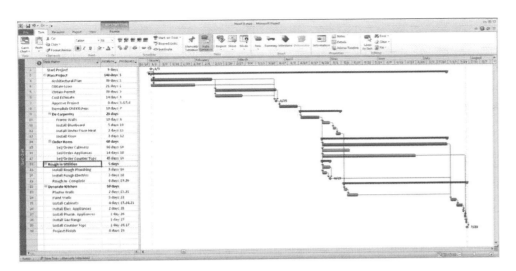

Figure 20.8: The Microsoft Project look in Gantt chart format.

A good example is the movement of the install tasks.[14] When creating Table 20.2, we placed them in the same order as they occurred in the WBS. Once we started working on the schedule, it became clear that installation of the appliances came at the end of the project, after most of the *Decorate* tasks. Therefore, we made the install tasks into sub-tasks of *Decorate Kitchen*.

Moving the install tasks produced a Gantt chart that flowed from top left to bottom right, which is easier to read and to manage.[15] This is an example of the analysis that occurs as the project planning proceeds.

Microsoft Project can produce a WBS automatically and this is shown in Figure 20.12.[16] However, because we moved the tasks around, this WBS is different from the previous version. We have two different WBS!

After all the design effort to create the WBS, the structure was ruined when the tasks were moved around to get a better network diagram. Our opinion at this point is that the original WBS is still the right one to use. Why? The original WBS was *designed* to help manage the project. Remember, we kept insisting that the construction of the WBS is a *creative* process, and that well-designed WBS was essential to a well-managed project.

We grouped activities so they could be managed coherently. For example, we collected all of the plumbing activities (and their deliverables) together so we could manage them effectively. Loosely speaking, everything to do with plumbing went

[14]We are using the word *task* here because *Project* uses it. Normally, we prefer to stick to the PMBOK terminology and use *activity*.

[15]If you don't move tasks around, the arrows begin to look like spaghetti, and you can't figure out what is going on.

[16]Right click on the column header, select *Add Column*, go to the bottom of the list that pops up, and select *WBS*.

285

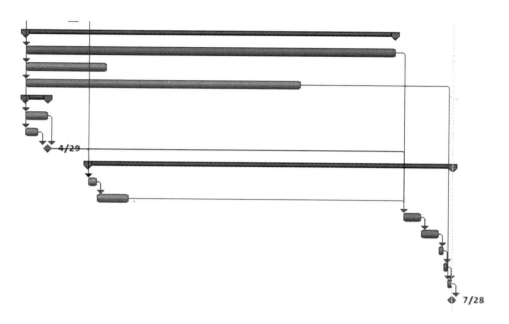

Figure 20.9: The Gantt chart for the end of the project.

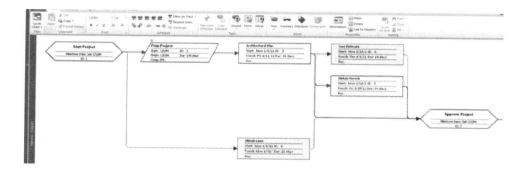

Figure 20.10: The network diagram for the start of the project.

into one box.

From the WBS, we estimated the costs for all plumbing activities, which made things easier for the plumber, who had a list of all plumbing-related things in one place. Also, when the plumbing work begins, the actual costs can be monitored against planned costs of the deliverables. If we had scattered the plumbing tasks

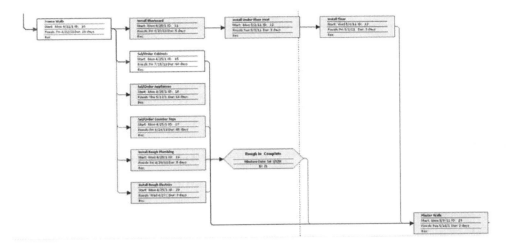

Figure 20.11: A portion of the network diagram that follows Figure 20.10.

throughout the WBS, it would be easy to miss something.

When we moved the tasks in the network diagram, *Project* re-numbered them. From a scheduling perspective, this was acceptable, as it made the *network diagram* clearer and easier to manage. However, the resulting WBS produced automatically from *Project* destroyed our carefully designed WBS![17]

So which WBS do we use? The well-designed version, of course! In our opinion, the WBS produced from *Microsoft Project* is not a real WBS, it is a merely a task numbering scheme that has some use in managing the schedule during the actual work of the project.

The WBS that was designed previously should be used to manage the project.[2]

---

[17]Which is why we refer to the *Project WBS* as the "lazy person's WBS."

	Task Name	Duration	Prede	WBS
1	Start Project	0 days		1
2	⊟ Plan Project	140 days	1	2
3	Architectural Plan	30 days	1	2.1
4	Obtain Loan	21 days	1	2.2
5	Obtain Permit	30 days	3	2.3
6	Cost Estimate	14 days	3	2.4
7	Approve Project	0 days	3,4,5,6	2.5
8	Demolish Old Kitchen	10 days	7	2.6
9	⊟ Do Carpentry	20 days		2.7
10	Frame Walls	10 days	8	2.7.1
11	Install Blueboard	5 days	10	2.7.2
12	Install Under Floor Heat	2 days	11	2.7.3
13	Install Floor	3 days	12	2.7.4
14	⊟ Order Items	60 days		2.8
15	Sel/Order Cabinets	60 days	10	2.8.1
16	Sel/Order Appliances	14 days	10	2.8.2
17	Sel/Order Counter Tops	45 days	10	2.8.3
18	⊟ Rough in Utilities	5 days		3
19	Install Rough Plumbing	5 days	10	3.1
20	Install Rough Electrics	3 days	10	3.2
21	Rough In Complete	0 days	19,20	3.3
22	⊟ Decorate Kitchen	59 days		4
23	Plaster Walls	2 days	13,21	4.1
24	Paint Walls	5 days	23	4.2
25	Install Cabinets	4 days	15,24,21	4.3
26	Install Elec. Appliances	2 days	25	4.4
27	Install Plumb. Appliances	1 day	26	4.5
28	Install Gas Range	1 day	27	4.6
29	Install Counter Tops	1 day	28,17	4.7
30	Project Finish	0 days	29	4.8

Figure 20.12: The WBS output from *Microsoft Project.*

20.6   Risks

Known unknowns were the risks identified during the planning stage. These included:

- *Cabinet Schedule Risk:* The longest activities on the critical path were the purchase, delivery and installation of the cabinets.[18] The cabinets could not be ordered until the kitchen studs were in place, because only then were the exact measurements available. Once ordered, the delivery time was 12 weeks.

  The mitigation strategy was for the contractor to work to get the kitchen studs up as soon as possible so the kitchen designer could finalize the measure-

[18]The longest critical path items should always be analyzed carefully.

ments and order the cabinets. After the studs were up, the contractor worked on other tasks while waiting for the cabinets.

- *Counter Top Schedule Risk:* We selected counter tops that were not in production, only pictures were available in brochures. They were scheduled to be delivered June 1st, but the company had not even delivered prototypes to the store for display.

  The mitigation strategy was to pick an alternate counter top design that was readily available.[19]

Unknown unknowns were the risks that actually occurred that we had no idea about during planning. These included:

- We realized that during construction there was nowhere to store the good china.[20] We hired a moving company to pack the china and put it in storage, which added storage costs of $100 per month for the length of the project.

- Mark applied for a gas permit from the city, but it took four weeks. Only after the city gas permit was granted would the gas company schedule the installation of the gas line, which took another three weeks. As a result, the installation of the new gas boiler was delayed three weeks.

The week things really went awry....

Projects often reach a point where frustrations boil over. In one week, the following happened:

1. On Monday morning the electrician called to say he had badly cut his hand and sent over his assistant. Eileen had planned to select sconces, and the junior assistant was not up to the task.

2. Over the weekend, the finish carpenter's roof was damaged in a storm, so he was at home fixing his roof. The substitute was not a finish carpenter and could not handle the week's activities.

3. The kitchen appliances were delivered on time on Tuesday morning. The refrigerator did not fit in the opening. The contractor called the appliance store, who condescendingly said, "You should have left an extra inch." The contractor yelled back "I left two inches!"

[19] This risk would occur as the company did not make samples available, and rather than wait two months, we selected the other design.

[20] Breakage would be catastrophic!

289

Investigation determined that the refrigerator specification was incorrect.[21] Fortunately, the refrigerator was carefully nudged into place using the leveling screws.

4. The insulation contractor showed up in a chemical protection suit. He said that everyone had to leave the house, which at the time included the contractor, plumbers, and electricians. Eileen was less than thrilled about having to leave the house when working on a writing deadline.[22,23]

20.6.1 Positive Risks

Risks can be positive or negative. A good example of a positive risk was the new gas boiler. During planning, the plumber examined the heating system and discovered an old and inefficient boiler. He proposed that we could save on heating bills by installing a new, efficient gas boiler.

After analyzing the efficiencies, we decided to purchase a new gas boiler.[24] This was a positive risk that we attempted to *enhance*.

20.7 Acceptance

The last few weeks of the construction involved a lot of negotiation about the remaining activities to be completed. Mark's original contract included a final payment upon completion of $8,000. We held back part of that payment until he had completed the "punch list."

This was not confrontational. Mark had his own punch list that he was working on. He also understood that when he finished our list, we would be happy, and he would get paid. We also understood that complaining at this stage would only annoy Mark and delay things even further.

Some of the items on our list were clearly *add-ons* and would increase the cost. But the entire process went smoothly, because we were in constant communication about what was to be done. The process dragged out several weeks because Mark had started another job and showed up intermittently, but he always told us what was happening. We had to accept that as the reality and concentrate on keeping the punch list up to date.

[21] Remember, spec errors are the most expensive if they are not caught until implementation. This is a good example.

[22] For the first time in 20 years, Eileen wrote a theater essay on a yellow pad with a pen, sitting in her car.

[23] When I explained it all to Vijay, he said, "Oh Cool. Communication risk. Be sure to put it in the book!

[24] Project management in action: Examine the proposed change for cost and schedule impacts before deciding!

CHAPTER 21

THE PICNIC CASE AND TEMPLATES

**If the rain spoils our picnic, but saves a farmer's crop,
who are we to say it shouldn't rain?**

Tom Barrett

In this chapter we present a complete set of templates for the graduation party picnic project. The technical concepts were covered previously in Parts I and II of the book. This chapter follows the order in the 5th Edition of the PMBOK, so a review of the chapters in *Part IV: The Process Groups, Processes and Knowledge Areas* will be helpful. Planning is particularly complex, so Chapter 24 will be especially useful as you study the project plan.

To help you quickly find a particular template, Table 21.1 summarizes where the Initiation and Planning templates are to be found in this chapter. Table 21.2 summarizes where the Executing, Monitoring and Controlling, and Closing templates are to be found.

21.1   The Picnic Project

Some graduating students who have studied project management decided to hold a picnic at the end of the academic year. The student council selected a *Classic American* theme: hamburgers, hot dogs and beer. The graduation party is an

Table 21.1: Summary Guide to the Initiation and Planning Templates.

Section	Process	Table or Figure	Page
20.2	**Initiating Process Group**		
.1.	Project Charter	21.3	294
.2.	Identify Stakeholders	21.4	295
.3.	Stakeholder Register & Engagement	21.5	296
20.3	**Planning Process Group**		
.1.	Project Management Plan	21.6	298
.2.	Collect Requirements	21.7	299
.3.	Project Scope Statement	21.8	300
.4.	Work Breakdown Structure (WBS)	21.1	302
.5.	Define Activities	21.10	301
.6.	Milestone List		
.7.	Estimate Activities & Resources	21.11	303
.8.	Estimate Activity Durations	21.12	303
	Risks		
.9.	Risk Register	21.13	304
.10.	Risk Contingency Plan	21.14	304
	Quality		
.11.	Quality Roles & Responsibilities	21.16	306
.12.	Define Quality	21.17	306
.13.	Measure Quality	21.18	307
.14.	Assure Quality	21.19	308
.15.	Control Quality	21.20	308
.16.	Quality Management Plan	21.15	305
.17.	Human Resources Plan	21.21	309
.18.	Team	21.22	310
.19.	Stakeholders	21.23	310
.20.	Communication Management Plan	21.24	311
.22.	Analogous Cost Estimation Template	21.25	312
.23.	Parametric Cost Estimation Template	21.26	312
.24.	Three Point Cost Estimation Template	21.27	313
.25.	Bottom-Up (WBS) Estimation Template		312

informal, evening picnic. An important goal of the party planning is to facilitate the socialization among the students. Entertainment will be provided by a DJ who will play student-selected music.

Table 21.2: Summary Guide to the Executing, Monitoring & Controlling, and Closing Templates.

Section	Process	Table or Figure	Page
20.4	**Executing Process Group**		
.1.	Acquire & Develop Project Team	21.29	314
.2.	Manage Project Team	21.30	315
.3.	Distribute Information	21.32	316
.4.	Manage Stakeholder Expectations	21.33	317
20.5	**Monitoring & Controlling Process Group**		
.1.	Update Project Schedule	21.2	319
.2.	Cost and Schedule Variance Analysis	21.35	321
.3.	Change Control	21.37	323
.4.	Quality Control Measurements	21.38	324
.5.	Update Risk Register	21.39	324
.6.	Administer Procurements		324
20.6	**Closing Process Group**	21.40	325

21.2 Initiating Process Group

21.2.1 Project Charter Template

The Project Charter Template is shown in Table 21.3.

21.2.2 Identify Stakeholders Template

The Identify Stakeholders Template is shown in Table 21.4.

21.2.3 Stakeholders Register & Engagement Strategy Template

The Stakeholders Register & Engagement Strategy Template is shown in Table 21.5.

How Did We Rank the Stakeholders?

We determined the rank of the stakeholders using the following approach. We identified who had substantial interest in the outcome and who had substantial power to help the project manager achieve the project's goals. Stakeholder power was summarized in Figure 23.6.

1. *High Power and High Interest in Project Outcome.* Only one stakeholder fits this group: Dr. Rebecca Johnson.

Table 21.3: The Charter Template.

Project Title:	**Picnic Project**
Organization:	The University
Start Date:	January 10, 2015
End Date:	May 15, 2015
Project Champion:	Student Council
Description: **Justification:**	It is an annual tradition for the graduating class to celebrate the earning of their degrees and the Student Council plans to organize a unique graduation party for the Class of 2015. 1) It is a school custom with benefits for the college and students. 2) The party builds lasting positive memories. The event encourages students to stay involved as alumni and builds solidarity in the class. 3) It is a reward for the students' hard work over the past four years and an opportunity for faculty and staff to appreciate this.
High Level Requirements:	A four to five hour party with food and entertainment. It will be organized on campus by the student council.
Success Criteria & Approvals:	1) High levels of participation and sign-up. (Participation thresholds approval: Student Council President) 2) Party runs smoothly. (Approval: Project Manager) 3) Follow-up survey, two days after completion of project, determines levels of satisfaction with the party. (Approval: Student council president & Project Manager)
Stakeholder List:	Executive stakeholder: Dean of students. Stakeholders: Student council president, Student class representative.
Budget: **Sponsor:**	$5,000. Dean of Students
Milestones:	Fundraising Complete: February 15th, 2015. Venue Selected and Approved: March 15th, 2015 Detailed Organization Plan for Logistics: April 15th, 2015 Preparation Complete: May 1st, 2015
PM: **Responsibility:** **Authority:**	Sandy Nestle. Sandy will report to Student Council President and Dean of Students during planning. Upon conclusion, PM to report project success. PM has the authority to charge students for participation; and to obtain additional funding from sponsors.
Signatures:	PM, Sandy Nestle; Dean of Students; Council President.

Table 21.4: The Identify Stakeholders Template.

Stakeholder	Interest
Dr. Rebecca Johnson	Dean of Students. Project Sponsor
James Burke	Student Council President. Project Sponsor
Jane Bedford	Head of Campus Security and Emergency Medical Services Liaison
Maria Sanchez	Director of On-Campus Catering Company
Dr. Kip Becker	Faculty member and Chair of Department
Neil Das	Student Representative. Possible project champion
Xin Li	Manager of Logistics for Venue
Julia Feinstein	IT Manager of resources for the project
DJ	Vendor who will provide entertainment

2. *High Power but Low Interest in Project Outcome* and *Low Power but High Interest in Project Outcome*: Several stakeholders fall in this group.

3. *Low Power and Low Interest in Project Outcome*: We classified Julia Feinstein in this group as IT is typically busy with several mission critical projects and will have low interest in the student party project. However, the project team can obtain the free web-based resources needed for the project.

Assessing Stakeholder Engagement

The project manager must engage all the stakeholders properly and at the correct project stage. For instance, Officer Bedford must be engaged twice: Once at the start of the project to inform her department about the event and to determine if there would be any issues with the venue or the nature of the party; and a second time the day before the party so that she, or her staff, can drive by and visit the party to check to see if there are any security issues.

The PMBOK 5th Edition introduces a stakeholder assessment matrix to plot where the team wants the level of engagement to be for each stakeholder. This ranges from a stakeholder being unaware to a stakeholder being very supportive and even leading. In the case of Officer Jane Bedford the PM has assessed the level of engagement as *Neutral*. In which case, no further engagement action needs to be taken in increasing her support for the project.

Now, however, let us review the case of the stakeholder, Dr. Kip Becker, who is the chair of the largest department with a large number of graduating students.

Table 21.5: Stakeholder Register & Engagement Strategy Template.

Stakeholder	Rank (Hi, Med, Lo)	Role	Goal
Dr. R. Johnson	High Power, High Interest	Approving Student Council's plans and signing off on them.	Guiding the student council's decisions for effective planning, anticipating obstacles, and correcting flaws in plans.
Xin Li	High Interest, Medium Power	Logistics of the venue	Making sure venue is available, sound system is working, & tech stuff is without glitches
Dr. Kip Becker	Medium Power, Medium Interest	Chair of the largest department	Participating in the event. Motivating his staff and faculty to participate in the party.
James Burke	Medium Power, High Interest	Sponsoring & funding project	Approves the scope.
Maria Sanchez	Medium Power, Medium Interest	Providing the hors d'oeuvres & refreshments	Providing good food, taking into consideration allergies, special dietary needs, etc.
Officer Bedford	Medium Power, Medium Interest	Securing the event	Making sure traffic is re-routed and providing student EMTs on scene for medical emergencies.
Neil Das	Medium Power, High Interest	Communicates with students and project organizers	Acts as a project champion. Identifies requirements for project and communicates the scope to the project manager.
Julia Feinstein	Low Power, Low Interest	Provides IT support	Project requires website, *MS Project*, and email tools. Julia has these resources.

From previous experience with college student parties, the PM has assessed that Dr. Becker's interest in the party project is *Neutral*.

Even though Dr. Becker has tentatively agreed to participate in the student graduation party, it is a good idea to engage him more closely for several reasons:

- Visibility of senior faculty is good for the image of the picnic and communicates commitment.

- Students typically like to take pictures with faculty and staff around the time of graduation.

- Dr. Becker is in a position to influence other faculty and staff to attend the event and make it successful.

- As someone who has attended many of these functions, his experience is invaluable.

The Project Manager should increase communications with Dr. Becker and convert him to *Supportive* or *Leading*. This can be accomplished by making him aware of the goals of the project, regularly reporting to him on the progress, and making him aware of any issues that arise. As an experienced department chair, Dr. Becker might have good ideas to contribute.

21.3 Planning Process Group

21.3.1 Project Management Plan Template

The Project Management Plan formally communicates the details of the project plans to all stakeholders, such as the project sponsor, company senior management, customers and the project team. The Project Management Plan Template is shown in Table 21.6. Like most plans, it is not a standalone document–it has links to other planning documents, which is the standard technique for avoiding duplication of information.

Scope Comments

The scope references several related documents. These are included *by reference,* which means that the content of the scope is considered to include explicitly all of requirements, conditions and goals in the referenced documents. It is as if they were actually included.[1]

It is important that scope information not be repeated–see the example in the Scope Chapter, section 7.6.2 Once the party has been planned, the core student group will receive some training and guidance to execute the party successfully.

21.3.2 Collect Requirements Template

The Collect Requirements Template is shown in Table 21.7.

21.3.3 Scope Statement Template

The Scope Template is shown in Table 21.8.

[1] Except, if they were included you would have duplicate information.

Table 21.6: Project Management Plan Template.

	Project: Graduation Party Picnic Project
1.	**Executive summary of project charter**, see section 21.1. Insert relevant excerpts from the charter here. Document any relevant additions to the charter.
2.	**Scope Management** See Scope Statement. See Requirements Document: Table 21.7.
3.	**WBS and Schedule** See WBS and *MS Project* Schedule Reports.
4.	**Milestones** (Preliminary: Estimated Time-frame) Fundraising Complete: February 15th, 2015 Preparation for Party Completed: Mary 15th , 2015 Completed Plan for party logistics: April 15th, 2015 Preparation for Party Completed: May 15th, 2015 Post Party Survey: May 17th, 2015
5.	**Subsidiary Plans** The following plans are included *by reference*: Schedule Management Plan Cost Management Plan Quality Management Plan Human Resource Management Plan Communications Management Plan Risk Management Plan
6.	Deployment Plan

21.3.4   The Priority Matrix Template

Table 21.9 shows the *Priority Matrix* for the picnic project. This is created during scope development, and its purpose is to establish the relative priorities between scope, cost, and schedule.

21.3.5   WBS Template

The WBS Template is shown in Figure 21.1.

21.3.6   Define Activities

The Define Activity Resources Template is shown in Table 21.10.

Table 21.7: Requirements Document (Specification) Template.

Category	Requirement	Stakeholder	Acceptance Criteria
Funding	Preliminary Funding	Dean of Students Student Council President	Sign off on the preliminary cost estimate.
Funding	Additional Funding	Students	Class representative signs-off on amount students will pay to attend.
Food	Hors d'oeuvres Dessert	Maria Sanchez Student body	To save money & make menu interesting this is planned as a "pot luck" event.
Food	Dinner	Maria Sanchez	Official contract signed off by *Completed Plan* milestone date.
Entertain-ment	Music selection Music system	DJ Student body	DJ Party Rentals Submits a signed contract.
Entertain ment	Volleyball Frisbee	Neil Das, Student body	Organized by students. Submits to PM detailed arrangements & costs.
Planning	Schedule & Budget	Sponsor & Student champion	Final Party details are formally approved by sponsors and student representatives & published on the website.
Party	Organization Committee	Student leaders assigned in charge of various activities.	A dry run meeting takes place with full participation of student activity leaders.
Party	Clean up	Student Clean up crew	No evidence of party on scene.
Satisfaction	Post-Party Survey	Sponsors will approve questions	Results of electronic survey will be provided to sponsors.

Table 21.8: Scope Statement Template.

Project: Graduation Party Picnic
Project Objective
Organize a party for graduating students on May 15th 2015 within a budget of $5000.
Deliverables
Cost Estimate
Party Plans and Logistics
Contract from Food Services for dinner
Entertainment contract for music
Party Invitations mailed formally
Post Party Survey (May 17th, 2015)
Milestones
Fundraising (February 15th)
Get a venue (March 15th, 2015)
Contract from Food Services for dinner being served (March 30th, 2015)
Entertainment contract for Music (April 5th, 2015)
Preparation for Party Completed. (May 7th, 2015)
Party completed (May 15th, 2015)
Post Party Survey (May 17th, 2015)
Techncial Requirements
DJ must be willing to accommodate a play list from students and play the "school's sports anthem song."
Catering must provide sample meals to volunteer group before final food contract is signed.
All dietary restrictions must be accommodated.
Assumptions
Student council and Dean of Students will provide some funding.
Additional funding will come from students participating in the event.
BU will provide party venue at no cost.
Limits and Exclusions
Entertainment: DJ is responsible for the audio equipment, special lighting, etc.
Food Services will provide plates, cutlery, napkins, etc.
The venue has time restriction which must be complied with.
Review of Final Deliverables
Customer and Sponsor:
Formal sign off Dr. Rebecca Johnson and James Burke.

Table 21.9: The *Priority Matrix* for the Graduation Party Picnic.

	Scope	Schedule	Cost
Constrain (Must Have)		No sacrifice on date	
Enhance (Nice to have)	Small details can be eliminated		
Accept			Some cost overrun ok

Table 21.10: Define Activities Template.

Activities
Prepare proposal for party and budget
Identify potential locations
Obtain Permission for Venue
Inform Security, Custodians
Identify Food Vendor
Select Menu
Identify music vendor (DJ)
Negotiate vendor contracts
Create Party Event Committee
Create invitations
Email invitations
Make guest list
Dry run the day before
Close all contracts
Document lessons learned
Send out survey
Identify key PM processes and complete documentation

21.3.7 Milestone List Template

Milestones occur in several sources. For example, high level project milestones are often introduced in the charter or business case, where they define strategic schedule constraints. For complex projects, more detailed milestones may also be provided, such as the end of each phase. In the picnic project, the milestones were listed in the scope. It is important to try to keep a single list of milestones so that when they change, only one document is updated. Tools such as *Microsoft Project* can print milestone reports.

301

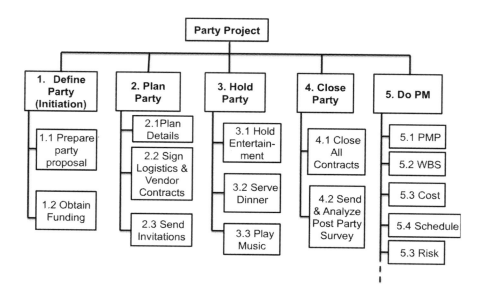

Figure 21.1: The WBS template

21.3.8   Estimate Activities & Resources Template

The Estimate Activities and Resources Template is shown in Table 21.11.

21.3.9   Estimate Activity Durations Template

The Estimate Activity Durations Template is shown in Table 21.12.

21.3.10   Risk Register Template

The Risk Register Template is shown in Table 21.13, where the first risk is that of under-age students consuming alcohol. The goal for this risk is "prevention," a much stronger category than "mitigation."

In risk prevention the goal is to move the risk completely outside the project scope. Banning alcohol consumption would do this. However, the students have selected an American theme, which includes beer, so this is not an option. Therefore, the

Table 21.11: Estimate Activities & Resources Template.

Activity	Resources		Quantity
	Type	Detail	
Create Requirements	Labor	Business Analyst	1
Estimate Funding	Labor	Cost Estimator	1
Website Development	Labor	IT specialist	1
& Invitations	Tools	Hardware & SW	1
Project Management	Labor	Project Manager	1
(Including procurement)			
Planning (All activities)	Labor	Student Leaders	4
Travel (Cost of identifying	Material	Actual travel costs	$500
Food, Catering, DJ			
Sports equipment	Material	Volleyballs, Nets, Frisbees	1
Sports Coordinator	Labor	Student	1

Table 21.12: Estimate Activity Durations Template.

Activity	Duration
	(days)
Create Requirements & Specifications	2
Estimate Party Funding	5
Website Development & Invitations	1
Project Management (All tasks)	8
Planning (All activities)	14
Sports Coordinator	3

risk prevention strategy is to check two IDs, which should make it difficult for underage students to consume alcohol. A student may have a fake ID, in which case a single ID check may not prevent the risk, and so would fall more in the mitigation category.

21.3.11 Risk Contingency Plan Template

The Risk Contingency Plan Template is shown in Table 21.14.

21.3.12 Quality Management Plan Template

Here, the project manager describes the roles and responsibilities of the project team, quality attributes and metrics, and the plans for quality assurance and quality control.

There are several ways to construct the Quality Management Plan (QMP). If the previous quality templates have already been developed, then the QMP need only

Table 21.13: Risk Register Template: Quantification and Risk Response Strategy.

Risk	Rating Before Risk Response H, M, L	Response Prevent, Mitigate Transfer or Accept
Alcohol consumption by under-aged attendees could cause legal liabilities	H	Prevent: Two IDs will be checked by security.
Rain will disrupt the party	M	Mitigate: Rent a backup tent to shelter the attendees
Dessert was planned as Pot-Luck. This might result in allergy, food poisoning, quality issues.	M	Transfer: Obtain Dessert from a reliable party
Sun burn, heat, insect bites, etc.	L	Accept: Develop contingency plan: Identify EMTs & post hospital numbers.
Good Risks	**Rating**	**Response** Exploit, Share, Accept
Advertise vendors on the back of the invitation card	H	Exploit. This is a good risk. It will result in a 5% pricing discount from the vendors.

Table 21.14: Risk Register Template: Quantification and Risk Response Strategy.

Risk	Rating After Risk Response H, M, L	Contingency Steps should the risk materialize
Alcohol consumption by under-aged attendees could cause legal liabilities	None	This risk was eliminated by risk analysis and response.
Rain will disrupt the party	None	The party committee will guide members into the sheltered tent area.
Dessert was planned as Pot-Luck. This might result in allergy, food poisoning, quality issues.	None	This item was outsourced to a reliable food vendor who provided desserts with clear labeling of ingredients.
Sun burn, heat, insect bites, etc.	None	Low $100 has been assigned to obtain medications from the local drug store. If serious complications arise, EMTs will be called and dial 911.

Table 21.15: Quality Management Plan Template.

	Project: Graduation Party Picnic
1.	**Overview:** Three metrics were identified for the project team to measure party quality: participation, engagement, and safety. Quality of food and music is tied to the engagement metric.
2.	**Quality Responsibilities and Quality Roles:** For each of the above drivers a dedicated team leader will be allocated.
3.	**Quality Assurance Approach:** Throughout the project QA will conducted. Audits of participation in the party by students and faculty will take place at key milestones.
4.	**Quality Control Approach:** Review of metrics at key milestones. On day of party, random communication with 10% participants will be conducted by the project manager or leader appointed by her.
5.	**Quality Improvement Approach:** Nothing is off limits. Walking tour of baseball park, which is nearby, and other minor tweaks to project scope will be considered to increase party attendance. On the day of the party, contingency plans will be made to increase party engagement.
6.	**Tools, Environment and Interfaces:** Website analytics, survey responses (survey monkey) will be used. Spreadsheets will be used for budgeting. Website will be used to communicate with participants.
7.	**Quality Reporting Plan:** Weekly team meetings will be used to obtain quality data.

reference the existing sub-components.[2] For a small project, the QMP can simply incorporate the sections directly. The Quality Management Plan Template is shown in Table 21.15.

21.3.13 Quality Roles and Responsibilities Template

The first step in the quality process is to identify quality roles and responsibilities, which include mentoring and coaching, auditing work products, auditing processes, and participating in quality assurance and quality control reviews. The Quality Roles and Responsibilities Template is shown in Table 21.16.

21.3.14 Define Quality Template

Here, the project manager:

[2] Again avoiding duplication of information.

Table 21.16: Quality Roles and Responsibilities Template.

Role	Responsibility
Project Manager	Obtain funding; manage budget and schedule. Ultimately responsible for project quality.
Sponsors	Provide funding. Additional funding will be raised from students who participate in the party or by other means.
Entertainment coordinator	Responsible for planning and coordination of sports and music.
Food & Refreshments	Responsible for coordinating the team in charge of this important activity, selecting the best vendors and ensuring timely delivery of food and refreshments.
Party Team coordinator	Responsible for planning and managing the hired & volunteer work force at the party.

Table 21.17: Define Quality Template.

Quality Goal/Attribute/Standard	Person or Entity Responsible
Participation	Project Manager
Safety	Entertainment Coordinator
Engagement on Event Day	Party Team coordinator

- Identifies the project's quality standards and expectations for customers, the parent organization, and government or industry observers.

- Defines customer and project goals, quality standards, and critical success factors

- Defines quality standards and continuous quality improvement and process innovation strategy, e.g., how team will undergo quality control training.

- Defines how organizational quality standards, such as ISO 9000 if applicable, and company policies and procedures will be used.

- Defines project management quality goals, e.g., meeting budget goals and delivering products on schedule.

The Define Quality Template is shown in Table 21.17.

Table 21.18: Measure Quality Template.

Metric	Definition
Participation	Percent of students who agree to attend the party.
Engagement	Percent of students who stay through the duration of the party.
Safety	Number of accidents and incidents playing sports at the party.

21.3.15 Measure Quality Template

The most important metrics measure product performance, project status and the acceptance criteria for deliverables. Along with identifying the metrics, the project manager defines the methods of data collection, the timeframe for conducting the measurements, and reports the results.

Examples are shown in the Measure Project Quality Template, which is shown in Table 21.18. For the party, the most important critical success factor is participation and engagement, so the RSVPs will be measured weekly by the techie and reported to the project manager.

21.3.16 Assure Quality Template

The project manager describes how the team will know if the project is achieving the established quality goals. If project quality is not acceptable, then there should be contingency plans to improve project quality. The Assure Quality Template is shown in Table 21.19.

21.3.17 Control Quality Template

Here, the project manager defines the quality tools that will be used to measure project quality and level of conformance to defined quality standards and metrics. Also, the project manager identifies those responsible for monitoring and improving project processes. The Control Quality Template is shown in Table 21.20.

21.3.18 Human Resources Plan Template

The Human Resources Plan Template is shown in Table 21.21.

21.3.19 Core Team Template

The Core Team Template is shown in Table 21.22.

Table 21.19: Assure Quality Template.

Metric	Definition
Participation	Participation is the biggest quality driver prior to the party. At each milestone, we will gather data about participation and interest. If participation is low, the party date, venue, or activities will be revised.
Engagement	Engagement is the big driver on the day of the party, and it includes quality of food and music. The project manager will gather party satisfaction and engagement data from random participants as the party is unfolding. If there are concerns, the committee will react in a timely manner. For example, if food is not satisfactory or sufficient in quantity, additional pizza will be ordered and served. Pictures taken by various participants will be shown at the party so that participants can enjoy the memories created by fellow classmates. Contingency plans will be made ahead of time for this.

Table 21.20: Control Quality Template.

Item	Action	Responsibility
Attendance	Weekly participation numbers will be monitored	Project Manager
Food	Food will be sampled before the event at the vendor for quality and taste. Preferences will be obtained ahead of time from participants (Chinese, Vegan, etc). On the day of the event, if possible, quality will tested on upon delivery.	Food and Refreshments Coordinator
Entertainment	Music quality/selection will be monitored. Playlists will be submitted ahead of time by participants. Quality of audio and music selection will be monitored by assessing participation on the dance floor.	Entertainment Coordinator
Engagement	Project Manager will randomly talk with participants about the party and gather intelligence.	Project Manager

Table 21.21: Human Resources Plan Template.

Project: Graduation Party Picnic

1. **Roles & Responsibilities:**

   - Project Manager (PM) is responsible for the success of the Party project. The PM must approve all project expenditures and communicate with the stakeholders. The team members will be responsible for timely execution of the assigned activities and the quality the work activities should meet established acceptability criteria.

   - Business Analyst (BA) is responsible for gathering requirements for the party project.

   - Student Leaders (SL) are responsbile for coordinating the various activities like entertainment, means, invitations, website and music.

   - Student Champion (SC) will communicate with students and get buy in on the party specifications.

2. **Organizational Structure:**
   All the above identified roles report the PM. The PM works with the Sponsors.

3. **Staff Acquisition:**
   The project staff will consist entirely of internal resources. There will be procurement or contracting of two functions: food, and music.

4. **Staff Release:**
   The project staff will be fully released from the project two days after the party.

5. **Training:**
   Dry run will be scheduled during the implementation phase and will be documented in the project schedule.

6. **Performance Reviews:**
   The PM will review each team member's assigned work activities at the onset of the project. Throughout the project the PM will communicate all expectations of work to be performed to the team.

7. **Regulations and Policy Compliance:**
   All BU Policies and Procedures for hiring and treatment of staff will be followed.

Table 21.22: Core Team Template.

Name	Title	Address	Email	Phone
Dr. R. Johnson	Dean of Students Project Sponsor	755 Comm Ave Room 217	rj@bu.edu	x3-3999
James Burke	Student Council President Project Sponsor	Dunce Hall Room 777	jb@bu.edu	999-3999
Jane Bedford	Head, Campus Security EMS Liaison	201 Comm Ave	bed@bu.edu	x3-4999 x3-4999
Maria Sanchez	Director, On-Campus Catering	117 Bedford St.	sz@bu.edu	x3-5999

Table 21.23: Stakeholders Template.

Stakeholder	Role	Goal
Dr. R. Johnson	Approving of the Student Council's plans and signing off on them	Guiding the student council's decisions for more effective planning and anticipating obstacles as well as correcting flaws
Dr. Kip Becker	Participating in the event.	Motivating his staff and faculty to participate in the party.
James Burke	Sponsoring and funding the project.	Approves the scope of the project.
Officer Bedford	Securing the event	Making sure traffic is rerouted, and providing student EMTs on scene for medical emergencies.

21.3.20 Stakeholders Template

The stakeholder information can be listed either in the HR plan or in the Stakeholder processes as part of the Initiating processes. The information should not be duplicated, but we repeat it here for convenience. The Stakeholders Template is shown in Table 21.23.

Table 21.24: Communications Management Plan Template.

Message	Description What is it about?	Audience Who is invited	Method Of comm- unication?	Frequency When & how?	Sender Who?
Kick-off Meeting	Stakeholders & Project Team discuss goals	Entire team Sponsors Stakeholders			
a) Announce- ment			Email & Phone	Once	PM
b) Minutes	Action Items		Email & Phone	Once	PM
Requirements Meeting	Identifying Party needs	Project Team Sponsors	Email & Phone	Once Once	Business Analyst
PM Meetings PM Meetings	Review Progress. Review deliverables. Update documents.	Team	Email	Every Friday at Noon	PM
Milestone Meetings	Team addresses progress on , entertainment, meals, etc.	Project Team Sponsors	Email	Each Milestone	PM
Dry Run	Meeting on site to go through all aspects of party.	Student Leaders	Email	Once	Project Champion
Completion Meeting	Administrative Closure.	Project Team	Email	Once	PM

21.3.21   Communications Management Plan Template

The Communications Management Plan Template is shown in Table 21.24.

21.3.22   Cost Estimation Templates

To estimate the cost of the picnic party, we use four methods of cost estimation: analogous, parametric, three point and bottom-up (from the WBS). All methods can be used early in the project. Even the scope statement will require a rough cost or effort estimate. Using more than one method is desirable because they check each other.

311

Table 21.25: Analogous Cost Estimation Template.

Previous Similar Project	Previous Project Effort / Cost	Multiplier	Current Estimate
The project manager managed a party graduation event last year. The party was formal and at a restaurant.	$10,000 party	0.5	$5,000

Table 21.26: Parametric Cost Estimation Template.

Unit of Measure Cost per student	Project Size Number of Students	Parametric Estimate
Column 1	Column 2	Column 1 * Column 2
$45	100	$45*100 = $4,500

Analogous Cost Estimation Template

The project manager uses previous similar projects as a benchmark for the analogous estimate. Using experience, the project manager applies a multiplier to a previous project.

For example, suppose last year's graduation party was a formal reception and cost $10,000. The project manager could use a multiplier of 0.50 to estimate the cost of this year's picnic, which is informal and a lot less complex. The Analogous Cost Estimation Template is shown in Table 21.25.

Parametric Cost Estimation Template

The Dean of Students provided the cost estimate, which is shown in the Parametric Cost Estimation Template, Table 21.26.

Three Point Cost Estimation Template

The Three Point Method, also called the PERT method, is described in detail in the chapter on cost, Chapter 11. The Three Point Cost Estimation Template is shown in Table 21.27.

21.3.23 Bottom-Up (WBS) Cost Estimation Template

In the bottom-up method you would typically add up the effort associated with all the work packages in the WBS. This estimate can be performed when the WBS has

Table 21.27: Three Cost Estimation Template.

WBS Item	Pessimistic, p (Highest) 1% Probability	Likely, l Estimate	Optimistic, o (Lowest) 1% Probability	Expected Cost $C = (p + 4*l + o)/6$
Total Cost	$7,000	$5,000	$4,000	$5,170

Table 21.28: Detailed Activity Cost Estimate.

Activity Cost Estimate				
WBS ID	**Start Date**		**End Date**	
12.1.6	3/15/2014		4/20/2014	
Description: Select Food Vendors				
Total Cost	**$275**			
Labor	Personnel Project Leader	Cost per hour $25	Hours 2	Total $50
Materials	Type Food Samples	Cost per unit $10	Quantity $7.50	Total $75
Costs	Item Taxi to Vendors	Description Three vendors will be visited to check the menu and sample the food.		Total $150

been created. For the picnic, we developed a detailed bottom-up estimate from the WBS, which can be found in the *Microsoft Project* Tutorial chapter.

Note: All of the estimates are in the range $4,000 to $5,000, which is within the budget established by the sponsor.

Detailed Activity Cost Template

Estimating costs requires consideration of expenses other than human labor. The categories of expenses are:

Human	Hourly Rate	Analyst, programmer
Materials	Cost per unit	Party tent, chair
Cost	Varies per unit	Travel expense, taxi

Table 21.28 shows an example of a detailed cost estimate for an individual activity. The costs for all activities would be rolled up to constitute the bottom-up WBS cost estimate.

Table 21.29: Staffing Assignments for the picnic project.

Date	Role	Resource	Commitment
2/10/2015	Student Leader	Jason Smith	1, Full time
2/10/2015	Business Analyst	Lisa Smith John Jones	2 Analysts, Half time
2/10/2015	Techie	Jay Bacaram Margaret Dell	2 Analysts, Half time

21.4 Executing Process Group

The executing process group contains the processes required to implement the project. The key activities conducted here are:

1. Acquiring and Developing the Project Team

2. Managing the Project Team

3. Distributing Information

4. Managing Stakeholder Expectations

21.4.1 Acquire & Develop Project Team

When the project was scheduled, a project resource plan was created to ensure that student leaders and volunteers would be available to perform the required tasks. During the execution phase, the project manager must ensure that the identified resources are actually available.

An important issue that tends to arise is that some of the staff might need training. The techie position is critical and an effort was made to hire a contractor who was very knowledgeable in all aspects of the web development task: email marketing, analytics, creating a website, and using *Microsoft Project*.

The PM consults the resource plan, which lists the required staff, and conducts a skills assessment. The PM then acquires the appropriate staff, assigns them to tasks such as entertainment leader and food services leader, and clarifies their responsibilities. A project staffing assignment form can be completed, such as the one shown in Table 21.29.

Table 21.30: Self-Assessment of team members.

Self Assessments:
Name of the Team Member:
Individual Assessment: Provide honest comments on: Attendance, communication, ability to listen, accepting responsibility, exceeding expectations, solving problems, making sure that team members can understand the solution you are working on, and whether you are completing work on schedule.

Team Assessment:
Comment on whether your team is:
   Feeling Empowered.
   Functioning in a collective manner or are some team members
     working independently.
   Spirit of Cooperation.
   Conflict Resolution and ability to handle differences of opinion.
   Balancing the workload evenly amongst all.
   Communication as a team.
   Driven to deliver on schedule.
   Motivated.

21.4.2 Manage Project Team

Once the project manager has acquired the team, the important ongoing task is to help the individual members of the team to improve. This can be accomplished by having each member of the team conduct a self-assessment. The project manager asks each team member to comment on their own individual performance, as well as their perspective on how the team is functioning. The project manager can then review these comments and suggest ways that the team member might improve.

The sample template shown in Table 21.30 can be used to improve the competency of the individual team members, to assess team performance, and to encourage team cohesion.

A review of the self-assessments can be integrated into the project manager's own observations. Individual extremes can be smoothed out and an honest assessment can be developed. The overall assessment of the individual team members should be communicated promptly at a private meeting. See Table 21.31. The assessment of the team as a whole should be communicated at a staff meeting.

If it appears that the team is not functioning well, the project manager will need to establish well-defined procedures and identify clear expectations for the team as a whole. Further, the project manager should explain the consequences of failing to follow procedures and of not meeting established goals.

Table 21.31: The PM's assessment of an individual team member.

Name of the Team Member:	Jason Smith
Assessment Date:	3/12/2015

Comments: You have not missed any meetings. That is outstanding dedication to the project. Your communication ability is outstanding; an essential skill for a lead. You have accepted several responsibilities that have abruptly come along. Great at solving problems and ensuring your team understands your approach. Exceptional performance!

Table 21.32: The "Who does what, when" report.

Resource Name	Task	Date
Techie	Create Website for Party	2/26/2015
Techie	Create custom invitations	3/31/2015

21.4.3 Distribute Information

The communication plan identifies all of the major deliverables, as well as *how they are to be distributed* to team members and stakeholders. Since the team is using *Microsoft Project*, one way to accomplish the distribution is to give password access to the various stakeholders.

Project contains several built-in reports that can be developed and distributed, and one that is popular is, "Who does what, when." That report shows the weekly assignments and it can be distributed to all team members. An example of the "Who does what, when" report is shown in Table 21.32.

21.4.4 Manage Stakeholder Expectations

This requires the project manager to work with all stakeholders to meet or exceed their expectations, and to handle issues as they arise. In the case of the party project, the project manager must communicate with stakeholders about issues stemming from cost over-runs and the change of the date of the party. Stakeholders will be extremely disappointed if the date changed is not immediately communicated to them.

After communication with stakeholders, the project manager should complete an issue log, such as the one shown in Table 21.33.

Table 21.33: The Stakeholder Issues Log for the picnic project.

Stakeholder Issues Log
Change Request: Picnic Party date change Date: 3/30/2015
PM Plan Updates: The entire plan needs to be updated and contract modifications need to be approved and signed by all stakeholders and vendors.
Project Document Updates: Update MS Project documentation and other templates.
Comments: Need to talk with all three stakeholders immediately!
Resolution Date: 4/5/2013

21.5 Monitoring and Controlling Process Group

Monitoring and controlling the project consists of:

1. Verifying Deliverables

2. Determining cost and schedule variances using reports from the information system, and leveraging Earned Value concepts.

3. Responding to threats and opportunities.

4. Managing changes, and using the change control procedures you have identified.

5. Controlling procurement

Monitoring is always approached at a particular point in time. At any point, there are completed tasks, tasks in process and pending tasks (not started). The actual status of tasks must be compared to what the plan says should be happening at that time. Also, the project manager must keep the project plan up to date.

A specific amount of funds have been spent from the budget, usually in the form of invoices received. The actual expenditures must be compared to the planned expenditures.

Therefore, we will assume that the picnic project has started and we have completed the "Planning Complete" milestone, which was due on April 30th, 2015. Email invitations were sent out and RSVPs have started coming back. A substantial amount of the planning is complete and contracts for food and entertainment have been agreed to and signed, so they will be hard to change.

At this time, the project manager observes that several schedule changes have occurred:

- The task "Obtain Funding" took two more days than planned.

- "Select Menu" took three more days than planned.

- "Identify Food Vendor" completed eight days earlier than planned.

- "Identity Music Vendor (DJ)" took six more days than planned.

- "Vendor Contracts" finished two days earlier than planned.

Also, there were variations associated with the costs. As it turned out, Food Services and Entertainment was more expensive than projected because it was the time of many convocations in the city when food services are in demand. Several hundred events take place in the in the month of May as many thousands of students graduate from local colleges. The caterer also wanted a large deposit of money up front.

The date was constrained because BU students tend to leave the city after graduation, so there was no flexibility in moving the picnic date. Also food quality could not be sacrificed, as the objective was to have a memorable event.

At this point the project manager should consult the priority matrix in the scope. We assume that Table 21.34 is the priority matrix for the picnic project. It says that the most important factor is the schedule (before graduation). After holding to the schedule, the project manager must attempt to enhance the performance (food and entertainment). Finally, of least importance is the cost.[3]

Table 21.34: The *Priority Matrix* for the picnic project.

	Scope	Schedule	Cost
Constrain		■	
Enhance	■		
Accept			■

The date is constrained by graduation and food quality cannot be sacrificed, so the project manager must accept the cost overrun. The stakeholders may not like the idea, but this is what was established when the requirements were developed and documented in the priority matrix, which is in the scope.

[3]Which does not mean that it is not important, only less so than the schedule and scope.

The following sections detail the typical sorts of analyses that might be conducted by the project manager.

21.5.1 Update Project Schedule

We use *Microsoft Project 2013* throughout this case study.[4] The project manager updated the picnic party schedule:

- The project manager first set the baseline (see *Project* Tutorial).

- The project manager set the Status Update date to Thu 4/30/2015 (the current date) and updated all tasks as complete. The command is: Project → Status Date.

- The tasks were updated to 100% complete by clicking the Update Project icon. These steps are illustrated in Figure 21.2.

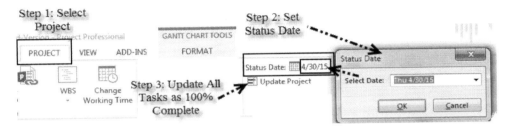

Figure 21.2: Updating the project tasks rapidly to the status date.

Since the duration and effort of some tasks were different from the baseline, the project manager updated them individually using the command: Task → Mark on Track, and the selected Update Task.

We illustrate how to enter that the vendor contract negotiation completed ahead of schedule by 2 days in Figure 21.3. The task duration was 2 days instead of the planned duration of 4 days.

21.5.2 Cost and Schedule Variance Analysis

The project manager uses variance analysis reports, and the scheduling software's cost and schedule reports, to obtain a snapshot of the project status.[5] Figure 21.4 shows a cost variance analysis report. The Actual Cost is higher than expected, due to the reasons explained earlier; however, the project is on schedule.[6]

Next, the project manager analyzed the work remaining, which is shown in Figure 21.5. The majority of the remaining work is assigned to event day coordinators, the

[4] For more details on *Microsoft Project*, see the tutorial in Chapter 28.

[5] Earned Value calculations can be done more easily and in more detail using a spreadsheet. However, *Project* can provide a quick snapshot of the status, which can be valuable.

[6] Remember, the Earned Value calculation uses cumulative costs.

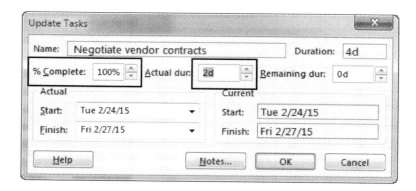

Figure 21.3: Individually updating tasks with a change in duration (variance).

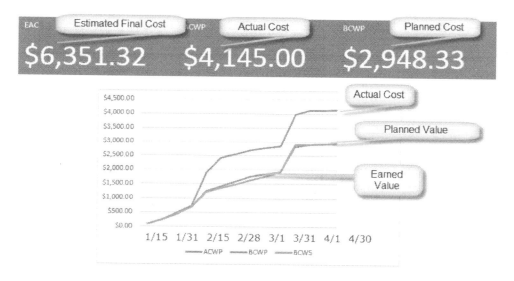

Figure 21.4: Cost variance analysis.

student leaders and the volunteer team. Only the student leaders are paid, so that is the only task on which there is an opportunity to reduce costs in the near future.

The percent Work Complete stands at 67%; the Remaining Work is 164 hours; and the Actual Work Completed is 327 hours.

The project manager has two options to deal with the cost overrun: Raise more funds (perhaps from sponsors) or spend less on the remaining tasks. The costs

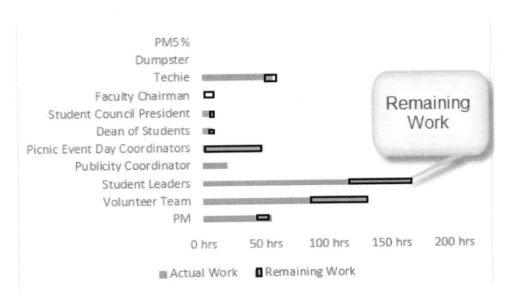

Figure 21.5: Remaining work on the picnic project.

associated with the remaining activities are primarily the payments to student leaders and event day coordinators. The project manager decided to explore the possibility of saving money on staff by studying the cost data in the resource sheet, which is shown in Table 21.35.

Table 21.35: The Resource Cost Sheet for the picnic project.

Name	Actual Work (hours)	Actual Cost	Standard Rate /hour
PM	41.87	$1,046.67	$25.00
Volunteer Team	85.33	$0.00	$0.00
Student Leaders	117.78	$1,766.67	$15.00
Publicity Coordinator	19.00	$285.00	$15.00
Picnic Event Day Coordinators	0 .00	$0.00	$0.00
Dean of Students	5.60	$0.00	$0.00
Student Council President	5.60	$0.00	$0.00
Faculty Chairman	0.00	$0.00	$0.00
Techie	52.33	$1,046.67	$20.00
Dumpster	0.00	$0.00	$50.00
PM @ 5%	0.00	$0.00	$0.00

321

Examining the resource cost sheet shows that the project manager has several options: The first is that voluntary student leaders might be hired to manage the project. Second, student leaders could be asked to work some hours as volunteers. Finally, the project manager might determine if the techie, who was hired as a consultant, can be replaced with someone from the IT department at BU who might take over the IT tasks for less money. In any of the above cases, a decision needs to be made quickly before the staff costs are spent.

The project manager documents the overrun by completing the template shown in Table 21.36.

Table 21.36: Variance Analysis and Work Performance Results.

Project Title:	**Picnic Project**	Prepared:	**5/20/2015**
Schedule Variance:			
Planned Result	Actual Result for Schedule	Variance	
$2,948	$4,145	$1,197	
Root Causes:			
#1	Catering expensive		
#2	Techie & leaders organizing the event were expensive.		
Planned Response:			
#1	Consider Volunteers		
#2	Consider substituting IT staff for techie (No cost to the project).		

21.5.3 Change Control

If a change is proposed, it should first be analyzed to determine the impact on the scope, cost and schedule. The project manager can perform a variance analysis to estimate how significant the impact of the change will be. The change is submitted to the Change Control Board (CCB), and if approved, the project manager creates a new baseline and updates all project documentation.

An example of a Proposed Change Form is shown in Table 21.37.

21.5.4 Quality Control Measurements

Table 21.38 shows some quality control measurements for the picnic project. The most important critical success factor is the percentage of students planning to

Table 21.37: Proposed Change Form for the picnic project.

Project Title:	**Picnic Project**	Prepared:	**5/20/2015**
Person Requesting:	Project Manager	Change ID:	1001

Category of Change:		
☐ Scope	☐ Quality	☐ Requirements
☐ Cost	☐ Schedule	☐ Documents

Detailed Description of Proposed Change: Invest in a dinner to invite student volunteers. Seeking $300 for the dinner meeting.

Justification for Proposed Change: Project budget is slipping and we will benefit from more volunteers.

Impacts of Change: Scope: Description: N/A	☐ Increase	☐ Decrease	☐ Modify
Quality: Description: N/A	☐ Increase	☐ Decrease	☐ Modify
Requirements: Description: N/A	☐ Increase	☐ Decrease	☐ Modify
Cost: Description: N/A	☐ Increase	☐ Decrease	☐ Modify
Schedule	☐ Increase	☐ Decrease	☐ Modify

Description: At the dinner meeting we will motivate the volunteers to join the project, bring them up to speed, and explain their roles and responsibilities.

Justification: If the volunteer pool increases, costs will go down.

Disposition:	☐ Approve	☐ Defer	☐ Reject

Change Control Board Signatures:			
Name	Role	Signature	Date
Dr. Rebecca Johnson	Dean of Students		4/1/2015
James Burke	Student Council President		4/1/2015

attend and returning RSVPs. Therefore, this metric is constantly measured and discussed at team meetings.

21.5.5 Update Risk Register

Table 21.39 shows the updates to the risk register for the picnic project. The "traffic light" indicator is used to summarize the status of the risks: Red means the risk is serious and needs to be dealt with immediately. Orange means the risk should be carefully monitored. Green means the risk is not of concern.

Table 21.38: Quality Control measurements for the picnic project.

Planned Result	Actual Result	Variance
RSVPs by milestone date:		
50% RSVPs	10% RSVPs	40% students not signed up.
Root Cause:		
Many students are leaving upon graduation. Also they want to be with their parents & family who are visiting from far away.		
Planned Response:		
Communicate venue planning to see if an earlier date is available immediately after final exams.		

Table 21.39: Risk Register Updates.

Risk ID	Risk	Response	Resource Responsible for Mitigation	Current Status Traffic Light
1	New Risk: Low RSVPs	Party date cannot be after convocation	Student Leader	Red
2	New Risk: Resource Costs high	Try to get volunteers for PM tasks	Student Leader	Orange

21.5.6 Administer Procurements

The project manager should pay close attention to the contractual relationships, such as those with the food and entertainment services. The vendors must be monitored to ensure that they meet their formal deliverables and perform according to the v conditions. Contract information, especially the deliverables, is documented in the Records Management System.

The project manager must also be aware of whether changes and corrections can be made to the contracts. For example, can the project manager delay the delivery of the food if there is a rainstorm?

The contract required the DJ to inspect the lights and power sources. The project manager should audit the DJ's activities to ensure that the inspections took place. If the project manager is unavailable, a student volunteer can be assigned to monitor the inspection. Also, the project manager must abide by the terms of the Dumpster contract by paying the deposit up front in a timely manner.

The project manager assigned student volunteers to audit the menu and they discovered the vendor changed the menu. The changes failed to account for the extensive interest in vegetarian and vegan food. The project manager called the food vendor and pointed out that these items had been contractually specified. The vendor agreed to add the vegetarian and vegan food.

It was proposed to move the picnic date to before graduation, which required updates to the contracts. The project manager communicated with the contractors and used the Change Control System (CCS) to propose a formal change to the project. The CCS Board discussed the date change and analyzed whether there would be an increase or decrease in the vendor costs. After discussion, the CCS Board approved the date change. The project manager then proceeded to negotiate the contract modifications with the vendors.

21.6 Closing Process Group

A major goal of the closing phase is to document lessons learned. However, the lessons are much more effective if they are collected as the project proceeds. It is good practice, therefore, for the project manager to continually monitor the project lessons.

Together with the team, the project manager can fill out the lessons learned template shown in Table 21.40. This should be performed continually, perhaps at the regularly scheduled staff meetings.

When the project is completed, there should be a comprehensive lessons learned meeting for the entire staff. This is generally part of the formal administrative closure of the project.

Table 21.40: Lessons learned from the picnic project.

Phase	What Worked?	What Did not Work?	Lessons for Next Project
Initiation	Good meeting with two key sponsors.	Failed to connect with faculty stakeholder early on.	Build proactively on stakeholder communication.
Planning	Good project planning by team.	Did not communicate well with students about menu preferences.	Early on, email all students asking for menu preferences.
Planning		Did not communicate well with leadership about party date	Early on, discuss party date with student leaders.
Monitoring & Control	Schedule Tracking.	Cost Overrun.	Techie expense was high. Should have planned more options.

Part IV

Process Groups, Processes and Knowledge Areas

22

THE PROCESS GROUPS

**When one has finished building one's house, one suddenly realizes
that in the process one has learned something that one really
needed to know in the worst way —before one began!**

Friedrich Nietzsche

The major components of project management are: Phases, Process Groups, Processes, and Knowledge Areas. In this chapter, we describe these components, and the interactions between them.

Each process produces deliverables. The expertise in the knowledge area is the skills, tools and techniques that a project manager needs to produce the deliverables effectively. Therefore the knowledge area chapters focus on the technical aspects of actually producing the deliverables. In this section, we focus on process groups and processes. Processes are associated with both *knowledge areas* and *process groups*, and their relationships are shown in Table 22.3.

22.1 Project Phases

Projects are divided into phases, which are logical divisions that allow for efficient development. Each project phase follows the process groups.[1]

[1] Note that project *phases* are not the same as *process groups*.

329

The number of phases depends on the size and complexity of the project, and they may occur in series or in parallel. Some phases may even be iterated or repeated. In the usual case, the phases are sequential, and the outputs from one phase are evaluated and the decision to proceed allows the next phase to begin.

Some phases can genuinely proceed in parallel. An example might be a system with software and hardware components. Once the formal specification is complete, and the interfaces defined, then the hardware and software development phases can proceed in parallel. Conducting the phases in parallel incurs risks, since mistakes can result in re-work of both hardware and software components. Therefore, when deciding whether to proceed with parallel phases, the project manager must spend time to precisely define the inputs to the phases.

Iteration is often imposed when changes are required. For example, a change to the scope will require the team to execute the same processes as when the scope was developed. The processes may be conducted in less detail than when the scope was first developed, but the steps are the same.[2] The cost and schedule impact of the proposed change must be estimated, and the risks assessed. Finally, a go/kill decision is made on whether to implement the proposed change.

Phases always share the same characteristics:

- *A phase is formally initiated and closed.* Phases typically produce specific deliverables, which are the basis for the decision of whether to continue to the next phase. For example, in the PMA growth strategy project, the end point of the first phase is a cost benefit analysis, which is the basis for the decision of whether to proceed with a membership growth phase or not, and if so, with which strategy. Note that one explicit outcome of a phase is whether to continue with the project or to kill it.

- *A phase is coherent and distinct.* The work of a phase should be as independent as possible from other phases or projects. This means that a phase uses specific skills (and organizational assets).[3]

- *A phase's major deliverables are carefully controlled.* The output is a go/kill decision, and so careful attention must be paid to the deliverables.

- *A phase follows the process groups.* See section 22.2

22.1.1 PMA Case: Growth Project Phases

Suppose PMA decides they want to increase their membership. This is not yet a project. First, they must study the problem and evaluate methods for increasing

[2]We believe that this is not really an iteration, but a kind of a mini walk-through of the steps. We have yet to find a situation where there is a genuine, complete iteration of a phase.

[3]If a phase is closely inter-related with another phase, the phase is badly specified— the phases probably should have been combined.

the membership (e.g., email blast, advertising, networking at conferences, etc.). Next, they evaluate the costs vs. potential growth from a particular strategy. Once they have analyzed the data, they can decide whether to proceed, and if so, with which method. This project, therefore, has two phases as shown in Table 22.1.

Table 22.1: PMA growth strategy phases.

Phase (Stage)	Deliverables	Gate
1. Select Growth Strategy	Growth Strategy Document Cost/Benefit Analysis	Growth Achievable?
2. Implement Strategy	Increased Membership	Target Growth Achieved

22.2 The Process Groups

If you want to build a ship, don't drum up people together to collect wood, but rather teach them to long for the endless immensity of the sea.

Antoine de Saint-Exupery

The PMBOK does not define the process group, it merely says that the 47 processes are combined into 5 process groups. For our purposes, a process group is a logical grouping of the project management processes.

The process groups are inter-dependent, and must be performed in the same sequence on each project. Many of these dependencies are intuitive; for example you cannot rank risks in order of importance unless you identify them first. And of course, you cannot create a risk response plan unless you have both identified risks and ranked them.

There are still some fuzzy areas, however. The PMBOK specifies that resources (people and materials) are identified before the activity durations are estimated. While desirable, we frequently have to estimate costs without having a list of resources available. In fact, companies often bid with "standardized" labor mixes, and actual resources are identified only when the project is underway.[4]

There are five process groups:

1. *Initiating Process Group*

   The purpose of this process group is to charter the project and to identify the stakeholders. The *initiating* process authorizes a new project, the start of a

[4]Note: Process groups are not project phases. The term *project phase* is used in the product life cycle.

331

phase of a multi-phase project, or the re-start of a halted project. This is also where a project is divided into phases and large projects into sub-projects.[5] There are only two processes in this group: *Develop Project Charter* and *Identify Stakeholders.*

2. *Planning Process Group*

The *planning* process group is the largest group with twenty four processes. It is the heart and soul of project planning: creating a successful road map for the project.

This process group defines action plan for the entire project, from start to finish. The processes in this group include defining and refining the scope, developing the project management plan, and identifying and scheduling all project activities. Many planning processes interact and, often, can be worked on concurrently. For example, *quality planning, risk management planning,* and *human resource planning* can all be done concurrently.

Changes to a project are inevitable and the planning processes allow for revisiting and re-planning one or more processes. In fact, planning is an iterative process and the incremental and progressive detailing of the project plan is referred to as *rolling wave planning.*

3. *Executing Process Group*

The *executing* process group dominates the work load and, therefore, the expenditure of funds. This is where the work on the project actually occurs. There are eight processes in this group and the key project management activities include acquiring and developing the project team, generally coordinating people and resources, and getting the work completed on schedule and within budget.

As work proceeds and the project is refined, other aspects of the project manager's job include distributing information, managing stakeholder expectations, and assuring quality.[6]

4. *Monitoring and Controlling Process Group*

In this group the project manager tracks, reviews, and regulates the performance. There are eleven processes in this group. The project manager identifies required changes, monitors and controls the cost, schedule, and risks, and manages any variances to the plan.

5. *Closing Process Group*

[5]Note: A significant portion of *initiating* is often accomplished outside the project, e.g., a project may be created and authorized by the company or the program office, often as part of the portfolio management process.

[6]Note that we are concerned here with managing the project, not doing the project. The project manager does not actually do the work!

332

The *closing* processes are those performed to formally terminate all activities of a project.[7] There are two processes in this group and the most important activity is to obtain acceptance of the project by customers, sponsors, or stakeholders. These processes may also be used to close a canceled project.

Table 22.2 presents research data, gathered from 860 project managers, on the average amount of effort spent by teams in the various process groups. [32] The results are intuitive and suggest that the executing processes, where the work is completed, consume most of the budget and effort on a project.

Table 22.2: Percent of effort spent in each of the project's process groups.

Process Group	Effort in Group		
Initiating Process:	1%	to	2%
Planning Process:	11%	to	21%
Executing:	69%	to	82%
Monitoring and Control:	4%	to	5%
Closing:	2%	to	3%

The relations between the process groups is shown in Figure 22.1. Each of the process groups is divided into *processes*. For example, the first process in the *Initiating* group is *Develop Project Charter*.

[7]Or phase of a multi-phase project.

333

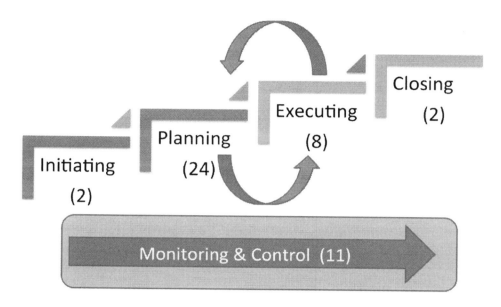

Figure 22.1: The process groups with the number of processes per group.

22.3   Processes

To live means to finesse the processes to which one is subjugated.

Bertolt Brecht

[8]This number changed in the current version of the PMBOK (5th Edition), so one should consider the PMBOK still in flux. In the 5th edition, *Stakeholder Management* became an entirely new knowledge area, while in the 4th edition, *Integration Management* changed drastically. In our view, the continuing changes to *Integration* means that PMI still hasn't quite figured out this knowledge area!

The PMBOK defines 47 processes.[8] The PMBOK defines a process as follows:

> *A process is a set of interrelated actions and activities performed to achieve a pre-specified product, result, or service. Each process is characterized by its inputs, the tools and techniques that can be applied, and the resulting outputs.*

For example, *Develop Project Charter* is a process. It is member of the *Initiating* process group and the *Integration Management* knowledge area.

More informally, a process is a project management step that helps you complete your project successfully. Processes fall into one of two major categories:

- *Project management processes:* These are selected, tailored, and followed to ensure a smooth and effective flow of work throughout the life of the project.

- *Product oriented processes:* These make up the product life cycle and vary by application domain, i.e., construction, information technology, defense, pharmaceutical, entertainment, etc. It is the product life cycle in which the product or service is created.

Processes have inputs, tools and techniques, and outputs, which are illustrated in Figure 22.2.

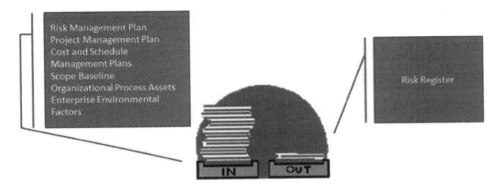

Figure 22.2: The inputs and outputs for the *Identify Risks* process.

As an example, we will focus on the process named *Identify Risks*. Before the project team can begin to identify the risks that may arise, they must have access to key information and data, which are the *inputs*.

The inputs to *Identify Risks* consist of examples of risks from historical projects and templates for their development. Risks may also exist as outputs from previous processes on the current project. For example, risks might have been identified in the *Define Scope* process.

Formally, the *Identify Risks* process requires the following information as inputs: Risk Management Plan, Project Management Plan, Cost and Schedule Management Plans, Scope Baseline, Organizational Process Assets, and Enterprise Environmental Factors.

The project team analyzes all of the above information and creates a *Risk Register*, which is the only output for this process, and consists of a list of risks that the team thinks might occur during the execution of the project.

Since developing and assessing the impact of risks is a creative process, the team uses a variety of tools and techniques to assist in the analysis. These might include interviewing stakeholders who might have experience on similar projects, brainstorming, and Delphi techniques.[9] Historical checklists from previous projects also help to identify risks and create the risk register.

22.4   The Knowledge Areas

If a man empties his purse into his head no one can take it away from him.
An investment in knowledge always pays the best interest.

Benjamin Franklin

The PMBOK defines knowledge as understanding a process, practice, or technique, or how to use a tool. Each *Knowledge Area* is an identified skill of project management, defined by its knowledge requirements and described in terms of its processes, practices, inputs, outputs, tools, and techniques. The relations between *Knowledge Areas*, *Process Groups*, and the individual *processes* are shown in Tables 22.3 and 22.4.

The *Knowledge Areas* are:

1. Integration Management

2. Scope Management

3. Time Management

4. Cost Management

5. Quality Management

6. Human Resource Management

7. Communications Management

8. Risk Management

9. Procurement Management

10. Stakeholder Management

[9]The Delphi technique is covered in section 11.5.1

Table 22.3: The relation between Project Management *Process Groups, Knowledge Areas* and *Processes*. Page 1 of 2.

| Knowledge Areas | Process Groups | | | | |
	Initiating	Planning	Executing	Monitoring and Controlling	Closing
Project Integration Management	Develop Project Charter	Develop Project Management Plan	Direct and Manage Project Work	Monitor and Control Project Work Perform Integrated Change Control	Close Project or Phase
Project Scope Management		Plan Scope Management Collect Requirements Define Scope Create WBS		Validate Scope Control Scope	
Project Time Management		Plan Schedule Management Define Activities Sequence Activities Estimate Activity Resources Estimate Activity Durations Develop Schedule		Control Schedule	
Project Cost Management		Plan Cost Management Estimate Costs Determine Budget		Control Costs	

Table 22.4: The relation between Project Management *Process Groups, Knowledge Areas* and *Processes*. Page 2 of 2.

Knowledge Areas	Process Groups				
	Initiating	Planning	Executing	Monitoring and Controlling	Closing
Project Quality Management		Plan Quality Management	Perform Quality Assurance	Control Quality	
Project Human Resource Management		Plan HR Management	Acquire Project Team		
			Develop Project Team		
			Manage Project Team		
Project Communications Management		Plan Communications Management	Manage Communications	Control Communications	
Project Risk Management		Plan Risk Management		Control Risks	
		Identify Risks			
		Perform Qualitative Risk Analysis			
		Perform Quantitative Risk Analysis			
		Plan Risk Responses			
Project Procurement Management		Plan Procurement Management	Conduct Procurements	Control Procurements	Close Procurements
Project Stakeholder Management	Identify Stakeholders	Plan Stakeholder Management	Manage Stakeholder Engagement	Control Stakeholder Engagement	

23

INITIATING PROCESS GROUP

**He who has begun has half done.
Dare to be wise. Begin!**

Horace

This is where we begin the project.[1]

Each process produces deliverables and the expertise in the *Integration* knowledge area is the skills, tools and techniques that a project manager needs to produce the *Integration* deliverables effectively. The *Integration* knowledge area processes and their associated *process groups* are shown in Table 23.1. The deliverables (outputs) from the processes in the *Integration* knowledge area are shown in Table 23.2.

The primary focus of the initiating process group is to authorize the project. A key point to note is that a project does not exist until the charter is created. Therefore, the charter is often developed by someone external to the project, such as the project sponsor. In reality, if a charter is not available, the designated project manager assists with its development.

The *Develop Charter* process is part of the *Integration* Knowledge Area and *Identify Stakeholders* is part of the *Project Stakeholder Management* Knowledge Area. See Figure 23.1.

Table 23.1: The *Integration* knowledge area processes and their associated *process groups.*

Initiating	Planning	Executing	Monitoring & Controlling	Closing
Develop Project Charter	Develop Project Management Plan	Direct & Manage Project	Monitor & Control Project	Close Project or Phase
			Perform Integrated Change Control	

Table 23.2: The deliverables (outputs) from the processes in the *Integration* knowledge area.

Process	Deliverable
Develop Project Charter	The Charter
Develop Project Mgmt Plan	Project Management Plan
Direct & Manage Project Execution	Deliverables, Change Requests
Monitor & Control Project	Change Requests
Perform Integrated Change Control	Change Requests Status Updates
Close Project or Phase	The final project, Lessons Learned

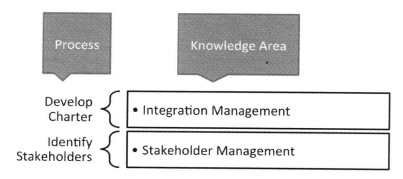

Figure 23.1: The *processes* contained in the *Initiating* process group.

These processes begin after project selection occurs. A formal project selection process, as described in section 2.6, would produce most, if not all, of the required inputs to these processes. In the unlikely scenario that a statement of work or business case is not available, it is left to the sponsor and project manager to describe the nature of the new project, how the project maps to the organization's goals, and the business case, including a cost benefit analysis.

Early in the project, there are two major deliverables from the *Integration* knowledge area, the *Charter* and the *Project Management Plan*. During execution, the major responsibility of *Integration* is to manage *Change Requests*. The deliverables associated with the *Integration* knowledge area are shown in Table 23.2.

All processes have inputs and outputs. Inputs are often an output from a previous process. Inputs also come from outside the project, such as from the business case or corporate goals. Outputs are often an input to a future process.

23.1 Develop Charter

A project does not exist until its charter is created, so someone outside the project usually develops it. We now describe the inputs, outputs, and tools and techniques of the *Develop Charter* process, which are summarized in Figure 23.2. The goal of the process is, of course, to produce the project charter.

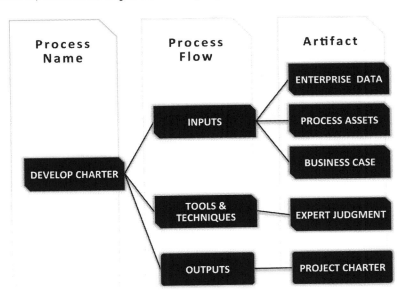

Figure 23.2: A summary of the *Develop Charter* process.

The *Develop Charter* process is defined in the PMBOK as:

341

The develop charter process formally authorizes the project (or phase), documenting initial requirements that satisfy the stakeholders' needs and expectations.

The key point is that the charter grants to the project manager the authority to spend money and acquire staff. Therefore, without a charter the project does not exist.[1] No charter, no project.

23.1.1 Develop Charter Inputs

The inputs to the *Develop Charter* process are summarized in Figure 23.3. Before the sponsor develops the charter, the following inputs must be available:

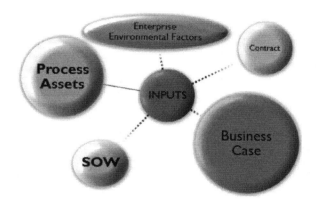

Figure 23.3: The inputs to the *Develop Charter* process.

It is not unusual for the person creating the charter to have to troll through many existing company documents to assemble the required information. For example, two important inputs to the charter are *Enterprise Environmental Factors* and *Organizational Process Assets*. These are not so much individual documents as collections of information. The following items can be used as a checklist to begin the search for the required *Charter* information.

1. **The Business Case**

   Why should the project be done?[2]

   The *Business Case* provides the data to establish that the project is worth its investment. There are many business reasons to do a project:

---

[1]We often suggest that when your boss calls you in and congratulates you as the new project manager for project X, you should immediately request a copy of the charter. "I can't be the project manager for a project that does not exist!"

[2]Every project manager should have an elevator speech that answers this question. You never know when you will run into your boss, who might ask, "Tell me again why are we doing that project?" Job survival depends on a really good answer!

342

- *Core Mission:* The development of a new product may be viewed as essential to maintain the company's position in the market space.

- *Market:* There is an untapped market the company believes it can satisfy.

- *Exclude Competition:* The company believes the project may prevent others from gaining entry into their market.

- *Core Technology:* The company wants to invest in a technology they believe will soon become important, and that will create a platform for future projects.

- *Image and Citizenship:* The project presents the company in a good light.

- *Unreliable Suppliers:* The project will diversify its suppliers and make deliveries more dependable.

- *Changing Regulations:* Upgrades to the information system are necessary to comply with changes to tax, environmental, or legal regulations.

As an example, we present the business case for the PMA project in Table 23.3. It specifies the key benefits of the project and makes a strong case for management to fund the project. It could also discuss the following topics: Problem the project addresses; a cost/benefit analysis; risks, including the impact of not doing the project; and an implementation strategy.

It is important for the project manager to periodically review the business case, particularly after major milestones. For example, when the scope is complete, it should be checked to ensure that it implements requirements that reflect the business case.[3]

2. **Enterprise Environmental Factors**

These arise from answering the following questions:

- How does the organization conduct the business?

- What are the various departments and how do they operate?

- What is the market place condition for the project?

- What is the organizational environment in which the project exists?

- What infrastructure exists?

Examples of *Environmental Factors* can also include:

[3]It is easy to get carried away in scope development and end up with a great project that does not satisfy the business case! Also, changing market conditions can invalidate the need for the project, so checking the business case is project management job security.

343

Table 23.3: The *Business Case* for the PMA web site.

Key Project Benefits
Provide a comprehensive site for project management activity and collaboration, which will include the latest news, tools to assist the project managers, PMI resources, introductions to research, evaluations of new practical tools, and employment postings from both employees and employers.
To become an online resource for the project management community.
Increase awareness of graduate programs in Project Management and increase exposure to new companies.
Attract potential students to the graduate program in Project Management by showing our leadership position in the project management community.
Further the *state of the art* of project management by providing access to research, tools, templates, hints and tips to visitors to the site.
Provide a resource for students and alumni to receive and post available jobs from companies looking for highly skilled project managers.
Increase visibility for the Project Management Institute to foster a better working relationship with students.

- Industry and government standards, such as ISO 9000, which specifies the fundamentals of quality management systems.

- Marketplace data and business intelligence.

3. **Organizational Process Assets**

    Examples of *Organizational Assets* include:

    - Company assets useful to the project, such as standards, policies and procedures, tools, templates, and information systems.

    - Historical information, lessons learned, knowledge bases relevant to project management, and any templates from previous projects. Data from previous projects is particularly valuable if available in a searchable knowledge base.

    - Past project data, metrics, and measurement guidelines in a project management information system (PMIS), particularly if supported by cost and schedule management tools.

4. **Statement of Work.**

    The SOW defines who is to do which tasks, and when. Often, there is no formal SOW when the charter is created. However, much of the information usually exists elsewhere. e.g., the completion date for the project may be in the business case; products must be available before the holidays; and an Olympic stadium must be available before the Olympics begin.

5. **Contracts.**

The sponsor may delegate aspects of the project to an external entity, in which case the contract is an input to the charter.

23.1.2   Develop Charter Tools and Techniques

The sponsor creates the project charter using existing assets, experience, and subject matter experts. A phrase used frequently in the PMBOK is *Expert Judgment*, and here this refers to any group or individual with specialized knowledge or training relevant to the creation of the charter. Such experts may include: stakeholders, potential customers, sponsors, professional organizations, subject matter experts, and staff from the project management office.

23.1.3   Develop Charter Outputs

There is only one output from this process, and that is the charter itself.

23.1.4   Charter Example

An example of a charter for the PMA website project is given in Table 23.4.

23.1.5   Charter vs. Scope

The 5th edition of the PMBOK provides some clarity on the differences between a Project Charter and Project Scope Statement—see Figure 23.4.

Table 23.4: The charter for the PMA web site.

Project Title	PMA Web Site
Organization	Project Management Association
Start Date	June 14, 2011
End Date	June 14, 2012
Project Champion	Dr. Vijay Kanabar
Purpose	The Project Management Association (PMA) is a networking group for current students and alumni of Boston University employed or interested in the Project Management profession. The PMA website project will create an environment for members of the community to share information, to be informed of current research, to obtain continuing education credits required to maintain certification, to learn about new employment opportunities and to get hints and tips on latest developments in the area of project management.
Description	The current Project Management website was implemented many years ago, and is not serving the needs of the PMA. The current website needs to be redesigned to keep up with new demands of the PMA, including access to research, changes in the project management profession, and improvements in tools and templates. This website project will create an environment that is both appealing and helpful to the project management professional, providing an equal balance of information sharing, tools and templates, and opportunities for networking.
Goals:	After installation, PMA should be able to: Increase the number of visits to the website by 50% over 2010 levels; decrease support costs of the website by 25%; and provide user friendly mechanisms to post, manage, update and remove content.
Success Criteria	1) Build a community of PMs. 2) Membership > 500 in the first year. 3) Analytics reveal popularity of site.
Project Budget:	$15,000
Milestones:	Initial Prototype to Stakeholders: 6/28/2011 Project Complete: 8/2/2011
Signatures:	Champion: PM: Stakeholders

Charter	Scope Statement
Project objectives	Project scope description (progressively elaborated)
Project justification	
Success criteria	Acceptance criteria
High-level project description & requirements	Project Deliverables
High-level risks	Exclusions
Summary milestone schedule	Constraints
Summary budget	Assumptions
Stakeholder list	
Approval requirements	
Name of the project manager	
Name of the sponsor	

Figure 23.4: The key differences between the charter and the scope statement.

23.2 Identify Stakeholders

**We must, indeed, all hang together,
or most assuredly we shall all hang separately.**

Benjamin Franklin

The *Identify Stakeholders* process begins the identification anyone who can influence the project. Stakeholders exist both within the organization (e.g., the team, upper management) and external to it (e.g., users, trainers, sponsors).

Managing the interests of stakeholders is a vital activity. A major risk to project success comes from not realizing who all the stakeholders are, or neglecting an important stakeholder. In fact, mismanagement of any single stakeholder can lead to a disaster because an angry or disillusioned stakeholder can hold up deliverables, make trouble for other interest groups, and generally cause havoc.

The definition of a stakeholder is:

A stakeholder is anyone actively involved in the project whose interests may be positively or negatively affected by the performance or the completion of the project.

Stakeholders are involved!

It is important to realize that not everyone will have a positive attitude to the project. Some individuals or advocacy groups might prefer that the project not be done at all. Such people are stakeholders because they have an *interest* in the project, but their negative interest can be really challenging. Also, some stakeholders may be in favor of the project once it is completed, but they may hold a negative view *during* the project.

For example, a project to repave a street might be viewed quite differently by different stakeholders. While a clean, modernized street is a goal supported by many, digging up the street may make a mess in front of stores and houses, angering the people who live and work there. This latter group can create challenges for the project manager.

During the *Identify Stakeholders* process, the project team identifies the stakeholders and their expectations. It is vital that the project manager actively manages stakeholder expectations, reduces conflict over competing requirements, and establishes unambiguous acceptance criteria for the project's deliverables.

348

Most likely, the process of stakeholder identification will continue throughout the planning process. This is a characteristic of project management: Processes are seldom completed in one pass, but are continually refined as more knowledge about the project is accumulated. This is an example of *progressive elaboration*, an important feature of project management.

Table 23.5: Stakeholders for the repaving project outside the classroom.

Stakeholder	Interest
Sponsor	Who pays for the project
Customer	The end user of the project. The customer (the city) may be different from the requesters of the project (the residents).
Project Manager	Wants to get the project done on time, on budget. Wants to keep the stakeholders happy.
Technical Director	Wants to get the project done right.
Project Team	Their jobs depend on the project. Even a simple construction project consists of many different subcontractors.
Trainers	Will train users when the project is over.
Students	During the project, are affected negatively by the disruption. Once completed, they will like the result.
Faculty	Hate the noise outside their window.
Police	Make extra money during construction.
Deans	Feel obligated to explain that construction will result in a better looking university.
The Mayor	Is happy the university will stop complaining about the poor street condition.
Shopkeepers	Complain business is down during construction
Residents	Complain there is less parking during construction.
Red Sox Fans	Miss the first inning because of the mess.

Identify Stakeholders is a critical activity, and it is quite easy to overlook some of them. Let's consider a relatively simple project to repave the street in front of the classroom in which we teach the project management course. Table 23.5 lists the stakeholders and their issues.

23.2.1 How Stakeholders Influence the Project

Stakeholders have varying levels of influence. Many stakeholders have specific requirements they want included and the team must strive to meet those needs. While not all stakeholder requirements can be fulfilled, the failure to meet a particular stakeholder's expectations is a major risk factor, e.g., you run the risk of failing an acceptance test. The key concept is "stakeholder expectations," and managing them is a key role for the project manager.

When conflicts arise, the project manager must take the long-term view, and treat stakeholders more as partners than adversaries. Short-term wins only make losers try harder in the future, they become better adversaries.[2]

23.2.2 Identify Stakeholders Inputs

Many of the process inputs are the same as for the *Develop Charter* process. The inputs to the *Identify Stakeholders* process are illustrated in Figure 23.5. [4]

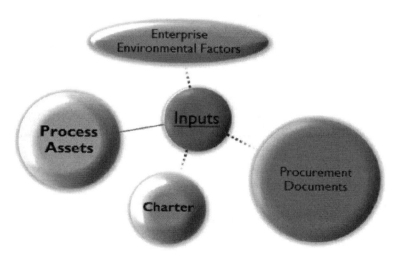

Figure 23.5: The inputs to the *Identify Stakeholder* process.

[4]Quite frequently, an output from a previous process is an input to the next process. That is true here: The *Charter* was an output from *Create Charter* and it is a key input to *Identify Stakeholders*.

23.2.3 Identify Stakeholders Tools and Techniques

The next step is to identify the stakeholders and their influence. The stakeholders are listed in the *Stakeholder Register*. Not all stakeholders have the same vested interest in the outcome of the project and not all have the ability to influence its outcome or override the interests powerful groups. Therefore, the goal is to create a strategy for managing the various stakeholders, which is a major output of the *Identify Stakeholders* process, and a tool to accomplish this is illustrated in Figure 23.6.

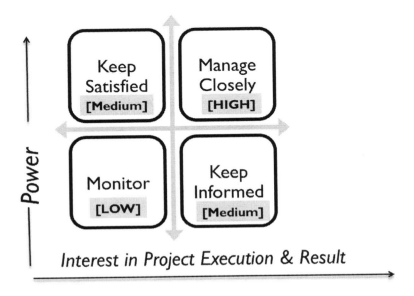

Figure 23.6: The tool to create the stakeholder management *strategy*.

In Figure 23.6 stakeholders are classified in two dimensions: The vertical axis indicates their power to influence the project and the horizontal axis indicates their interest in the project, e.g., their desire to take part in meetings and evaluate outputs. Stakeholders are ranked as either "Low" or "High" in both categories. Every entry in the *Stakeholder Register* is assigned to a box in Figure 23.6. The actions of the project manager towards the stakeholder groups are also shown in each of the four boxes and constitute the *Stakeholder Management Strategy*.

For example, stakeholders with high power and high interest are assigned: *manage closely*. They should be frequently consulted and their views acknowledged, particularly with respect to deliverables. On the other hand, stakeholders with low power and low interest should be assigned: *monitor*. Stakeholder analysis takes place continually and the *Stakeholder Register* is likely to be updated frequently.

23.2.4 Identify Stakeholder Outputs

The inputs, tools and techniques, and outputs for the *Identify Stakeholders* process are shown in Figure 23.7. The important outputs are the *Stakeholder Register* and the *Stakeholder Management Strategy*. Table 23.6 is an example of a tool that can be used to identify the expectations of important stakeholders and to develop a strategy to manage them.

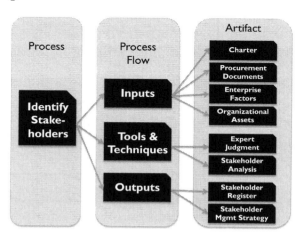

Figure 23.7: The inputs, tools and techniques, and outputs for the *Identify Stakeholders* process.

Table 23.6: Stakeholder Register & Management Strategy.

Stakeholder	Role	Goal	Expectations
Joe Brown	President, PMA	Web site to promote social network and organization growth.	Complete before conference.

23.3 Summary

We provided a detailed analysis of the *initiating* process group.[5] The *inputs* are used to create the process deliverables—the outputs. The tools and templates illustrate how to create those outputs. Throughout Part IV, we repeat this approach, defining the inputs, tools and techniques, and outputs. By covering this simple Process Group in detail, we hope that the more complex process groups will be easier to understand.[6]

[5]However, we have covered just two of the forty seven processes.

[6]Planning, alone, has 24 processes.

24

PLANNING PROCESS GROUP

**Give me six hours to chop down a tree and
I will spend the first four sharpening the axe.**

Abraham Lincoln

In this chapter we focus on the *planning* process group, which is the largest group the project manager must deal with.[1]

An overview of the *planning* process group is shown in Figure 24.1. The technical aspects of the documents (e.g., how to write the scope, the technical details of the network diagram) are covered in the knowledge area chapters.

Planning begins by carefully defining the scope of the project in concert with the stakeholders, and then developing the cost and schedule estimates. Planning also involves: analyzing the risks to the project; defining how to assess the quality of the deliverables; establishing the communications between all parties; acquiring and training the team; and finally, deciding on the approach to sub-contractors.

The technical aspects of the planning processes are extensive, and include: collecting the requirements and writing the project scope; evaluating constraints and creating the work breakdown structure; estimating costs, identifying resources, and developing the network diagram; and determining the project schedule.

[1] We might also suggest that these are the most important processes for the project manager. Maybe not for the project, but for the project manager. A badly planned project is doomed.

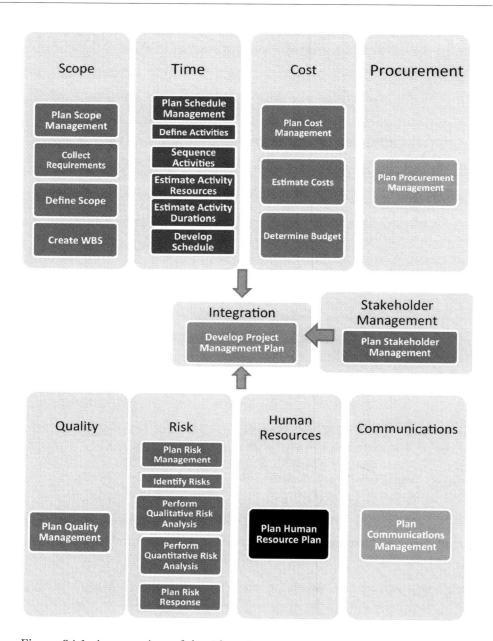

Figure 24.1: An overview of the *Planning* process group and its processes.

The primary outputs of the planning process group are the components of a comprehensive Project Management Plan, which consists of multiple sub-documents.

It is important to realize that planning is inherently iterative in nature. As stakeholder needs are refined, changes to the plan will be proposed, and not just technical or content requests, but also the real-world demands of cost and schedule. The progressive evolution of planning is referred to as *rolling wave planning*.

For each process we identify the key inputs, because you can only start a new document when all the preceding documents (the inputs) are completed. We also identify the outputs, because future processes can only be started when the key deliverables (the outputs) are complete.

Since planning covers so many disciplines, we divide our discussion into the following major sections:

- *The Project Management Plan*: This defines the entire plan, both technically and managerially.

- *Scope Planning*: The *scope* contains the user requirements and is the most important document in the project.

- *Time Planning*: Here the project schedule is developed, and the *critical path* emerges, the most important concept in project management.

- *Cost Planning*: These are the steps required to develop the project cost estimate, and the budget.

- *Risk Planning*: The risks are identified, their impacts assessed, and how to mitigate them.

- *The Sub-Plans*:

    - *Quality Plan*: This defines the quality standards for the project, both the process and the content.

    - *Human Resources Plan*: This defines how the project team is to be acquired and developed.

    - *Communications Plan*: This defines the distribution of information to stakeholders.

    - *Procurement Plan*: This defines the role of sub-contractors.

    - *Stakeholder Management Plan*: The strategic approach to identifying and managing stakeholders.

24.1 Develop Project Management Plan

The *Develop Project Management Plan* process is where the *Project Management Plan* is created. It is the major document used throughout the project to explain precisely how the project will be planned, managed, executed, assessed, and eventually, closed.

Table 24.1 shows the inputs to and outputs from the *Develop Project Management Plan* process. The inputs consist of the *charter*, the preliminary, pre-project work (rationale, business case, the desired cost and schedule, etc.), and any existing assets (the company's tools, technology, and templates) and environmental factors. The output is the *project management plan*.

Table 24.1: The *Develop Project Management Plan* process inputs and outputs

Input	Process	Output
Project Charter	**Develop Project**	Project Management Plan
Outputs from project planning	**Management Plan**	
Environmental factors		
Organizational assets		

Table 24.2: The components of the *Project Management Plan* and the associated processes.

Process	Output
Plan Scope Management	Scope Management Plan
Plan Schedule Management	Schedule Management Plan
Plan Cost Management	Cost Management Plan
Plan Quality Management	Quality Management Plan
Plan Human Resource Management	HR Management Plan
Plan Communications Management	Communications Management Plan
Plan Risk Management	Risk Management Plan
Plan Procurement Management	Procurement Management Plan
Plan Stakeholder Management	Stakeholder Management Plan

Unlike many project documents, the *Project Management Plan* is actually a compendium of documents and should be really considered as a high level reference to all of the sub-plans. We summarize the components of the *Project Management Plan* and the processes that produce the component planning documents in Table 24.2. Figure 24.2 illustrates how developing the project management plan requires integrating sub-plans from several knowledge areas.

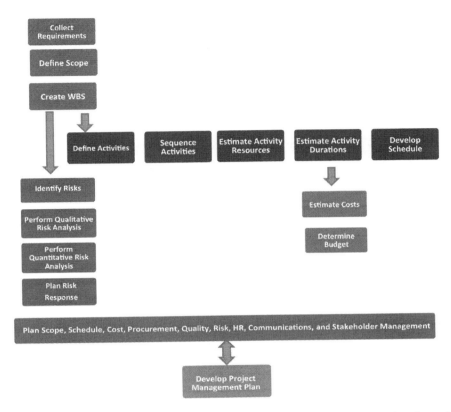

Figure 24.2: The *Project Management Plan* requires integrating sub-plans from several knowledge areas and their processes.

24.1.1 Template for Project Management Plan

A template for the *Project Management Plan* is shown in Table 24.3. The template illustrates that the PM Plan does not repeat other documents, but provide links to the other plans.[2]

---

[2]In the modern world, the references can be hyperlinks.

357

Table 24.3: A template for the *Project Management Plan*.

Project Management Plan
PMA Membership Growth Project

1.	Executive summary of Project Charter a. Abstract from the charter. b. Document any updates to the charter including assumptions and constraints. c. Scope Management plan.
2.	Scope Statement.
3.	WBS and Schedule.
4.	Milestones and Estimated Completion Timeframe. a. Major milestones. b. Major deliverables.
5.	Subsidiary Plans. a. Schedule Management Plan b. Cost Management Plan c. Quality Management Plan d. Human Resource Management Plan e. Communications Management Plan f. Risk Management Plan g. Procurement Management Plan h. Stakeholder Management Plan
6.	Deployment Plan a. Describe the rolling out the application to the sponsors. b. Describe how the end users will be provided training.

24.2 Scope Planning

**By looking at the questions the kids are asking,
we learn the scope of what needs to be done.**

Buffy Sainte-Marie

Scope planning is a major topic and has its own Knowledge Area called *Project Scope Management* with a total of six processes, four of which are in the *Planning* process group and two in the *Monitoring and Controlling* process group. While the *Scope* is produced as part of the plan, it is the first major deliverable on the project and it is the most important document in the project.

Once the project charter has been created and the stakeholders have been identified, the project manager can begin the four scope planning processes: *Plan Scope Management, Collect Requirements, Define Scope,* and *Create WBS.* We describe each of these processes, along with their required inputs and outputs. Major documents are also defined.

24.2.1 Plan Scope Management

The *Plan Scope Management* process produces a key output document, the *Scope Management Plan.*[3] This document provides a road map for creating the scope and for managing changes to it.

The key inputs for this process are the project charter, the project management plan, process assets and enterprise environmental factors. The tools and techniques used to create a Scope Management Plan are simply expert judgment and meetings.

A *Scope Management Plan* typically contains the following information:

1. The procedures to follow when developing the scope statement.

2. The components of a scope statement, i.e., its table of contents.

3. How the WBS is to be created from the scope statement, i.e., traceability of requirements to WBS activities.

4. A process for formal acceptance of the scope by the customer and sponsor.

5. The process for managing changes to the scope and its ties with the integrated change control process.

24.2.2 Collect Requirements

Collect Requirements is the process of clearly defining and documenting all stakeholder's goals, objectives, and needs for the project. The key inputs and outputs associated with this process are shown in Table 24.4. The outputs—the deliverables from the process—are described in the following sections.

The Requirements Document

The requirements document is sometimes called the *Specification.* An easy way to begin thinking about the stakeholders' requirements is to answer the following questions:

[3]This is a new process in the 5th edition of the PMBOK.

359

Table 24.4: The *Collect Requirements* process inputs and outputs

Input	Process	Output
Project Charter	**Collect**	Requirements Document
Stakeholder Register	**Requirements**	Requirements Traceability Matrix
Stakeholder Management Strategy		
Requirements Management Plan		
Scope Management Plan		

- *What?* What do the stakeholders want?

- *When?* When do the stakeholders want it?

- *Who?* Who is going to do what?[4]

Other information included in the requirements document might include:[5]

- *Traceability information.* The name of a stakeholder is associated with each key functional requirement.

- *Acceptance criteria.* These are the specific, measurable properties of the delivered project. They form the basis of the tests to ensure that the stakeholder requirements have been met. One has to be able to answer questions such as: What are the criteria for satisfying the stakeholder? How are the requirements to be tested?

- *Priority of the Requirements.* Different stakeholders have different priorities, which can be classified as "must have" or "nice-to-have." This is a useful way to separate the priorities.

- *Non-Functional Requirements.* These include such items as security, performance, and supportability issues. Specific examples of non-functional requirements are:

    - *Usability,* e.g., the system should be compliant with U.S. Department of Justice Americans with Disabilities Act (ADA).

    - *Availability,* e.g., the website should be hosted with a reliable provider that ensures access 99.9% of the time.

[4]Another question might come to mind: How? This question is not answered here, because *How?* answers the design question, i.e. how are the requirements to be met. We will discuss the difference between requirements and design in Chapter 7–Scope.

[5]For small projects, these should be considered as a checklist. That is, a simple one line statement may be all that is necessary to explain the role of these issues in a small project.

As an example, we present the requirements document for the PMA web site in Table 24.5.

Table 24.5: *Requirements document* for the PMA case study.

Category	Requirement	Stakeholder	Acceptance Criteria
Functional Requirements	A form to register new members	PMA Director	Should be user friendly form
	Email Newsletter to members	Marketing Director	Ability to send up to 3,000 emails to members
Maintainability Requirements	Edit Registration form	IT Staff	Easy to add and edit fields in registration form
	Update web site	IT Staff	System easily updated by IT staff
Security	Membership data will be encrypted in the database	Information Assurance Staff	Membership data secure against hacking tests

Requirements Management Plan

The *Requirements Management Plan* is the document that specifies the way in which requirements will be *managed* throughout the life of the project. It describes attributes such as requirements collection, traceability, and configuration management. Configuration management is important, as it specifies the process to be followed when someone proposes to change a requirement.

As projects evolve, there is an overwhelming temptation to give in to user requests to add functionality.[6] The impact of any change on both cost and schedule must be weighed against the proposed functionality improvement.

In this context, it is important to distinguish between refinements (good) and enhancements (bad). Enhancements usually increase the cost and delay the project. This process is described in more detail in Chapter 7—Scope.

Requirements Traceability Matrix

After the Work Breakdown Structure (WBS) is completed a *Requirements Traceability Matrix* can be constructed. This matches the attributes in the *Requirements Document* to the WBS deliverables and allows for Verification and Validation of the requirements. Verification is the process that tests the *technical* validity of the requirements. Validation is the process that ensures the *value* of the individual requirements to the stakeholders.

[6]"Can we *please* just add this minor function?"

For the PMA case, Table 24.6 shows a *Requirements Traceability Matrix*, which links the requirements to the WBS items.

Table 24.6: *Requirements Traceability Matrix* for the PMA case study

Requirement	Status	Acceptance Criteria	WBS ID
Form to register new members	Completed	Form tested and approved by QA department	2.1
Email Newsletter to members	Not Started	Test designed for 3,000 emails	2.2

24.2.3 Define Scope

As expected, the *Define Scope* process defines the scope of the project and produces the *Scope Statement*, one of the most important documents that the project team will produce. The scope can be started once the *charter* and *requirements document* are completed.

The *Scope Statement* is the fundamental document that describes all aspects of the project, both the managerial process and the desired content to be delivered. The *Scope Statement* is also the basis for a macro (or top-down) cost estimate. The inputs to and the outputs from the *Define Scope* process are shown in Table 24.7.

Table 24.7: The *Define Scope* process inputs and outputs

Input	Process	Output
Project Charter	**Define**	Project Scope Statement
Requirements Documentation	**Scope**	Project Document Updates
Process Assets		
Scope Management Plan		

Project Scope Statement

Typically, the scope includes the following sections: Description of the project; its justification; the business case, including return on investment arguments; deliverables; acceptance criteria; exclusions; constraints; and assumptions. The detailed contents and the technical aspects of preparing a scope statement are covered in Chapter 7—Scope. A major section of the scope defines what the project will do, and is referred to as the *specification*, or "spec."

Project Document Updates

While developing stakeholder requirements, it is expected that changes to the documents will occur. For example, as requirements are refined, new stakeholders may be identified, requiring updates to the *Stakeholder Register*. Therefore, one should expect *Project Document Updates*, which is an output from this process. Also, one may need to refine the *Requirements Traceability Matrix*.

This is an illustration of the iterative nature of project planning, which is not a one-time-through, cascading waterfall process. Project planning requires the project team to evolve: to continually examine the existing documentation, and as required, to carefully update all the previously published documents. In particular, each time a new plan or sub-plan is created, the project team should revisit all related documents and assess the wider impact of the new plan.

24.2.4 Create WBS

The *Work Breakdown Structure* (WBS) is created once the project scope statement is complete. The WBS is derived from the scope baseline and generates individual *activities*, as well as the elements of the WBS dictionary. The inputs to and outputs from the *Create WBS* process are shown in Table 24.8. The outputs, which are deliverables, are described in the following sections.

Table 24.8: The *Create WBS* process inputs and outputs

Input	Process	Output
Project Scope Statement	**Create WBS**	WBS
Requirements Documentation		WBS Dictionary
Process Assets		Scope Baseline
Scope Management Plan		Project Document Updates

WBS

The WBS is a deliverable-oriented hierarchy and defines each deliverable. The WBS further decomposes major deliverables into smaller work packages.

The high level WBS is typically presented in graphical form, and an example is given in Figure 20.6. This is suitable for managing the project and tracking the costs. The low level WBS is usually presented in outline form (see Figures 8.4 and 8.5). The low-level WBS is also the foundation for a bottom-up estimation of the project cost. The detailed contents and the technical aspects preparing the WBS are covered in Chapter 8–WBS.

A sample WBS for the PMA project is given in Figure 24.3.

Figure 24.3: The graphical *WBS* for the PMA case.

WBS Dictionary

The *WBS Dictionary* is a repository that contains the detailed description and data for the work required for each element of the WBS. The *WBS Dictionary* includes: activities, milestones, start and end dates, the organization responsible for the element, quality requirements, performance measurement criteria, resource requirements, cost estimates, and contact information. For the PMA project, we provide an example of a *WBS Dictionary* in Table 8.1.

Scope Baseline

The approved combination of the project scope statement, the WBS and the WBS dictionary constitute the *Scope Baseline*. You can expect the *Scope Baseline* to be updated often. Therefore, *Update Scope Baseline* appears frequently as a process output as the scope evolves.

24.3 Time Planning

> **Lost time is never found again.**
>
> *Benjamin Franklin*

Time Planning covers the processes required to manage the timely completion of the project.[7] There are six processes associated with time (or schedule) planning, and these are shown in Table 24.9, along with the inputs and outputs. The important outputs are in bold. It is clear from Table 24.9 that the outputs from one process are often the inputs to the next process.

Time Planning begins with the *Plan Schedule Management* process, which describes the policies, procedures and documentation for planning, developing, and managing the project schedule. The output from this process is the *Schedule Management Plan*, which can be either a formal document (usually on larger projects) or brief set of procedures informally documented in the Project Management Plan.

Time Planning is a complex and important activity, as it results in an estimate of the project schedule, which is one of the most important aspects of project planning. Everyone wants to know: When will it be finished?

The data for *Time Planning* is most conveniently captured, documented, and reported in a software system that includes project management scheduling, such as *Microsoft Project*®, *GANTTER*®, or *Primavera*®. Another alternative is *ProjectLibre*, which is open source project management software that is compatible with Microsoft Project 2010.[8]

We illustrate the use of project management software by providing samples from the PMA case study using *Microsoft Project*. The technical aspects of developing the project schedule are covered in Chapter 10.

The outputs from *Time Planning* are:

1. *Activity List*

[7] The PMBOK uses "time," but we believe that a more appropriate word is "schedule." After all, who can plan *time*? One is really developing the *schedule*.

[8] Initially released in August 2012, ProjectLibre was developed by the founders of the abandoned OpenProj, which it is still available for free.

Table 24.9: The *Time Planning* processes with their associated inputs and outputs. Important outputs are in bold.

Inputs	Process	Outputs
PM Plan Charter Environmental Factors Process Assets	Plan Schedule Management	Schedule Management Plan
Scope Baseline Environmental Factors Process Assets Schedule Management Plan	Define Activities	**Activity List** Activity Attributes Milestone List
Activity List Activity Attributes Milestone List Activity List Schedule Management Plan	Sequence Activities	**Schedule Network Diagram** Project Document Updates
Activity List Activity Attributes Resource Calendars Environmental Factors Process Assets Schedule Management Plan	Estimate Activity Resources	Activity Resource Requirements **Resource Breakdown Structure** Project Document Updates
Activity List Activity Attributes Activity Resource Requirements Resource Calendars Activity duration estimates Project Scope Statement Environmental Factors Process Assets Schedule Management Plan	Estimate Activity Durations	**Activity Duration Estimates** Project Document Updates
Activity List Activity Attributes Schedule Network Diagram Activity Resource Requirements Resource Calendars Activity duration estimates Project Scope Statement Environmental Factors Process Assets Schedule Management Plan	Develop Schedule	**Project Schedule** Schedule Baseline Schedule Data Project Document Updates

The *Activity List* is created from the WBS. An *activity* is any task that takes time, and you start by generating an activity from each element of the WBS. An illustration of the *Activity List* for the PMA project is presented in Table 24.10.

Table 24.10: *Activity List* for the PMA Case

Initial Design of Membership Form
Create the Requirement Specification
Create User Interface Design
Create Database Table to Store Membership Data
Review Specification and Prepare Test Cases
Review User Interface Design documentation
Documentation of all Systems Documentation
Update Project Management Documentation
Completion of Initial Design Phase

2. *Activity Attributes*

Activity Attributes are the properties and characteristics of activities. These include their predecessor and successor activities, the logical relationships between activities, leads and lags, constraints, resources, and assumptions. The activity attributes develop as the planning process matures.

The most important *Activity Attributes* are:

- *Identification:* The name of the activity (and, perhaps, its number).

- *Duration:* How long it will take to complete.

- *Predecessors:* The activities required to be completed before it can start.

Once these attributes are determined, they can be entered into a project scheduling system, such as *Microsoft Project*, and the schedule drops out.

3. *Milestone List*

Milestones play a key role in assessing the actual schedule against the plan as the project progresses. The accomplishment of major deliverables at specific milestones shows whether the schedule agrees with the stakeholders' planned expectations. It is useful to provide additional attributes for milestones, such as clarifying if the milestone date is Internal or External, and if it is Mandatory or Flexible.[9]

Table 24.11, gives an example of a *Milestone List* for the PMA project.

[9] The technical details of these terms are covered in Chapter 8—WBS.

367

Table 24.11: *Milestone List* for the PMA case.

Milestone	Date	Type
Initiation Phase Complete	1/15	Internal, Flexible
Project Planning Complete	2/1	Internal, Flexible
Initial Design Phase Complete	2/15	Internal, Flexible
Prototype Implementation Complete	2/28	External, Flexible
Full Website Complete	3/10	External, Mandatory
Closing Processes Complete	3/15	Internal, Mandatory

4. *Project Schedule Network Diagram*

Once we have a list of activities and milestones, they can be entered into a software scheduling system to produce a visual network diagram. The network diagram displays the timing relationships between the activities, identifies the critical path, and shows which activities can be worked in parallel. We can also include additional information such as leads and lags. The network diagram is the fundamental tool used to generate an accurate estimate of the project schedule.

For the PMA case, we illustrate the high level portion of a network diagram in Figure 24.4.

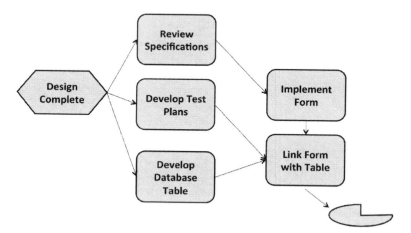

Figure 24.4: A portion of the high-level network diagram for the PMA case.

24.3.1 Estimate Activity Resources

In the *Estimate Activity Resources* process you estimate the types and quantities of resources required for each activity. Resources include people (the team, external consultants, subject matter experts, etc.), material, equipment, and supplies.

Table 24.12 shows examples of resource estimation for the PMA project. Note that the resource types are matched with the activities using them.

Table 24.12: Some examples of *Estimate Activity Resources* for the PMA case.

Activity	Resource Type	Quantity
Create Requirement Specification	Business Analyst	2
Create User Interface Design	Systems Analyst	1
Create Database Table	Database Developer	1
Review Specification and Prepare Test Cases	Test Developer	1
Review User Interface Design Documentation	Design Specialist	1
Writing Systems Documentation	Programmer	1
Update Project Management Documentation	Project Manager	1
Database & Programming Activities	High End Work Stations	6

Resource Breakdown Structure

The *Resource Breakdown Structure* (RBS) hierarchically categorizes the available resources according to different functions, types, or categories. As an illustration, Figure 24.5 presents an RBS in hierarchical format for the PMA project.

24.3.2 Estimate Activity Durations

Estimate Activity Durations is the process in which the time to complete an activity is estimated. The required resources are considered to be an input.[1]

Many techniques are available for estimating the duration of an activity, including both top-down and bottom-up. Popular methods for estimating durations include parametric estimating, analogous or experience-based estimating, the three-point (PERT) method, and the Delphi approach.[10]

An example of *Activity Durations* is shown in Table 24.13 for the PMA case.[11]

[10]This is an important knowledge area and we have dedicated an entire chapter to duration (and cost) estimating–Chapter 11—Cost.

[11]Note that activities with zero duration are considered to be *milestones*.

369

```
0    Project PMA RBS
    1.    Personnel Resources
         1.1    Business Analyst (2)
         1.2    Database Developer (1)
         1.3    Test Developer (1)
         1.4    Design Specialist (1)
         1.5    Programmer (4)
         1.6    Project Manager (1)
    2.    Equipment
         2.1    High End Workstations (6)
         2.2    Printers (3)
    3.    Materials
         3.1    DVDs, USBs, etc.
         3.2    Books, Online Tutorials, etc.
    4.     Services
              4.1    Web Hosting
              4.2    High Speed Networks
```

Figure 24.5: *Resource Breakdown Structure* for the PMA case.

Table 24.13: *Activity Durations* for the PMA case

Activity	Duration (days)
Design	
Review preliminary software specifications	2
Develop functional specifications	5
Develop prototype based on functional specifications	4
Develop prototype based on functional specifications	4
Review functional specifications	2
Incorporate feedback into functional specifications	1
Obtain approval to proceed	0.5
Design complete	0
Development	
Review functional specifications	1
Identify modular/tiered design parameters	1
Assign development staff	1
Develop code	15
Developer testing (primary debugging)	15
Development complete	0

24.3.3 Develop Schedule

**The sooner you fall behind,
the more time you'll have to catch up.**

Steven Wright

In the *Develop Schedule* process, the scope statement, activity list, milestone list, activity resource requirements, and duration estimates are all analyzed to produce the *Network Diagram*.

The single most important concept that emerges from the *Network Diagram* is the *critical path*. An example of a piece of the network diagram is shown in Figure 24.6 for the PMA case, and we can immediately see that the activity *Review Functional Specification* is on the critical path. Critical path boxes are bold.

Further, three activities can start upon completion of the design phase, and we can now see their start and completion times, their durations, and the resources required. As the start and completion times for the activities emerge, we can add these dates to the WBS Dictionary.

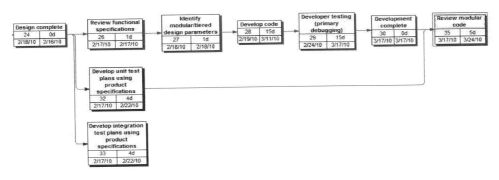

Figure 24.6: A portion of the network diagram for the PMA case.

Modern software systems make it relatively easy to generate such network diagrams.[12] The project schedule shown in the network diagram is called a Gantt chart, and it is widely used to communicate the schedule information.

A Gantt chart is easily understandable by anyone, even if they have no formal training in network diagrams. An example of a Gantt chart is shown in Figure 24.7 for the PMA project.

Schedule Baseline

Once the schedule has been estimated, it can be saved as a *Schedule Baseline*. This baseline, which is a component of the *Project Management Plan*, must be communicated to all stakeholders. Before project execution starts, an official sign-off on the baseline is recommended.

[12] We insist there is no excuse for not using them.

371

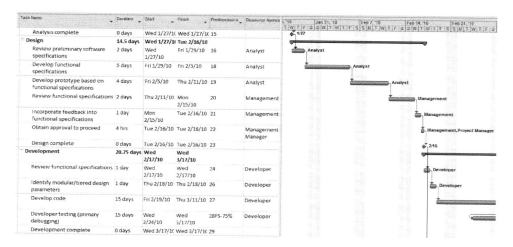

Figure 24.7: A portion of the Gantt chart for the PMA case.

> *The Schedule Baseline is a specific version of the project schedule that is accepted and approved by the team, with committed start and finish dates.*

In Figure 24.8 we illustrate the schedule baseline graphically using the Timeline Tool from *Microsoft Project.* Typically, however, it is the Gantt chart that is submitted to stakeholders to communicate the schedule baseline.

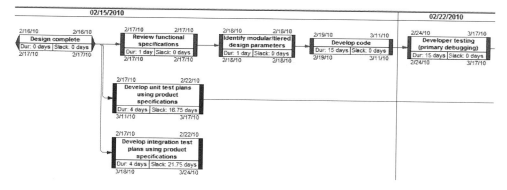

Figure 24.8: A portion of the Timeline diagram for the PMA case.

Before we continue to *cost planning,* we summarize in Figure 24.9 where we are in the planning process. The figure highlights the important processes and deliverables that most project teams would have completed at this point. We have completed the user requirements and the project scope; we have designed the WBS; and we have developed the network diagram, which gives us the schedule. The next step is *cost planning*, in which we develop the project cost estimate.

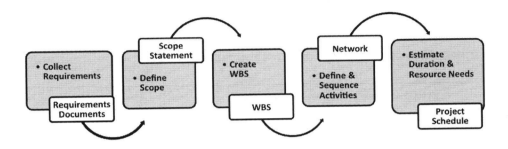

Figure 24.9: A summary of the status after completing *Scope* and *Time* planning.

24.3.4 Cost Planning

The cost of living has gone up another dollar a quart.

W. C. Fields

After the project schedule is created we progress to Cost Planning, which can range from being formal and highly detailed to informal and general. While the team hopes to produce accurate estimates of the cost and schedule, the reality is that these will contain uncertainty, depending upon the quality of the scope and the chance of unknown risks materializing.

The accuracy of the cost and schedule varies over time. Early on, the accuracy may be quite low, but it should improve as the project proceeds.[13] It is important, therefore, to establish a good communication framework that clearly disseminates to the stakeholders the cost and schedule estimates, the current views on their accuracy, any variances, and the assumptions involved. Chapter 11—Cost is dedicated to cost estimation, a very important knowledge area.

The processes associated with cost planning are: *Plan Cost Management, Estimate Costs* and *Determine Budget*. The inputs to and outputs from the *Cost Planning* process are presented in Table 24.14.

[13]A useful rule of thumb is that the project cost is known to within 20% once the project is 20% complete. The interesting issue is that the internal team almost always knows this. Whether the customer is informed is an ethical and political issue!

Table 24.14: *Cost Planning* processes, inputs, and outputs.

Inputs	Process	Outputs
Charter PM Plan Environmental Factors Organizational Assets	**Plan Cost Management**	Cost Management Plan
Cost Management Plan Scope Baseline Project Schedule Human Resource Plan Risk Register Environmental Factors Organizational Assets	**Estimate Costs**	Activity cost estimates Basis of estimates Document Updates
Cost Management Plan Activity cost estimates Basis of estimates Scope Baseline Project Schedule Resources Calendars Contracts Organizational Assets	**Determine Budget**	Cost performance baseline Funding Requirements Document Updates

Plan Cost Management deals with establishing the policies and procedures for estimating costs, budgeting and controlling costs. The primary inputs are the charter and the project management plan, along with process assets and enterprise factors. Meetings and expert judgment are used to create the primary output, which is the *Cost Management Plan*. The *Cost Management Plan* contains the following information:

- Techniques that will be used to estimate the cost

- Experts who will participate in the estimating process

- Units of measure for cost estimates

- Account codes for cost accounting purposes

- Control thresholds for cost variance during execution.

24.3.5 Estimate Costs

> **Large increases in cost with questionable increase in performance can be tolerated only for racehorses and fancy women.**
>
> *Lord Kelvin*

The first step in *Estimate Costs* is to develop a rough, approximate estimate of the resources needed to complete **each activity**.[14] This requires the project manager to consider alternative implementation approaches in both the technical approach and the management process.

An example of technical alternatives might be: Should a prototype be developed, and the project requirements incrementally developed in concert with user feedback, or, is the scope to be carefully defined, and the project developed using the waterfall approach? There are also options for the management approach: Which activities can be processed in parallel? Should we build the activity in-house or outsource the development?

For example, for the PMA project, we might analyze whether to outsource the website development to an experienced engineer or build the website in-house. This is a classic "make versus buy" decision.

Like many processes, *Estimate Costs* is an iterative process, and the accuracy of the cost estimate increases as time goes by. Early on, it is important to label the cost estimate clearly as an *Order of Magnitude* estimate. History suggests that the variation in early cost estimates is often ±50%![15]

As the project proceeds, and the scope is refined, the cost estimate becomes more reliable. As the accuracy improves, the estimate may be relabeled as a *Budget Estimate*. Eventually, when the project manager is confident about the project scope and potential risks, the cost estimate becomes a *Definitive Estimate*.[16]

Cost estimates are expressed either in units of currency or in units of effort, such as staff hours or staff months. Estimates in units of effort are more useful, as they are not subject to inflation.

Cost estimates also include the costs associated with materials, equipment, and services. Finally, there is the entire issue of the overhead costs (benefits, office, utilities, etc.), and these are also covered in Chapter 11–Cost.

Finally, cost estimation should include an allocation for risks, which is called a *contingency*. Risk analysis is the topic of Chapter 17—Risk.

[14] Note that at this point, we are estimating the costs of the **individual activities**, not the entire project. In reality, one may estimate the entire project cost from the scope parameters.

[15] Data also suggest that the larger the project, the larger the initial error. Beware though, this is often a political error, in that people, particularly politicians, are often reluctant to release the true cost.

[16] Only a foolish project manager would be so confident.

Depending upon the industry, worksheets may be available to help the team estimate the costs of activities. For example, for a construction project in the City of Boston, there are detailed worksheets available.[2]

Basis of Estimates

The *Basis of Estimates* document contains a description of how the cost estimate was obtained for each WBS element. Such details are important to note, and if detailed, may be listed in a separate appendix to the cost estimate.

24.3.6 Determine Budget

After completing the cost estimate, the *Determine Budget* process occurs. This is defined as:

> *Determine Budget is the process of aggregating the estimated costs of the individual activities, or work packages, to establish an authorized cost baseline.*

There are two outputs: The *Cost Performance Baseline* and the *Project Funding Requirements*.

Cost Performance Baseline

This is defined as:

> *The cost performance baseline is the time-phased budget that is used to measure, monitor, and control the cost performance for the project.*

The inputs to the *Cost Performance Baseline* are the scope baseline, project schedule, and the cost estimates.

In order to create the *Cost Performance Baseline*, we must add up both direct and indirect costs. (Direct and Indirect Costs are covered in chapter 11—Cost.) A typical baseline consists of the following information: Work Package ID and name, cost per time period, and cumulative cost.

Microsoft Project can output the time-phased costs by resource, and an example is shown in Table 24.15 for the PMA project.

This is only part of the cash flow analysis. It is only the outflow of cash that comes from paying the team. The incoming cash payments from the sponsor must also

Table 24.15: *Time Phased Costs by Resource* for the PMA project. Output from Microsoft Project

Resource	1/3/10	1/10/10	1/17/10	1/24/10
Management	$1,200			$400
Project Manager	$1,60		$2,000	$2,000
Analyst	$840	$2,800	$1,680	$1,400
Tester	$2,800	$2,800	$2,800	$2,800
Total	$6,440	$5,600	$6,480	$6,600

be added. As an example, we present the project costs and payments for the PMA project website in Figure 24.10.

The next step in cost budgeting is to add all of the cash inflows and outflows, since workers, subcontractors, and suppliers need to be paid in a timely fashion. On most projects this requires a detailed cash flow analysis, as the customer may not pay until specific milestones are completed. Meanwhile, bills and invoices may accumulate and may require the project manager to borrow funds to pay the bills. Therefore, synchronizing cash-flow is as important an issue as the total amount of money required.

Figure 24.10 shows the outflow of cash as payments are made to the team (black). It also shows the inflow of cash from the sponsor (grey). The inflows are separated in time because they are tied to deliverables. For example, there is a payment from the sponsor in week 0, representing a payment upon signing of the contract. The payment in week 4 is for the successful completion of the scope.

In Figure 24.11, we have added the weekly cash flows to produce the cumulative net cash position over the life of the project (shaded). The cash flow is initially positive due to the payment in week 0, at contract signing. The net cash position fluctuates as team members are paid, deliverables are completed, and sponsor payments are received.

In weeks 7 and 10, the net cash position turns negative, representing a situation where the project manager will have to borrow money to pay the bills. In weeks 12-17, the project manager will need a line of credit approaching $20,000. Note that the project will eventually end up in a positive situation, but not until well after week 20.

The occurrence of risk events can impact the project cost and schedule. There are usually considered to be two types of risks: *Known-unknowns* and *unknown-unknowns*. The known-unknowns are listed in the *Risk Register* and can be quanti-

377

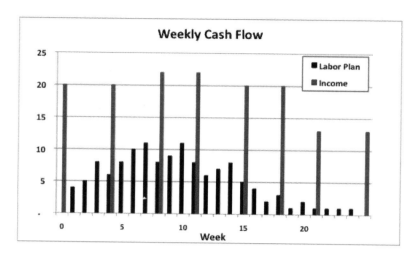

Figure 24.10: The time-phased budget for the PMA project

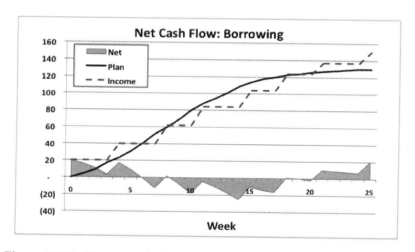

Figure 24.11: The cumulative net cash position for the PMA project

fied.[17] The unknown-unknowns are those events that are totally unexpected, and are much more difficult to deal with.[18]

During the process of risk quantification the team calculates and sets aside contingency reserves for known-unknowns. These reserves can be integrated into the project budget baseline. The PMBOK suggests that funds also be allocated for

[17]Well, it is assumed that they can be quantified.

[18]"No one could have expected that .... (insert your favorite event here)."

unknown-unknowns, depending upon the risks and uncertainty existing in the project.[19] A project manager may keep a separate account with the contingency funds to be spent as needed.

24.4 Risk Planning

> **Risk comes from not knowing what you're doing.**
>
> *Warren Buffett*

Risk management is a large component of the project management plan, with several processes and outputs, and significant technical work. The technical aspects of risk management are covered in Chapter 17—Risk.

Risk management is both an art and science, and deals with planning for the management of the risks; identifying risks; quantifying them; and planning a response in case the risk occurs.[20]

An overall view of risk management is given in Table 24.16, which lists the risk processes, as well as their inputs and outputs.

24.4.1 Plan Risk Management

In this process, the overall plan for risk management is developed. The inputs to and the outputs from the *Plan Risk Management* process are given in Table 24.16. The major deliverables are described below.

Risk Management Plan

The *Risk Management Plan* documents the project team's approach to managing uncertainty, threats or opportunities, stakeholder risk tolerance, resources for assisting with risk analysis, identification of risk categories, assigning weights for risk probabilities and their impact, details about risk management funding, and risk audit approaches.

Before you can create the *Risk Management Plan* you must have access to the project scope statement, the schedule, the cost management plan, the communications management plan, and the enterprise and organizational assets. The risk management plan is a key input to the risk register.

A sample *Risk Management Plan* is shown in Figure 24.12 for the PMA web project case study.

[19]Unfortunately, it is very difficult to convince upper management to set aside funds for things you don't know anything about.

[20]It should be noted that in the PMBOK, the risk processes come after quality and before procurement. We have combined the HR, quality, and procurement processes into the *Sub-Plans* to make what we think is a more organized and easily understood approach.

Table 24.16: The Risk Management Processes, Inputs and Outputs.

Inputs	Process	Outputs
Scope Statement Cost Mgmt. Plan Environmental Factors Process Assets	**Plan Risk Management** **HR Plan**	Risk Management Plan
Risk Management Plan Cost Estimates Environmental Factors Scope Baseline Stakeholder Register Cost Mgmt. Plan Schedule Mgmt. Plan Quality Mgmt. Plan Project Documents Environmental Factors Process Assets	**Identify Risks**	Risk register
Risk Register Risk Mgmt. Plan Scope Statement Process Assets	**Perform Qualitative Risk Analysis**	Risk register updates
Risk Register Risk Mgmt. Plan Cost Mgmt. Plan Schedule Mgmt. Plan Process Assets	**Perform Quantitative Risk Analysis**	Risk register updates
Risk Register Risk Mgmt. Plan	**Plan Risk Responses**	Risk register updates Risk related contract decisions Project Mgmt. Plan updates Document updates

Risk Register

The *Risk Register* plays a key role in the risk management planning process. Creating the *Risk Register* is the first step in the process, and evolves as more activities are completed. During the *Identify Risks* and *Quantify Risks* processes, the risk register might simply consist of the worksheet, as in Table 24.17:

Risk Register Updates

The risk register is updated as the risk management activities evolve. The register is updated as plans for dealing with the identified risks emerge. These typically

---

Risk Management Plan

Project Title: **PMA Website**   Version: **1.2**   Date: **4-15-2011**

Methods and Approaches:

1. The PMI methodology and best practices will be followed for risk management, including the adoption of identifying, quantifying, identifying responses, and monitoring and controlling risks.
2. The team will use an Agile approach to reduce risk by breaking the project into small modules and iterating, with each iteration each lasting only a week.
3. Escalation of risk to senior management shall occur promptly.

Tools and Techniques:

Risks will be classified in the Risk Breakdown Structure (RBS), which is illustrated in the Risk Categories section below. Techniques used to identify risks will include: Brainstorming, risk auditing, the Delphi technique, interviewing experts, and survey of like projects.

Risk Categories:

From our experience with similar projects, we have identified the following categories of risks:

Category	Risks
Schedule	Tight Schedule, Scope Creep, Poor Estimation
Resource	
Communication	Communication skills, Previous Experience
Budget	
Technical	Software quality and browser compatibility risks

Stakeholder Risk Tolerance:

High tolerance=3; medium=2; and low tolerance=1

Issue	Sponsors	Project Manager	Team Members
Performance	1	0	1
Budget	1	1	1
Schedule	2	0	1

Definitions of Probability:

Fuzzy labels of High (H), Medium (M) and Low (L) will be used. High will imply risks above 80%, Medium will be risks at 40% to 80% and Low will be risks below 40%.

Risk Management Funding: Contingencies and Reserves:

Upon completion of a quantitative risk analysis, contingency funding may be requested. If the project risk is high, senior management may set aside a management reserve as well. For example, the quantitative risk analysis may estimate a contingency budget of $10,000 to cover the known unknowns. In addition, a 5% contingency budget may be set aside for unknown unknowns, and a 6-week schedule buffer for schedule risks.

Frequency and Timing:

Risk Analysis will be conducted every week at the project team meeting.

Figure 24.12: *Risk Management Plan* for the PMA case.

involve the following approaches: Prevent/Avoid the risk, Transfer the risk, Mitigate the risk, or Accept the risk, i.e., absorb the risk and do nothing for now, just monitor the situation. Once the strategy for dealing with the risks is assigned, Table 24.17 can be updated as shown in Table 24.18.

Table 24.17: *Risk Identification* for the PMA case.

Risk ID	Risk	Rating (H, M, L)
1	Technical Risk: Lack of WordPress programming knowledge	M
2	Communication Risk: Various stakeholders geographically separated.	H

Table 24.18: *Risk Identification Updates* for the PMA case.

Risk ID	Risk	Rating (H, M, L)	Response
1	Technical Risk: Lack of WordPress programming knowledge	M	Training will be provided to mitigate risk.
2	Communication Risk: Various stakeholders geographically separated.	H	Accept risk–we are unable to do anything about this. Mitigate by providing virtual teaming skills

The technical aspects of risk management are described in chapter 17–Risk.

24.4.2 Identify Risks

The goal is simply to identify risks and add them to the *Risk Register*. To start, a list of risks can often be found in existing resources: lessons from comparable projects or searches in a knowledge-base of historical projects.

As with cost estimation, we can identify risks using either a top-down or bottom-up approach. Early in the project life cycle, we capture risks using top-down risk identification. The advantage of the top-down approach is that it is conducted early in the planning process, and the team has time to change the scope of the project to mitigate or eliminate risks. This technique is called *Risk Prevention*, and mitigating risks early on can make the project significantly less costly.

We recommend the Post-It® approach to risk identification: Provide each member of the project team Post-It notes and ask them to write down all the risks they can come up with. They should be encouraged to briefly document the risk, and add attributes such as: Risk Category (e.g., Technical, Scope, Communication); and Project Impact (e.g., Cost, Schedule). The risks are then entered into the *Risk Register*, which at this stage may simply appear as:

1. Lack of programming knowledge. Risk Category: Technical.

2. Some team members are geographically separated. Risk Category: Communication.

There are many popular methods to help identify risks:

- *Historical databases* and *Lessons learned:* These are typically recorded in a debriefing at the end of projects. They identify "What worked?" and "What did not work?" The former is a good source for the under-appreciated *good risks*, while the latter is a source for threats (bad risks).

    For example, on the PMA project we identified a good risk called "Expedite purchase of new hardware and software." The team identified this as a way to enhance both the cost and schedule.

- *Checklists:* These provide a useful starting point in risk identification.[21] Typically, a checklist will stimulate the team to come up with useful ideas.

    Checklists have received a huge boost in popularity, thanks to a best-seller entitled *The Checklist Manifesto* by Dr. Atul Gawande.[3] [33]

- *Risk Breakdown Structure (RBS):* The RBS is a tool to classify risks according to their category, e.g., technical, scope, etc. Several RBS templates are available in the public domain and can be used as a starting point.

- *Cause and Effect Diagrams:* These are also called Ishikawa diagrams, or Fishbone diagrams. They provide a useful method of identifying and classifying risks, as well as the responses. This tool is described in Chapter 14—Quality.

24.4.3 Perform Qualitative Risk Analysis

In this process we assesses the risks listed in the risk register and prioritize them *qualitatively.* For each risk, this requires determining the likelihood that the risk will occur, and the impact upon the project objectives.

Our preferred approach is to use a scale from 1-5, for both the likelihood and the impact.[22] The risks are then plotted on a grid. The advantage of using a 1-5 scale is that it provides useful bands—see Figure 17.2. The project manager needs to establish agreed-upon definitions for both the likelihood and the impact. Examples help to clarify categories, such as those shown in Table 24.19 for the PMA project.

At this point in the PMA project we could extend the Post-It® approach as follows: The risks the team identified earlier using Post-It notes can now be placed on a flip

[21] Of course, anything missing from the checklist is also a risk!

[22] We prefer to use the term *likelihood* rather than probability. Using the term probability tempts people to assign numbers such as 73% which, at this stage, are meaningless.

383

Table 24.19: Definition of *impact* of risks for the PMA case.

Value	Definition	Examples
1	Unacceptable, or Catastrophic Risk:	The system is compromised, and data is visible to hackers.
3	Minor Damage, or Acceptable Risk:	Project completion date slips by a week. Delay in receiving hardware by a week.

chart to create the likelihood/impact chart. The results are then transferred into the risk register.

24.4.4 Perform Quantitative Risk Analysis

This process provides a numerical, or quantitative, estimate of the impact of the risks under discussion. The impact is usually measured in dollars, although the same techniques can be used for schedule slippages.

For example, we might be interested in identifying a contingency budget reserve for the risks associated with the Lack of Programming Knowledge on the PMA project. We would perform the quantitative risk analysis calculations as follows:

Risk:	Probability	Impact
Lack of Programming Knowledge:	50%	$10,000

If the risk occurs, the estimated contingency fund that must be set aside to pay someone to finish the project is:

$$Contingency\ Fund = 0.5 * \$10,000 = \$5,000. \qquad (24.1)$$

24.4.5 Plan Risk Responses

In this process we develop a plan for what to do if the risk actually occurs. We attempt to reduce the impact of the risk by planning a smart response. Risk responses typically fall in the categories shown in Table 24.20:

Table 24.20: Risk response categories.

Risk Response	How
Prevent	Changing the scope of the project.
Mitigate	Reducing the likelihood or impact., Or both!
Transfer	Passing the risk on to a third party.
Accept	Do nothing. Set aside a budget to deal with the risk.

24.5 The Sub-Plans

Here we cover the sub-plans that make up the final pieces of the Project Management Plan. These are the plans for managing Quality, HR, Communications, Procurement and Stakeholders.

24.5.1 Plan Quality

The quality, not the longevity, of one's life is what is important.

Martin Luther King, Jr.

The output of the *Plan Quality* process is the *Quality Management Plan*, which describes how the quality requirements for the project will be met. The definition is:

> *Plan Quality is the process for identifying quality requirements and standards, and documenting how to demonstrate compliance.*

The inputs to and outputs from the *Plan Quality* process are listed in Table 24.21.

Table 24.21: The *Plan Quality* inputs and outputs.

Inputs	Process	Outputs
Scope Baseline	**Plan**	Quality management plan
Stakeholder Register	**Quality**	Quality metrics
Cost Performance Baseline		Quality checklists
Schedule Baseline		Process Improvement Plan
Risk Register		Document Updates
Environmental Factors		
Process Assets		

Quality Management Plan

In order to create a *Quality Management Plan,* you must have completed the all of the input documents listed in Table 24.21. This plan is used in all subsequent quality management processes and is also consulted when creating the *Project Management Plan.*

As an example, we present a sample quality management plan for the PMA project, which is shown in Figure 24.13.

Quality Metrics

Quality Metrics provide specific measurements of project attributes, and are identified in the *Plan Quality* process. Every industry has its own metrics, e.g., many companies have "customer satisfaction" metrics that are tracked over time.

For service-oriented applications, such as call-centers, metrics might include the time to answer the call, average time to satisfy the customer, percent of 'very satisfied' customers, etc. For software industries, metrics of interest are: code defects per thousand lines; mean time to failure; mean time to repair; and test coverage.

As an example, for the PMA website project, response time was identified as a key metric. Response times to a user request for information was demanded to be less than 2 seconds for all minor requests, and less than 5 seconds for major database-oriented requests. These are examples of specific, measurable attributes of the web site, and make excellent metrics.[23]

Quality Checklists

Quality is enhanced if *Quality Checklists* are used to ensure that the project team produces all documents and does not miss a process. Well-designed checklists actually simplify the project manager's life. For example, for a small project full-scale plans may not be required. A checklist serves as a reminder that all issues have been covered without writing a long bureaucratic plan.

Organizational process assets will typically include checklists that can be tailored for the current project. Some examples of checklist items are listed below. For each item, the project manager can simply indicate whether the issue has been considered with a 'Yes' or 'No', and a brief comment.

- Are project management activities identified for the project?

[23]Of course, there is an issue here: Does fast response make the web site friendly? Not necessarily. More metrics would be needed to measure "user friendly,"

386

QUALITY MANAGEMENT PLAN FOR THE PMA PROJECT

A. Overview:
This plan describes the information required to effectively manage PMA project quality from planning through delivery. It defines quality policies, procedures, roles, responsibilities and the authorities involved.

B. Quality Responsibilities and Quality Roles:
Design and User Interface
> Test User Interface specification – Design Team

Development Environment
> Unit Testing – Development Team
> Functional testing – Test Team

Staging Environment
> Testing – Test Team
> Compliance Testing – End User including an Impaired End User
> Performance Testing – Performance Tester
> Execute Training Exercised– Trainers, End Users

Production
> Production Testing – Test Team

C. Quality Assurance Approach:
Validate: Requirements & functionality of the system; the transition from the requirements specifications to functional & detail designs; and the application is correct and accurate. Adhere to DoJ ADA Compliance Requirements. Customer satisfaction will be measured by industry standard usability practices.

D. Quality Control Approach:
The Test Plan will describe the processes, methods, tools and techniques to be used in performing quality control, specifically supporting the following objectives:

Metrics: Identify the items that should be targeted for testing.
Types: Outlines the testing types that will be executed.
Resources: Identifies the required resources and estimates test efforts.
Deliverables: Lists the deliverable elements of the test project.

E. Quality Improvement Approach:
Proactively identify approaches to improve processes, and techniques, and provide training to all resources.

F. Tools, Environment and Interfaces:
List tools, tool description, and industry recognized benchmarks.

G. Quality Reporting Plan
The communication matrix will identify all stakeholders, who will be informed continually about all aspects of quality and performance.

Figure 24.13: PMA Quality Management Plan.

- Do we have measurable and prioritized goals for managing the quality of the products?

- Have the following been considered: Functionality, reliability, maintainability, and usability?

- Has the project team received training in project management, quality management, and risk analysis?

24.5.2   Plan Human Resources Management

The human mind is our fundamental resource.

John F. Kennedy

Human Resources (HR) Management deals with processes for organizing, managing, and leading the project team. The *Plan Human Resources Management* process has one key output: The *Human Resources Plan.* The HR plan is a comprehensive document made up of several subsidiary plans, including such items as: Roles and Responsibilities, Project Organization and Staffing Management.

The HR Plan identifies the people with the necessary skills to complete the activities, and documents their roles and responsibilities. This is often accomplished with a project organization chart. The staffing plan includes timetables for staff acquisition and release, training needs, team building strategies, recognition and rewards, compliance considerations, and safety issues.

The inputs to and outputs from the *Plan HR Management* process are shown in Table 24.22.

Table 24.22: The *Plan HR Management* process inputs and outputs

Inputs	Outputs	Outputs
Activity Resource Requirements	**Plan HR**	HR Plan
Environmental Factors	**Management**	
Process Assets		

We present a sample *Organizational Chart* for the PMA project in Figure 24.14. We also present a sample *HR Management Plan* in Figure 24.15.

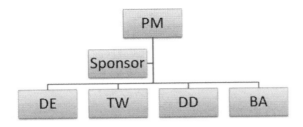

Figure 24.14: The organizational chart for the PMA project.

24.5.3 Plan Communications Management

> **The single biggest problem in communication is the illusion that it has taken place.**
>
> *George Bernard Shaw*

Project communication is essential for successful project management. Communication ensures timely and appropriate generation, collection, distribution, storage, retrieval, and disposition of project information. The project manager must communicate effectively with internal and external stakeholders, and with personnel from different cultural and organizational backgrounds.

There is only one process: *Plan Communications Management,* which has one deliverable: The *Communications Management Plan.*

The inputs to and the outputs from the *Plan Communications Management* process are shown in Table 24.23.

Table 24.23: The *Plan Communication Management* process inputs and outputs.

Inputs	Process	Outputs
Stakeholder Register	**Plan**	Communications Management Plan
Stakeholder Strategy	**Communications**	Document Updates
Environmental Factors	**Management**	
Process Assets		

The communications management plan describes the communication needs of the project, including audiences, messages, methods, and other relevant information. It also defines the approach to be used for those communications. Typical information includes: The sender; the messages to be communicated, and the frequency

---

HUMAN RESOURCES PLAN.

ROLES AND RESPONSIBILITIES

The Project Manager (PM) is responsible for the success of the PMA Website project. The PM must authorize and approve all project expenditures and communicate with the stakeholders. The team members will be responsible for timely execution of the assigned activities and the quality of their work (the activities) should meet established acceptability criteria.

The Design Specialist (DS) is responsible for the design specification & gathering coding requirements.

The Technical Writer (TW) is responsible for training users and the sponsoring IT staff in how to maintain the website. The TW will produce the training manuals, and document configuration changes to the software.

The Database Developer (DD) will implement the backend database connections to the website and will design and build the data tables. The DD must be proficient in PHP and MySQL.

The Business Analyst (BA) is responsible for: Gathering website requirements; building the test cases; and the test plan.

ORGANIZATIONAL STRUCTURE

STAFF ACQUISITION

The project staff will consist entirely of internal resources. No procurement or contracting will be performed. The PM will identify and assign resources in accordance with the organization structure.

STAFF RELEASE

The project staff will be released from the project upon completion and all accounts will be disabled according to information assurance procedures.

TRAINING

Training will be scheduled during the implementation phase and will be documented in the project schedule.

PERFORMANCE REVIEWS

The Project manager will review each team member's assigned work activities at the onset of the project and communicate all expectations of work to be performed. A bonus of 15% of the project cost will be distributed as bonus to recognize team member performance for timely completion of all deliverables within the quality benchmarks.

REGULATION AND POLICY COMPLIANCE

The Department of Justice, American Disabilities Act, will be strictly adhered to. This will require effort in human resources for both development and testing.

Figure 24.15: HR Plan for the PMA case.

with which they will be distributed; the audience; and the media or method to be used.

A sample communication management plan for the PMA project is illustrated in Table 24.24.

The project manager may want to tailor the above plan by adding communication guidelines, including the reason for the communication. For example:

Table 24.24: The PMA *Communication Management Plan*.

Message	Description	Audience	Method	Frequency	Sender
Kickoff Meeting	Introduce team Review goals objectives & processes	Sponsor Project Team Stakeholders Sponsor	Video Conf.	Once	PM
Team Meetings	Review project status	Project Team	Conf. Call	Weekly	PM
Technical Meetings	Status of deliverables	Project Staff	Conf. Call	Weekly, or as required	Project Lead
Monthly Project Status Meetings	Report status of project & technical deliverables	Customer Stakeholders PMO Staff Upper Mgmt.	Face to Face	Monthly	PM

Kick Off Meeting. This is an important meeting, and the objective is to get to know the stakeholders and communicate the project objectives.

Meeting Agenda. The Agenda will be distributed two days ahead of the meeting, and will specify the presenter for each subject, along with a time limit to prevent meeting overruns. Meeting minutes will be recorded by a team member on a rotating basis, and emailed to all members who attended the meeting within 48 hours.

24.5.4 Plan Procurement Management

**The universe never did make sense;
I suspect it was built on government contract.**

Robert A. Heinlein

Procurement planning is all about contracts and their administration. This is a highly specialized area and a good example of the diverse knowledge required by a project manager. The project manager does not need to know all the legal details, but does need an understanding of the risks of the various contract types (covered in Chapter 18—Procurement). Also, a project manager needs to pay special attention to what is to be delivered by whom, which is detailed in the Statement of Work (SOW), which is the most important contractual document.

There is only one process: *Plan Procurement Management*. The inputs to and outputs from the *Plan Procurement Management* process are shown in Table 24.25.

Table 24.25: The *Plan Procurement Management* process inputs and outputs

Inputs	Process	Outputs
Scope Baseline	**Plan**	Procurement Mgmt. Plan
Requirements Doc.	**Procurement**	Procurement SOW
Teaming Agreements	**Management**	Make-or-buy decisions
Risk Register		Procurement documents
Risk-related contract		Source selection criteria
decisions		Change Requests
Activity Resource Reqs.		
Schedule		
Activity Cost Estimates		
Cost Perf. Baseline		
Environmental Factors		
Process Assets		

The important output is the *Procurement Management Plan*, which typically includes the following: contract type, statement of work, procurement roles and responsibilities, contracts, seller lists, selection criteria, bonding and insurance requirements, and constraints and assumptions.

The PMA case study does not have any procurement–all the project work is done with internal resources. This is an example where the item could be checked off with no further work required.

24.5.5   Plan Stakeholder Management

> **Don't live down to expectations.**
> **Go out there and do something remarkable.**
>
> *Wendy Wasserstein*

The *Plan Stakeholder Management* process is defined as follows:[24]

[24]This is one of the major additions to the 5th edition of the PMBOK, the elevation in importance of *Stakeholder Management.*

Developing appropriate management strategies to effectively engage stakeholders throughout the project life cycle, based on the analysis of their needs, interests, and potential impact on project success.

Since stakeholders are so critical to the success of any project, the goal of the *Plan Stakeholder Management* process is to provide a comprehensive and structured approach to the interaction with management of stakeholders.

The key inputs to the *Plan Stakeholder Management* process are the project management plan and the *Stakeholder Register*. The *Stakeholder Register* was an output of the *Identify Stakeholders* process, which is in the *Initiating* process group.

The tools and techniques to develop the stakeholder management plan are simply brainstorming or analytical meetings, typically using expert judgment. The stakeholder management plan can be either formal or informal and usually contains the following information:

- Identities of the stakeholders, their interrelationships and overlaps.

- A benchmark of the desired engagement level (e.g., supportive or leading). A higher engagement level will require more resources and greater communication effort.

- Communication time frames and frequency of interactions.

An interesting point to note is that, unlike most previous knowledge area planning processes, *Plan Stakeholder Management* is the second process in the sequence, not the first! That is, the *Plan Stakeholder Management* process is part of planning and it follows the *Identify Stakeholders* process, which is part of the *Initiating* process group.[25] In other words, one identifies the stakeholders before developing a plan to manage them.

The inputs to and the outputs from the *Plan Stakeholder Management* process are shown in Table 24.26. The primary output is the *Stakeholder Management Plan*.

Table 24.26: The *Plan Stakeholder Management* process inputs and outputs

Inputs	Process	Outputs
PM Plan	**Plan**	Stakeholder Mgmt. Plan
Stakeholder Register	**Stakeholder**	Document updates
Environmental Factors	**Management**	
Process Assets		

[25] *Develop Charter* comes before *PM Planning*, in contrast to *Plan HR Management*, which is the first process in the HR cycle.

25

EXECUTING PROCESS GROUP

Everything should be made as simple as possible, but not simpler.

Albert Einstein

The *Executing Processes Group* is where you actually implement the project.[1] A summary is given in Figure 25.1, which shows that the bulk of the work for the project manager is in managing:

- *People and resources:* Acquire, develop and manage the project team.

- *Communications:* Distribute information and manage the expectations of the stakeholders.

- *Changes:* Manage updates to project documents through change requests.

- *Quality:* Audit the quality requirements and quality control measurements.

- *Procurements:* Evaluate subcontractors and award contracts.

---

[1] Phew, finally!

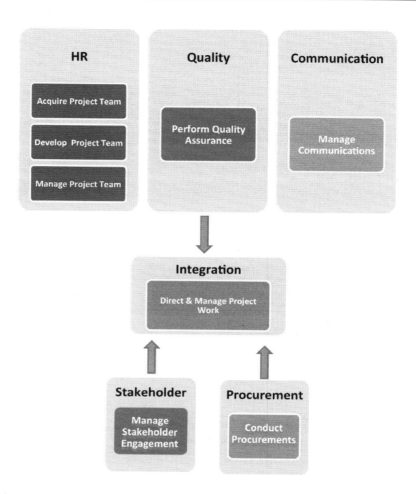

Figure 25.1: The *Executing Process Group* and its associated *Processes.*

25.1 Direct and Manage Project Work

We cannot direct the wind, but we can adjust the sails.

Unknown

During this process the project manager manages the creation of the deliverables, and ensures that they meet project objectives. The project manager also measures the cost and schedule performance against the plan, and manages all communications, risks, quality, and human resources.

The key process in the *executing* process group is *Direct and Manage Project Work*. The primary inputs are from the *project management plan* and the outputs are the actual project deliverables. A vitally important output is the project performance information: whether the project spending is on track, and whether the project is on schedule.

The inputs to and outputs from the *Direct and Manage Project Work* process are shown in Table 25.1. The innocent sounding output, *Work performance information*, is where all the action is. It is the focus of the entire Earned Value chapter.

Table 25.1: The *Direct and Manage Project Work* process inputs and outputs.

Inputs	Process	Outputs
Project Management Plan	**Direct and Manage**	**Work performance information**
Approved Change Requests	**Project Work**	Change Requests
Environmental factors		Project Mgmt Plan updates
Organizational assets		Document Updates

A thread that re-occurs in all the planning processes is the management of change. When the need for a change is detected, there are three possible actions:

- *Corrective action:* The project manager needs to bring the performance of the project into line with established objectives.

- *Preventive action:* The project manager can take action to reduce the probability of negative consequences arising from risks.

- *Defect repair:* The project manager needs to fix the problem.[2]

As an example, in the PMA project, the project manager directs and manages activities such as:

> Creating web pages.
> Training staff in web technology.
> Reassigning best staff to the critical path.
> Managing communications with stakeholders.
> Generating work performance information, i.e., costs and schedules.
> Managing risks.
> Updating the project notebook with lessons learned.

[2] There will inevitably be a lot of debate about whether it is really a defect or the customer's mistake in specifying the requirement. In other words, who is going to pay for it?

25.2 Perform Quality Assurance

Excellence, then, is not an act but a habit.

Will Durant

Many organizations use the term quality assurance to describe the activities that are undertaken to ensure quality results. The *Perform Quality Assurance* process therefore deals with auditing the quality of deliverables and analyzing the results from quality control measurements. The goal is to ensure that the project meets all appropriate standards.[3]

Quality Assurance (QA) is typically conducted through a series of audits, and what results from the audit is a description of good practices to share, deficiencies or defects, and areas for improvement. This generally results in change requests and updates to project documents.[4]

The inputs to and outputs from the *Perform Quality Assurance* process are shown in Table 25.2.

Table 25.2: The *Perform Quality Assurance* process inputs and outputs.

Inputs	Outputs	Outputs
Project Management Plan	**Perform**	QA Change Requests
Quality metrics	**Quality**	Areas for Improvement
Quality control measurements	**Assurance**	Organizational Assets Updates
Information on completed		Updates to project
Deliverables		documents

[3]Essentially, this process is an audit of the quality standards and processes themselves. Remember also that quality assurance covers every stage of project development, not just the implementation phase.

[4]Quality control is technically different from quality assurance. Quality control involves monitoring project results, while quality assurance is about compliance to the customer's needs. It is best to keep the two terms separate, as they have very specific definitions.

As an example, a QA audit for the PMA case might go as follows: The motivation for the audit was that the project manager was concerned about the quality standards in place for the website, which might result in vulnerabilities to cyber-security threats. Therefore, with the assistance of the QA team, a quality audit was conducted and the results are presented in Table 25.3:

Table 25.3: PMA Quality Assurance Audit Results

QUALITY ASSURANCE AUDIT		
☐ Project	☐ Project processes	☐ Project documents
☐ Product	☐ Organizational Policies	☐ Quality Management Plan

As a consequence of the audit, updates were made to the organization's quality assurance processes and the project management plan. Also, areas for improvement were suggested:

Software Design: Focus on best practices to ensure that design specification produces a secure website code.

Hosting Environment: Ensure that the website hosting site is secure.

Software Development Life cycle: Introduce software quality assurance steps, including maintenance recommendations.

Personnel: Schedule constraints on programmers will be watched and training will cover proper configuration and security of the software.

Process: A layered system of security will be introduced into the existing plan.

25.3 Acquire Project Team

Talent wins games, but teamwork and intelligence wins championships.

Michael Jordan

When the project schedule was developed, a resource plan was created to ensure that adequate staff would be available for all required activities. During the execution phase, the project manager must identify the required resources and ensure that they are available, a process known as *Acquire Project Team*. The inputs to and the outputs from *Acquire Project Team* are shown in Table 25.4.

Table 25.4: The *Acquire Project Team* process inputs and outputs.

Inputs	Outputs	Outputs
HR Management Plan	**Acquire**	Project Staff Assignments
Enterprise Environmental Factors	**Project**	Resource Calendars
Organizational Process Assets	**Team**	PM Plan Updates

Tools and techniques used to create staff assignments include:

- *Pre-assignment:* This is typical with larger procurements where the sponsor may have approval rights over major staff assignments, particularly the project manager.

399

- *Negotiation* with stakeholders, particularly functional managers, for best resources.

- *Acquisition* of new project staff with the relevant skills.

- *Create a virtual team*: Some members may be geographically distributed.

For example, the PMA project manager consulted the resource plan, which contained information about team skills, an assessment of their capabilities, roles and responsibilities, and their availability. From this information, the project manager developed the project *staffing assignment* form shown in Table 25.5:

Table 25.5: PMA Staffing Assignments

Calendar	Resource	Commitment
Quarter 1, 2012	Project Manager	1 – Full time
Quarter 2, 2012	Business Analyst	2 – Half time
Quarter 3, 2012	Programmer	2 – Half time, 1 – Full time

Like many software scheduling systems, Microsoft Project supports *Resource Calendars*. The above information could be entered into such a tool as soon as the functional managers commit to the staffing assignments.

25.4 Develop Project Team

> **A person will sometimes devote all his life to the development of one part of his body — the wishbone.**
>
> *Robert Frost*

Once the team is assigned, the job of the project manager is to develop it. This is accomplished in the *Develop Project Team* process, where the goal is to improve the competency of the various individual team members and to generate team cohesion. The inputs to and outputs from the *Develop Project Team* process are shown in Table 25.6.

If the assigned staff does not have the required technical skills, the project manager is responsible for providing training.[5]

[5]Did you squirrel away training funds for this eventuality? You didn't assume that all of the staff would be exactly what you needed, did you?

400

Table 25.6: The inputs and outputs for the *Develop Project Team* process.

Inputs	Process	Outputs
Project staff assignments Human Resources Plan Resource Calendars	**Develop Project Team**	Team performance assessments Environmental factors updates

Typical examples for the team directory, operating agreement, and performance assessment are shown in Tables 25.7, 25.8, and 25.9. Each team member should complete all of these forms.

Table 25.7: PMA Team Directory

Name: **Role:** **Contact Information:**	Victor King Project Manager 617-555-1212 vking@somewhere.com
Name: **Role:** **Contact Information:**	Mary Contrary Systems Analyst 780-111-1212 mcontrary@somewhere.com
Name: **Role:** **Contact Information:**	Bruce Lee Web Programmer 978-555-1212 blee@somewhere.com
Name: **Role:** **Contact Information:**	Maya Banker Cost Analyst 977-555-1212 blee@somewhere.com

Table 25.8: PMA Team Operating Agreement

Purpose:	This team operating agreement provides ground rules to help the team work productively together. Updates to this agreement will be made only after team discussions and obtaining consent from all participants.
Guidelines:	Project team members will report status at each team meeting. Frequency of team meetings and location of meetings. The preferred meeting platform and system for sharing documents, Procedure for managing issues and change requests. Procedure for reviewing action items and updating them. The responsibility of each team member if they miss a meeting.
Communication & Decision Making:	Each team member will be encouraged to bring their area of expertise to the table and communication will be encouraged. All team members will be empowered to make decisions. Also any voting procedures will be covered here to resolve a conflict.

Table 25.9: PMA Team Performance Assessment

Technical Performance:	Rated as *Meets Expectations* or *Needs Improvement*. Example: Programmers: Need Improvement. They do not have experience with WordPress programming and customization.
Interpersonal Skills:	Rated as *Meets Expectations* or *Needs Improvement*. Example: The team members will benefit from some exposure to communication, collaboration, and conflict resolution.
Areas for Development:	*Describe the approach and actions for improvement:* Example: The team will be given half day training in project communication. Programmers will be provided three days' training, either online or at a local company, in WordPress, PHP, and MySQL.

25.5   Manage Project Team

> **As a coach, I play not my eleven best, but my best eleven.**
>
> *Knute Rockne*

The ongoing process of *Manage Project Team* deals with tracking each individual team member's performance, providing feedback, and resolving any issues that arise. The inputs and outputs are shown in Table 25.10. An individual team member's performance should be documented in an assessment form that includes their strengths, weaknesses, areas for development, and actions to be taken by both the project manager and the team member.

Table 25.10: The *Manage Project Team* process inputs and outputs.

Inputs	Process	Outputs
Project staff assignments	**Manage**	Environmental factors updates
Human Resources Plan	**Project**	Organizational asset updates
Team performance assessments	**Team**	Change requests
Performance reports		Project Mgmt Plan updates
Organizational assets		
Issues Log		

25.6 Manage Communications

> **The speed of communications is wondrous to behold.**
> **It is also true that speed can multiply the distribution**
> **of information that we know to be untrue.**
>
> *Edward R. Murrow*

Manage Communications is where information is sent to all stakeholders on a regular, planned basis.[6] The inputs and outputs are shown in Table 25.11.

Table 25.11: The *Manage Communications* process inputs and outputs.

Inputs	Process	Outputs
Communication Mgmt Plan	**Manage**	Project Communications
Work Performance Reports	**Communications**	PM Plan Updates
Enterprise Environmental		Project Document
Factors		Updates
Organizational Process		Organizational Process
Assets		Assets Updates

25.7 Manage Stakeholder Engagement

> **Oft expectation fails, and most oft there where most it promises;**
> **and oft it hits, where hope is coldest; and despair most sits.**
>
> *William Shakespeare*

Manage Stakeholder Engagement is the process of communicating with both internal and external stakeholders, especially about project progress and any issues that have arisen. This engagement usually results in change requests, which require

[6]The tools for *Manage Communications* are covered in detail in Chapter 16, Communications.

403

processing through integrated change control and documentation updates. The capabilities required are strong communication, interpersonal and management skills. The inputs to and outputs from the *Manage Stakeholder Engagement* are shown in Table 25.12.

Table 25.12: *Manage Stakeholder Expectations* inputs and outputs.

Inputs	Process	Outputs
Stakeholder Management Plan	**Manage**	Issue Logs
Communications Management Plan	**Stakeholder**	Change Requests
Change Log	**Engagement**	PM Plan Updates
Organizational Process Assets		Organizational Process Assets Updates

A *Stakeholders Issues Log* can be used to document communications from stakeholders, and an example of for the PMA case is given in Table 25.13.

Table 25.13: The PMA *Stakeholders' Issues Log*.

Issue #	103
Date Reported:	02/10/2012
Reported By:	Bruce Lee, Programmer.
Issue Description:	Web site assets (videos and images) not provided to team in a timely manner.
Ranking & Classification:	High: Impacts critical path. Programming concludes in one week and we urgently need the media.
Impact to Project:	Delay of project schedule.
Resource Assigned To: Assignment:	Systems Analyst, Mary Contrary. Investigation & Resolution
Current Status: **Date Resolved:**	Team plans placeholders for graphics and media as intermediate step. May require website redesign if media quality is poor. Open. We hope to have this issue resolved by 02/17/2012
Resolution, Comments	Systems analyst Mary Contrary has been assigned to work with sponsor to get the media urgently. If sponsor does not respond within 3 days, the PM will escalate this issue.

25.8 Conduct Procurements

> **I'm not going to buy my kids an encyclopedia.
> Let them walk to school like I did.**
>
> *Yogi Berra*

The final *Executing* process is *Conduct Procurements*, which deals with requesting seller responses, selecting a vendor, and awarding a contract. The inputs to and the outputs from *Conduct Procurements* are presented in Table 25.14.

Table 25.14: *Conduct Procurements* Inputs and Outputs.

Input	Process	Output
Procurement Management Plan	**Conduct Procurements**	**Selected sellers**
Procurement documents		**Procurement Contract award**
Source selection criteria		Resource calendars
Qualified seller list		Change requests
Seller proposals		Project Mgmt Plan updates
Project documents		Project document updates
Make or buy decisions		
Teaming agreements		
Organization assets		

26

MONITORING AND CONTROLLING

Kirk: You're not exactly catching us at our best.
Spock: That much is certain.

Star Trek IV

In the *Monitoring and Controlling* process group, the project's deliverables are reviewed, which means they are compared to the established baselines. The project manager monitors the big three: cost, schedule, and scope. However, the project manager must also continually check the status of risks and review quality.[1]

An important part of the *Monitoring and Controlling* process group is the management of changes. Each time a change is proposed, the project team should revisit all related documents, which is accomplished in the *Perform Integrated Change Control* process.

If there are significant variances from the plan, the project manager must take immediate corrective action, following the established change control process. The important question, as always, is: Are the required changes refinements or additions? Changes are submitted to the change control board to determine if they are to be implemented or not.

Monitoring and controlling also involves forecasting. For example, using earned value analysis techniques, the project manager can estimate a revised cost and

[1] Questions to ask here include: How is the project progressing against objectives? Milestones? Schedule? Budget?

schedule for completing the project. During the monitoring and controlling process, the project manager must:

- Validate and verify deliverables.

- Measure deliverables against the cost and schedule baselines.

- Determine variances and return to cost and schedule.

- Respond to threats and opportunities.

- Manage changes through established change control procedures.

- Leverage tools and techniques such as Earned Value.

- Monitor and control procurements and sub-contractors.

- Use Configuration Management and Integrated Change Control systems.

A summary of the processes in this group is given in Figure 26.1.

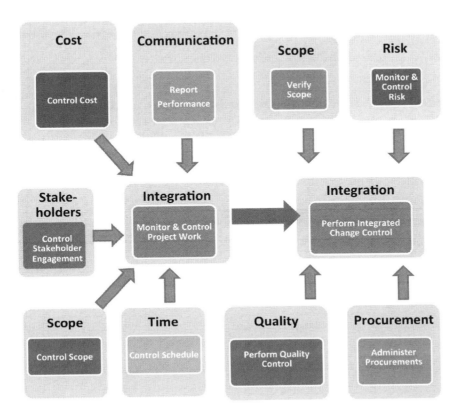

Figure 26.1: The *Monitoring and Control* process groups and the associated *Processes*.

26.1 Monitor and Control Project Work

If everything seems under control, you're just not going fast enough.

Mario Andretti

The *Monitor and Control Project Work* process is where the tracking, reviewing, and regulation of progress occur. The status of the project is determined from the status reports, which are analyzed to determine actual vs. planned progress. If necessary, revised forecasts of the cost and schedule are generated.

A common theme throughout the monitor and controlling process is the tracking of the scope, cost, and schedule, and reporting on the performance, which is

409

illustrated in Figure 26.2. The inputs to and outputs from the *Monitor and Control Project Work* process are shown in Table 26.1.

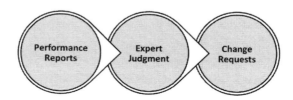

Figure 26.2: Monitoring and controlling project work is about tracking, reviewing, and regulating project progress.

Table 26.1: The *Monitor and Control Project Work* inputs and outputs

Inputs	Process	Outputs
Project Mgmt Plan	**Monitor and**	Change Requests
Work Performance Information	**Control Project**	Project Mgmt Plan updates
Environmental Factors	**Work**	Document updates
Process Assets		
Validated Changes		
Cost & Schedule Forecasts		

The project manager monitors and controls project work throughout the project. As an example, for the PMA project, the project manager's activities include:

- Producing cost and schedule variance reports using Earned Value.

- If there is a significant variance, issuing a change request.

- Updating plans when approved by sponsors and stakeholders.

- Using earned value techniques, revising forecast estimates for the cost (e.g., a new estimate to complete) and schedule.

[2]Notice that the analysis of the change request is not conducted here, it is performed in the *Perform Integrated Change Control* process.

As an example, consider the PMA case. Suppose a key programmer left the project and this required corrective action. This would be uncovered during the *monitor and control project work* process. In the PMA project, keeping to the schedule is important, and the project manager proposed a thorough analysis of the issues, which were documented in a change request.[2]

410

26.2 Perform Integrated Change Control

Change is inevitable ... except from vending machines.

Steven Wright

Perform Integrated Change Control is the process that describes how changes are documented, approved, and managed. This is accomplished through a *Change Control System*, CCS, which is summarized in Figure 26.3.

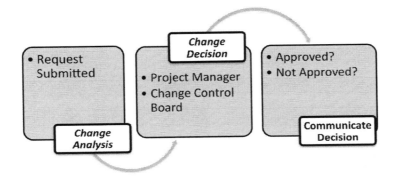

Figure 26.3: The Change Control System (CCS).

This is the process of reviewing all change requests, which may apply to either the deliverables or the documentation. All change requests must be formally documented, approved by stakeholders, carefully implemented, and monitored.

Each proposed change is reviewed for its cost and schedule impact, and then either rejected or approved. Only *approved changes* are incorporated into a revised baseline.

As an example, consider again the above PMA case, where a key programmer left the project. The project manager created a *change request* during the *monitor and control project work* process. In the *Perform Integrated Change Control* process, the *change request* is reviewed and analyzed in consultation with stakeholders. The team came up with the following proposed solutions:

1. Hire and train a new team member.

2. Move team members to different activities.

411

3. Change the scope slightly to reduce the effort.

Keeping to the schedule is most important, and the first two proposed solutions will result in a delay. Only the third option will maintain the schedule, and so it was selected. After everyone agreed to the reduction in scope, the change was approved. The project manager documented all of the potential impacts of the change request, in all relevant plans, and also requested that the team members update the baseline configuration of the system.

Why do changes occur, and what causes them?

Changes occur for many reasons and, typically, by stakeholders requesting additional functionality. This results in scope creep, which is the uncontrolled growth of the project.

Even the project team can be responsible for scope creep as they implement improvements to the project by providing features that the sponsor did not request.[3] Sometimes, changes occur due to some unknown risks materializing and these may result in changes to the project cost or schedule.

What happens when we need to make a change?

In practice, before changes are made, they need to be approved by the stakeholders. A formal process is required, as documenting the change helps the various stakeholders understand the nature of the request and the potential impact. The change is documented in a *Change Request*, which is the initiator of the *Perform Integrated Change Control* process.

Usually, a project has a Change Control Board that analyzes the *change request*, and decides whether to approve it or not. [4]

Once the change is approved, the project manager performs a variance analysis, which will document how significant the impact of the approved change is. The project manager will need to revise the scope based on the approved change, and create a new baseline. Once the new baseline is created, all relevant project documentation must be updated, especially cost and schedule baselines.

The definition of the *Perform Integrated Change Control* is:

> *The process of reviewing all change requests, approving and managing changes to the deliverables, organizational process assets, project documents and the project management plan.*

[3]This is often called gold plating.

[4]If the scope change was not documented then it was not requested.

The word "integrated" reminds us that any changes have to be considered from a global project perspective, since even a small change can affect many different areas. Therefore, a change control system is employed to ensure that changes do not result in chaos.

The first requirement for any proposed change is to determine if it is a refinement or an addition. Refinements are desirable, and a natural part of the progressive elaboration process. Additions however, require a totally different attitude. Any proposed change that will add to the scope should be immediately halted, and thoroughly evaluated.

Formally, the group responsible for approving or rejecting a change is the *Change Control Board* (CCB). The stakeholders should be informed of the potential cost and schedule impacts, and in particular, the customer and sponsor, who will have responsibility for the cost and schedule. These constituencies are represented on the CCB.

The inputs to and outputs from the *Perform Integrated Change Control* process are shown in Table 26.2. An example of change management in the PMA case is given in Figure 26.4.

Table 26.2: The *Perform Integrated Change Control* inputs and outputs.

Input	Process	Output
Project management plan Work performance information Change Requests Environmental Factors Organizational assets	**Perform Integrated Change Control**	Change request status updates Project Mgmt Plan updates Document updates

---

Change Requests
During the PMA project, changes will be requested through a formal system. A standard *Change Request* document will be prepared, which contains the proposed change; its rationale; and the potential cost and schedule impacts. The process for reviewing potential changes is outlined below.

- Change Request submitted formally using a form.

- Project Manager performs initial triage and studies impact.

- Stakeholders review the proposed change and assessed impacts.

- Change is either accepted, rejected or deferred by CCB.

- All stakeholders are notified.

Figure 26.4: The *Change Management Plan* for the PMA web site

26.3 Validate Scope

The *Validate Scope* process is where the scope is formally accepted as a completed deliverable. Accepting completed deliverables requires the project team to interact with stakeholders, and have them formally declare that the requested work has been satisfactorily accomplished.[5]

The inputs to and outputs from the *Validate Scope* process are shown in Table 26.3.

Table 26.3: The *Validate Scope* process inputs and outputs.

Input	Process	Output
Project management plan	**Validate**	Accepted deliverables
Requirements documentation	**Scope**	Change requests
Requirements traceability matrix		Project document updates
Validated deliverables		Work Performance Information
Work Performance Data		

The primary tool used to validate the scope is inspection: That is, the team determines whether the deliverables meet the acceptance criteria. Inspections are described by other keywords, such as reviews, audits and walks-through. Whichever words are used, stakeholders and sponsors examine the work produced by the team, and indicate if it is satisfactorily completed.

The *Requirements Traceability Matrix* can be used as a baseline to help verify the scope. The *Configuration Management System* (CMS) documents the results of scope verification. For example, the CMS documents project updates, and specifies if the scope has been verified; whether the deliverables were accepted, and how the change requests were processed.

For the PMA case, we present a simple example of the *Scope Verification* process and results in Table 26.4.

Table 26.4: PMA Scope Verification

ID	Requirement	WBS ID	Verification	Validation
1	Home Page useful information to members & non-members	1.2.2 1.2.2	Review of page with Sponsor	Sponsor acceptance
2	Section to increase social networking capability of PMA	1.3.2.1.7 1.3.2.1.8 1.3.2.1.10	Walkthrough	Sponsor acceptance

[5]Note that the customer's needs and wants were validated previously, so now we are verifying their elaboration in the scope.

In reality, of course, new desires will show up here!

414

26.4   Control Scope

The *Control Scope* process is where the scope is controlled, i.e., changes to the scope baseline are carefully managed.

The principle method used to analyze a deliverable is *Variance Analysis*. The team analyzes the deliverables for compliance with customer requirements, while also assessing if they are within the planned cost and schedule. If changes need to be made to the scope baseline, *Change Requests* are generated. Variances between the planned and actual cost and schedule may also require corrective actions, and those too may result in *Change Requests*.

The inputs to and outputs from the *Control Scope* process are shown in Table 26.5.

Table 26.5: The *Control Scope* process inputs and outputs.

Input	Process	Output
Project management plan Work performance information Requirements documentation Requirements traceability matrix Organizational assets	**Control Scope**	Work Performance measurements Organizational assets updates Change requests Project Mgmt Plan updates Document updates

26.5   Control Schedule

In the *Control Schedule* process, you monitor the project schedule, producing updated progress reports, which may result in changes to the schedule baseline. The approach is similar to that of the *Control Scope* process, but the focus is on the schedule: Updating changes to the schedule baseline after the impact of the change has been considered by the Change Control Board.

The inputs to and outputs from the *Control Schedule* process are shown in Table 26.6.

The project manager uses variance analysis (for technical assessment) and performance reviews (for cost and schedule assessment) to determine and report project progress. The project management information system can be used to determine an updated schedule.

For the PMA case study, we illustrate a *Variance Analysis* with a sample report shown in Table26.7.

415

Table 26.6: The *Control Schedule* process inputs and outputs

Input	Process	Output
Project management plan Project Schedule Work performance information Scope baseline Project Calendar	**Control Schedule**	Change requests Work performance measurements (eg., Update all EV metrics) Work Performance Metrics (e.g., updated SPI) WBS documentation updates Change requests

Table 26.7: Variance Analysis and Work Performance Results

Project:	PMA	
Date:	05/20/2011	
Planned: **Schedule:**	**Actual** **Schedule**	**Variance**
Package 1: 20 out of 47 project deliverable reports, documents expected completed by 4/15	Only 13 deliverables were completed by 4/15/2011	
Planned Value: $PV = \$4,000$	Earned Value: $EV = \$3,000$	Schedule Variance: $SV = -\$1,000$
Package 2: First iteration of website scheduled to be completed by 4/15	Only 80% of the site pages complete	
$PV = \$2,500$	$EV = \$2,000$	Schedule variance: $SV = -\$500$
Total PV = $6,500$	Total EV = $5,000$	Variance: $1,500$ $SPI = 0.77$ **Behind schedule.**

Root Cause:
(#1) One member of the team was on medical leave of absence.
(#2) Detailed Design delayed by team member on a different page

Planned Response:
New team member requested to pick up the slack.
All documents will be updated to reflect this change.
Existing team will work extra hours until the new resource is up to speed.

26.6 Control Costs

Project costs are monitored in the *Control Cost* process, which involves updating the project budget and managing changes to the cost baseline. The process is similar in nature to the *Control Schedule* process, except the focus here is on costs. Both involve following the flow of events: review of reports and analyze performance data, such from earned value analyses. The inputs to and outputs from the *Control Costs* process are shown in Table 26.8

Table 26.8: The *Control Costs* process inputs and outputs.

Input	Process	Output
Project Mgmt Plan	**Control**	Work performance measurements
Project Funding Requirements	**Costs**	Budget forecasts
Work performance information		Organizational assets updates
Organizational assets		Change requests
		PM Plan updates
		Document updates

Using tools such as Earned Value Management (EVM), an estimated budget is generated, along with any necessary changes to the *Project Management Plan.*

For the PMA case study, we illustrated this process with the sample report that was shown in Table26.7. This is an example of using one report to cover multiple topics. This is efficient and helps eliminate errors by reducing redundancy.

26.7 Control Quality

In the *Control Quality* process, the team monitors the deliverables and assesses the performance of the project. Project deliverables are monitored for quality and technical defects or deviations from planned cost and schedule necessitate corrective action. The inputs to and the outputs from the *Control Quality* process are shown in Table 26.9.

Table 26.9: The *Control Quality* process inputs and outputs.

Input	Process	Output
Project Mgmt Plan	**Control**	Quality control measurements
Quality metrics	**Quality**	Validated changes
Quality checklists		Validated deliverables
Work performance measurements		Organizational assets updates
Approved Change Requests		Change Requests
Deliverables		PM Plan updates
Organizational assets		Document updates

417

In the PMA case study, the project team conducted *Verification and Validation*. The purpose verification was to find defects in documents such as specifications or test cases, but not to fix them. Verification was accomplished through reviews, meetings, inspections, and walks-through.

Validation occurred after verification. Validation was the testing of the functionality of the product, i.e. does the product meet the customers' requirements. The output of the *Verification and Validation* was the *Quality Control Measurements* document, which is shown in Table 26.10.

Table 26.10: PMA Quality Control Measurements.

Planned Result	Actual Result	Variance
Page load 3 seconds.	Average Page Load 10 seconds	7 seconds
Link Navigation 5 seconds.	Average Link Navigation 15 seconds	10 seconds
Root Cause:		Slow response time attributed to the hosting provider.
Planned Response:		Communicate with hosting company. Contingency: Investigate new hosting company immediately.

26.8 Control Communications

Control Communications is a communications process, where the project manager is responsible for collecting and disseminating status reports, forecasts, and technical performance information. The inputs to and the outputs from the *Control Communications* process are shown in Table 26.11.

There are two kinds of reports: A *Performance Report* and a *Forecast Report*. Examples of these are given for the PMA case: The performance report is the *Earned Value Status Report*, which is shown in Figure 26.5. The *Forecast Report* for the PMA case is a calculation of the new *Estimate at Completion*, which is shown in Figure 26.6.

The initial budget for the PMA project was $12,500, but the reports show a revised estimate of $12,900. The project is over budget, with $CPI = 0.97$.

418

Table 26.11: The *Control Communications* process inputs and outputs.

Input	Process	Output
Project Mgmt Plan	**Control**	Performance reports
Work performance information	**Communications**	Organizational assets updates
Work performance measurements		Change Requests
Project Communications		
Organizational assets		

EARNED VALUE STATUS REPORT

Project Title: _____ **BUPMA** **Date Prepared:** 4/20/

Budget at Completion (BAC): $ _____ 12,500.00 **Overall Status:** Almost on budget behind schedule

	Current Reporting Period ($)	Cumulative ($)	Past Period Cum
Planned value (PV)	6,500	10,000	
Earned value (EV)	5,000	8,500	
Actual cost (AC)	5,250	8,750	
Schedule variance (SV)	(1,500)	(1,500)	
Cost variance (CV)	(250)	(250)	
Schedule performance index (SPI)	NA	0.850	
Cost performance index (CPI)	NA	0.971	

Root Cause of Schedule Variance:
(#1) One member of the team was on medical leave.
(#2) Team not on same page on design and implementation issues.

Impact on Deliverables, Milestones, or Critical Path:
There is a chance that project deliverables for this week and subsequent weeks will get dela

Figure 26.5: A *Performance Report* showing the status of the PMA project, which uses Earned Value to determine that the project is over budget.

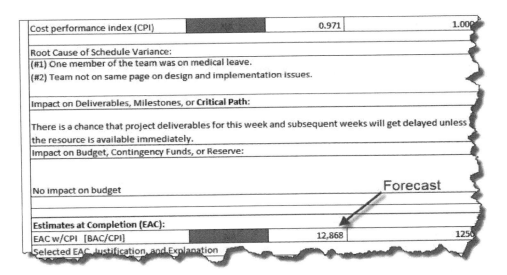

Figure 26.6: A *Forecast Report* showing the revised forecast for the estimate at completion (EAC).

26.9   Control Risks

In the planning phase we covered the risk planning processes: *Plan Risk Management, Identify Risks, Perform Qualitative Risk Analysis, Perform Quantitative Risk Analysis,* and *Plan Risk Responses.* Once the project begins executing, the *Control Risks* process describes how the project team will track and manage the risks that have already been identified.

The *Control Risks* process also describes how to deal with any new risks that appear in the execution phase of the project. Finally, the team evaluates the effectiveness of the *Risk Management Plan.* The inputs to and the outputs from the *Control Risks* process are shown in Table 26.12

Table 26.12: The *Control Risks* process inputs and outputs.

Input	Process	Output
Risk Register	**Control**	Risk Register Updates
PM Plan	**Risks**	Process Assets Updates
Work Performance information		Change requests
& reports		Project Document Updates

The activities associated with this process require the team to monitor residual risks through the risk mitigation process, as well as to identify, quantify, and respond to new risks. The project manager also has to ensure that risk policies and procedures are followed and that all project assumptions remain valid.

For the PMA case study we show an updated *Risk Register* in Table 26.13. This is an extension of the *Risk Register* illustrated in the Planning phase.

The *Risk Audit* is a tool that is used to monitor and control project risks, and it is illustrated in Table 26.14.

Table 26.13: Updated Risk Register

Risk ID	Risk	Response	Responsible Resource Mitigation	Rating (H,M,L)	Current Status (Traffic Light)
1	Technical Risk: Lack WordPress programming knowledge	Training provided to mitigate	Mary	L	Green
2	Communication Risk: Various stakeholders geographically separated	Accept risk: Unable to do much. Mitigate with virtual team training	Mary	L	Green
			Dave	M	Orange

Table 26.14: PMA *Risk Audit* tool.

Audit of Process	Rating	Actions to Improve
Risk Identification and Mitigation	Satisfactory	Risk analysis could be improved by the PMA agenda item at weekly team meetings and communicating to stakeholders

26.10 Control Procurements

The *Control Procurements* process describes the relationship with sellers and how to monitor the contracts with them to assure appropriate performance. It also describes how changes and corrections can be made to a contract.

The inputs to and outputs from the *Control Procurements* process are shown in Table 26.15.

Table 26.15: The *Control Procurements* process inputs and outputs.

Input	Process	Outputs
Procurement documents	**Control**	Change requests
Contract Performance reports	**Procurements**	Updated documentation
PM Plan		
Procurement documentation		

In our PMA case study we do not have any external contracts or procurement relationships, so for this section of the plan, we can simply note: Not Applicable.[6]

[6]This is not unusual in project management, as not all processes apply to all projects. The processes are used as checklists, and if one is not needed, it is OK. Just be sure to note this in the PM plan.

26.11   Control Stakeholder Engagement

The *Control Stakeholder Engagement* process is defined as follows:[7]

> *The process of monitoring overall project stakeholder relationships and adjusting strategies and plans for engaging stakeholders.*

This process is necessary because, as the project environment changes, new stakeholders might appear. The project manager must be constantly on the lookout for new, emerging stakeholders. As new stakeholders are identified, they must be immediately classified as to their engagement level and their potential to disrupt the project as currently organized.

The inputs to and the outputs from the *Control Stakeholder Engagement* process are shown in Table 26.16

Table 26.16: The *Control Stakeholder Engagement* process inputs and outputs.

Input	Process	Outputs
PM Plan	**Control**	Work Performance Information
Issue Log	**Stakeholder**	Change Requests
Work Performance Data	**Engagement**	PM Plan Updates
Project Documents		Organizational Process Assets Updates

The key tools that the project manager needs to monitor stakeholder engagement are expert judgment and meetings with various individuals or groups, such as senior management, other units in the organization, subject matter experts and industry consultants.

---

[7]This is a new process in the 5th edition of the PMBOK.

27

CLOSING PROCESS GROUP

**Acceptance of what has happened is the first step
to overcoming the consequences of any misfortune.**

William James

In the *Closing Process* group, the customer formally accepts the project deliverables.[1] and it is the job of the project manager to complete the project (or phase). Activities at this stage consist of:

- *Formal Acceptance of the Project.* The project manager must obtain final acceptance of the project.

- *Post Implementation Activities.* These include soliciting and documenting the lessons learned; releasing all project resources; archiving project materials; and conducting post-project reviews.

- *Closing Out Contracts.* If a seller was involved, the final procurement details are completed.

Projects come to an end when they have completed their deliverables and satisfied their stakeholders.[2] Sometimes projects are suspended or killed for business

[1] The deliverables were previously validated–an output of the *Perform Quality Control* process.

[2] Hopefully, successfully!

425

reasons or for failure of the team to perform adequately. We will cover the scenario of early project termination when we discuss the *Close Procurements* process. Whether successful or not, the project manager must complete the project closure processes–see Figure 27.1.

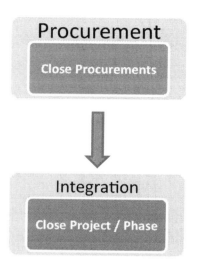

Figure 27.1: The *Closing* process group and its associated *Processes.*

The following questions need to be asked at the start of project closure:

- *Organizational Issues.* Who will be involved in the project closure phase? When and where will project closure be conducted?

- *Project Evaluation.* How did the project perform against its stated objectives? How did the cost and schedule compare against the plan?

- *Lessons.* What lessons were learned? What could have been done differently?

A team meeting at this stage will be a good learning experience for everyone. Typically this meeting might involve asking questions such as:

- How well did we plan the project?

- How well did we execute the project?

- How well did we monitor and control the project?

- How well did we communicate internally and externally?

- How would you rate your satisfaction working on this project?

- How can we improve on the above aspects?

There are two processes: *Close Procurements* (associated with the *Procurement* knowledge area) and *Close Project or Phase* (associated with the *Integration* knowledge area). This is indicated in Figure 27.1.

27.1 Close Project or Phase

Close Project or Phase is the process of formally completing the project or phase. The formal name includes "close phase" because the project management process groups may be applied repeatedly in a multi-phase project.

Close Project or Phase involves administrative closure, which is the name given to the collection and archiving of project reports and documents; creating project archives; and the capturing of lessons learned from the project. The inputs and outputs are illustrated in Table 27.1.

Table 27.1: The *Close Project or Phase* inputs and outputs.

Input	Process	Output
Project Mgmt Plan	**Close Project or Phase**	Final product, service or result transition
Accepted Deliverables		Process assets updates
Organizational assets		Organizational assets updates

First, what are accepted deliverables? This is the list of final deliverables accepted through the *Verify Scope* process, which is part of the *Monitoring and Controlling* process group. Process assets include documents such as the project audit guidelines, project evaluation requirements, and transition criteria.

The completion of the project results in a final product, service or result, and the outcome is described in the formal sign-off document.[3] This process is widely known as *Formal Acceptance*, and involves documenting the stakeholder comments that emerged during the acceptance process.

The output *Organizational Asset Updates* refers to updates to the project management plan, risk registers, change management documentation, and the cost budget. Together with lessons learned, these documents constitute historical information,

[3] The sign-off document does not refer to the physical project, only the process outcomes.

427

and should be transferred to the organizational knowledge base for use by future project managers.

Another useful document the project manager may decide to write is the *Transition Plan*, which guides the sponsors in the future use the product. This will also help the transition of the project into its operational role.

A final face-to-face meeting with the sponsor is desirable and it is where the final product and transition plan are discussed. This will create a positive lasting experience for the stakeholder.[4]

A key problem with this phase of the project is that the team members are very busy and they are released from the project to work elsewhere. Therefore, lessons learned from a project are frequently not captured. To resolve this problem, organizations should commit to continual improvements by budgeting time for the process of lessons learned and disseminating them.

The project manager may be responsible for some post-project activities, such as working with the functional managers, in a matrix structure, to release and re-assign personnel. Also, the project manager may want to write an honest performance assessment for each team member for consideration by the functional manager. The project manager should discuss such appraisals personally with each team member.

Another suggested post project activity is to follow up with the customer several weeks or months after the product is in use. As well as generating goodwill, it can help determine if the strategic business reasons for undertaking the project actually materialized.[5]

Lessons Learned

The project manager should create a *Closeout Report*, which includes an executive summary of the project and highlights of the scope. The report should also document the project management processes, commenting on any significant schedule, cost, quality and communication issues. The lessons learned should also be recorded here. Finally, the *Closeout Report* should be widely disseminated so that people in the organization can benefit from the accumulated wisdom.

[4]The last impression is the best impression!

[5]A good project manager would celebrate success and reward participants with a party.

A sample project *closeout report* document containing some lessons learned from the PMA project is illustrated in Figure 27.2.

428

> **Closeout Report** containing lessons learned from the PMA project
>
> Project Name: PMA   Date Prepared: 5/9/11   Project Manager: V. Kanabar
>
> **Summary:**
> The PMA project was a successful project: It fully met its objectives. The scope and sponsor requirements were fully implemented and accepted. Product quality was verified and validated and the project stayed within the planned schedule and cost baselines.
> The sponsors communicated during acceptance they were happy with the deliverables. The team members communicated that the project was a great learning experience for all. They attribute this in part to the excellent collegiality and communications among team members. They also observed that team members were willing to pick up slack for each other, especially when one of the team members was on medical leave of absence.
>
> **Lessons learned:**
>
> 1. The project was well-planned and the team executed it very well.
>
> 2. The project team's focus on cost estimation and risk management paid off. Since the estimates were on target, the project schedule stayed on track. Since a comprehensive risk response plan was created, issues and risks were mitigated satisfactorily.
>
> 3. Very few technical risks materialized, which appeared due to good risk management.
>
> 4. We communicated with the sponsor about the project scope and requirements early on. This was very important for the final success of the project.
>
> 5. We created a code of conduct for the team, which dictated how communications should take place and how conflicts were to be resolved. This helped avoid conflicts.
>
> 6. We conducted team-building exercises early on. Since some team members were working virtually, it was very important to investigate and implement virtual team-building techniques. Personality issues were resolved early on according to the code of conduct.
>
> 7. We were honest about problems, and so we resolved many early before they became difficult issues.
>
> 8. We completed project deliverables in a timely manner and engaged stakeholders on a regular basis. This involved final updates to all documentation, and migration of the new website to the production server for live use.

Figure 27.2: Project Closeout Report and Lessons Learned

27.2 Close Procurement

Close procurement involves the closure of contracts and procurement relationships with the various sellers. The inputs and outputs are shown in Table 27.2.

The following options exist for closing a procurement:

Table 27.2: The *Close Procurement* inputs and outputs.

Input	Process	Output
Project management plan	**Close**	Closed Procurements
Procurement documentation	**Procurement**	Process assets updates

All deliverables have been completed and meet expectations.
Termination of the project early by mutual agreement.
Termination the project by default when the buyer has
unresolvable problems with the seller.

Procurement is an area dominated by the legal implications. Therefore, the project
manager must be aware of the contents of all contracts, as well as the financial and
legal procedures, and follow them strictly. Two key inputs are needed: The project
management plan and the procurement documentation, which is used to verify
that all contractual requirements have been met.

Even if the project closes abruptly, either by mutual consent or otherwise, the *Close
Procurement* process must occur. Typically, this is guided by the close procurement
clause in the contract that the buyer and the seller agreed to.

What comes out of the walk-through, audits and final negotiations is the signing
of the legal close procurement papers, which document the process.[6] Company
assets are updated, and the following items are typically added to the repository:

> *Acceptance Notice.* This formally acknowledges the acceptance of the
> deliverables by the buyer.
> *Warranty.* Assurance of warranty is kept for future reference.
> *Contract Documentation.* This includes all closed contracts.
> *Lessons Learned.* Experience with the project, deliverables, and vendors
> are documented for future reference by the organization.

PMA Closure Example

[6]When we remodeled our
kitchen we conducted a walk-
through with the contractor
to inspect the finished construction. We had agreed to
hold back $5,000 to be paid
upon successful completion
of the work. We went through
the "punch list" to ensure
that everything was indeed
completed.

Suppose during the PMA case study, the design of the member database was sub-
contracted out to an expert. Below is a sample of issues to be included in the
contract closeout document, which evaluated the services delivered:

> Vendor performance analysis: What worked? What can be improved?
> Record of contract changes.
> Record of contract disputes.

Part V

Microsoft Project® Tutorial

28

MICROSOFT PROJECT TUTORIAL

Software is like entropy. It is difficult to grasp, weighs nothing, and obeys the second law of thermodynamics; i.e. it always increases.

Norman Ralph Augustine

In this chapter, we present a tutorial in the use of *Microsoft Project*®. We implement the Graduation Picnic Project case study introduced in the Chapter 21. [1]

28.1   Start Project

Open *Microsoft Project 2013*. To do that, click the "Start" button on the task bar, click "Programs" and then "Microsoft Office Project 2013." You will see the Main Project Window—see Figure 28.1.

On the Main Project Window you will see various templates and on the left side of the screen you have the opportunity to open recent projects you have worked on. On the right side of the screen are icons. Select "Blank Project" and you will see The Main Task Window (Figure 28.1).

We explain some of the components of the main dashboard here. The "Quick Access Toolbar" is at the very top, and is a place for you to add short cuts to your frequently

[1] In this chapter, we follow the *Project* notation, which uses the term *task*. Previously, we have followed standard project management vocabulary by using the term *activity*

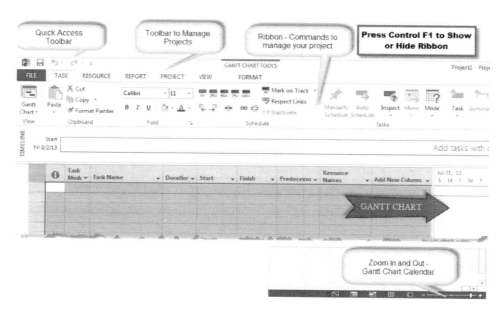

Figure 28.1: The *Project* Main Window.

used functions.

For example, you will see an icon for file save.[2] Two other icons, there by default, are arrows for "Redo" and "Undo." These have short cuts of Control-Z and Control-W and give you a chance to cancel any changes you made or to reapply them. These are very useful options. Don't be afraid to click on buttons and make changes while you are learning—you can usually undo any ghastly mistakes.[3]

You should also see the "Toolbar" with menus options such as "Task," "Resource" and "View." When you click on one of the menu options, you will see additional menu options.

For example, the "Scroll to Task" icon is in the "Task" menu. This is a useful feature that is frequently asked for by students: It scrolls the Gantt time scale and shows the bar for the task you select. The Report menu option is new in *Project 2013*.

If you want more room on your screen, you can collapse the Ribbon. To do that, right mouse click anywhere and select the "Collapse Ribbon" option. Or you can use the "Control F1" command. To see the Ribbon again, hover over the menu bar at the top and uncheck "Collapse Ribbon." The Ribbon automatically adjusts itself based on the width of your window.

[2] Frequent saving is even more important in *Project* than in other programs.

[3] But not always!

28.2 Change Project Settings

Before you get going with *Project*, there are two settings you may want to change:

1. *Setting up Project Options*: Click on "File" and then select "Options." Here, you can change the calendar date format, the currency, the project start and end dates, the number of work hours per day or per week, the week's start day, the language, and more exotic options such as the cloud storage location. You may want to change the default storage location to your own computer, instead of "Microsoft Skydrive."

2. *Auto Schedule vs. Manual Schedule*: The most important option that you should change is to "Auto Schedule."

Before you start entering data into *Project*, you should change the default setting of the scheduling engine to *Auto Schedule*. In earlier versions of *Project* prior to 2010, the scheduling engine defaulted to scheduling project dates automatically. This is called auto-scheduling. When a new task is inserted, say with duration of two days, the project finish date is updated automatically by two days. Furthermore, dependent tasks dates are adjusted appropriately with new start and finish dates.

The other option is *Manual Schedule*, which is the default setting. This can be viewed as "do-it-yourself scheduling." When *Manual Schedule* is active, you can insert new tasks and they will not impact the schedule, you have to manually insert task start and end dates. Manually scheduled tasks have unique indicators and the task bar indicates how the task is scheduled.

Especially for beginners, it is much easier to understand *Project* when tasks are automatically scheduled. Therefore, we strongly recommend changing the default to *Auto Schedule* as shown in Figure 28.2. You should also learn what manually scheduled tasks look like and how to change them to Auto Scheduled scheduling.

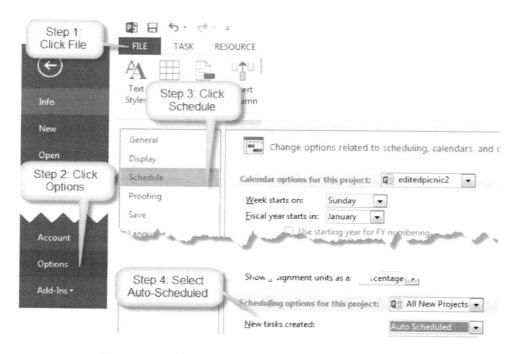

Figure 28.2: Changing the Default Scheduling Setting.

28.3   Enter Project Information

You are now ready to start entering your project data. One of the first things to do is to select a name for your project and save it with an appropriate file name, e.g., "Picnic Project-1."[4] Next, you set the start date and your scheduling preference: either forward from the "Start Date" or backward from the "Finish Date."[5]

To set the project start date, click the "Project" menu option in the Ribbon. Then select the "Project Information" option (see Figure 28.3). In this chapter we will indicate such commands by: Select Project → Project Information.

Notice that the default project start date is the current date. We changed it to January 1, 2015, which is when we wish to start working on the project.

You have the option to schedule your project forward from the "Start Date" or backward from the "Finish Date. In our example, we have a specific end date in mind: The picnic is to be held before graduation in the middle of May. Therefore, we entered the project "Finish Date" as 5/19/15, as shown in Figure 28.4. We also selected "Schedule from: Project Finish Date."

[4]We encourage you to use lots of version numbers as you progress (-1, -2, etc.) so as not to lose your work.

[5]For beginners, we recommend selecting forward from the "Start Date."

436

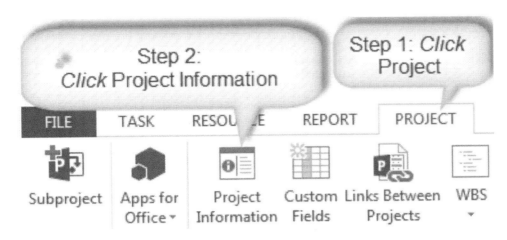

Figure 28.3: Setting the project Start Date.

Figure 28.4: Scheduling from the project Finish Date.

28.4 Enter the Tasks

Before entering tasks, you must already have developed a work breakdown structure (WBS). Since we already have a WBS for the picnic from the project plan templates (Chapter 21), we will use that and proceed to enter the key tasks into the default Gantt View window.

As illustrated in Figure 28.1, the main project window consists of the Gantt chart calendar and a spreadsheet-like entry table. A split bar separates the entry table on the left from the Gantt chart form on the right. You can move this bar to make more or less room for the Gantt chart.

Use the entry table to enter the Picnic Project task information shown in Table 28.1

437

Table 28.1: Tasks, their ID, durations and predecessors.

Task ID	Task Name	Duration (days)	Predecessors (ID from col 1)
3	Prepare proposal for party and budget	5	
4	Obtain Funding for party	5	3
	Charter & Funding Complete	0	
6	Identify potential locations	5	4
7	Obtain Permission for Venue	2	6
8	Inform Security & confirm venue	1	7
	Venue Obtained	0	
9	Identify Food Vendor	30	8
10	Select Menu for the Party	3.75	9
11	Identify music vendor (DJ)	1	8
12	Negotiate vendor contracts	4	11, 10
13	Create Party Event Committee	1	9
14	Create invitations	1	13
15	Email invitations	2	14
	Party Planning Completed	0	
16	Dry Run for the Picnic 1	1	15
18	Manage the Party	1	16
	Party Completed	0	
33	Close all Contracts	1	29
34	Send out survey	1	29
24	Identify key PM processes & IS Needs	20	
25	Complete & Maintain PM templates	60	24
26	Implement & Maintain Project IS	30	24
21	Document lessons learned	0.5	26, 34

by simply typing the names of the tasks into the box. You can also import your tasks from Excel or copy and paste them from just about any other source document.

Click on the "Task" menu option in the ribbon and enter the tasks shown in Table 28.1.

The information in Table 28.1 is interpreted as follows: In the first column, *Project* has assigned the unique ID = 12 to the task named "Negotiate vendor contracts." The second column contains the "Duration" of Task 12, which is estimated at 4 days. The third column contains the predecessors and Task #12 has two of them: Tasks #10 and #11. This means that Task #12 cannot start until both #10 and #11 are complete.

Tasks with duration of zero are milestones and have no predecessors, e.g., "Charter & Funding Complete."

We have also entered a summary task for the entire project, called "Party Project," which is the top level of the WBS tree. In addition, we have included activity tasks that will be designated as lower level subtasks. Later, we will show how to indent these lower-level tasks and create subtasks, so that the structure will be more understandable.

28.5 Creating Summary Tasks and Subtasks

A summary task is made up of two or more lower level tasks, which are called subtasks. To create subtasks:

1. Select the tasks you want to designate as lower level or subtasks.

2. Create the subtasks by clicking on the "Indent" button, identified by the arrow key icon ($\rightarrow$), which indents the tasks and designates them as subtasks.

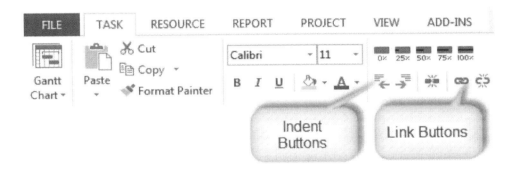

Figure 28.5: Indent and Link Task Menu Buttons.

An indented task becomes a subtask of the task above it, which is now the parent task. Figure 28.5 shows the "Indent" button. The "Indent" button was used to create the summary tasks and subtasks, which are illustrated in Figure 28.6.

Once you have created summary tasks you can collapse the subtasks by clicking on the small triangle that appears to the left of the "Party Project" and "Define Party" tasks. This gives you a summary view of your project by including only the high-level tasks. If you click the triangle again, you will see the subtasks. The small triangles are shown in Figure 28.6.

Click the "Outdent" icon (the left arrow), which is next to the "Indent" icon, to move a task back to the level of the task above it; now they are no longer subtasks.

439

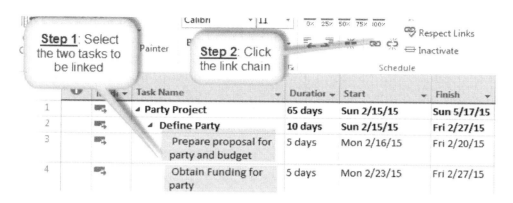

Figure 28.6: Linking Tasks.

28.6   Link Tasks

The next step is to add network dependencies by using the "Link" button, which is shown in Figure 28.6.

When you link a task to other tasks, you answer the question "For this task, which predecessor tasks must be completed before it can start?" There are two steps to linking tasks and we show them in Figure 28.6.

Consider the task, "Obtain funding for the party." Before it can start, the predecessor task "Prepare Proposal for party and budget" must be completed.[6]

To link tasks, select (i.e., highlight) the predecessor and then select the successor task so that they are both highlighted. Next, click on the "Link" button. A link arrow will be created in the Gantt chart.

It is very important to select the tasks in the correct order—select predecessor and then successor, i.e., select "Prepare Proposal for party and budget" and *then* select "Obtain funding for the party." If you select them in the wrong order, the tasks will be linked incorrectly.

Upon completing the link steps, study the project start and finish dates and you will notice that they have updated appropriately.

If you make a mistake, you can unlink tasks by clicking the "Unlink" icon, which is to the right of the "Link" icon, see Figure 28.5.

As an alternative to using the icons, you can also double click on the "Task Information" and a dialog box opens. Click the "Predecessors" tab where you can enter the

[6]We remind the reader of that this is the definition of the network arrow, and the finish-to-start constraint.

440

dependency information for the task.

You can also change the link to a different type. The default link type is Finish-to-Start (FS). You can change the link type by adding the abbreviation for a start-to-start (SS), finish-to-finish (FF), or start-to-finish (SF) link.[7]

Once you have linked all of the tasks, you have your first project plan. It should show that you could successfully finish the party project by the 17th of May, which is in agreement with the proposed plan.

28.7   Displaying the WBS ID

It is easier to read and understand the task hierarchy if you introduce a column called "WBS," as shown in Figure 28.7. When you insert the WBS column, it automatically creates an outline number for each task based on where the task appears in the hierarchy.

We illustrate the three steps required to insert the WBS column in Figure 28.7. Here, we see that the "Create Invitations" task has a WBS ID of 1.2.9.

[7]We highly recommend against this. Stick with the standard finish-to-start (FS) task type.

441

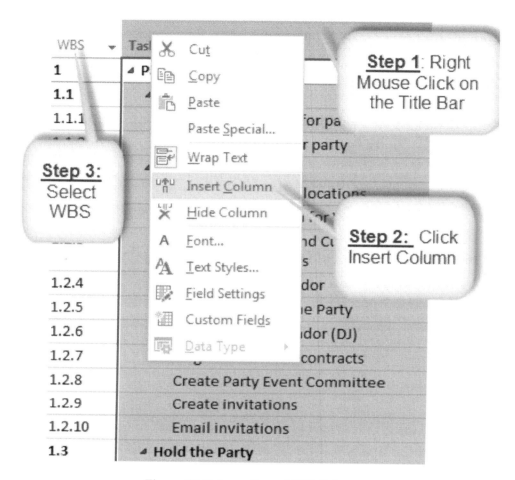

Figure 28.7: Inserting a WBS Column.

28.8 Assign Durations

You assign a duration to a task by simply typing a number in the duration column. Figure 28.8 shows the durations of the tasks, as well as indented subtasks.[8]

When you enter a task, *Project* automatically assigns it a duration of one day, followed by a question mark. To change the duration, type a number in the duration column. Durations are measured in units (days, weeks, etc.), which are shown in Table 28.2.

The duration consists of both a number and an appropriate duration units symbol.

[8]Remember, at this point, these are still estimates.

Task Name	Duration	Start	Finish
⊟ **Party Project**	**80 days**	**Wed 1/28/15**	**Tue 5/19/15**
⊟ **Define Party**	**23 days**	**Wed 1/28/15**	**Sat 2/28/15**
Prepare proposal for party and budget	5 days	Wed 1/28/15	Tue 2/3/15
Obtain Funding for party	5 days	Wed 2/4/15	Tue 2/10/15
Charter & Funding Complete	0 days	Sat 2/28/15	Sat 2/28/15
⊟ **Plan Party**	**45 days**	**Wed 2/11/15**	**Wed 4/15/1!**
Identify potential locations	5 days	Wed 2/11/15	Tue 2/17/15
Obtain Permission for Venue	2 days	Wed 2/18/15	Thu 2/19/15
Venue Obtained	0 days	Sun 3/15/15	Sun 3/15/15
Inform Security, and Custodians & formalize	1 day	Fri 2/20/15	Fri 2/20/15
Identify Food Vendor	30 days	Mon 2/23/15	Fri 4/3/15
Select Menu for the Party	3.75 days	Mon 4/6/15	Thu 4/9/15
Identify music vendor (DJ)	1 day	Mon 2/23/15	Mon 2/23/15
Negotiate vendor contracts	4 days	Tue 2/24/15	Fri 2/27/15
Create Party Event Committee	1 day	Mon 4/6/15	Mon 4/6/15
Create invitations	1 day	Tue 4/7/15	Tue 4/7/15
Email invitations	2 days	Wed 4/8/15	Thu 4/9/15
Party Planning Completed	0 days	Wed 4/15/15	Wed 4/15/15
⊟ **Hold the Party**	**2 days**	**Wed 5/13/15**	**Fri 5/15/15**
Dry Run for the Picnic	1 day	Wed 5/13/15	Wed 5/13/1!
Manage the Party	1 day	Thu 5/14/15	Thu 5/14/15
Party Completed	0 days	Fri 5/15/15	Fri 5/15/15
⊟ **Close Party**	**3 days**	**Fri 5/15/15**	**Tue 5/19/15**
Close all Contracts	1 day	Tue 5/19/15	Tue 5/19/15
Send out survey	1 day	Fri 5/15/15	Fri 5/15/15
⊟ **Project Management**	**80 days**	**Wed 1/28/15**	**Tue 5/19/15**
Identify key PM processes & Project Information System Needs	20 days	Wed 1/28/15	Tue 2/24/15

Figure 28.8: Duration estimates for the picnic project for tasks and subtasks. Milestones have duration zero.

When you type a number into the duration column, the units are automatically

Table 28.2: The units, and their symbols, for task durations in *Project*.

Unit Symbol	Unit
d	days (default)
w	weeks
m	minutes
h	hours
mo, or mon	months

assigned in days.

If you are unsure of the duration estimate, and want to review it again later, enter a question mark after it. Do not enter durations for summary tasks as these are automatically calculated based on the subtasks. In fact, *Project* will not allow you to enter or change the duration of a summary task.

28.9   Inserting Milestones

In the task ribbon you will see the milestone icon. To create a milestone, click the icon and enter a task name such as, "Charter & Funding Complete." Another way to create a milestone is to select a task and just enter its duration as *zero* days. The task symbol changes from a bar on the Gantt chart to the symbol for a milestone, which is a triangle. The milestones for the picnic project are shown in Table 28.3.

In *Project*, milestones are actually tasks, they just have a zero duration. However, because they are tasks, they can be linked to other tasks. Therefore, there are different ways to implement milestones:

- You can link an important milestone to the tasks that precede it. That way, if any of the tasks are delayed, the milestone moves to the time of the completion of the last linked task.

- You can insert the milestone date directly, so that its date is fixed and it does

Table 28.3: The milestones for the picnic project.

Task Name	Date
Charter & Funding Complete	Sat 2/28/15
Venue Obtained	Sun 3/15/15
Party Completed	Sun 5/17/15
Project Complete	Sun 5/17/15

not move. If tasks get delayed, they might extend beyond the milestone, indicating trouble. However, since the milestone is not linked to the delayed tasks, you may miss the fact that the milestone is actually late.

You can also use multiple milestones assigned to a single event. That way, you get the best of both options: One milestone linked to its predecessor tasks, which will be the best estimate of when the milestone will occur, and a static milestone, which will not move, for the planned date (from the scope).

We recommend that you enter the milestones for important events as "manually" scheduled tasks with a hard date. After you have entered all your tasks and fine-tuned your schedule, link the milestone to the predecessors. Otherwise, your milestone will keep moving as you tweak your schedule.

Note: If you want a milestone with finite (i.e., non-zero) duration, you can use the task properties box. After entering the task duration, just double click the task, and click on the "Advanced" tab of the "Task Information" dialog box. Click the "Mark Task as Milestone" check box and click OK.[9]

It is important to continually analyze the emerging network as it develops. For example, after we inserted milestones from the project scope statement, we noticed an issue: The 2/15 milestones appears to be after its planned date, see Figure 28.9. Either we have to start the project earlier or we must move the milestone to a later date.

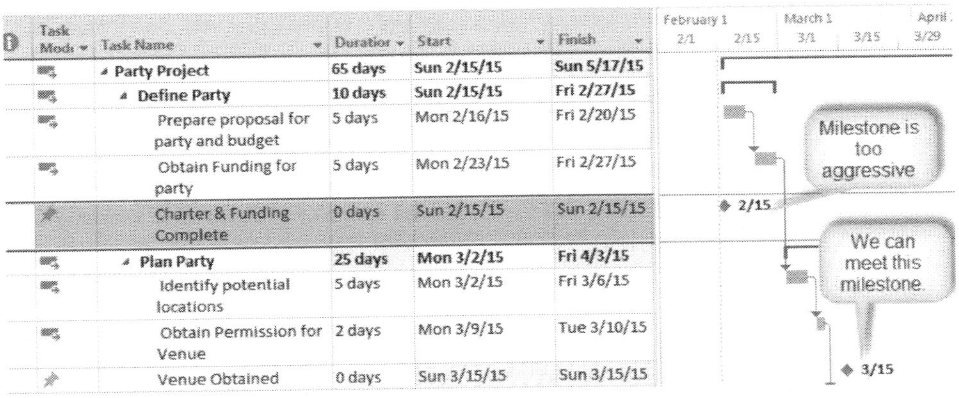

Task Mode	Task Name	Duration	Start	Finish
	Party Project	65 days	Sun 2/15/15	Sun 5/17/15
	Define Party	10 days	Sun 2/15/15	Fri 2/27/15
	Prepare proposal for party and budget	5 days	Mon 2/16/15	Fri 2/20/15
	Obtain Funding for party	5 days	Mon 2/23/15	Fri 2/27/15
	Charter & Funding Complete	0 days	Sun 2/15/15	Sun 2/15/15
	Plan Party	25 days	Mon 3/2/15	Fri 4/3/15
	Identify potential locations	5 days	Mon 3/2/15	Fri 3/6/15
	Obtain Permission for Venue	2 days	Mon 3/9/15	Tue 3/10/15
	Venue Obtained	0 days	Sun 3/15/15	Sun 3/15/15

Figure 28.9: Milestones in the Picnic Project.

[9]We do not recommend using a milestone with a finite duration. The formal definition of a milestone says that it is an *event*, which, by definition, has zero duration.

28.10   Showing and Hiding Summary Tasks

If you want to hide the summary tasks, you can uncheck the option "Summary Tasks" in the Format menu on the ribbon. You will only see tasks that are low level, i.e., usually work packages. To show the summary tasks again check the "Summary Tasks" again as illustrated in Figure 28.10

Figure 28.10: Showing and Hiding Summary Tasks.

If you checked the option called "Project Summary Task," you will see that a root-level summary task was inserted with the WBS ID of 0. In our project, we created a summary task and we hard-coded the root WBS with an ID = 1.0.

If you have many tasks, say more than 40 tasks or a page full, do not create a root WBS for the project. Let *Project* create the root summary task and provide the summary view of the project whenever you need it.

28.11   Resources

Projects use resources, such as people, materials, and even cash, such as money for travel and training. You can define resources and assign them to tasks. *Project* then allows you to produce reports that specify the total resource requirements, their cost, and even to balance and level their consumption.

All resources are defined with the "Resource" menu option in the ribbon. Here you can add people, create a resource pool, and manage and level the workload.

The following menu options are used to manage resources:

1. *Resource Menu:* This is used to define the resources, i.e., to name them and to assign their costs.

2. *Task Menu:* This is used to assign particular resources to individual tasks.

3. *View Menu.* This is used to view the resource sheet and the usage of resources over time.

Before entering resource data into *Project*, you should have a clear picture of the costs of each resource. Here is a brief summary of resource costs:[10]

- *Direct Costs:* Direct costs are those billed directly to the project, and include labor for team members as well as material, supplies and equipment used wholly by the project. Direct costs also include travel to perform specific project work and procurement costs associated with subcontracts.

- *Overhead Costs:* These are costs not directly associated with a specific task but are required to run the organization. Overhead costs include occupancy costs, e.g., mortgage or rent, utilities, supplies, etc. In the picnic project case study, a storage room will also be used to store party supplies, computers and more. This room is not dedicated to the picnic project.

- *General and Administrative (G&A) Costs:* These include company-wide expenses, such as payroll processing, information technology, legal and accounting.

We will assume, as is usual, that direct labor costs include overhead and G&A, since total labor rates are typically what is presented to the customer. In other words, we use *Project* in a way that presents cost information to the customer in a familiar and comfortable way.[11]

28.11.1   The Resource Sheet

Entering resource data begins with the "Resource Sheet." When you entered the tasks into the Gantt view, you started identifying the resources for your project. Most of them were probably of type "Work," i.e., labor. There are other resource types, such as the costs associated with the procurement of goods and services, e.g., Music and Food.

You can click on View → Resource Sheet to see the resources defined for the party project, which are shown in Table 28.4.

We now discuss the resource types:

[10]We remind the reader that labor and overhead costs are all defined in section 11.8.

[11]If you told the customer that the project manager costs $30 per hour, then that is the number to use in *Project*. The fact that the project manager only takes home $10 per hour is irrelevant.

447

Table 28.4: Resource sheet for the picnic project.

Name	Type	Material	Std. Rate	Cost/Use
Project Manager	Work		$30.00/hr	$0.00
Volunteer Team	Work		$0.00/hr	$0.00
Student Leader	Work		$20.00/hr	$0.00
Publicity Coordinator	Work		$20.00/hr	$0.00
Event Day Coordinator	Work		$20.00/hr	$0.00
Dean of Students	Work		$0.00/hr	$0.00
Student Council President	Work		$0.00/hr	$0.00
Faculty Chairman	Work		$0.00/hr	$0.00
Techie	Work		$20.00/hr	$0.00
Dumpster	Work		$50.00/hr	$100.00
Food Services	Cost			
Music DJ Cost	Cost			
Printing Cost	Cost			
Taxi Cost	Cost			
Container for Trash	Material	Can	$50.00	$0.00
Tables	Material	Table	$50.00	$0.00
Chairs	Material	Chairs	$10.00	$0.00
Tent	Material	Tent	$0.00	$500.00

1. *Work Resources*: Resource costs for labor, such as the project manager and other project team members, can make up the majority of a project's costs. The proposed labor rate for the project manager is $30 per hour and $20 per hour for the other student coordinators. Later, you will assign these student coordinators to the appropriate tasks, i.e., the ones they will perform.

In our picnic project, in order to cut down on labor expenses, we are using unpaid student volunteers. Also, the Dean and the Department Chair are assigned zero cost, since their management oversight is considered part of their normal job assignment.

Project uses an hourly rate to calculate the cost of an assignment to produce a cost report. For example: If the project manager works 5 hours on the "Prepare proposal for party and budget" task, the cost is calculated as:

$$Cost = \$30 \times 5 = \$150. \tag{28.1}$$

You can also use non-labor resources here. For example, in our party we plan to use a "Dumpster" for all the trash. This Dumpster has a charge of $100 per use, and an additional $50 per-hour rental cost. Therefore, the dumpster cost

Table 28.5: Material resources for the picnic project.

Resource Material	Cost/Use
Container for Trash	$50.00
Tables	$50.00
Chairs	$10.00

estimate is:

$$\$50 \times 6 \; hours + \$100 \; charge = \$300 + \$100 = \$400. \qquad (28.2)$$

Note that *Project* automatically prorates costs over time. You can, however, change this default setting so that you pay for the resource either at the start or at the end of the task. For example, the Dumpster provider may ask for the entire rental fee up front.

2. *Material Resources*: Many resources are classified as "Material." You do not assign material resources over time, as we did with work resources. Instead, material resources are assigned by quantity.

   For example, chairs, tables and the tent are all assigned as material resources for the picnic project. We simply enter a cost per unit as shown in Table 28.5. Therefore, if your party uses three tables, the cost estimate is:

$$Table\; Cost = 3 \times \$50 = \$150. \qquad (28.3)$$

3. *Cost Resources*: Cost resources are used when a resource is not associated with an hourly rate or quantity. Unlike work or material resources, we assign cost resources directly to tasks, and not on the resource sheet. This also allows you to change the costs assigned to a task each time the resource is used.

   Consider, for example, a taxi, which might be used for visits to the DJ, the Food Catering Company and to pick up food. Depending upon the distance traveled, the taxi cost will vary by task, and different amounts will be assigned to different tasks.

28.12 Assigning Resources to Tasks

Once you have completed the resource sheet, the next step is to assign resources to the tasks. Go to the Gantt View and select the "Resources" column of the task for which you want to assign resources. You will see a drop-down box showing the resources. Select a resource. Put a check mark next to the resource, and you are done, see Figure 28.11.

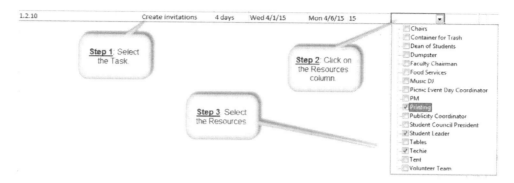

Figure 28.11: Assigning Resources to Tasks.

If you look at the Gantt chart you will now see the assignments (i.e., the names) of the resources to the tasks in the bar chart, see Figure 28.12.

Figure 28.12: Resources Displayed in Gantt View.

The above process only allocates a quantity of one resource. To assign more resources, double click on the task, select the resources column, and change the quantity. For example, if we need three tables for the party, we double click on the task, select the resources column, and change the quantity to '3,' see Figure 28.13.

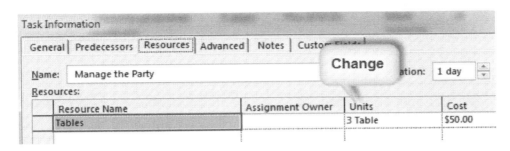

Figure 28.13: Changing the Quantity of Resources.

28.13   Changing Assigned Resources

You can change the resource name. For example, we started with a generic resource name, i.e., "Student Leader." Once we have assigned the leader we can use his or her real name. You can also replace a resource with another one. Reasons to replace a resource are that someone is no longer available or that they are over allocated.

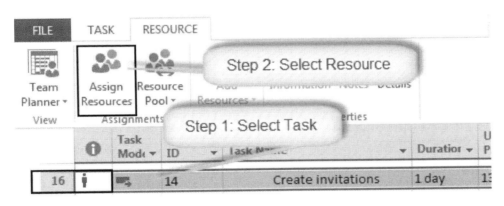

Figure 28.14: Changing the Over-Allocated Resource.

To replace a resource, highlight the task and then use the command: Resource → Assign Resources. Select the appropriate resource. See Figure 28.14.

One of the valuable options is the ability to query *Project* for resources with time available. Figure 28.15 shows how to search for an alternate resource that has two hours available to replace the Student Leader, who is over-worked.

451

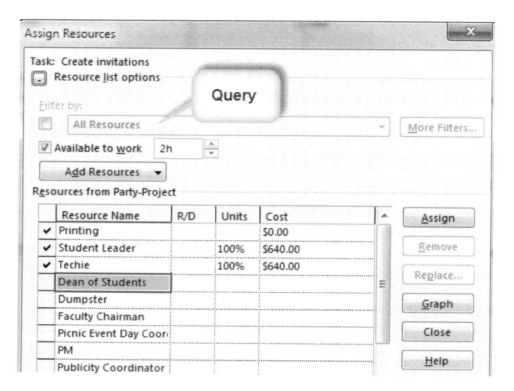

Figure 28.15: Query for Available Resources.

28.14 Project Calendars

Scheduling a project and assigning resources requires you to understand project calendars. A project calendar defines the working time, the non-working time, holidays, vacations and more. There is a standard calendar that comes with *Project* and it defines the typical work schedule: Monday to Friday, eight hours per day.[12]

Calendars are used when a particular resource is only available for a specific time interval. For example, the Techie may only be available for picnic project web site work during the month of April.

If you wish, you can change the standard calendar and create a new one. For example, you may want to consider the fact that on the picnic project the students are busy with schoolwork during the day time. In that case, you can assign the working time as being from 7 PM to 11 PM. Also, since the students are truly dedicated to the picnic project, you can even make it a seven days-a-week schedule.

[12]The standard calendar is more than adequate for simple projects.

452

There are various types of calendars in *Project*. They include the Standard Calendar (comes with the default install); the Base Calendar (defines new working hours and working days); the Resource Calendar (can be created for each resource, with variations from the base calendar to accommodate things like annual vacations); and the Task Calendar (used, for example, for board room meetings), which is similar to the Resource Calendar.[13]

28.15   The Work Column

So far, we have not explained the Work column, as we have done all our scheduling using durations in days. For example, the estimate for the very first work package, called "Prepare Proposal for Party & Budget," is 5 days. There is only one person, the project manager, who is allocated to perform this task. Since the project manager is working full time over this 5-day period (8 hours per day), the task will consume 40 hours of work.

The project manager may have an "Assistant Project Manager" to help with the preparation of the proposal. With two people on the task, its duration could be reduced to 2.5 days. However, the task's work, or effort, will remain at 40 hours.

28.15.1   Units

In the above examples, we assumed that the resources work full time on a task. Therefore, they are considered as 100% resource units. If a resource were assigned to work only half time on a task (50%), the Work effort would be only 20 hours per week instead of 40.

Resources are assigned in what *Project* calls "units." A half time resource assignment will appear on the Gantt chart as: **Project Manager [50%]**, which is a half unit.

Suppose a task is estimated to take 10 days and the project manager assigned to the task has a rate of $30 per hour. The default is a full-time resource (100%), so that the cost is 10 days × 8 hours × $30 = $2,400.

If the task were smaller, then the project manager might only need to work half-time, and so the cost of the task would be at a 50% work rate: 10 days × 8 hours × $30 ×50% = $1,200. For a larger task with two full-time people assigned, then the cost doubles to $4,800.

The mathematical relationship between duration and Work is:

$$Duration = \frac{Work}{Unit}. \qquad (28.4)$$

[13]We do not cover the details of the calendars in this tutorial. However, you will find more information about changing the calendars in *Project Help*. Click F1.

453

This can be switched around to calculate Work as: Work = Duration × Unit. Also, *Project* can calculate the resource units if the duration and work are available: Unit = Work / Duration.

For example, the project manager takes 40 hours to finalize the project plan. The duration is two weeks (80 hours). Therefore,

$$units = \frac{40 \ work\text{-}hours}{80 \ hours} = 0.5. \tag{28.5}$$

This 0.5 unit is 50%, which means that the project manager works half-time on the task "Finalize the Project Plan" over a period of two weeks.

We have an example of this for the "Project Management" activity. The project manager works only 10% of the time on the tasks listed there, such as: "Identify key PM processes & Project Information System Needs," and "Complete & Maintain PM templates."

When we talk about Work (also called Effort) we do not include holidays or non-working days, such as weekends. However, you can use the term "Elapsed Time" if you want to refer to calendar time, which is the span of time associated with the actual elapsed duration of a task. For example a week of work is 5 days, but a week of elapsed time is 7 days.

28.16   Fine Tuning the Schedule

We are almost done with our first cut at the project plan for the picnic project. At this stage, it is a good idea to take a step back and analyze the schedule. This might include the following activities:

1. Align Milestones with the Project Plan: Study the planned milestone dates and see how well they align with the proposed schedule.

2. Change the Gantt Chart Timescale.

3. Investigate Resource Conflict: Study over allocated resources.

4. Study the Critical Path: Provide resources to the critical path if needed to compress the schedule.

5. Examine Costs: See if they fall within the budget proposed by the sponsor.

6. Identify Bottom up Risks: While we have looked at system level risks, we now have the opportunity to identify risks at the task level and mitigate them. For example, risks on critical path tasks may delay the schedule.

Table 28.6: Milestones output from *Project*.

Task Name	Milestone Date
Charter & Funding Completed	Sat 2/28/15
Venue Obtained	Sun 3/15/15
Party Planning Completed	Wed 4/15/15
Party Completed	Sun 5/17/15

7. Create a Baseline.

These topics are explored in more detail below.

28.16.1   Aligning Milestones with Project Plan

We have identified several milestones, which are tasks with zero duration. Our first goal is to see how well these milestones compare with the planned milestone dates, which we promised to our sponsors in the charter and scope statement. The milestones in the scope statement are presented below:

Fundraising Complete:	February 15th, 2015
Preparation for Party Completed:	May 15th, 2015
Completed Plan for party logistics:	April 15th, 2015
Preparation for Party Completed:	May 15th, 2015
Post Party Survey:	May 17th, 2015

We can now compare this to the output from *Project*, which seems to fit in pretty well so far, see Table 28.6. A key indicator is that the planning should be completed a month before the party. Fundraising has slipped by 15 days, but since the sponsors provide a large amount of the party funding, this is not a risk.

Displaying Milestones with Filters

It is easy to display the milestones in your project. You can filter and sort dates before viewing and printing them. Filtering also allows you to see just the tasks you want. In our milestone table shown above we have taken the following steps:

1. In the ribbon click: View → Filter and select "Milestones" from the drop down box. See Figure 28.16.

2. Click: Form → Uncheck Summary Tasks.

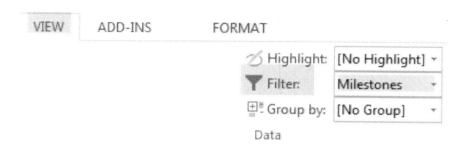

Figure 28.16: Project Filters.

28.16.2 Changing the Gantt Chart Timescale

Changing the Gantt chart timescale is very helpful when studying the project schedule. You can adjust the timescale to show the schedule on smaller or greater time unit scales, from minutes to years. This gives you an opportunity to compress your project onto one or two pages and to get a birds-eye view of the bar chart. There are three tiers of timescales and you have to ability to format each of them.

In Figure 28.17 you see the key steps required to change the timescale. The command is: View → Timescale. There are three tiers you can format: top, middle and bottom. For example, in Figure 28.18, we formatted the middle tier to show quarter years (i.e., three months) as the time-scale. This middle tier will appear above the bottom tier, which is in months. A preview of what the three tiers will look like is shown at the bottom of Figure 28.18.

In this context, the scroll-to-task function is useful. The command is: Tasks → Scroll to Task (or Control-Shift-F5). This will center your view on the task you are interested in. You can also use the zoom button, at the bottom right corner, to get a detailed view of your project bar chart.

Finally, you can right mouse click anywhere in the Gantt chart and change the display options of the bar styles. For example, you can show and hide critical tasks, slack, late tasks, baseline, and slippage.

28.16.3 Investigate Resource Conflicts

A resource is over-scheduled when a person is expected to work more than the allocated eight hours per day. In that case, we have a resource conflict.

Analysis revealed that the project manager was assigned to several activities in

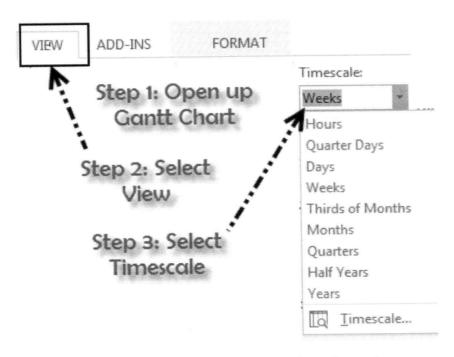

Figure 28.17: Formatting the Gantt Chart Timescale.

parallel, and the total utilization exceeded 100%, or more than 8 hours per day. *Project* flags these resource conflicts for you, see Figure 28.19. Therefore, we added Student Leaders to some tasks, which removed the conflict.

Project provides a tool that uses "resource leveling" to resolve resource conflicts. The command is: Resource → Level Resources from the Project ribbon. The dialog box that appears gives you several options to resolve resource conflicts. Over-used resources are spread out, so that, invariably, resource leveling will increase the project duration.[14]

Another approach to resolving a resource conflict is simply to add resources. In this case the resource conflict was obvious: We only had one resource unit—the leader or coordinator—for several key tasks. See Figure 28.20.

We added the following resources:

1. Five members who will play a key role in the Volunteer Team. These are unpaid volunteers.

[14]In real projects, we strongly recommend against using *Project* to do automatic resource leveling. It often destroys the look of the network and results in a mess. Also, the results are difficult to understand, which means the PM loses control. We suggest the project manager add and subtract resources by hand to get the desired result.

457

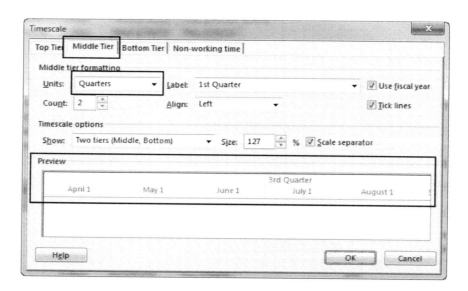

Figure 28.18: The three tiers of the Gantt Chart Timescales.

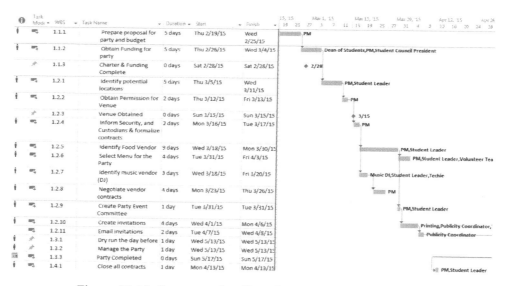

Figure 28.19: Resource Conflicts flagged in the Gantt View.

		Resource Name	Type	**Mater Label**	Max Units
1	◈	PM	Work		100%
2	◈	Volunteer Team	Work		100%
3	◈	Student Leader	Work		100%
4		Publicity Coordinator	Work		100%
5	◈	Picnic Event Day Coordinator	Work		100%
6		Dean of Students	Work		100%
7		Student Council President	Work		100%
8		Faculty Chairman	Work		100%
9		Techie	Work		100%
10		Food Services	Cost		
11		usic	Co		

Figure 28.20: Over allocated Resources as they appear in the Resources Sheet.

2. Student leaders: In the project plan we had budgeted leaders for various aspects of the project such as Music, Food, and Entertainment. These were paid positions.

3. Picnic Day Event coordinators: These are additional volunteers who will help the leaders.

After adding resources (units), and re-balancing the project manager's workload, we have no flags and a reasonable resource listing, see Figure 28.21. Recall that the 500% you see in the figure refers to five units or five resources.

28.16.4 Study the Critical Path

The critical path is the sequence of tasks that are critical to the timely completion of the project. Several techniques allow you to see just the tasks that are on the critical path. The simplest approach is to use filters: In the ribbon, click: View → Filter, and then select Critical. You will see the critical path tasks.

Alternatively, click: View → Highlight, and then select Critical.

Resource Name	Type	Materi Label	Max Units
PM	Work		100%
Volunteer Team	Work		500%
Student Leaders	Work		500%
Publicity Coordinator	Work		100%
Picnic Event Day Coordinators	Work		500%
Dean of Students	Work		100%
Student Council President	Work		100%
Faculty Chairman	Work		100%
Techie	Work		100%
Food Services	Cost		
Music DJ	Cost		
Printing	Cost		

Figure 28.21: Balanced Resource Listing.

Our project schedule is quite comfortable and so we don't need to add additional resources to the critical path tasks to shorten it. However, once the project starts, the project manager should carefully manage tasks on the critical path.

28.16.5 Examine Costs

While we have a good grip of the project schedule and its duration, we have not looked at the estimated costs to see if they are in line with the project sponsors' expectations, i.e., the budget.

Assuming the costs for resources have been entered correctly, it is easy to view the overall project cost and determine if it is within budget. Our favorite approach is to simply insert a new column called "Cost."

Table 28.7: Picnic project cost report.

Task Name	Work (hrs)	Cost	Duration (days)	Start	Finish
Party Project	374	$4,773	80	1/28/15	Tue 5/19/15
Define Party	16	$200	23	1/28/15	Sat 2/28/15
Plan Party	179	$2,467	45	2/11/15	Tue 4/14/15
Hold the Party	126	$1,090	23	4/15/15	Sun 5/17/15
Dry run for the Party	6	$30	1	4/15/15	Wed 4/15/15
Manage the Party	120	$1,060 0	1	5/15/15	Fri 5/15/15
Party Completed	0	$0	0	5/17/15	Sun 5/17/15
Close Party	12	$280	2	5/18/15	Tue 5/19/15
Project Management	40	$736	80	1/28/15	Tue 5/19/15
Charter & Funding Cmplt					Sat 2/28/15
Venue Obtained					Sun 3/15/15
Party Planning Complete					Wed 4/15/15
Party Completed					Sun 5/17/15

Table 28.7 shows the new Gantt View with the addition of the Cost column. The Picnic Party Project has a total budget of $4,773. This is well within the amount allocated to plan and hold the party. Therefore, we do not need to tweak the project costs anymore.

Table 28.7 displays five summary tasks: Define Party, Plan Party, Hold the Party, Close Party and Project Management. It also shows the sub-totals for various subtasks. We expanded "Hold the Party" to reveal three subtasks.

The top level summary task provides comprehensive statistics about the entire project: The total effort is 373 hours, the duration is 80 days, the project start date is January 28th, the party is executed on May 15th, and the entire project is fully wrapped up by May 19th. The total cost is $4,773.

28.16.6 Identify Bottom up Risks

While creating a project plan we identified risks and developed plans for mitigating them. For example, we set aside funds for a tent in case a drenching rainstorm was forecast. Now we have to the opportunity to identify additional risks by reviewing the *Project* version of the plan.

From our experience, we recommend flagging risks associated with "Email Invitations." Such tasks should be analyzed, especially if they are on the critical path or involve dependencies external to the project, e.g., a student might not receive the invitations as it might end up in the Spam folder. To mitigate this risk, the project manager might decide to mail invitations out via regular mail as well.

The project manager should also examine the tasks that are on the critical path to determine if they are considered high risk. For example, a problem in "Venue Selection" might cause a delay in the schedule.

28.16.7   Baseline the Project

Now that the project plan has been analyzed and we are happy with it, we can set a baseline. This is done using the command: Project → Set Baseline, and selecting "Entire Project."

Creating a baseline is a very important activity, and you should communicate the baselined project schedule and budget to the sponsor. This should be done formally, as the baseline represents a commitment between the project manager and the sponsor to the estimated project cost and schedule.

Prior to the execution phase of the project, you can delete a baseline at any time. If you update the schedule, you can create a fresh baseline. With the establishment of the baseline, the planning phase of the project is complete and you are ready to enter the execution phase.

28.17   Tracking Project Progress

This section explains how to track the progress of your project as it evolves, which is accomplished using various project reports. *Project* uses three terms:

1. *Baseline*: The planned dates developed prior to project start.

2. *Actual*: Completed and partially completed tasks as of a given date.

3. *Schedule*: Tasks that have not yet started as of a given date.

Project data such should be updated regularly, but no later than the end of each week. *Project* recalculates and reschedules your entire project as you enter task completion data.

First, we will show you how to update the project schedule. Then, we will show you some reports.

28.17.1   Updating the Schedule

Progress is measured by entering completion data for tasks. We can enter actual start and finish dates for a task, or we can enter progress information as percent complete. The best approach is to have each team member report actual work completed, and then also to estimate the percent complete of tasks still in progress. We will look at several approaches to updating project progress.

Quick Approach: Right mouse click on the task and indicate it as 100% complete. Alternatively, you can right mouse click on the bar graph on the right side inside the Gantt Chart and select 0%, 25%, 50% or 100% complete. See Figure 28.22.

Figure 28.22: Updating Project Progress Data.

Update using the Ribbon: In the ribbon, select the command "Task" and then select one of the choices you see there: 0%, 25%, 50% or 100% complete.

Update Tasks Window: In the ribbon you can activate the Update Tasks window by entering the command: Task → Mark on Track, and select "Update Tasks." You will see a window where you can you can enter percent complete, along with the Actual Duration and Remaining Duration. Alternatively, you can simply enter the Actual Finish date and the percent complete. See Figure 28.23.

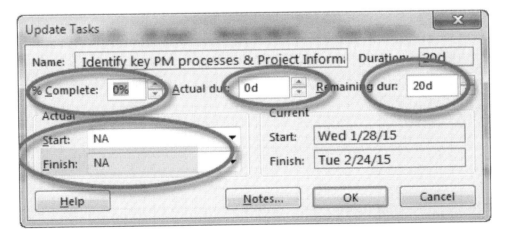

Figure 28.23: Alternate Approaches to Updating Progress.

463

Table 28.8: Actual vs. Baseline report.

Task	Work (hrs)	Baseline (hrs)	Variance (hrs)	Actual (hrs)	Remaining (hrs)	Percent Complete
Prepare proposal & budget	4	4	0	4	0	100%
Obtain Funding	24	12	12	24	0	100%

28.18   Comparing Actual Progress against the Baseline

We set a baseline before the picnic project started and we can now monitor how well we are progressing by using filters and the Tracking Gantt Chart view.

In order to see values for task variance, we set the actual duration for the task "Obtain Funding for Party" to 10 days–double the baseline value of 5 days. We also entered it as 100% completed. See Figure 28.24.

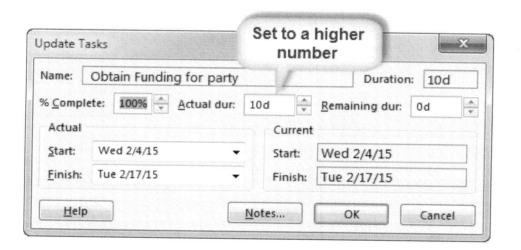

Figure 28.24: Updating a task with variance.

Next, from the ribbon, select View → Table → Work. Next select View → Filter and select "Completed Tasks." We do not want to see summary tasks, and so select Format → (Uncheck) Summary Tasks. You should see the "Actual vs. Baseline" report, which is shown in Table 28.8:

We note the following points: Work refers to the effort put in and is a combination of values found in the Actual plus Remaining columns. Variance is the difference between the values found in the Work and the Baseline columns. In the second task, this is 24 - 12 = 12.

Project provides several visual reports, such as the one shown in Figure 28.25, which displays a summary overview of cost overruns by resource. This report can be obtained by simply clicking the following commands in the ribbon: Report → Cost → Cost Overruns.

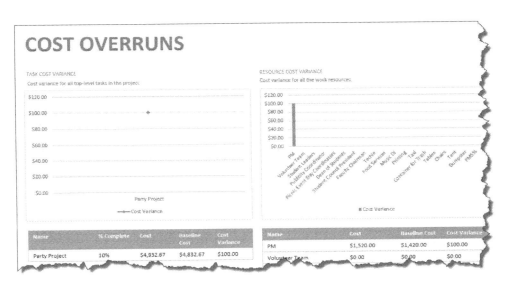

Figure 28.25: Cost Overrun: An example of a Visual Report.

28.18.1 Tracking Gantt Chart

The Tracking Gantt Chart provides graphical representation of Actual vs. Baseline for the entire project. In the ribbon, select the following commands: View → Tracking Gantt. This icon is usually in the same location as the Gantt Chart icon. If you do not see it, click "More Views" and then select "Tracking Gantt." The Tracking Gantt Chart provides a nice bar chart that shows when tasks are either slipping or ahead of schedule.

465

28.19 Printing Reports

Project contains an extensive set of predefined reports and dashboards under the "Report" menu option in the ribbon. An example was shown in Figure 28.25. Any view or screen that you work with can be printed.

To print a report Click File → Print → Print.

However, you must do some work to generate a report that is clear and engaging. First format the view:

- Pick the view you want.

- Change the view so it shows only the data you want to display. Hide sub-tasks to show only top-level tasks. Sort tasks or dates to highlight specific information. Hide columns temporarily so they do not appear in the printout.

- Click File → Print.

- Under Settings, choose how much of the project to print. You can print the whole thing or pick date and page ranges.

- Set other printing options, like the number of copies, page orientation, and paper size.

- Add a header, footer, or legend.

You can also simply do a "Screen Print" of your screen. This keystroke copies the contents of your screen to memory, and you can then simply paste it into Word or Excel. There, you can crop, shape and magnify the relevant parts of the screen. This allows you to build a comprehensive report highlighting important project features, such as the critical path. The report can also be printed.

Finally, don't forget that instead of printing, you might want to save the project report as a PDF file.

29

ACKNOWLEDGMENTS AND COPYRIGHTS

Quotes are slippery things and, like any currency, they get passed around. We've made every attempt here to give credit where credit is due and to respect the rights of everyone quoted, but for some quoted remarks it hasn't been possible to identify the original use, or even to confirm the author with certainty.

In an interview with Tasha Robinson, Steven Wright[1] described the widespread misattribution of quotes, commenting, "Someone showed me a site, and half of it that said I wrote it, I didn't write. Recently, I saw one, and I didn't write any of it." Wright also expressed the distress this can cause for an author: "I wish it was just my material, and people could like it or not like it. Just as long as it was really mine."

Our goal in presenting this information is to honor the contributions and rights of all the authors quoted, so if you have concerns about the accuracy of an attribution or the appropriateness of use, please contact the authors.

Preface

I like prefaces. I read them. Sometimes I do not read any further.

Malcolm Lowry (1909-1957), British poet and novelist. Original publication unknown, but the line is referenced by Lowry in a 1947 letter to Jonathan Cape.[2]

Lowry paraphrases this quote himself in a letter to his editor, pleading for more time to write a preface. He writes, "I like prefaces. I read them. Especially if they come at the end of the book." The authors of this text appreciate the advances in publishing technology that have made this pleading unnecessary, but are still grateful for the patience of their editors.

[1] Wright, S. (2003, Jan 29) Interview by T. Robinson. Retrieved from http:// www.avclub.com/ articles/ steven-wright, 13796/.

[2] Grace, S. (1997). Sursum Corda: The Collected Letters of Malcolm Lowry. Toronto: University of Toronto, p. 5.

Introduction

The important thing is not to stop questioning. Curiosity has its own reason for existence.

Albert Einstein (1879-1955). German theoretical physicist who derived the most famous equation, ever: $E = mc^2$.[3] From Miller, W. (1955, May 2),"Death of a genius: His fourth dimension, time, overtakes Einstein." *Life*, **38(19)**, p.64.

Chapter 1: Projects

Don't undertake a project unless it is manifestly important, and nearly impossible.

Edwin Herbert Land (1909-1991). American scientist who invented inexpensive filters for polarizing light and the Polaroid instant camera, which first went on sale in 1948.

I think it's wrong that only one company makes the game Monopoly.

Stephen Wright (born 1955). American comedian, actor, writer, and famous Red Sox fan.

You want to study project management? Read more, sleep less!

Mr. John Cable is the Director of the Project Management Program at the A. James Clark School of Engineering at the University of Maryland. John is a superb speaker who brings astute and pithy observations to the teaching of project management.

Managing is essentially a loser's job, and managers are about the most expendable pieces of furniture on the earth.

Ted Williams (1918-2002). The Splendid Splinter, American baseball player and manager. From Williams, T. & Underwood, J. (1969, revised edition 1988). *My turn at bat: The story of my life.* New York: Simon & Schuster, p. 241-242.[4]

Chapter 2: The Project Environment

There are two ways of being creative. One can sing and dance. Or one can create an environment in which singers and dancers flourish.

Warren G. Bennis (born 1925). American scholar, widely regarded as a pioneer in the field of Leadership. In 2005, James O'Toole claimed that Bennis developed the "then-nonexistent field that he would ultimately make his own—leadership." He further observed that Bennis "challenged the prevailing wisdom by showing that humanistic, democratic-style leaders are better suited to dealing with the complexity and change that characterize the leadership environment."

I don't know the key to success, but the key to failure is trying to please everybody.

Bill Cosby (born 1937). American comedian, actor, author, television producer, educator, musician and activist.

If it doesn't matter who wins or loses, then why do they keep score?

Vincent Thomas "Vince" Lombardi (1913-1970) is best known as the head coach of the Green Bay Packers during the 1960's. He led the team to three straight league championships and five in seven years. Under Lombardi the Packers won the first two Super Bowls and the Super Bowl trophy is named in his honor. He was enshrined in the NFL's Pro Football Hall of Fame in 1971.

[3]Except the first time he actually wrote $L = mc^2$, and then crossed out the L and wrote E.

[4]Williams actually made this statement in a description of his years as the manager of the Washington Senators. But it seems likely he was still thinking of newly appointed Red Sox manager Lou Boudreau's 1950 remark that all players, including Williams, were expendable (ibid, p.172).

468

Chapter 3: Deliverables and Milestones

Life isn't a matter of milestones but of moments.

Rose Fitzgerald Kennedy (1890-1995). American philanthropist and matriarch of the Kennedy family.

It's a funny kind of month, October. For the really keen cricket fan it's when you discover that your wife left you in May.

Denis Norden (born 1922). British comedy writer and television presenter.[5]

Chapter 4: Projects and Companies

There's no crying in baseball!

Tom Hanks. From Marshall, P. (Director); Wilson, K., Candaele, K., Ganz, L., & Mandel, B. (Writers). (1992). *A League of Their Own.* USA: Columbia Pictures.

A nation's culture resides in the hearts and in the soul of its people.

Mohandas Karamchand Gandhi (1869-1948), known as Mahatma Gandhi, was the leader of Indian nationalism in British-ruled India. Employing non-violent civil disobedience, he inspired movements for non-violence, civil rights and freedom across the world.

As leader of the Indian National Congress in 1921, Gandhi campaigned to ease poverty, expand women's rights, build religious and ethnic amity, and end untouchability. Gandhi protested the salt tax by marching 250 miles, the Dandi Salt March, in 1930 for which he was imprisoned.[6] He was assassinated on 30 January 1948. January 30 is observed as Martyrs' Day in India and his birthday, October 2, is commemorated worldwide as the International Day of Non-Violence.

Peace is a daily, a weekly, a monthly process, gradually changing opinions, slowly eroding old barriers, quietly building new structures.

John Fitzgerald "Jack" Kennedy (1917-1963). The 35th President of the United States, serving from 1961 until his assassination in 1963.

After military service as commander of the Motor Torpedo Boats PT-109 and PT-59 during World War II in the South Pacific, Kennedy represented Massachusetts's 11th congressional district in the U.S. House of Representatives from 1947 to 1953 as a Democrat. Thereafter, he served in the U.S. Senate from 1953 until 1960. Kennedy defeated then Vice President Richard Nixon in the 1960 presidential election. Kennedy is the only president to have won a Pulitzer Prize.

Chapter 5: Project Life Cycles

Life is what happens to you while you're busy making other plans.

John Lennon (1940-1980). British musician, artist and writer. From *Beautiful Boy (Darling Boy)*, Double Fantasy (1980).

Chapter 6: Integration

I'm not for integration and I'm not against it.

[5] Like the baseball season, the cricket season also runs April through September.

[6] Winston Churchill ridiculed him as a "half-naked fakir."

Richard Pryor, American comedian and actor. From a 1977 interview with New York Times writer Guy Flatley, accessed 6/1/2012 at http://www.moviecrazed.com/outpast /pryor.html. The full quote is "I'm not for integration and I'm not against it. What I am for is justice for everyone, just like it says in the Constitution."

Chapter 7: Scope

If you can't explain it simply, you don't understand it well enough.

Albert Einstein (1879-1955). German theoretical physicist.

Sometimes I can't figure designers out. It's as if they flunked human anatomy.

Erma Louise Bombeck (1927-1996). American humorist and newspaper columnist. From 1965 to 1996, Bombeck wrote over 4,000 humorous newspaper columns chronicling the ordinary life of a mid-western suburban housewife. Bombeck also published 15 books, many of which became best-sellers.

The most essential gift for a good writer is a built-in, shock-proof sh**t-detector.

Ernest Hemingway (1899-1961). American novelist and author. From an interview with Hemingway in *The Paris Review* (**18**), Spring 1958.

Chapter 8: WBS

The secret of getting ahead is getting started. The secret of getting started is breaking your complex overwhelming tasks into small manageable tasks, and then starting on the first one.

Unknown. The origin of this comment has not been found. Several online sites attribute the first sentence to Agatha Christie but more cite Mark Twain; the quote as a whole is always attributed to Twain. In rebuttal, a number of sites devoted to Twain specifically identify this as a misattribution. Since the second sentence sounds surprisingly unskeptical for Twain, we are going with "Unknown."

Chapter 9: Time

Time is nature's way of keeping everything from happening at once. Space is what prevents everything from happening to me.

John Wheeler (1911-2008). American theoretical physicist who coined the term "black hole." The first sentence is often attributed to Einstein, Pauli, and others. The second sentence, however, is pure Wheeler, so Wheeler gets the credit.

Chapter 10: The Network Diagram

Even if you are on the right track, you'll get run over if you just sit there.

Will Rogers (1879-1935). American humorist of the vaudeville stage and of silent and sound films.

Life can only be understood backward, but it must be lived forward.

Søren Kierkegaard (1813-1855). Danish philosopher and author.

The show doesn't go on because it's ready. It goes on at 11:30.

Lorne Michaels (b. 1944), Canadian-American television producer, writer, and comedian. Quoted by Tina Fey (born 1970), American comedian, writer, actress, and television producer. From the section headed "Things I Learned from Lorne Michaels" in Fey, T. (2012). *Bossypants* (paperback edition). New York: Reagan Arthur / Back Bay Books (p. 23).

Chapter 11: Cost

The first 90% of the job took the first 90% of the money. The remaining 10% of the job took the other 90% of the money!

Anonymous.

If I had asked people what they wanted, they would have said faster horses.

Henry Ford (1863-1947). The founder of the Ford Motor Company and innovator in mass production. His Model T automobile revolutionized transportation and American industry.

It's tough to make predictions, especially about the future.

Yogi Berra (born Lawrence Peter Berra, 1925). American baseball player and manager. This comment has the distinction of being attributed to both Yogi Berra and Niels Bohr. A debate on the authorship in the Letters section of *The Economist* (July 15, 2007) offers some evidence in favor of Bohr, but it sure sounds like something Berra would say. Of course, as Yogi himself noted "I really didn't say everything I said!"

A dollar per horse per mile.

Paul Parnegoli is a carpenter who works in Rhode Island. On his lunch break he once regaled the crew about how he used to haul horses for a living. Always on the lookout for unusual cost estimation metrics, RW asked him how he bid the cost of hauling a horse from Kentucky to Boston.

Beware of the little expenses; a small leak will sink a great ship.

Benjamin Franklin (1706-1790). From Franklin's 1758 essay, *The Way to Wealth*.

The real problem is not the overhead. What is really stifling is the underfoot.

Little is known of Bill Carlson, other than that he is quoted in *Augustine's Laws*, p. 44.

Price is what you pay. Value is what you get.

Warren Buffett (born 1930). From the 2008 Berkshire Hathaway Letter to Shareholders (p. 5), where Buffett attributed the origin of the idea to Benjamin Graham, author of the classic text, *The Intelligent Investor*. Accessed 6/1/2012 at http://www.berkshirehathaway.com/ letters/ 2008ltr.pdf.

Chapter 12: Earned Value Management

The more education a woman has, the wider the gap between men's and women's earnings for the same work.

Sandra Day O'Connor (born 1930). The first woman to be appointed to the United States Supreme Court. She served as an Associate Justice from 1981 until her retirement from the Court in 2006.

The only way to enjoy anything in this life is to earn it first.

Ginger Rogers (1911-1995). American stage and film actor and dancer, noted primarily as the partner of Fred Astaire in motion-picture musicals.[7]

Once our customers start using earned value, we will no longer be able to fudge the cost!

Roger Warburton in a lecture to the Project Management Institute's Massachusetts Bay Chapter entitled *Miss the Memo? How TCPI makes customers tougher and smarter*, February 18, 2010.

Data is what distinguishes the dilettante from the artist.

George V. Higgins (1939-1999) was an American author, lawyer, newspaper columnist, and college professor who is known for his bestselling crime novels. He wrote for the Associated Press, the Boston Globe, the Boston Herald American, and the Wall Street Journal. Later in life, he practiced of law, represented several famous figures, such as Eldridge Cleaver and G. Gordon Liddy. He was a professor at Boston College and Boston University.

Chapter 13: Explaining to the Stakeholders

If you guys were women, you'd all be pregnant. You just can't say no.

Patricia Nell Scott Schroeder (1940-) was the first woman elected from Colorado to the United States House of Representatives, and served from 1973-1997. Born in Portland, Oregon, she graduated from the University of Minnesota with a B.A. in history and in 1964 earned a law degree from Harvard Law School. At age 31, Schroeder was the second-youngest woman ever elected to Congress. She became the first woman to serve on the House Armed Services Committee and her frustration with escalating Pentagon arms spending led to the above comment. For a fascinating biography, see [34].

There are some people who have trouble recognizing a mess.

Bill Cosby (born 1937). American comedian, actor, author, television producer, educator, musician and activist.

I cannot help it–in spite of myself, infinity torments me.

Alfred Louis Charles de Musset-Pathay (1810-1857) was a French dramatist, poet, and novelist.

Simple solutions seldom are. It takes a very unusual mind to undertake analysis of the obvious.

Alfred North Whitehead, OM FRS (1861-1947) was an English mathematician and philosopher who is best known as the defining figure of the philosophical school known as process philosophy. His most famous work is the three-volume *Principia Mathematica* (1910-13), which he co-wrote with former student Bertrand Russell. *Principia Mathematica* is considered one of the twentieth century's most important works in mathematical logic.

I am definitely going to take a course on time management... just as soon as I can work it into my schedule.

Louis E. Boone is the author of several books on contemporary marketing. He was a Professor of Marketing and Transportation at the University of South Alabama from 1983-1999.

We've been running a little behind schedule. But only by about 15 years or so.

Matthew Abram Groening (1954-) is an American cartoonist, screenwriter, animator, comedian and voice actor. He is the co-creator of *The Simpsons* and *Futurama*. Groening has won 12 Primetime Emmy Awards, 10 for The Simpsons and 2 for Futurama, and has a star on the Hollywood Walk of Fame.

[7]In a 1982 Frank and Ernest comic strip, award winning cartoonist Bob Thaves wrote about Fred Astaire: "Sure he was great, but don't forget that Ginger Rogers did everything he did, backwards ... and in high heels."

What's here? The portrait of a blinking idiot. Presenting me a schedule!

William Shakespeare (1564-1616), The Merchant Of Venice. Prince Arragon gets what he deserves.

Chapter 14: Quality

Be a yardstick of quality. Some people aren't used to an environment where excellence is expected.

Steve Jobs (1955-2011). American businessman, designer and inventor. Co-founder of Apple.

A small fraction of participants produce a large fraction of the accomplishments–Pareto. ' A small fraction of participants also produce a large fraction of the problems–Augustine's Corollary

Business-management consultant Joseph M. Juran suggested the principle and named it after Italian economist Vilfredo Pareto, who first discussed the phenomenon in his 1897 *Course of Political Economics*. Supposedly, Pareto developed the principle by observing that 20% of the pea pods in his garden contained 80% of the peas.

However, the *Encyclopedia of Human Thermodynamics* claims that the 80-20 rule has since been applied *baselessly* to a number of non-wealth scenarios, e.g. 20% of one's effort produces 80% of the results, among others.

For Augustine, see below.

Chapter 15: Human Resources

Never hire anyone you wouldn't want to run into in the hallway at three in the morning.

Lorne Michaels (b. 1944), Canadian-American television producer. Quoted by Tina Fey in *Bossypants*.

Chapter 16: Communications

It is better to keep your mouth closed and let people think you are a fool than to open it and remove all doubt.

Mark Twain (born Samuel Langhorne Clemens, 1835-1910). American author and humorist. This quotation is widely attributed to both Mark Twain and Abraham Lincoln, among others. Whoever said it was probably paraphrasing Proverbs 17:28, "Even a fool, when he holdeth his peace, is counted wise: and he that shutteth his lips is esteemed a man of understanding."

Everyone is entitled to his own opinion, but not to his own facts.

According to Barry Popik's blog (July 30, 2009), "Every man has a right to his own opinion, but no man has a right to be wrong in his facts" is credited to American financier Bernard M. Baruch (1870–1965), who said it in 1946. James R. Schlesinger, United States Secretary of Defense from 1973 to 1975, is credited with saying: "Each of us is entitled to his own opinion, but not to his own facts." Daniel Patrick Moynihan (1927-2003), United States Senator from New York from 1976 to 2000, is also often credited with saying, "Everyone is entitled to his own opinion, but not his own facts."

Chapter 17: Risks

Risk! Risk is our business!

Captain Kirk. From Roddenberry, G. & Kingsley, J. (1968, Feb 3). *Star Trek: Return to Tomorrow* (Television program). Los Angeles: Paramount Television.

Chapter 18: Procurement Management

I wish to be cremated. One tenth of my ashes shall be given to my agent, as written in our contract.

Groucho Marx (Julius Henry Marx, 1890-1977). American comedian and film and television star.

Thoroughly read all your contracts. I really mean thoroughly.

Bret Michaels (born Bret Michael Sychak, 1963). American musician and television personality.

Chapter 19: Ethics

Relativity applies to physics, not ethics.

Albert Einstein (1879-1955). German theoretical physicist.

Chapter 20: A New Kitchen

You're not using that project management stuff on me are you?

Eileen Warburton, writer and independent scholar.

Few things are harder to put up with than the annoyance of a good example.

Mark Twain (born Samuel Langhorne Clemens, 1835-1910). American author and humorist. From Twain, M. (1894). *Pudd'nhead Wilson*. Hartford, CT: American Publishing Company (p. 246).

Chapter 21: The Picnic Templates

If the rain spoils our picnic, but saves a farmer's crop, who are we to say it shouldn't rain?

Thomas Mark Barrett (1953-) is an American politician. He is the 40th, and current, Mayor of Milwaukee, Wisconsin, serving since 2004.

Chapter 22: The Process Groups

When one has finished building one's house, one suddenly realizes that in the process one has learned something that one really needed to know in the worst way—before one began!

Friedrich Nietzsche (1844-1900). German philosopher.

If you want to build a ship, don't drum up people together to collect wood, but rather teach them to long for the endless immensity of the sea.

Antoine de Saint-Exupery (1900-1944). French pilot and writer

To live means to finesse the processes to which one is subjugated.

Bertolt Brecht (1898-1956). German poet, playwright, and theater director.

If a man empties his purse into his head no one can take it away from him. An investment in knowledge always pays the best interest.

Benjamin Franklin (1706-1790). One of the Founding Fathers of the United States. A major scientist for his theories on electricity, he invented the lightning rod, bifocals, the Franklin stove, and a carriage odometer. He formed the first public lending library in America and earned the title of "The First American" for his early campaigning for colonial unity.

Always proud of his working class roots, he became a successful newspaper editor and printer in Philadelphia, played a major role in establishing the University of Pennsylvania, and was elected the first president of the American Philosophical Society. Later in life, he freed his slaves and became a prominent abolitionist.

Chapter 23: Initiating Process Group

He who has begun has half done. Dare to be wise. Begin!

Horace (65 BCE-8 BCE). Roman lyric poet, satirist, and critic. In Latin, "Dimidium facti qui coepit habet: sapere aude, incipe." Horace. (20 BCE). *Epistles* **1.2.40** (Letter to Lollius).

We must, indeed, all hang together, or most assuredly we shall all hang separately.

Benjamin Franklin (1706-1790). Comment made in the Continental Congress just before signing the Declaration of Independence, 1776.

Chapter 24: Planning Process Group

Give me six hours to chop down a tree and I will spend the first four sharpening the axe.

Abraham Lincoln (1809-1865), 16th president of the United States. Though the original source of this quote has not been found, Lincoln's expertise in building rail fences with raw timber was well known and frequently referenced in his political life. In 1860 he ran for president as "The Rail Candidate," playing on his frontier background, and later in his presidency was frequently referred to as "The Rail Splitter," so presumably he knew something about chopping down trees!

By looking at the questions the kids are asking, we learn the scope of what needs to be done.

Buffy Sainte-Marie (born 1941). Canadian musician and activist. From Silber, S. (1998, June 1). Sharing the fire online. *Wired*, accessed 6/1/2012 at http://www.wired.com/culture/ lifestyle/ news/ 1998/ 06/ 12630.

Lost time is never found again.

Benjamin Franklin (1706-1790). From Franklin's 1758 essay, "The Way to Wealth."

The sooner you fall behind, the more time you'll have to catch up.

Steven Wright (born 1955). American comedian, actor and writer

The cost of living has gone up another dollar a quart.

W. C. Fields (1880-1946). American comedian, film star, and vaudeville performer.

Large increases in cost with questionable increase in performance can be tolerated only for racehorses and fancy women.

William Thomson, Lord Kelvin (1824-1907). British mathematical physicist. Unsourced, though widely quoted. Still, this seems a strange remark for a life-long bachelor and scholar who was devoted to his research and teaching at the University of Glasgow. [8]

Risk comes from not knowing what you're doing.

Warren Buffett (born 1930). CEO of Berkshire Hathaway, investor, and philanthropist.

The quality, not the longevity, of one's life is what is important.

Martin Luther King, Jr. (1929-1968). American clergyman, activist, and prominent leader of the Civil Rights Movement.[9] From America's Gandhi: Rev. Martin Luther King, Jr. (Man of the Year cover story, unsigned.) (1964, Jan 3). *Time*, **83(1)**.

The human mind is our fundamental resource.

John F. Kennedy (1917-1963). 35th president of the United States. From Kennedy's Special Message to the Congress on Education, February 20, 1961.

The single biggest problem in communication is the illusion that it has taken place.

George Bernard Shaw (1856-1950). British literary critic, playwright and essayist.

The universe never did make sense; I suspect it was built on government contract.

Robert A. Heinlein (1907-1988). American author and winner of the first Grand Master Award from the Science Fiction Writers of America From Heinlein, R. (1980). *The Number of the Beast.* New York: Fawcett Publications (p. 6).

Don't live down to expectations. Go out there and do something remarkable.

Wendy Wasserstein (1950-2006). Brooklyn born, American playwright was the Andrew Dickson White Professor-at-Large at Cornell University. She received the Tony Award for Best Play and the Pulitzer Prize for Drama in 1989 for her play *The Heidi Chronicles.* Also authored the books: *Shiksa goddess, Sloth,* and *Bachelor Girls.*

Chapter 25: Executing Process Group

Everything should be made as simple as possible, but not simpler.

Albert Einstein (1879-1955). German theoretical physicist.

We cannot direct the wind, but we can adjust the sails.

Unknown. The comment is attributed a number of people. However, all online sites that have investigated this in detail conclude that the source is unknown.

Excellence, then, is not an act but a habit.

Will Durant (1885-1981), American writer, historian, and philosopher. Commenting on a quote from Aristotle (384 BCE-322 BCE), Greek philosopher, student of Plato, and teacher of Alexander the Great. From Durant, W. (1926) *The Story of Philosophy: the Lives and Opinions of the Greater Philosophers.* New York: Simon & Schuster, revised edition 1933 (p. 98).

In commenting on Aristotle's philosophy, Durant added this interpretation of his own, which is now widely quoted as coming directly from the Greek philosopher. Durant actually wrote, "[W]e do not act rightly because we have virtue or excellence, but we rather have these because we have acted rightly;

[8] Far from being born into aristocratic circles, Kelvin was raised to the peerage only when he was 68 years old.

[9] Boston University's most famous alumnus.

476

'these virtues are formed in man by his doing the actions'; we are what we repeatedly do. Excellence, then, is not an act but a habit." The internal quote from Aristotle ("these virtues are formed...") comes from *Nicomachean Ethics*, **ii**, 4.

Talent wins games, but teamwork and intelligence wins championships.

Michael Jordan (born 1963). American NBA Basketball Player. From Jordan, M., Vancil, M. & Miller, S. (1994). *I can't accept not trying: Michael Jordan on the pursuit of excellence*. San Francisco: Harper San Francisco (p. 24).

A person will sometimes devote all his life to the development of one part of his body—the wishbone.

Robert Frost (1874-1963). Pulitzer Prize-winning American poet, teacher and lecturer.

As a coach, I play not my eleven best, but my best eleven.

Knute Rockne (1888-1931). American football player and coach who played and coached exclusively for the University of Notre Dame.

The speed of communications is wondrous to behold. It is also true that speed can multiply the distribution of information that we know to be untrue.

Edward R. Murrow (1908-1965). American broadcast journalist and producer. On receiving "Family of Man" Award (1964).

Oft expectation fails, and most oft there
where most it promises; and oft it hits,
where hope is coldest; and despair most sits.

Helena in *All's Well That Ends Well*. William Shakespeare (1564-1616). English poet and playwright. The "Bard of Avon" is widely regarded as the greatest writer in the English language.

I'm not going to buy my kids an encyclopedia. Let them walk to school like I did.

Yogi Berra (born Lawrence Peter Berra, 1925). American baseball player and manager.

Chapter 26: Monitoring and Controlling

Kirk: *You're not exactly catching us at our best.*
Spock: *That much is certain.*

Captain Kirk and Mister Spock are the captain and science officer respectively of the starship Enterprise in the Star Trek series of television shows and movies (though Spock holds other titles as the series matures). From Nimoy, L. (Director). Meerson, S., Krikes, P., Bennett, H., & Meyer, N. (Screenplay writers). (1986). *Star Trek IV: The Voyage Home*. USA: Paramount Pictures.

If everything seems under control, you're just not going fast enough.

Mario Andretti (born 1940). Italian American racecar driver, the only person ever to win the Indy 500, the Daytona 500, and the Formula One World Championship.

Change is inevitable....except from vending machines.

Steven Wright (born 1955). American comedian, actor and writer

Chapter 27: Closing Process Group

Acceptance of what has happened is the first step to overcoming the consequences of any misfortune.

William James (1842-1910). American psychologist and philosopher.

Chapter 28: Microsoft Project Tutorial

Software is like entropy. It is difficult to grasp, weighs nothing, and obeys the second law of thermodynamics; i.e. it always increases.

Norman Ralph Augustine (1935-). A U.S. aerospace businessman who started as a Research Engineer at the Douglas Aircraft Company in 1958 and rose to become president of Lockheed Martin, retiring as chairman and CEO in 1997. He is popularly known for "Augustine's Laws," a series of tongue in cheek aphorisms, the most famous of which is, Law #16: "In the year 2054, the entire defense budget will purchase just one tactical aircraft. This aircraft will have to be shared by the Air Force and Navy 3.5 days each per week, except for leap year, when it will be made available to the Marines for the extra day."

Notes

Chapter 0 Introduction

1. This is a chapter note for Chapter 0, the Introduction. The extra information being provided here is that this is how a chapter note looks.

Chapter 2 The Project Environment

1. For an excellent practical book on new product development, see the book by Cooper.[35]

2. We are actually quoting research on what makes successful new *products*, not projects. There is little research to report on what makes successful projects, but there is a significant, growing body of evidence for what makes a successful product. Since each new product development is a project, we feel comfortable presenting this as "project selection."

Chapter 3 Deliverables and Milestones

1. This definition is a technical convenience, which makes milestones equivalent to activities. This allows the linking of milestones to activities, which is useful. If the completion of an activity has a linked milestone, and the activity is delayed, then the milestone is also delayed.

Chapter 4 Projects and Companies

1. For an excellent set of references on the topic of corporate culture, see Gray and Larsen, page 81. [8]

Chapter 5 Project Life Cycles

1. More information on the pharmaceutical life cycle can be found in [36].

2. This is based on a template for Microsoft Project [37].

3. The approach was pioneered by Barry Boehm in his *Spiral Model* [38].

4. *The Agile Manifesto* consists of 12 philosophical statements, which were first described in the *Manifesto for Agile Software Development* by Beck, Kent; et al. in 2001. [39]

5. The name *scrum* is borrowed from the game of rugby, and was first described by Peter DeGrace, Leslie Stahl, and Leslie Hulet in *Wicked problems, righteous solutions*, Peter DeGrace and Leslie Hulet Stahl. [40]

6. We have adapted the attributes from earlier research conducted by Mo Mahmood. [41] Table 5.3 was adapted from Richard Fairley's *Managing and Leading Software Projects*. [42] Note that Fairley has a more liberal interpretation of the waterfall as he includes incremental builds.

Chapter 6 Integration

1. This Charter was developed as a homework assignment by Vicky Morrissey in Fall 2011 in the undergraduate PM class. We are grateful to Vicky for allowing us to use this excellent example of a charter.

Chapter 7 Scope

1. As described by our colleague *Steve Leybourne* in [10]. People unfamiliar with the complexity and magnitude of superyacht projects may learn more by visiting www.feadship.nl and www.lurssen.com.

Chapter 8 The WBS

1. We are burying the answer to this claim in this note to give you a chance to think about it. The answer is: The *Project Management* is missing from the WBS!

Chapter 10 The Network Diagram

1. We have been issuing the following challenge to our students for several years: How do we know that "The critical path typically includes only a small fraction of the activities in a project"? This is so important that it really deserves a reference and a backup.

What kinds of projects does this apply to? All? Large projects only?

This assertion occurs in many textbooks and journal articles, all without a reference, and has been driving us crazy for years. Finally, Boris Cailloux, one of our undergraduate students, found the original reference and it is fascinating. The statement that only a minority of tasks are on the critical path occurred in a 1963 *Harvard Business Review* article entitled "The ABC's of the Critical Path Method" by F. K. Levy, G. L. Thompson and J. D. Wiest.

Project management arose in military applications and this was one of the first generally available, public articles. Almost casually, they say, "In many projects studied, it has been found that only a small fraction of jobs are critical ..." We see that there is not much support for such a strong statement but given that it was 1963, they can be excused.

Thus was born the urban legend. Thank you Boris.

Chapter 11 Cost Estimation

1. This example comes from our colleague Steve Leybourne, a professor at BU, who studied the nature innovation in super yachts. See [10].

2. Thanks to Andrew Korda for this elegant parametric cost estimation example. Andrew took the undergraduate Project Management course in the Fall of 2012.

3. The data is summarized in an article by Frank Sietzen Jr. in *Space Ref* [43]. The actual data comes from an Appendix to a technical report by Barry Watts at the Center for Strategic and Budgetary Assessments in 2001. [44]

4. The city of Boston has a comprehensive worksheet at their web site: www.cityofboston.gov, in the section dnd/PDFs. See NSP_Preliminary_ Cost_ Estimate_ form.pdf.

Chapter 12 Earned Value Management

1. One of the techniques for addressing the issue of the time-dependence in the SPI is called *Earned Schedule*, and was pioneered by Walter Lipke.[45]

2. To show that equations 12.11 and 12.14 are equivalent, consider 12.14 and substitute for $CPI = EV/AC$:

$$EAC(t) = AC(t) + \frac{BAC - EV(t)}{CPI(t)} = AC(t) + \frac{BAC}{CPI(t)} - EV(t)\frac{AC(t)}{EV(t)} = \frac{BAC}{CPI(t)}, \quad (29.1)$$

which is equation 12.11.

3. Christensen has conducted several landmark studies on the accuracy of the CPI. Using Department of Defense data he found that, "without exception, the CPI does not improve during the period 15% to 85% of the contract."[19, 21]

4. For a theoretical justification of this statement, see [20].

Chapter 13 Explaining it to the Stakeholders

1. If we substitute the EAC from equation 12.14 into the $TCPI$ formula, we get:

$$TCPI = \frac{BAC - EV(t)}{EAC - AC(t)} = \frac{BAC - EV(t)}{AC(t) + \frac{BAC - EV(t)}{CPI(t)} - AC(t)} = CPI! \quad (29.2)$$

The EAC version of the $TCPI$ formula is an identity: $TCPI = CPI$. Presumably, this is what the PMBOK means by: "If it becomes obvious that the BAC is no longer viable .... the EAC effectively supersedes the BAC as the cost performance goal."

2. The expression probably dates from much earlier, but Einstein quoted it a lot and so is credited with it.

3. Lipke deserves credit for convincing the project management community that "Schedule is Different." [45] In practice, ES has been shown to work well [46]. However, the concept of ES is not without its problems–see Book [47].

481

There is also confusion at the end of the project where the earned value and the planned value are equal. When all value that has been planned has been earned, $SV = 0$. That is, the measure of the project's lateness is zero, even if the project's completion is far beyond the planned date.

4. The usual equations for ES, for example found in Lipke's book [23], are:

$$ES(i) = U + \Delta, \quad \Delta = \frac{EV(i) - PV(u)}{PV(u+1) - PV(u)}, \qquad (29.3)$$

where i represents the current time and U is an integer representing the number of time units where the $EV < PV$, so the project is behind schedule; EV represents earned value and PV represents planned value. The index, u, represents the point in time where the horizontal projection back from the point $EV(i)$ intersects the $PV(t)$ curve.

The conventional argument for Δ (not to be confused with δ) is that the intersection occurs between u and $u+1$ and, so, it represents a fraction of that time-interval. If the project cost data is collected daily or weekly, it is unlikely that the fraction of the data collection interval will be significant. Only monthly data (or longer) would seem to require Δ.

The dimensionless ratio, Δ, presents an algebraic difficulty and to clarify the issue, we write the denominator in (29.3) as the slope of the planned value curve between u and $u+1$:

$$m(u) \equiv \frac{PV(u+1) - PV(u)}{(u+1) - u}. \qquad (29.4)$$

Using the standard schedule variance, SV, evaluated at time u gives:

$$ES(u) = U + \frac{SV(u)}{m(u)}, \qquad SV(u) \equiv EV(u) - PV(u). \qquad (29.5)$$

This expression shows that ES depends on the slope of the planned value curve as well as the performance of the project represented by the current $SV(t)$. This showcases an important conceptual problem: Why should the performance of the system depend on the average planned value cost *rate* at the intersection time, u? Arguments could presumably be made for a dependence on some thoughtfully chosen *average* over previous points rather than the arbitrarily chosen immediately succeeding or immediately past points.

Many projects are assumed to follow S-shaped cumulative labor curves, and so the slope of the cumulative planned labor curve varies over time. Therefore, unlike the schedule variance, SV, which is at least a cumulative measure summed over all project activities to date, it is hard to see how the *instantaneous* slope at that one point can legitimately characterize the entire project. At a minimum, one can argue that a longer time scale would at least average the noise in the data and give a better estimate of the slope of the cumulative planned value curve. Further, numerical slope calculations are notoriously erratic and the denominator in Δ causes considerable undesirable scatter in the schedule estimate.

Thus, it is worth pointing out that equation (29.3) is actually based on a hidden assumption: A linear slope in the local region, which will generally not apply globally. Since most project labor curves are S-shaped, this introduces a question about the theoretical applicability of the formula for ES.

For S-shaped labor curves, which are generally considered to apply to more complex projects, the cumulative $PV(t)$ curve approaches a constant (the budget) towards the end of the project. Thus, at the end of the project, the expression for Δ in (29.3) becomes undefined because the slope of the cumulative planned value curve goes to zero. *ES* itself, however, is perfectly well defined at the end of the project because one can always draw the line from the earned value curve to the planned value curve.

Chapter 14 Quality

1. We think it is hard to find an example from project management. For example, cost and schedule variances can be tracked against their goals and flags raised if they depart from acceptable upper and lower limits. However, control charts are based on the idea that things are independent, and the *CPI* is a cumulative measure and so correlates the variables. Personally, we don't see how they apply to PM at all!

2. We have already established that all *CPI* charts values are less than 1.0, which says that the "process is out of control!"

Chapter 17 Risks

1. For example, Metzger's *Managing a Programming Project* (1996) [48] does not even make reference to the practice of risk management!

2. Even worse, scientists develop a hypothesis to be tested, and then in an ideal situation perform experiments that are at-best designed to test the null hypothesis. At the outset the researcher does not know whether or not the results will support the null hypothesis. However, it is common for the researcher to believe that their result will be within a range of known possibilities. Occasionally, however, the result is completely unexpected—it was an unknown unknown! [49]

3. For an interesting discussion of the use of decision trees in medicine, see Farrokh Alemi's web page, *http:// gunston.gmu.edu/ 730/ DecisionTrees.asp*. The page is based on a chapter with the same name in the book *Systems to Support Health Policy Analysis: Theory, Model and Uses.* [50]

Decision trees can be very useful in the analysis of medical issues because there is often lots of data on the cost of a treatment or drug, along with actual probabilities for patient outcomes, e.g., cure rates, death rates, etc.

Chapter 18 Procurement Management

1. For example, see an interesting discussion of contracts in the Iraq war at http://www.dodig.mil/ audit/reports/ fy06/06-007.pdf

Chapter 19 Ethics

1. I want to thank Nestor Taffor, an undergraduate at Boston University, for allowing me to use his real name. His presentation was so moving that it stuck with me (RW).

Chapter 20 A New Kitchen

1. This is a simplified account of the design and construction of Roger's new kitchen. The conceptual and design work was done by his wife, Eileen. We took the opportunity to record what was happening as an example of a project. Fortunately for this book, but not so for the real implementation, the new kitchen project seemed to go through all the typical project management issues.

2. The perfect tool would help you to create the graphical WBS diagram and then add outline format for the lower levels of the hierarchy, and with automatic numbering. These activities (along with their WBS numbers) would then automatically populate a network diagram in which tasks can be moved around without destroying the WBS numbering. I can dream!

Chapter 23 Initiating Process Group

1. Quintus Horatius Flaccus, known as Horace, was the leading lyric poet during the time of Augustus. In Horace's first book of Epistles the epigraph to this chapter is the moral of a story where a fool waits for the stream to stop before crossing it. Horace values human endeavor, persistence in reaching a goal, and the need for effort in overcoming obstacles.[51]

Sapere aude is Latin for "Dare to be wise." It challenges us to experience discovery and to be passionate about it. But thinking is not enough, one must also, "Begin!"

Kant suggested that *Sapere Aude* was the motto of enlightenment: "Have courage to use your own understanding!" Kant charged his readers to follow a program of intellectual self-liberation, the tool of which is *reason*. Kant suggested the mass of "domestic cattle" have been bred by unfaithful stewards not to question what they've been told. It is the courage of individuals to follow *Sapere aude* that will break the shackles of despotism and, for the benefit both of the population and the state, reveal through public discourse better methods of governance or legitimate complaints.

In other words, we start as we intend to continue, *Challenge Everything!*

2. For an excellent book on the softer skills of project management, see Meredith and Mantel [52].

Chapter 24 Planning Process Group

1. There is considerable debate as to whether the activity resources are estimated before or after the activity durations. In the text, we have presented the standard PMBOK approach, which says that resources are estimated first, then durations. The argument to support this is that you can't realistically estimate how long it takes to do a job unless you know what type of person is working on it. Is the assigned person an expert or a novice? The duration obviously depends on the skill.

However, many organizations have an estimating procedure that estimates activity costs directly from the parameters in the scope. For example, a painter may estimate the time to paint a room based on the number of square feet. The cost is then determined by assigning a person (the resource) to it, and by multiplying by their hourly cost, the activity cost is determined.

Software cost estimation does not follow the PMBOK either. Typically, one first determines the program parameters (e.g., number of function points, or forms and screens) and then derives the estimated number of hours to complete the job. After that, an allowance is made for the type of staff assigned.

2. See the NSP Preliminary Cost Estimate form at cityofboston.gov in the dnd/ PDFs/ section.

3. Dr. Gawande is a surgeon at the Brigham and Women's Hospital in Boston, a staff writer for The New Yorker, and an assistant professor at Harvard Medical School.

BIBLIOGRAPHY

[1] Paul McDonald. It's time for management version 2.0: Six forces redefining the future of modern management. *Futures*, 43:797–808, 2011.

[2] S. Leybourne, R. D. H. Warburton, and V. Kanabar. Is project management the new management 2.0? In *Proceedings of the PMI Research and Education Conference*, Limerick, Ireland, July 2012. Project Management Institute.

[3] *A Guide to the Project Management Body of Knowledge*. Project Management Institute, 5th edition, 2013.

[4] V. Kanabar and R. D. H. Warburton. *MBA Fundamentals: Project Management*. Kaplan Publishing, New York, NY., 1st edition, 2008.

[5] K. Jugdev and R. Muller. A retrospective look at our evolving understanding of project success. *Project Management Journal*, 36(4):19–31, 2005.

[6] The Standish Group. The CHAOS report. Web page: www. projectsmart. co. uk/ docs/ chaos-report.pdf, 1995.

[7] L. Eveleens and C. Verhoef. The rise and fall of the chaos report figures. *IEEE Software*, 27(1):30–36, January/February 2010.

[8] Erik Larson and Clifford Gray. *Project Management: The managerial process*. McGraw-Hill Irwin, NY, NY, 5th edition, 2011.

[9] James Wilson and Michelle Harrison. The necessity of driving to Abilene. *Organization Development Journal*, 19(2):99–109, 2001.

[10] Stephen Leybourne. Project Management and high-value superyacht projects: An improvisational and temporal perspective. *Project Management Journal*, 41(1):17–27, 2010.

[11] T. DeMarco. *Software State-of-the-Art: Selected Papers*. Dorset House Publishing, New York, NY, 1990.

[12] R.S. Pressman. *Software engineering: A practitioner's approach*. McGraw Hill: Higher Education. McGraw-Hill, 2005.

[13] PMI. *Practice standard for project estimating*. Project Management Institute, Newtown Square, PA, 2011.

[14] V. Kanabar and R.D.H. Warburton. Leveraging the new practice standard for project estimating. In *PMI World Congress, Dallas*, October, 2011. PMI.

[15] EunHong Kim. *A Study on the Effective Implementation of Earned Value Management Methodology*. PhD thesis, The George Washington University, 2000.

[16] Quentin W. Fleming and Joel M. Koppleman. *Earned Value Project Management*. Project Management Institute, Newtown Square, PA, 3rd edition, 2005.

[17] Q. W. Fleming and J. M. Koppelman. The two most useful earned value metrics: the CPI and the TCPI. *PM World Today*, XI(VI), June 2009.

[18] F. T. Anbari. Earned value project management method and extension. *Project Management Journal*, 34(4):12, 2003.

[19] David S. Christensen and Scott Heise. Cost Performance Index Stability. *National Contract Management Journal*, 25(Spring):7–15, 1993.

[20] Roger D. H. Warburton. A time-dependent earned value model for software projects. *International Journal of Project Management*, 20:1082–1090, 2011.

[21] David S. Christensen, Richard C. Antolini, and John W. McKinney. A review of estimate at completion research. *Journal of Cost Analysis*, 25(Spring):41–62, 1995.

[22] Elizabeth Kubler-Ross. *On Death and Dying*. Scribner, New York, NY, reprint edition, 1997.

[23] Walter H. Lipke. *Earned Schedule*. Lulu (R) Publishing, Lexington, KY, 2010.

[24] W. Allen. A pragmatic approach to using resource loading. production and learning curves on construction projects. *Canadian Journal of Civil Engineering*, 21:939–953, 1994.

[25] Project Management Institute. Code of ethics and professional responsibility. Technical report, 2006.

[26] B. W. Tuckman and M. A. C. Jensen. Stages of small-group development revisited. *Group and Organization Studies*, 2(4):419, 1977.

[27] A. Maslow. A theory of human motivation. *Psychological Review*, 50(4):370–396, 1943.

[28] S. R. Covey. *The 7 Habits of Highly Effective People*. Free Press, 1st edition, 1990.

[29] PMI. *Practice standard for Risk Management*. Project Management Institute, Newtown Square, PA, 2011.

[30] Louis Mercken. Ethics has proven a useful tool for the project management profession. *PMI Today*, page 3, December 2011.

[31] S. Susanka and K. Oblensky. *The not so big house: A blueprint fort he way we live*. The Taunton Press, Newtown, CT, 2nd edition, 2008.

[32] Andrew Crowe. *Alpha Project Managers*. Velociteach Press, GA., 2006.

[33] A. Gawande. *The Checklist Manifesto: How to Get Things Right*. Metropolitan Books, 1st edition, 2009.

[34] Joan A. Lowy. *Pat Schroeder: A Woman of the House*. University of New Mexico Press, Albuquerque, NM, 2003.

[35] Robert G. Cooper. *Winning at New Products: Accelerating the process from idea to launch*. Perseus Publishing, Cambridge, MA, 3rd edition, 2001.

[36] Oracle. Oracle agile product lifecycle management pharmaceuticals. Web page: http://www.oracle.com/ us/ products/ applications/ agile/ index.html, Oct 2011.

[37] Microsoft. Home construction project plan. Web page: http://office.microsoft.com/en-us/templates, June 2014.

[38] Barry Boehm. A spiral model of software development and enhancement. *ACM SIGSOFT Software Engineering Notes*, 11(4):14–24, August 1986.

[39] Kent Beck. Manifesto for agile software development, 2001.

[40] P. DeGrace and L. H. Stahl. *Wicked problems, Righteous solutions: A Catalog of Modern Engineering Paradigms*. Prentice Hall, 1990.

[41] Mo A. Mahmood. A comparative investigation of system development methods. *MIS QUARTERLY*, 11(3), 1987.

[42] R. E. Fairley. *Managing and Leading Software Projects*. Wiley, IEEE Computer Society, 1st edition, 2009.

[43] Frank Sietzen Jr. Spacelift Washington: International space transportation association faltering: The Myth of $10,000 per pound. *Space Ref.*, March 2001.

[44] Barry Watts. The militray use of space: A diagnostic assessment. Technical report, Center for Strategic and Budgetary Assessments (CSBA), Washington, DC, February 2001.

[45] W. H. Lipke. Schedule is different. *The Measurable News*, pages 31–34, Summer 2003.

[46] M. Vanhoucke and S. Vandevoorde. A comparison of different project forecasting methods using Earned Value metrics. *International Journal of Project Management*, 24:289–302, 2006.

[47] Stephen Book. Earned Schedule and its possible unreliability as an indicator. *The Measurable News*, pages 24–30, Spring 2006.

[48] P. W. Metzger and J. Boddie. *Managing A Programming Project: Processes and People*. Prentice Hall, 3rd edition, 1996.

[49] David Logan. Known knowns, known unknowns, unknown unknowns and the propagation of scientific enquiry. *Journal of Experimental Botany*, 60(3):712–714, 2009.

[50] D. H. Gustafson, W. L. Cats-Baril, and F. Alemi. *Systems to Support Health Policy Analysis: Theory, Model and Uses*. Health Administration Press, Ann Arbor, Michigan, 1992.

[51] Wikipedia page for "sapere aude". Web page: wikipedia.com, 2014.

[52] Jack Meredith and Samuel Mantel Jr. *Project Management: A Managerial Approach.* John Wiley & Sons, Hoboken, NJ, 8th edition, 2012.

[53] Lars Madsen. *Various chapter styles for the memoir class.* MemoirChapStyles.pdf, 2009.

[54] Peter Wilson and Lars Madsen. *The Memoir Class for Configurable Typesetting: User Guide.* The Herries Press, Normandy Park, WA, 8th edition, August 2009.

INDEX

Colophon

This book is set in Computer Modern Roman, 11 point size using the LaTeX typesetting system created by Leslie Lamport. The layout follows the *memoir* class with Lars Madsen's chapter styles. [53] Acknowledgments go to Peter Wilson for creating the memoir class and to Lars Madsen for maintaining it. [54] And of course, none of this would be possible without Donald Knuth who wrote the original TeX. The bibliography was produced in BibDesk. LaTeX produced the final POSTSCRIPT file that was sent to the printer.

Made in the USA
Middletown, DE
11 August 2017